Culloden

THE LAST CHARGE OF THE HIGHLAND CLANS 1746

Culloden

THE LAST CHARGE OF THE HIGHLAND CLANS 1746

JOHN SADLER

TEMPUS

To Christine

First published 2006

Tempus Publishing Limited
The Mill, Brimscombe Port,
Stroud, Gloucestershire, GL5 2QG
www.tempus-publishing.com

British Library Cataloguing in Publication Data.
A catalogue record for this book is available from the British Library.

ISBN 0 7524 3955 3

Typesetting and origination by Tempus Publishing Limited
Printed in Great Britain

CONTENTS

ACKNOWLEDGEMENTS

It would be fair to say that this book has been forty years in the making. It was forty years ago that I was first taken to the battlefield on Culloden Moor by my father and then read John Prebble's superb account of the battle, which, for me, has never been improved upon in terms of dramatic impact. This sparked a life-long interest in the Jacobites and the events of 16 April, 1746. At about the same time the BBC produced the dramatised documentary, filmed with an amateur cast and in grainy black and white. Arguably it was one of British television's finer moments; those attempts that have followed have all been desultory in the extreme.

All my childhood holidays were spent in the western Highlands, so I can validly claim to have visited virtually all the locations mentioned in this history, from the dark, atmospheric wynds of Edinburgh to the golden strands of the West Coast and the islands. My concurrent interest, or perhaps obsession, with Highland arms and armour has led me to study most of the major collections.

Thanks are due to the following, without whose assistance this book could not have been written: Christine Browell, who drew the maps; Philip Walling, for assistance with the photographs; Alan Magnus Bennet; Iain C. Bowden of Armourclass; Ian Jones of the National Army Museum; Dr Tobias Capwell of Kelvingrove Museum, Glasgow; Alexandra Speirs of Tyne and Wear Museums; Deborah Hawthorne of Bailiffgate Museum; Jonathan Reeve, my editor at Tempus; and lastly, as ever, my wife Ruth for her enduring patience and sensibility.

All errors remain entirely the responsibility of the author.

Belsay, Northumberland, *autumn 2006.*

TIMELINE

1371   Robert II becomes the first Stuart King of Scotland.

1436   James I assassinated at Perth.

1461   James II killed at the siege of Roxburgh.

1488   James III killed after the Battle of Sauchieburn.

1513   James IV killed at the Battle of Flodden.

1542   James V dies shortly after the Scots are defeated at the Battle of Solway Moss.

1547   The Rough Wooing and the Battle of Pinkie.

1587   Execution of Mary, Queen of Scots.

1603   James VI of Scotland becomes James I of England.

1638   Signing of the Solemn League and Covenant.

1639   First Bishop's War.

1640   Second Bishop's War.

1642   Outbreak of civil war in England.

1644   Marquis of Montrose raises the Royal Standard at Blair; battles of Tippermuir, Aberdeen and Fyvie.

1645   Montrose's 'Year of Miracles': Battles of Inverlochy, Auldearn, Alford, Kilsyth and Philiphaugh.

1649   Execution of Charles I.

1650   Battles of Carbisdale, Dunbar and Worcester.

1660   Restoration of Charles II.

1678   The beginning of the 'Killing Time': Battles of Drumclog and Bothwell Brig.

1688   Year of the 'Glorious Revolution'.

1689   27 July: Battle of Killiecrankie.
       21 August: Battle of Dunkeld.

1692   13 February: Massacre of Glencoe.

1707   Act of Union.

1715   6 September: Mar raises the Jacobite standard at Braemar.

13 November: Battle of Sheriffmuir: Northumbrian Jacobites surrender at Preston.

1719 9 June: Battle of Glenshiel.

1725 12 May: The raising of six independent Highland companies is authorised.

1739 25 October: The independent companies are formed into 43rd Highlanders.

1745 25 July: Charles Edward Stuart lands at Loch nan Uamh.

19 August: The Jacobite standard is raised at Glenfinnan.

20 August: Sir John Cope marches from Stirling, but reaches Inverness avoiding an encounter.

17 September: Edinburgh falls to the Jacobites.

21 September: Cope defeated at Prestonpans.

31 October: The invasion of England is underway.

15 November: Carlisle falls.

29 November: The Jacobites reach Manchester, then press on to Derby.

6 December: The retreat from Derby begins.

18 December: Skirmish at Clifton.

20 December: The Jacobites cross the Eden back into Scotland.

23 December: Jacobites defeat Loyalists at Inverurie.

30 December: Jacobites at Carlisle surrender.

1746 8 January: Siege of Stirling castle begins.

17 January: Jacobites defeat Hawley at Falkirk.

6 February: Hanoverians reach Perth.

11 February: Jacobites take Ruthven Barracks.

18 February: Jacobites occupy Inverness.

27 February: Hanoverians halt at Aberdeen.

5 March: Jacobites capture Fort Augustus.

20 March: Loyalists under Loudoun defeated at Dornoch, Jacobites 'take up' Keith.

12 April: Hanoverians cross the Spey.

15 April: Abortive night attack by Jacobites on Hanoverian camp at Nairn.

16 April: Battle of Culloden.

18 April: Rump of Jacobite army disbanded.

30 April: Naval engagement in Loch nan Uamh.

17 May: Hanoverians reoccupy Fort Augustus.

19 September: Charles Edward flees Scotland aboard *L'Heureux*.

1

THE MOOR

We see every day gentlemen born here; such as the Mackenzies, McLeans, Dundonalds, Gordons, Mackays and others who are named amongst the clans as if they were Barbarians, appear at Court and in our Camps and Armies, as polite and finished gentlemen as any from other countries, or even among our men, and if I should say, outdoing our own in many things, especially in arms and gallantry as well as abroad as at home.

Daniel Defoe

Jacobite: a supporter of the deposed James II and his descendants in their claim to the British throne after the Revolution of 1688.

Concise Oxford English Dictionary

Dawn on 16 April 1746 carried little intimation of spring; the day was cold with a stiff wind and showers of stinging sleet. The ground beneath the feet of the marching – or, as was often the case, stumbling – men was wet and miry. Gathered on the rise of Culloden Moor was the last Jacobite field army, depleted, demoralised and hungry. The men who, with their Hanoverian opponents marching toward them from Nairn to the east, were about to fight the last significant land battle on British soil.

In a diagonal line the army of Charles Edward, known as the Young Pretender and later as Bonnie Prince Charlie, the hero of romance if not of history, was deployed between the walls of Culloden Park to the north and east and the Culwhiniac Enclosure in the south-west.

By noon Lieutenant-General Lord George Murray, previously regarded as the guiding genius of the rebels' tactical successes, watched the bodies of red-coated infantry moving from column into line. Today he would fight as a brigade commander only, having been relieved by the Prince of his wider responsibility. He had no illusions as to the Jacobite army's prospects for success and is said to have remarked resignedly to Donald Cameron of Lochiel: 'we are putting an end to a bad business'. The majority of men from both armies gathered now on the moor would, most probably, have agreed wholeheartedly.

The scene was thus being set for a famous and bloody battle. It was to be the denouement of the Jacobite saga which had begun with the Glorious Revolution of 1688 when James II of England, VII of Scotland, a determined Roman Catholic, was deposed in favour of his Protestant son-in-law William of Orange.

War had been the immediate consequence, both in Ireland and in Scotland, where James Graham of Claverhouse, Viscount Dundee, 'Bonny Dundee' (or 'Bloody Clavers', depending on which side of the religious debate the speaker stood), had raised the Stuart standard. His army, mainly comprised of Highlanders from the clans of the North-West, had won a stunning victory over Hanoverian forces at Killiecrankie the following year. But, with the ill luck that was to dog the Jacobite cause, Dundee fell in the very moment of his triumph, leaving the rebellion leaderless and doomed. Killiecrankie was, in part, redeemed by a heroic defence of Dunkeld, conducted by the radical Cameronians under their colonel William Cleland who, like Dundee, succumbed to his wounds in the heat of the fight.

Culloden was not just the end of the Jacobites but also sounded the death knell for the rump of the old Norse-Gaelic clan society. It is not often that history shows such a tidy sense of irony by fixing the very moment that an ancient way of life comes to a close. The clan system was undoubtedly faltering before 1745 and was clearly in terminal decline, but the battle and the subsequent harrying of the glens accelerated a process that the Clearances would, half a century later, complete.

The battle has become both a romantic symbol and a talisman for Nationalist and Gaelic sentiment in which the English are the undoubted villains, the Duke of Cumberland labelled a butcher. A whole raft of iconography, most of it fallacious, has arisen to misinform and obfuscate. Culloden was not just a clash between noble Highlander and base English; the reasons which brought men to the field were varied and complex.

Throughout Scottish history from the early fifteenth century onward an element of polarisation did occur in Scottish society. The author has previously charted the origin of this in an earlier work.[1] It is questionable as to how viable this divide remained by the mid-eighteenth century and whether the Lowlander's perceived virulent hatred of his Highland contemporary, the '*mi run mor nan gall*', was as prevalent as has been assumed.

Depending upon interpretation, the defeat of the clans and their subsequent treatment could be likened to that odious expression of atrocity 'ethnic cleansing'. It could be argued that the Jacobite clans were increasingly marginalised by their remote and anachronistic way of life, their religion, language, dress and dogged adherence to a failing system. Those who did not espouse the Whig cause were regarded as entirely pernicious by a rapidly developing Lowland culture increasingly alienated from and ashamed of their Gaelic compatriots.

Within the last few years the author has listened to a respected Scottish academic express a pejorative view on national radio: that the brutality meted out by the English after Culloden so hardened the clansmen that, seeking a new life in America, they were easily moved to inflict similar treatment on native American tribes. What nonsense!

It has been argued that it may well have been in the interests of the Whig faction that dominated the progressive society of the Lowlands, centred on the increasing influence and prosperity of burgeoning Edinburgh society, to promote the idea of a divide. Their purpose being to show that they stood firmly behind the Hanoverian administration and apart from the aberration of Jacobitism.[2]

Throughout the whole period that the Jacobite movement proved a constant or near constant threat to the Whig government, the problem was by no means uniquely Scottish. The threat was just as real in England, even though it tended to draw its primary military resources from the Highland clans.

Much suspicion that the unchecked martial tendencies of young blades from the disaffected clans, disinclined to or denied gainful employment, might spark further disturbances, was allayed within a decade of the '45. William Pitt the Elder conceived the notion that this pool of available manpower could be tapped as a resource for the British army whose imperial commitments were already burgeoning. Restless young men from the heather were thereafter recruited into scarlet to win and police the empire's swelling frontiers. They fought through India and the Americas and became almost the very backbone of the army. The Duke of Wellington thought highly of his kilted Highlanders and they did him good service in the Subcontinent, Spain, and on the bloody ground at Waterloo.

Sir Walter Scott and the nineteenth-century Romantic revival completed the clansman's transition from Popish outlaw to Noble Savage and ushered in the Victorian flowering. George IV postured in absurd tartan and laid the foundation for the present-day tourist industry, which peddles every manner of 'clan' memorabilia to a gullible trade. Those involved in promoting Scotland's heritage have every reason to be thankful both to 'Bonnie Prince Charlie' and to his later hagiographers – his fame has filled many a tour.

Unquestionably the most famous book to have been written about the battle is John Prebble's classic account of 1961. Despite the passage of over forty years this remains one of the best battle narratives ever written; the immediacy of the action is compelling and dramatic. Throughout the book, however, he favours the stance earlier taken by Katherine Tomasson[3] which casts Lord George Murray as the hero and Colonel John William Sullivan, the Jacobite Adjutant-General, as the incompetent villain. These roles were already defined by Lord George's memoir.[4] Sullivan's own account was largely overlooked, and subsequent analysis in recent years by other historians, particularly Stuart Reid,[5] has tended to cast doubts on this somewhat partisan view. Murray was possibly not quite the successful, charismatic figure thwarted by the unstable Pretender and his Irish cronies, and Sullivan less of the bombastic fool.

This book, therefore, is about a battle, about the men who fought and why they were there on that bleak, rain-lashed heath on that fateful day in a wet and distant spring. It is about who led them, how they were armed, motivated and disciplined, how they stood the terrible ordeal of fire, who lived and who died. To understand why so many would hazard their lives and property for what, at best, seemed a forlorn hope, requires a considerable amount of investigation.

Loyalty to the Stuart case was undoubtedly waning by 1745; the most likely prospect for a restoration occurred in the early days and flared again in 1715. The key occurrence that alienated many Scots during the early years of the eighteenth century was resentment at the passing of the Act of Union, a stripping of nationhood and subservience to what was, for many, a foreign parliament. Nearly four decades on this had significantly abated as the advantages of Union were realised and Scotland entered an era of economic prosperity and cultural and economic development.

It has been claimed that the Scots invented the modern world in the great age of Scottish enlightenment. If so then Culloden was surely the last act in the old world that had gone before.

2

THE HOUSE OF STUART

Robert II was still, according to the romantic reckoning, the ninety-ninth King of Scots from the mythical Fergus; he had been a good fighter in his youth, and his descendants, who carried the blood of Bruce, were some of them good fighters too. Again, he represented the opposition to the English whose tyrannies were not forgotten...

J.D. Mackie.[1]

The Stuart kings of Scotland ruled from 1371 to 1688, in excess of three centuries. From 1603 they also ruled England – the only serious interregnum being after the Civil Wars, from the execution of Charles I in 1649 to the restoration of his son eleven years later. The intervening experiment in republicanism was not a success.

Theirs was an ancient lineage: the family could trace its roots back to the era before the Norman Conquest of England[2] to Dol in Brittany, where they held the important post of stewards to the local Count. One of their number followed the Conqueror's path a generation after Hastings and, a further generation on, Walter Fitzalan fell in with the future David I of Scotland during the King's long sojourn at the court of Henry I. Walter was made baron of Renfrew and did the King good service when he saw off a major incursion from the Norse-Gaels of the West, killing their legendary chief Somerled. His grandson was active on the field of Largs in 1263 and cemented the family's swelling list of honours from the Scottish court.

Their role as High Stewards placed their name at the heart of the Scottish polity. Robert Bruce, in turn, was well served by two generations and the younger, another Walter, sixth High Steward, scooped the hand of the King's daughter, a very great prize. It was their son, called Robert after his illustrious grandfather, who was destined to assume the mantle of kingship.

In the event the succession came as something of a surprise. Bruce was succeeded by his son David II, at a time when the security of the realm was again threatened by internal strife and the English. Throughout his life

Robert, older than his uncle, had a difficult and at times strained relationship with the King. He was blamed for the defeat of the Scots army at
Neville's Cross, insofar as it was felt his brigade quit the field with unseemly
haste, leaving David II to ruin and capture.

During the King's lengthy captivity in England Robert acted as Regent,
no easy task and one which he appears to have gone about with no particular
enthusiasm – he seemed to be in no great haste to raise the substantial ransom
demanded! On David's final release the relationship may have deteriorated.
Robert's faction were implicated in civil disturbances amongst disaffected magnates and in the rather brutal murder of the King's mistress Katherine Mortimer,
who fell to an assassin's dagger like a doomed heroine from Webster or Ford.

When David II died suddenly in 1371, in his mid-forties but without
an heir, the crown passed to Robert who was a decade older, already aged
by the standards of the times and perceived by many as 'yesterday's man'.
Froissart gives an unflattering description of the King as an elderly man
thirteen years later in 1384. He describes him as worn out and world-weary,
overwhelmed with his responsibilities.[3] This pejorative image has stuck and
is probably unfair; sixty-nine was a great age for the medieval era and the
King had in fact achieved a considerable amount, through diplomacy and
cunning rather than force of arms. The example of his predecessor's debacle
may well have guided his strategy. He succeeded in gradually winning back
the territories occupied by the English under Edward III, secretly encouraging the young hawks of the war party, untainted by the disaster at Neville's
Cross, whilst avoiding a major rift with England.

Attrition proved a highly effective policy and the old King lived long enough
to see Scottish arms triumph on the moonlit field of Otterburn in 1388. His
son, originally named John but who changed his name also to Robert,[4]
acceded on his father's death two years later. The new King was of a generally
melancholy disposition, prone to depression, and much of the government
was carried on by his able and unscrupulous younger brother, confusingly
also called Robert, Earl of Fife and later Duke of Albany. This Robert was as
capable as he was ruthless and held on to the reins of power into his eighties.

Otterburn had offered the Scots the tantalising prospect of military
hegemony on the borders, a state which had not obtained since the heady
years after Bannockburn (1314). This advantage was squandered by the
third Earl of Douglas, who led a national army to catastrophe at Homildon
(Humbleton) in 1402 against Henry Percy 'Hotspur' and his exiled rival the
Scottish Earl of March.[5]

Albany succeeded in disposing of his nephew the Duke of Rothesay who briefly and rashly challenged his power,[6] and the ageing King tried to send his younger son James to France for safekeeping. The lad never arrived for he was captured, in defiance of the prevailing truce, by English privateers and sold on to a delighted Henry IV. James I remained in captivity for many years, growing to manhood as a hostage at the English court. He was at least treated as a prince and furnished with a first-class education. When he was subsequently ransomed the payment was artfully couched as school fees rather than brigandry!

It was during this captivity that, in July 1411, the celebrated Battle of Harlaw was fought near Inverurie, generally hailed as a clash between the 'wild' Highlanders and civilised Lowlanders. While there may have been an element of truth in this, the causes of the conflict were varied and, in large part, resulted from a feudal dispute over succession to the earldom of Ross, exacerbated by the Regent's mighty avarice.

When he returned to Scotland in 1424, a confirmed anglophile like his predecessor in captivity David II, the young King was determined to make a difference and bring some order to his realm. He was at least partly successful and is rightly remembered as a lawgiver. He fell foul of several of the magnates, though he had dealt effectively with the power of the Albany stewards, and his reign was cut short by assassins at Perth in 1437.[7]

His untimely death left the kingdom with another minority. James II ('James of the fiery face')[8] had a difficult upbringing whilst the magnatial families squabbled over who should exercise the reins of power. He developed a particular suspicion concerning the all-powerful, altogether too powerful, Black Douglas. The young King's violent temper got the better of him during or immediately after the final entrée of a dinner at Stirling early in 1452, where he stabbed the 8th Earl of Douglas to death.[9]

Civil war with the Black Douglas followed, culminating in their defeat at Arkinhom three years later. By now England too was slipping into the near anarchy of the first phase of the Wars of the Roses. James sought to profit from England's disorder when, in 1461, he laid siege to the great bastion of Roxburgh Castle. To prosecute the siege he had assembled a formidable artillery train, fascinated as he was by the new science of gunnery. Ironically he was fatally injured when one of the great guns exploded during a cannonade intended to celebrate the arrival of his queen, Marie de Gueldres.

Once again the kingdom was left with an infant king, James III. Pious, learned, something of an aesthete and, very possibly, with homosexual tendencies, the King oversaw a rash of major building projects and championed the arts. His court, to the disgust of his nobles, was filled with architects, poets and others, many of questionable sexuality.

This time it was the Red Douglas, Archibald 'Bell the Cat', who took the lead and orchestrated a mass cull of the King's detested cabal, who were unceremoniously done to death by hanging[10] in the course of a supposed military expedition to relieve Berwick-upon-Tweed. Richard of Gloucester, the future Richard III of England, was laying siege to the fortress which had changed hands more than a dozen times since 1296. While the Scottish nobles enjoyed themselves by getting rid of the King's catamites, Berwick was allowed to fall – finally lost to England. James III remained uneasily on the throne for another six years until a final quarrel with the magnates led to his rather abrupt 'taking off' after a skirmish at Sauchieburn. The rebel lords were led, at least in name, by the King's eldest son who now ascended as James IV.

The new monarch ruled for a quarter of a century and achieved much. He was catholic in his interests, which included medicine, the arts, law, shipbuilding and armaments. In 1493 he finally did away with the moribund office of the Lordship of the Isles and attempted, with modest success, to extend the Crown's authority over the fissiparous clans of the West and North. Unhappily for James he is best remembered as the architect of the disaster at Flodden (9 September 1513) which resulted in his own death and those of a great swathe of the magnates and gentry, together with several thousand commons. His magnificent artillery train, which had consumed so much of the nation's treasure, was lost. The battle was a defeat of epic proportions, eclipsing even the worst of earlier losses. Despite the slaughter amongst the upper echelons the mechanics of government did not fold completely and the administration was able to continue, even remaining bellicose.

The dead King had been married to Margaret Tudor, a daughter of Henry VII and sister to his successor, Henry VIII. The widowed queen stunned opinion by marrying the Red Douglas Earl of Angus, and the royal minor, James V, spent much of his youth hostage to the ruthlessness of the Angus faction. Like his predecessors his relations with the magnates were not always cordial. His first wife, a sickly daughter of France, failed to survive the Scottish climate and he then wed the more robust Marie de Guise[11] who produced a daughter: the future Mary, Queen of Scots.

James's brittle temperament could not withstand the shock of the fresh disaster which engulfed Scottish arms at Solway Moss in 1542. An invasion force, some ten thousand strong, was cut up by the English Border Horse, ably led and brilliantly deployed. Already demoralised and virtually without any command structure, the Scots army simply disintegrated into mass capitulation and rout. Already physically ill, James, having wandered aimlessly for a while from castle to palace, gave up the struggle and died.

Mary Stuart, still a small child, came to the throne in challenging times. Henry VIII had already taken the step of breaking with Rome and the pressure for religious reform in Scotland was gathering momentum. Henry now perceived the opportunity to win a major coup by brokering the marriage of Mary to his own young son, the future Edward VI. With the Angus faction in his pocket Henry might just have succeeded, but he seriously overplayed his hand and the moment passed. Infuriated by this unreasonable intransigence Henry instigated a more forceful policy, based on intimidation – 'The Rough Wooing'. More battles were fought: at Ancrum Moor in 1545, when Angus, returning to his natural allegiance, trounced the invaders; and at Pinkie two years later, when Protector Somerset won a tactical if ultimately hollow victory.

The Scottish Reformation was to prove crucial to the development of Anglo-Scottish relations. Marie de Guise remained a champion of the Church of Rome and the ancient if faltering alliance with France, but the tide of reform could not be checked and the Protestant lords would prove victorious. The infant Mary, invincibly wed to Catholicism, had been married off to the Dauphin and only returned to her Scottish inheritance when her husband died.

Scotland proved to be unfamiliar and unfriendly territory for a young Popish queen more used to the sophistication of the French court. She began well, steering a difficult path through the minefield of factions, even joining her Protestant half brother Moray as he put down the Catholic Gordons of the North. Her judgement faltered when it came to her choice of consort. The first, Darnley, a weak and vicious degenerate, was unfortunate; his probable assassin, James Hepburn, Earl of Bothwell, an even more disastrous second.

As luckless in war as in matrimony, Mary, her followers thrashed by Moray at Langside, was forced to flee and throw herself on the mercy of her cousin Elizabeth. This was both a surprise and an embarrassment, and the exiled Queen's twenty-year captivity was a sorry tale of conspiracy and threadbare plots which inevitably led her to the block. Whatever Mary lacked she did not want for courage, and the crowd that gathered to watch her execution at Fotheringay was not disappointed. The Stuarts knew how to die, in Mary's case wearing a dress of red, colour of the Catholic martyrs.

Even as Mary, Queen of Scots took her last bow and sowed the seeds for her own posthumous cult, history had moved on. The Treaty of Berwick, agreed between England and Scotland as two Protestant nations faced with a formidable and threatening array of Catholic powers, ushered in a period of more cordial relations. As he grew into his kingdom the young James VI, firmly of the reformed persuasion, increasingly cast his eyes southward where the ageing Elizabeth, childless, was in need of a successor. When, in 1603, the Union of the Crowns did take place and James VI became also James I of England, the long enmity was finally resolved, at least outwardly. For so long the Kings of England had sought to exercise sway over the smaller realm. It was a fitting irony that three centuries of near continuous strife should be ended by a Scottish king sitting at Westminster.

James had been an effective and largely successful ruler in Scotland, though he would be judged less favourably in England. He was physically unprepossessing, learned but not always wise, eternally fearful of the assassin's blade and with an unfortunate liking for young men. Early in his reign the more extreme elements of the Catholic faction, disappointed in their hopes of greater tolerance, plotted to blow up King and Parliament in the Gunpowder Plot. This may have been a genuine conspiracy or possibly a 'put up' job by Cecil, the Earl of Salisbury, intended to bring further opprobrium on the Catholic minority. If so, it was successful.

If he failed to win the hearts of his English subjects, James was always a wily politician; his son Charles I was not. He was both tolerant and courageous, a tiny man who married a French Catholic and encouraged the Episcopalian church championed by Archbishop Laud. Having stirred up resentment among his Scottish subjects by excluding the Lords of Session from his Privy Council, he then caused near panic by threatening to recover all lands sequestered since Mary's accession almost a century earlier!

'Laud's Liturgy' – the popular name for the Book of Canons, considered by many Scots to smack of Popery – led to a spate of disorders and spurred enthusiastic support for the Solemn League and Covenant of 1638. This was a clear statement of Scotland's religious affiliation and stimulated resistance to the Bishops. The Covenanters, as the signatories were labelled, with the bit now firmly between their teeth, sought, through the Scots Parliament, to abolish the Episcopacy altogether. This sparked the fiasco known as the First Bishop's War, though Charles failed to raise a viable force and a second attempt in 1640 resulted in a humiliating debacle in the Battle (or, more correctly, Rout) of Newburn Ford with the temporary loss of Newcastle to the Scots. The Covenanters, led by Alexander Leslie, an experienced general who had served his apprenticeship in the Thirty Years War under the Swedish paladin Gustavus Adolphus, fielded a well-drilled and disciplined army of over twenty thousand foot, horse and guns. Buying back Newcastle cost Charles some £200,000 sterling.

One of the King's early political opponents in Scotland who was destined to become his most ardent champion was James Graham, 5th Earl and later 1st Marquis of Montrose.[12] Like some of those who would follow him in the service of the Stuarts, Montrose remains a supremely romantic figure, successful in the field yet politically naïve. He would fall foul of the problem of reliance on an army, modest in size, composed either of Irish regiments or Highland clans. Such a Popish following might serve to conquer Scotland, but the anathema attached to Rome would ensure no viable political consolidation. A string of victories, however brilliant, could be undone by a single reverse.

In 1639 the Committee of Estates became alarmed at the power of Huntly and the Gordons, notorious recusants in the North-East. Montrose was, at the start of the year, given a commission to raise sufficient men to ensure the back door was kept firmly bolted. Leslie took both key bastions of Edinburgh and Dumbarton, which secured any easy access for Royalist reinforcements from Ireland. Huntly, however, scored an easy and largely bloodless victory at Turriff but was, by early April, sufficiently alarmed to submit to Montrose at Inverurie.

Undeterred, the Royalists, led by an experienced officer, struck at the Covenanters before Turriff and in the ensuing scrimmage drove them from the streets – the 'Trot of Turriff'. Montrose was able to restore the situation when he appeared with fresh levies, but his over-optimistic assessment of the royalists' morale left Aberdeen exposed and the city was soon occupied.

Lord Aboyne, Huntly's son, moved out to confront the Earl Marischal and Montrose at Stonehaven. The fight was untidy and confused; the Covenanters' guns did some execution but they failed to follow up their initial success. When Montrose did move on Aberdeen he was stopped at the Bridge of Dee by the Strathbogie men under Nat Gordon. After a stiff fight the Covenanting artillery found its mark and flayed the defenders crowding the bridge. Montrose had won his first major victory; Royalist resistance was now all but broken.

In England the Civil Wars began with the raising of the King's standard at Nottingham in the summer of 1642. Four years of civil strife followed with a great expenditure of blood and treasure on both sides. The King, who on several instances proved himself no mean opponent, held off his enemies until losing the North after the Battle of Marston Moor on 2 July 1644.[13] Before then the

General Assembly in Scotland had accepted the terms of an alliance with the Parliamentarians, putting the Scots army under Leslie (now Earl of Leven) into the field. Despite these setbacks the King remained undefeated, trouncing Essex in Cornwall and fighting Sir William Waller to a standstill at Cropredy Bridge. The Covenanter army, which had performed indifferently at Marston Moor, became bogged down during the autumn at the Siege of Newcastle, the city obstinately holding out for the King though there was no hope for its relief.

A year earlier Montrose, in Scotland, had found himself increasingly at odds with the majority of the Covenanting faction led by the Marquis of Argyll, MacCailean Mor, a wily politician and head of Clan Campbell. Though one of the first to sign the Covenant, the Graham was essentially a royalist at heart – opposing the policies of the King's unpopular ministers was a very different matter to taking up arms against the Sovereign. Montrose had latterly been a party to the Bond of Cumbernauld, the signatories of which were alarmed by Argyll's perceived personal motives and boundless ambition. The outbreak of war in Ulster and then in England continued the process of estrangement.

It was not until 1644 that Charles confirmed Montrose as his Lieutenant-General in Scotland and conferred his marquisate. The forces at his disposal, besides himself, included a total of two others. It was scarcely an encouraging beginning. Yet an Irish brigade, under the youthful paladin Alistair MacColla,[14] had been landed on the wild reaches of Kintyre and was harassing Clan Campbell on the Ardnamurchan Peninsula.

The Irish brigade comprised no more than three under-strength regiments and a tail of followers. MacColla, barely twenty-one, was already a veteran and is often credited with the development of the Highland charge as a tactical initiative. Probably he simply improved upon an existing arrangement. The partnership with Montrose was nonetheless a viable one and destined to achieve great things.

MacColla was not pursuing any identifiable strategy at this point other than to raid Argyll's territories. He had escaped from the potential trap of Ardnamurchan[15] to descend on Lochaber. The two men at Blair and their combined forces, the Irish together with those the Marquis had raised, barely topped two thousand.

His first objective was Perth, where Lord Elcho, with a crop of raw levies, prepared to make a stand. The clash occurred by the village of Tippermuir. The Covenanters, enjoying a distinct numerical supremacy, deployed with foot in the centre and their horse, perhaps eight hundred strong, securing the flanks, a perfectly conventional formation. As well as numbers the

Lowlanders had the advantage of seven field pieces. Montrose drew up his meagre forces along a similar frontage – his men standing only three ranks deep as opposed to the Covenanters' six.

The fight began with an exchange of musketry. Elcho's skirmishers recoiled and caused some confusion; Montrose chose the moment to order a general assault along the line. The veteran Irish showed their mettle and the Highlanders, notoriously reluctant to withstand cavalry, managed to see off the horse who charged them. The encounter ended in a complete rout and the Royalists entered Perth.

Alarmed by the debacle at Tippermuir, the burgesses of Aberdeen made haste to see to their defences. Levies from the county, from Moray and Banffshire were summoned and command given to Lord Balfour of Burleigh – the more capable Lord Gordon was, as a recusant, politically unacceptable. Though Montrose was to find the Bridge of Dee once more barricaded against him, he succeeded in crossing the river at Mills of Drum. Battle was joined on 13 September; Montrose deployed his Irish troops in the centre while the Covenanters appear to have, as before, stationed their foot in the middle with bodies of horse on the extreme flanks. A confused fight raged around a gaggle of buildings at Justice Mills with the Royalists, commanded on that flank by Colonel Hay, driving out the defenders and then holding their gains against a rather weak counterattack. Again it was the Royalists who advanced, swapping volleys with the Covenanter foot until the fight came to 'push of pike'. The melee persisted for some time until the Irish broke through and drove the defenders back, through the streets, in a corpse-strewn rout.

Despite these fresh laurels, Montrose was far from secure. Argyll, alarmed at the unexpected threat developing in his rear, was on the march with substantial forces. The Marquis, whose scouting and intelligence-gathering left much to be desired, was obliged to withdraw smartly from the city. MacColla had already been detached to reinforce the slender garrisons left in the West. The Campbells caught up with him at Fyvie, depleted in both numbers and supply. The fight which followed was a series of extended skirmishes as the Covenanters sought to overcome the Royalists' hurried defences; it finally spluttered out in a muted war of outposts and sniping.

Montrose got away, but Argyll would give him no rest. The Gordons cannily stood aside, but when his remnant arrived at Blair Atholl they were rejoined by MacColla who brought in substantive reinforcements from the clans. The Royalists were now bolstered by MacDonalds of Keppoch, Glengarry, Clanranald and the Isles, MacLeans, Stewarts and Farquharsons.

It was time for sport. Montrose led his army in an extended chevauchée through the heart of the Campbell country. For Clan Donald, this was the stuff of dreams, emptying Argyll's fat byres, harrying his terrified tenantry and, supreme joy, torching his capital at Inveraray, all whilst MacCailean Mor[16] appeared impotent to intervene. It was a fine time indeed. Inevitably, once sated and laden with spoil, many Highlanders saw no need to continue and quietly slipped off home. Very soon Montrose was reduced to two thousand men at most.

As he was preparing to march down the length of the Great Glen and deal with Seaforth at Inverness, the Marquis was made aware that Argyll was mustering at Inverlochy, poised to bottle the Royalists in the confines of the Glen with both ends firmly sealed. It was now that Montrose showed his genius as a commander of irregular forces. In the depths of a bitter winter he led his remaining forces on a desperate march over the high ground to outflank Argyll and recover the initiative.

On 2 February 1645, Candlemas Day, the grey blades of Clan Donald swept down through the swirling mist to seek out the astonished Campbells by the shores of Loch Linnhe. Merciless and swift as wolves, the Highlanders closed the gap. The Covenanters, led by Campbell of Auchinbreck, still outnumbered their attackers by perhaps two to one. With the defiant Cameron rant 'Sons of Dogs, come and we will give you flesh' sounding in the still air the fight was joined, the veteran Irish and Highlanders smashing through the levies. Auchinbreck, and many of his name, sold their lives as dearly as they could but the day was soon decided. Argyll, safe aboard his galley, hoisted sail and cruised sedately away from the stricken field.

Having seen off Argyll, Montrose now stormed the length of the Great Glen to take Inverness and Elgin. Lord Gordon, inspired by the Royalist triumphs, finally came off the fence. Aberdeen, Brechin and Dundee all fell. Once again, however, Montrose was nearly surprised by a fresh Covenanting army under Hurry and Baillie who obliged him to withdraw hurriedly towards Brechin.

Hurry was to prove more energetic than his predecessors, a more worthy opponent. He was able to again surprise the Royalists by the village of Auldearn, near Nairn, on the evening of 8 May. The Covenanter commanded a formidable force, comprising a number of veteran regiments which had seen hard service at Marston Moor – he had perhaps 3,000 foot and 300 horse.

Auldearn was scarcely more than a ribbon of rustic cottages astride a rise. Hurry was already deploying for the attack by the time the Marquis realised his peril. The Irish were, for once, discomfited, and pushed back into the village, where an untidy and savage fight raged around cottage and garden. MacColla's attempted counterstroke foundered. A royalist cavalry attack succeeded in driving off Drummond's horse and relieving pressure on the Irish. The Covenanters stood their ground even as the rest of their horse were chased off. The fight was hot and long disputed before the Royalists gained the upper hand and won the victory. Hurry may have left as many as two thousand dead on the field and was quick to dump the blame squarely on the wretched Drummond who was speedily dispatched by firing squad before the battered remnants struggled into Inverness.

From the wrack of their enemy's baggage the Royalists harvested much-needed muskets, powder and shot, pikes and provisions. The victory, though dramatic, was not yet conclusive. Both sides in the struggle were labouring under specific disadvantages. Apart from his redoubtable Irish regiments Montrose was obliged to recruit primarily from the Highland clans and the Gordon affinity in the North-East. There was virtually no support from the Lowlands. Equally, the Covenanters' main strength was with their army in England; they had difficulties in raising sufficient forces from those remaining and such additional levies as could be pressed into service. Though Hurry was chastened, General Baillie with yet another army was mustering. Like his predecessors, Baillie was constantly frustrated by the intermeddling of the Estates who appear to have learnt nothing from their catalogue of defeats.

Throughout the month of June the two sides jockeyed for advantage. On 24 June Montrose nearly pinned his opponent, but Baillie placed his men into such a formidable defensive position that the Marquis refused to oblige by attacking. On 1 July the Royalists splashed over the somnolent summer waters of the Don to make camp, appropriately enough at a place known as Gallows Hill adjacent the hamlet of Alford.

Baillie remained cautious; Montrose had finally achieved parity of numbers and the battle, which the Covenanting general would probably have preferred to avoid, began with a clash instigated by Lord Gordon. He was, it is said, incensed by the galling spectacle of so many head of his prize cattle penned behind the Lowland foot!

The cavalry melee became general on both flanks and the Covenanters were worsted, leaving the foot exposed. Though Baillie's regiments had disputed the Royalist advance to push of pike, with their flanks gone they gave way and Alford became yet another victory for Montrose, who now appeared well nigh unstoppable.

Once MacColla rejoined the army with yet more Highland recruits, the road south lay open. Montrose now commanded perhaps 4,500 foot and 500 horse, the largest force he was destined to lead. Bolstered by an alleged atrocity which occurred when Hurry's cavalry cut up a party of camp followers foraging for fuel in Methven Wood, the Royalists prepared for the deciding bout.

The Covenanter general was still beset by the relentless and pernicious interference of Argyll and the Estates. He was sufficiently demoralised to offer his resignation, an offer that was declined. The battle was fought on 15 August 1645 near Kilsyth, with Baillie's forces drawn up in a strong defensive deployment, ultra-cautious but secure. Argyll, favouring a more aggressive stance, suggested a general move to the right. This suggestion would have placed the Covenanters on good ground for an advance should such a move become practicable.

In order to achieve the new position the army was obliged to echelon to the right, moving north-west; a commanded party was dispatched to secure the high ground, followed by the horse and then, lastly, the foot. By swift degrees the plan came unstuck: Haldane, leading the van, turned to meet Highland skirmishers and the clash drew in more clansmen. This in turn prompted Home's foot regiment to charge in support of Haldane.

Despite the fact that Baillie's army was splitting into three disconnected formations the fight was not yet critical as the maze of enclosures denied the Highlanders ground upon which to launch a decisive charge. The horse, commanded by Balcarres, were quickly in difficulties, assailed by the Gordons. More of the Royalist cavalry were committed until the Covenanters were overwhelmed and broken. With Montrose's foot now pressing hard, Baillie's disjointed army began to unravel, and though some regiments managed to retire in reasonable order, the day was lost.

Kilsyth was the only star in the slipping Royalist firmament. In England, King Charles's veteran Oxford army had been utterly defeated by the Parliamentarians under Fairfax and Cromwell, the New Model or 'New Noddle' Army winning decisively at Naseby. The King now entertained great hopes that his invincible Scottish General would lead an army into England. In this he was to be sadly disappointed.

The plain fact was that Montrose did not really have an army, the Highlanders were already stealing back toward their own glens, MacColla was again detached to secure the West whilst the Marquis sought to recruit in the borders. The Douglas brought in a thousand riders, hardy borderers, descendents of the Steel Bonnets of Elizabeth's day. But that was largely it. Few others came forward and faulty scouting once again precipitated a crisis.

And this time there was to be no escape, no familiar warren of hills into which the army could retire. On 13 September Montrose was surprised at Philiphaugh near Selkirk and his slender force overwhelmed. The Border Horse promptly deserted, dooming the Irish foot who managed to surrender only to be butchered en masse along with their womenfolk. The Kirk and its vituperative ministers browbeat David Leslie into breaking his word. The surviving male prisoners were shot in batches against the courtyard wall of nearby Newark Castle[17] and the women, to save the cost of powder, were drowned. Leslie, even if he had besmirched his honour, had saved the Estates. The Year of Miracles was over.

Montrose had succeeded in escaping the field of Philiphaugh, though it might have been better had he fallen there. He spent the best part of the next twelve months skulking in the Highlands seeking to salvage whatever he could. In May 1646 Charles surrendered, not to Parliament but to the Scots before the walls of Newark. One of his final commands was to his loyal lieutenant in Scotland advising he should shift for himself. Montrose fled to the Continent.

With hostilities over, at least for the moment, the relationship between the Committee of Estates in Scotland and Parliament in England, at best a marriage of convenience, began to founder. As the power of the New Model Army and the demands of the radical sectaries grew, Charles sought to exploit the differences. The Covenant was no longer as popular in Scotland and there were those who tired of the ministers' ranting.

A resurgent Royalist faction, the 'Engagers' – partisans of a proposed compromise or 'Engagement' with the King – were gaining ground. Hamilton, their leader, was able to influence the Estates and, in 1648, led an army into England on behalf of Charles I. Hamilton's folly proved disastrous; his struggling and straggling regiments, blundering down the western side, were finally smashed at Preston.

Having got the better of the Kirk party led by Argyll, at least temporarily, the Engagers were still, for political reasons, unwilling to admit the Royalists who had been 'out' with Montrose and MacColla. Their army needed to be composed of the pure and godly, there was no room for recusants.

With the Engagers defeated and Hamilton executed, Argyll soon recovered the reins of power. Any chance of a lasting settlement with the English Parliament was dashed when the Regicides there decided to cut off King Charles's head, which they did on 30 January 1649. This was too much and the Scots rallied to the cause of the young Charles II.

Even whilst he was in the midst of tortuous negotiations with Argyll and the Estates, Charles was prepared to authorise Montrose to raise an army in the Highlands. This last, quixotic campaign finally ended with the Marquis being betrayed by his hosts at Ardvreck Castle on the shores of Loch Assynt.[18] His ramshackle force had earlier been utterly routed at Carbisdale. Charles had no wish to be little more than a pawn of the Kirk party and, had Montrose been successful, the spectre of another Year of Miracles might quickly have brought Argyll to heel.

For the Marquis of Montrose, all that now remained was for him to bear the ruthless humiliations heaped on him by his enemies and the sham of his trial with resolute and steadfast courage. Correspondence produced at the hearing, ostensibly from the King, stridently denied that Montrose had acted on instructions. This was inevitable given that the Marquis had failed to produce the expected trump. When King Charles II entered his Scottish capital, he would have passed the Tolbooth where the severed head of his most loyal servant looked down.

Oliver Cromwell proved a good deal less easy to dispose of. On 3 September 1650, despite being isolated in what appeared a most unfavourable position at Dunbar, he exploited Leslie's mistake and won a stunning victory. Regardless of the magnitude of this disaster the Estates pressed on and Charles was crowned at Scone on 1 January 1651. As Cromwell's inexorable advance continued, and with Perth threatened, Charles boldly resolved to strike directly into England.

His invasion finished in the streets of Worcester where Cromwell won yet another dazzling success. In Scotland, General Monck continued the mopping up, Stirling fell, the Committee of Estates were mainly made prisoner, and Dundee was stormed and ruthlessly sacked on 1 September, though it was not until 25 February 1652 that Dunnottar castle, the final bastion, capitulated.

It might have seemed that the Stuart tenure, both in England and Scotland, was at an end, but the great English experiment with republicanism did not long survive the death of its creator in 1658 and it was General Monck who set about organising the King's return. In April 1660 the wheel turned full circle and Charles Stuart recovered his throne. He was to rule for quarter of a century but showed little or no interest in the northern kingdom. He never even set foot north of the border but preferred to leave matters in Scotland in the hands of a series of commissioners, to all intents provincial governors: Middleton, Rothes, Lauderdale and, latterly, his own brother James, Duke of York, a convinced Roman Catholic.

The Committee of Estates, so rudely interrupted by Monck at Alyth, was reconvened and, in accordance with the strongly Episcopalian mood of the administration, now forbade ad hoc gatherings of worshippers or 'conventicles'. These were open air meetings, where services were conducted by Presbyterian ministers, away from the Episcopalian pulpits favoured by the government.

Another casualty of the new face of Scottish politics was Argyll, whose supposed treachery justified his execution. The Act Recissory was then passed and, at a stroke, removed the statutory privilege the Kirk enjoyed; the legislative position was returned to that which had prevailed in 1633, before the Covenant.

James Sharp, the ambitious Archbishop of St Andrews and Primate of Scotland, proved the perfect instrument to undertake the new policy. To those who had supported the Solemn League, bishops smacked of Popery and were to be resisted. Those ministers who demurred were progressively purged, and in November 1666 popular outrage spilled into an insurrection. Harried by Sir Thomas Dalyell of the Binns,[19] the rebels headed for the Pentland Hills where they were dispersed in a skirmish at Rullion Green; perhaps half a hundred were killed by the dragoons.

In the short term the rattled administration reacted sharply. Thirty-three men who had been 'out' with the Pentland Rising, as the affair was known, were hanged, and more shipped to the Colonies. Though Lauderdale's time saw something of a relaxation, the business of the Bishops had triggered deep resentment, particularly amongst the more radical Presbyterians in Galloway.

By 1679 matters in the South-West were sliding out of control, and a show of force involving billeting Highland companies forcibly in the area did not prove conducive. The Highland Host, though apt to be light-fingered, were not unduly savage, but to the radicals the mere idea of a force of savage clansmen, most likely Catholics, on their very doorsteps was an added injury.

In that year Archbishop Sharp, the perceived instrument of repression, was ambushed and done to death by a group of extremists. This was the signal for a further and far more serious insurrection. The conventicle that assembled on Loudon Hill on 1 June comprised perhaps fifteen hundred protesters, armed with an array of miscellaneous weapons. While the ministers exhorted, a young firebrand named William Cleland assumed some form of military control.

He was to be opposed by James Graham of Claverhouse, latterly Viscount Dundee, hero or villain depending on conscience. Kneller's portrait shows

a handsome, even slightly effeminate young man, arrogant, perhaps petu-
lant but, for many, the ideal *beau sabreur*. He was prone to contention but
considered loyal to his friends, amongst whom he had numbered the slain
archbishop and James, Duke of York.

Cleland made the best use of both ground and manpower; Claverhouse
rashly chose to make a frontal attack, dismounting his dragoons in a skirmish line. As they advanced, secure in their superior musketry, the rebels
surged forward on the flanks. Withdrawal became a rout as Claverhouse's
wounded horse bolted. Three dozen troopers lay dead, at least one prisoner
was murdered and the body of one of Graham's relatives mutilated.

In his subsequent report Claverhouse put the best gloss on the debacle:

> In the end (they perceiving that we had the better of them in skirmish), they
> resolved a general engagement, and immediately advanced with their foot,
> the horse following. They came through the loch, and the greatest body of all
> made up against my troop. We kept our fire until they were within ten paces
> of us; they received our fire and advanced to shock.[20]

The rebels surged forward to assault Glasgow but were seen off after a stiff
fight. As the government forces regrouped at Stirling and cast about for
recruits, Charles sent his illegitimate son James, Duke of Monmouth as
Commander-in-Chief. As the administration recovered its nerves the rebels
fell to wrangling. The Duke was able to assume the initiative and a confrontation ensued at Bothwell Bridge.

After some attempts at conciliation firing broke out and a firefight raged
for the next couple of hours. Finally the bridge was successfully stormed
and the royal guns deployed to rake the rebels with a storm of round shot. A
rout ensued, amidst much slaughter in the pursuit.

On the day following the battle Tam Dalyell rode into the government
lines with a commission to supersede Monmouth. The Duke's well-
intentioned attempts at clemency did not impress the ageing warrior; had
he had conduct of the fight, 'The rogues should never more have troubled
the King or country'.[21]

Lauderdale's career was a further casualty of the insurrection and he was
succeeded by Monmouth who, admirably, persisted with attempts at reconciliation, including an Act of Indemnity. He, in turn, was followed by the
Duke of York, not only the King's brother but his likely successor should
Charles, as appeared likely, die childless.

James was possessed of both integrity and courage but lacked either wisdom or tolerance. His appointment was a dangerous choice: a rabid Catholic was bound to stir yet further resentment in a divided realm and his authoritarian measures, including a 'test' for clerics, alienated even staunch Episcopalians.

In the hills and glens of the South-West a guerrilla-style war of murder and repression continued with Claverhouse, supported by the Duke's principal agent 'Bluidy' Mackenzie.[22] This was the 'Killing Time' – a dark era of relentless harrying. Richard Cameron, something of an extremist even by radical standards, was one of the rebel leaders. He was killed in a scrimmage in July 1680 and bequeathed his name to Angus's regiment who became the Cameronians. In time they would serve the government well, but that would be an altogether different administration.

When Charles II died in 1685 he was replaced, as expected, by James, the seventh Stuart King of Scots to bear that name and destined to be the last. James VII of Scotland and II of England had no talent for compromise. He failed to take that part of the Coronation Oath guaranteeing the Anglican supremacy, and conventicles in Scotland were again proscribed, attendance now being made a capital offence.

Monmouth launched his doomed rebellion in the South-West, his makeshift army destroyed at Sedgemoor and his head lost with it. James's daughter Mary was married to the Stadtholder William of Orange, the staunchest of Protestants, indefatigable enemy of Frenchmen and Catholics. The Dutchman, sensing the mood and aware of discontent in England, prepared his ground carefully, quick to reassure Scots that the Presbyterian Church would be safe.

James Stuart found he had few allies remaining in Scotland and even fewer in England. The 'Glorious Revolution' of 1688 was largely bloodless and William sent his father-in-law fleeing into exile. The Protestant champion was soon writing to the Estates and the Convention, summoned in March the following year, voted on 9 April, to nobody's surprise, in favour of William.

There was, however, at least one dissenting voice. Claverhouse, now Viscount Dundee, remained unshakeable in his loyalty to James. With characteristic élan he stormed out of the Convention and refused all pleas to return. These entreaties soon turned to threats, and when he maintained his obduracy he was, on 30 March, proclaimed a traitor at the Mercat Cross.

It is unlikely that many of his former colleagues believed they had heard the last of Bonny Dundee.

3

THE WHITE COCKADE

O last and best of Scots! who didst maintain
Thy country's freedom from a foreign reign...
Scotland and thou didst in each other live
Thou wouldst not her, nor could she thee survive.

Archibald Pitcairn

Behave yourselves therefore like true Scotchmen; and let us, by this action, redeem the
credit of this nation, that is laid low by the treacheries and cowardice of some of our
countrymen...

Viscount Dundee, speech to the army prior to the Battle of Killiecrankie
27 July, 1689.

Dundee was to draw heavily on the loyalty of the Highland clans to the house of Stuart, yet the Highlanders had not always been considered so distinctly faithful. The Norse-Gaels, under their great chief Somerled, had in the twelfth century established an almost autonomous state. His successors, as chiefs of Clan Donald, styled themselves Lords of the Isles, living and acting as free princes, their administration based on their palace complex at Finlaggan.

Clan Donald backed Bruce during the Wars of Independence but resorted to arms in 1411 over a disputed claim to the earldom of Ross. Although the Battle of Harlaw counts as a defeat, the Lordship, increasingly in decline and reduced in status to a feudal holding, hung on until James IV finally abolished it in 1493.

With this stabilising influence removed the field was open for a period of internecine violence known as 'The Age of Forays'.[1] It proved no easy matter for the Stuart kings to assert their authority and the struggle for supremacy between Clan Donald and the Campbells produced a bitter legacy. Finlaggan had been unwalled, a civil rather than a military settlement, but endemic strife in the sixteenth century implied that gentlemen needed strong stone towers.

By the end of the century matters did, to an extent, begin to cool, and increasingly the chiefs came to rely on their lawyers to a greater extent than their swords; both had the capacity to exacerbate. The Year of Miracles had ultimately achieved nothing for the Gaels. They had won victories but, in the final analysis, had crushed neither Campbells or Covenanters.

Their participation brought the clans out of their dark and brooding glens and nearer to a national stage. Charging with MacColla had been for a greater cause than individual enrichment. True, there was great satisfaction to be had from sparring with the Campbells and even more from spreading fire and sword through Argyll's wide and gilded lands. Their stand in part championed Catholicism, and in some cases the Episcopalian face of Protestantism, but above all they fought for their king.

It has been suggested, most persuasively, that Tippermuir in 1644 ushered in a major change in clan society that continued to hold, even falteringly, until 1746 and the reckoning on Culloden Moor. '…in the long run the real significance of [Montrose's] wonderful campaign was its effect on the Highlanders. These astonishing victories put fresh heart in them.'[2]

This view could be challenged in that Montrose was, of course, a Lowlander and Argyll had plentiful support from the Highlands besides his own clan, including the Mackenzies. The image of a Highland army, dressed outlandishly, muttering strange oaths in their heathen tongue and looting indiscriminately, became something of a bogeyman for Lowlanders and may have deepened the cultural gap.

Though the Highlanders opposed Argyll and could thus have shared a platform with the Royalist Engagers, the need, on Hamilton's part, to maintain political support in the Lowlands precluded any pact with 'malignants' who had fought with Montrose and MacColla. The defeat suffered by the Engagers at Preston and their subsequent collapse removed any possibility of cooperation, though an attempt by the Kirk party to establish some form of control over Inverness by the installation of a garrison there produced an armed response from the Mackenzies, who had previously proved loyal.

When the Regicides took the final step of executing Charles I, the Kirk party set its face permanently against England and thus presented the Highlanders with a dilemma: should they engage with the Argyll faction as the lesser of two evils? Despite the long history of antipathy, perhaps even Clan Campbell was preferable to English republicans! The Kirk would only bend its collective knee to Charles II if he would accept the Covenant, itself an anathema to the clans.

It was this crisis that led to Montrose's last, ill-fated attempt, which even though it failed utterly did motivate the Kirk to offer some scope for compromise; terms had been reached even before the disastrous encounter at Carbisdale removed the Marquis from the board. The Regicide had stimulated the swell of popular discontent with the Kirk, which had, after all, only recovered with English aid. Their moral tirades were wearisome and the popular mood shifted in Charles's favour.

Cromwell's invasion of 1650 proved a further stimulus. The Kirk might rant over religion but, to the majority of Scots, the matter was one of resisting the ancient enemy; having the person of their King at their head added further weight to his legitimacy. Despite the odds the Kirk steadfastly, if foolishly, stood by its refusal to admit recusants and malignants into its hallowed ranks. With Cromwell triumphant at Dunbar and the Kirk's star visibly waning, Charles was moved to consider raising a Highland force to seize power. This near coup, 'The Start', did not proceed but the possibility frightened the Kirk into opening its ranks to the untouchables.

From December 1650 Highlanders began to be actively recruited, and bled for their King at the Battle of Inverkeithing in July 1651, where the MacLeans suffered grievous loss, and later in the streets of Worcester, where the MacLeods, amongst others, took many casualties.[3] Despite this support many of the clansmen stayed at home. Some had been financially wasted by the earlier wars, more feared that to quit their own areas would be to invite their harrying by less scrupulous neighbours. Many chiefs still preferred a purely parochial over the national interest. For instance Argyll, in April 1651, did not raise his tenants from Lochaber and this spread the suspicion, based on precedent, that once the Camerons and others had quit their glens the Campbells would be emptying the byres. At the same time Cameron of Lochiel[4] was robustly enforcing his feudal rights against MacDonald of Glengarry and Keppoch, collecting loan instalments at swordpoint.[5]

Despite these obsessions with largely domestic matters the clans were generally moved to support the King. His rule was preferred to that of the Covenanters and certainly to the English yoke. Once Argyll had submitted, the traditional hatred of Macailean Mor could once again be coupled to support for the house of Stuart. In spite of this, continued opposition to the English invader foundered, due in no small part to poor leadership, but also to natural friction between clansman and Lowlander. Officers and men quarrelled, duels were fought, the common purpose was subverted.

By the time English troops began to penetrate into the West, resistance spluttered and failed in a welter of petty rivalries and the conquest proved easy. Ironically the occupation of the Highlands during the Commonwealth brought some benefits in the form of an even-handed administration, unfettered by local jealousies and archaic feuds. As the chiefs accepted the inevitable, they entered into terms with the English, finding caution[6] and calming their followers.

The invader's policy was one of stick and carrot. As a reward for acquiescence the chiefs retained all of their privileges, even the right of them and their 'tail' to continue to bear arms for self-defence.[7] Old disputes were dealt with through arbitration. If this was tyranny it was not without its merits. The stick came in the form of a string of outposts, the largest of which was at Inverlochy. Lochiel's Camerons refused to accept such an imposition tamely and the garrison was not established without loss.

Cannily, Lochiel soon came to appreciate the beneficial aspects of English rule. To secure his cooperation, the English were inclined to provide often generous incentives and mitigate his own indebtedness by settling his outstanding arrears to the Mackintoshes. He also did not scruple to act against Glengarry when the latter rebelled. Later he claimed to have been holding the confiscated lands in trust for their rightful owner. It is unlikely that Glengarry would have derived any comfort from this – there had been bad feeling between the two men and the MacDonald went on to accuse Lochiel of profiting from the rents due to him.

This was not the only way the Cameron chief managed to profit. His was the only sept permitted to carry weapons; anyone found in arms could be sure of immunity if they took the name and became Cameron adherents. Thus he could maintain a monopoly on armed force. For Lochiel the Restoration did not bring the rewards he had anticipated; given his conduct as, at worst, a collaborator, certainly an opportunist, this is perhaps unsurprising.

Even Glengarry, considerably more active, though he earned a peerage and a pension, was denied his prime objective, the Earldom of Ross. Perhaps this was an echo of the old claim before Harlaw, but no administration would be likely to grant such a major boost to Clan Donald.

With Argyll shorn of life and lands it would have appeared that the day of Clan Campbell was over, but Lord Lorne, the dead Marquis's son, despite being in disfavour and under sentence of death himself, did manage to avoid the axe and begin clawing back his lost lands. Ultimately it did not suit the Crown to emasculate the Campbells completely: as the generally preferred tool of government in the Highlands their extirpation would have left a dangerous vacuum.

Lord Lorne, who succeeded to his father's title, had a significant financial burden in that the Huntly lands, confiscated by the Covenanters, now reverted, but the transfer of the Gordon's indebtedness which Argyll had assumed to legitimise the grant, at least in part, remained and imposed a crushing liability. This crippling legacy necessitated some ruthless cash-flow management in the West where he, in turn, oppressed his debtors to make up the losses. This rapacity did nothing to endear him to the clans. His position was not a happy one: the son of a traitor, and therefore continuously under suspicion, yet at the same time a principal agent of the government.

The Earl's need for cash ignited a local feud with one of his principal debtors, MacLean of Duart. Argyll had tried to assign the benefit of MacLean's mortgages directly to his own creditors, though MacLean refused. This sparked what amounted to a local war as the two squabbled and sniped. Duart was massively in debt and the cost of defying his principal creditor only swelled the burden. As the two sides allowed the conflict to escalate, inevitably other clans were drawn in. Argyll had few allies and MacLean found support amongst the other Royalist clans.

In law Argyll was in the right and, as mortgagee, entitled to enforce possession of the MacLean lands in Morvern, title to which was encumbered by the debt. Though this was a vicious little war of raid and counter-raid, such as any of their ancestors would have recalled from the Age of Forays, there was a significant difference. Argyll, for his part, had only taken up arms to enforce his legal rights; he had the law and the authority of the Crown on his side. Nonetheless, the feud with MacLean alarmed the other chiefs who were deeply suspicious of Argyll's motives and methods. Keppoch, Glengarry and Lochiel all dispatched broadswords to aid MacLean (generally for a price, of course), which exacerbated his already dire fiscal problems.

Highland chiefs of the late seventeenth century were markedly more reluctant than their heroic forbears to rely on their swords. They now liked to have at least some legal pretext before taking up arms. Many had dispensed with force altogether and relied on their lawyers. Clan society was becoming less militaristic but considerably more litigious.[8] In part this was due to the widening role of the chiefs. The events of the 1640s had thrust them onto a national stage; the idea that they were serving their anointed King had taken root. They themselves, as they moved from being Gaelic chieftains to Scottish gentlemen, came to perceive the notion of clan warfare as backward, embarrassingly so, harking back to a savage past which earned nothing but scorn from their Lowland contemporaries.

This increasing sophistication did not necessarily mean the glens were more peaceful. There remained a pernicious infestation of broken men and caterans. The troubles of the Civil Wars had left many homeless and destitute, while economic developments, which might be thought beneficial, in fact served to aggravate the problem.[9] The English garrisons had been withdrawn to assuage national pride and this removal acted as a further inducement to lawlessness. Even MacDonald of Keppoch, seeking to impose some order within the sept, fell foul of the rougher element and was, with his brother, murdered in 1663. His successor was one of the prime culprits.[10]

A remedy proved impossible to find. Garrisons could not be maintained and the raising of Highland companies foundered, as did efforts to compel the chiefs to act on their own initiative. Despite the rising tide of anarchy the Highlands, at this time, were not considered a priority. The ruthless nature of the religious establishment meant that the government's eyes were firmly fixed on the disturbances in the South-West.

Conventicles were considered a far greater threat that the clans and the dispatch of Highlanders as unwelcome guests billeted on their dissenting Lowland contemporaries was an example of the administration's trust in their loyalty. Lauderdale obviously had no fears the rot would spread, nor did it. Even the traditional links with Ireland, which had tended to promote fissiparous tendencies, had withered in the 1650s.

The presence of the Highland Host, some 5,000 or 6,000 strong, did nothing to improve the Lowlander's perception. The clansmen plundered at will but, in many cases, returned as swiftly as they had come for fear one of their neighbours might be doing likewise at home!

By 1678 opposition to Argyll's oppressions was growing, and not just in the Highlands. This might never have amounted to a viable threat, but the equanimity of the nation was upset by the 'Popish Plot' of that year. This was a fiction but one which caused panic in the breasts of all true Protestants who feared that the King was to be murdered along with many of their persuasion and the Catholic James installed. This led the Privy Council in Edinburgh to review their relaxed approach to the Highland clans, so many of whom comprised recusants.

Argyll was now viewed as the paladin who would suppress these rebel-
lious tendencies, despite the entreaties of Glengarry and others that they
were utterly loyal. In the prevailing climate of paranoia these overtures were
seen as nothing more than cunning posturing.[11] Argyll's mercantile assault
on MacLean thus gained a new and wider legitimacy. The Earl pursued his
second attempt to gain Morvern with vigour but a fresh panic arose when
the Conventiclers rose and Argyll was ordered to desist and prepare to head
south into Galloway. He did nothing of the sort and doggedly pursued his
goals in the Highlands.

Lauderdale's fall, in the wake of the rebellion, removed one of the principal props securing the Campbell's position and, when he was replaced by
James, circumstances shifted unfavourably. The Duke of York had primarily
been sent to Scotland to remove him from the centre of controversy in
England. His aims were divergent from those pursued by his predecessor.
His eyes were firmly fixed on the English throne; to ensure his accession he
would, as a Papist, need the support of the clans, as they were the obvious
resource. Permitting Argyll to oppress them at will was clearly contrary to
his policy of courting the chiefs.

By the early part of 1680 James had devised a proposal or 'Scheme' which,
whilst it would not emasculate the Earl, would certainly clip his wings, and
provide for wider distribution of authority in the Highlands. The 'extraor-
dinary favours and partialities formerly shewn to the Lord Argile, could
neither be answer'd nor without much difficulty amended, since that family
had been so much advanced and with so much power put imprudently
into their hands'.[12] He proposed that the Crown should pick up MacLean's
burden and free him from the crushing burden of his debts; this investment
would doubtless secure the grateful MacLean's eternal loyalty and reduce
Argyll's holdings. He further proposed that the policing of the Highlands
should become the joint responsibility of the four leading magnatial
families, Argyll, Atholl, Huntly and Seaforth, each of whom would become
a paid officer of the Crown.

Argyll's arrogance buoyed his opponents' cause, and opposition was growing. James was not necessarily amongst these: he had no personal antagonism
and indeed resisted a proposal that the Earl's conduct should be subjected to
a parliamentary enquiry.[13]

What brought matters to a head was the Test Act, a draconian move that
required, in effect, all men to swear to support the likely succession of James.
Argyll opposed the measure, thus suddenly raising the spectre of his father's

appeal to ultra-conservative Protestantism. This was a very dangerous situation, and one which naturally alarmed James. Very soon the Earl was on trial for his life which was found to be forfeit. It remains highly doubtful that James, or for that matter his brother, intended to carry out the full sentence of the law. Rather Argyll was being taught a lesson: they sought to 'make use of this occasion to get him more into their [Charles's and James's] power, and forfeit certain jurisdictions and superiorities which he and his predecessors had surreptitiously acquir'd and most tyranicaly exercised'.[14]

The whole sorry business proved a serious blunder. Argyll's refusal struck a chord with all Scots who feared a Catholic succession; his previous excesses and unpopularity were forgotten; worse, he escaped from confinement and fled to the Low Countries, which vitiated any hope of a compromise. The outlawed Earl's son, another Lord Lorne, was permitted to come into part of his inheritance, though his father's sprawling legacy was vastly shrunk. He lost titles, most of the lands held through feudal superiority, and a significant part of his income – these confiscations were used to pay off his father's outstanding debts. This was undoubtedly music to the ears of Macailean Mor's legion of enemies.

James was still struggling to find an effective policing system for the Highlands. His scheme to employ the magnates came to nothing; he recruited two more independent companies, their complement drawn mainly from the Lowlands,[15] though these achieved little or nothing. Lastly, he briefly planted a garrison at Inverlochy before Lochiel sent them packing. An attempt to set up a panel of commissioners to mete out justice in the turbulent glens began well, particularly in the East, but foundered when the justices came into contact with the wily Lochiel.[16] To strengthen their authority Lieutenant General Drummond was detailed to provide the commissioners with some military muscle. He was presently sending back wildly optimistic reports of his and the commission's successes.

Charles II died in 1685; the work of Drummond and his colleagues became redundant when Monmouth's abortive rising in England was accompanied by a landing in the Highlands, led by the fugitive Argyll. The Earl's adventure was a still-born thing; he was as doomed as his principle. His track record as a rack-renting landlord was inauspicious, he had no natural charisma or military credentials and the government had already installed Atholl as Lieutenant in Argyllshire. His zeal and the enthusiasm of the clans in receiving carte blanche to harry the Campbells ensured that the venture

quickly collapsed. Argyll was taken and the sentence of death, which had
hung over his head for the previous four years, was now carried out.

Determined to stamp out any embers of dissent, the government authorised draconian measures against any Campbells remaining in arms. The
disturbances spawned a new wave of lawlessness, private grudges were
cloaked as loyal endeavour, swarms of landless men emerged to loot and
burn. The painstaking work of the earlier commission was washed away in
a fury of violence. Drummond, now Lord Strathallan, was sent back with
more troops to bring the situation under control. As before he responded
with enthusiasm, but achieved little success. By the time of the 'Glorious
Revolution', three years later, matters had scarcely improved.

James showed a partiality toward Lochiel, whose record, as a loyal servant
of the state, was distinctly mixed. It appears that the Duke was impressed
by his swashbuckling manner and easy charm. Certainly his cunning and
ready wit served to extricate him from a number of scrapes. Lochiel may
have succeeded, at least in part, in convincing James that much of the trou-
ble in which he had been embroiled was caused by the mire of confused
land holdings and the complexities of an outmoded feudal system. This
would not explain why he harried the garrison of Inverlochy or so readily
obstructed the work of the commissioners!

One anecdote, which illustrates the Duke's perhaps reluctant fascination
with his Highland subject, concerns the conferring of a knighthood on
Lochiel in 1681, the year of Argyll's fall. As a gesture, James offered to dub
the Cameron with his own sword, which, embarrassingly, refused to budge
from the scabbard. The chief was obliged to free the blade and offer it, hilt
first, to the future King. James wittily observed that Lochiel's sword obeyed
no hand but his own. There was a barb within the humour; the Duke was
well aware that Lochiel was motivated entirely by personal goals.[17]

James may have viewed the Camerons as partial successors to the
Campbells, once the latter had been stripped of much of their authority,
a natural counterpoise. Lochiel, generally, had the ear of the other chiefs
though his relations with Argyll were cordial. Perhaps too cordial, as there
was suspicion that the wily chief was playing a double game during the
Earl's abortive revolt. Sufficient mud stuck for Lochiel to mount a hasty
dash to the Court to reinforce his loyalty to James, who jovially, if pointedly,
referred to his guest as 'the King of Thieves'.[18]

Throughout the Restoration period, as Professor Stevenson relates, the
government had been far more occupied by the threat posed by Lowland

conventicles than any from the Highland chiefs. Some attempts to stamp out lawlessness had been undertaken but these had, at best, been half-hearted and largely starved of resources.

It appears correct to assert that James, as King, gave little thought to any fundamental reform of the pernicious web of feudal complexities that obfuscated property matters. When in exile, however, he was quick to promise that he would 'free them from all manner of vassalage and dependence on the great men their neighbours'.[19] He was prepared to undertake that all would be free of feudalism and subject only to the rights of the Crown.

Destroying the overweening power of Argyll and the Campbells, notwithstanding the fact it had largely come about as a result of miscalculation, put heart into the Royalist clans. Not only did they discern the practical benefits, they were able to conflate the twin ideals of support for the Stuarts with detestation of the Campbells. It proved a far reaching set of circumstances. James VII, therefore, had both destroyed the beast of oppression and had, at least in part, recognised the efforts of the loyal clans during the civil wars.

These events, which occurred during the 1680s, caused many of the clans to see their loyalty to the dynasty in terms of personal loyalty to James – the Jacobite faction[20] could therefore be said to have been born at this time in the Highlands. The happy coincidence of disposing of the Campbells cemented the loyalty of the Royalist clans, who traditionally associated the Argyll faction with radical anti-monarchist tendencies. They saw the Campbells as a major and continuing menace, and so any government of which they were an active part must, inevitably, also constitute a threat.

In reality the Stuarts had, in historical terms, done little to stimulate loyalty amongst the Gaels. They had been the instrument of Clan Campbell's rise after the demise of the Lordship and, in general, had found little to interest them in the Highlands. Neither Charles I nor Charles II found any appeal in their native realm whatsoever, far less the Gaelic Fringe.

The early alliance between the ruling house, through its generals Montrose and MacColla, and the Highland clans, had largely been directed by expediency. The echoes of that alliance with changing circumstances forty years on forged a much closer bond.

Professor Stevenson points out that the problem posed by the fissiparous tendencies of the Gaels changed in the course of the seventeenth century. James VI was plagued by the endemic lawlessness of the clans and their extreme reluctance to bow to central authority. Merely defying, or, more usually, ignoring the King did not imply that the chiefs disputed his right to rule. That was never in question; it was more a matter of how much interference could be tolerated.

After 1688, William III and his Hanoverian successors were to be disturbed by an altogether different problem – the archaic loyalty of the clans to a redundant royal family and a threatened way of life. This loyalty to the Stuarts was largely one-sided and dictated, as before, by a measure of expediency. The exiled dynasty was to prove cynical in their use of their Highland sympathisers. They wished to bring their cause onto the national stage, to recover the thrones of both England and Scotland; the latter alone would never suffice. The clans were a source of manpower, a reserve of natural fighters who could form the core of a Stuart army. They saw the Highlands as a jumping-off point, firstly for the Lowlands, then the whole of Scotland and finally for the greater prize of England.

As time passed these became increasingly unrealistic goals and, by adhering to them, the chiefs only succeeded in widening the gulf separating Gael and Lowlander. Even if the *Mi run mor nan gall* has been overstated, the general contempt for the 'Mackes' or 'Maks' persisted, and loyalty to the House of Stuart in an age of Whig supremacy could only serve to deepen this divide. Worse, when the cause finally expired, the reaction of a nervous administration would result in a brutal and bitter repression.

It was this fountain of sentiment that Dundee now hoped to tap. He had few friends in the Lowlands – the Estates had effectively marginalised his faction completely. With a mere handful of diehards he raced first for his seat at Dudhope, before withdrawing into the Highlands to avoid the net that was fast closing. Pausing in Glen Ogilvy to preach the gospel of revolt amongst his wife's people, he went next to Keith, then on to Elgin and Forres. Whatever his limitations, Dark John of the Battles did not lack charisma: he had that essential pull which Argyll had so noticeably lacked.

The government was far from blind to the growing threat and had appointed Hugh Mackay of Scourie as local commander; he could immediately field three regiments of foot and one of horse. Having captured one of his gallopers at Cairn o' Mount and learnt of his imminent peril, Dundee made a dash for the relative sanctuary of Castle Gordon; here he was joined by a body of north-eastern gentry under the Earl of Dunfermline.

Now the western clans began to respond; Keppoch chose the moment to descend upon Inverness and extort a ransom, which he preferred to call a debt, from the burgesses. Outraged, the wronged citizenry demanded redress from Dundee, since this piece of banditry had been carried out in the name of James VII. All he could do was offer a receipt in the King's name and promise future redress. It is unlikely this would have sufficed to win many friends in the town!

From near Dalwhinnie the rebel Viscount issued a summons for a general muster in Lochaber on 18 May. Again, he slipped past Mackay's patrols and relieved government tax collectors of their funds at Perth. Having redistributed this sudden wealth and warned off some of the local lairds who might have been leaning toward the Williamites, he approached Dundee to try and suborn his own former regiment. The men were more than willing, but the government's watchful eye was too close to facilitate a mass defection.

Mustering beneath the standard at Killiecrankie was a fine array from the Jacobite clans: Lochiel, MacLean of Duart (who had ample cause for gratitude to James), Clan Donald, Stewart of Appin, MacNeil of Barra, MacLeods from Skye and Raasay, Frasers, MacNaughtons, MacAllisters, MacLachlans and Lamonts. The pride of the Gael, a great, ranting host, vivid in saffron and plaid.

Mackay was now forced onto the defensive as the Jacobites took Ruthven Castle,[21] and Keppoch found time to settle another outstanding matter by harrying the Mackintoshes at their stronghold at Dunachton. The Williamites were chased into Strathbogie where Mackay might hope to better employ his cavalry. He was also reinforced with a further two foot battalions and Dundee fell back into Badenoch. On 9 June several hundred MacLeans took on the government dragoons and saw them off in a sharp little skirmish; the panicked Williamites obligingly left most of their weapons and gear behind.

Blighted by the inevitable defections Dundee retired into the relative fastness of Lochaber. Despite the slenderness of his support he resisted offers of mediation and found the price on his head raised to the very considerable sum of £20,000, a measure of the government's alarm.

At this time Blair Castle, seat of the Marquis of Atholl, was held by his son, Lord John Murray. Blair was a key position and best kept out of the hands of the Williamites with whom, it was feared, the peer's true sympathies lay. Stewart of Ballochie, the Marquis's factor and a convinced Jacobite, was detailed to seize the place. On 26 July Dundee arrived with two and a half thousand broadswords at his back. Mackay, whose numbers were greater, had not been able to advance past Dunkeld.

Should the clans risk a general engagement? A number of the chiefs preferred to retire but Dundee advocated making a stand, supported by Lochiel
who, despite the weight of his sixty summers and his somewhat chequered
history, still commanded widespread respect. Their counsels carried the day;
the Jacobites would test their resolve in battle.

In the quickening glow of a summer's dawn Mackay marched his battalions from Dunkeld, a great slew of scarlet, toiling toward the narrow defile
of the pass of Killiecrankie. By mid-morning the lead elements were at the
foot of the narrow ascent, where the Garry foamed over brown speckled
stones and the path wound uphill for nearly two miles, a wilderness of rock
and scrub.

Once the men had rested they commenced the tortuous climb. For the
horse and guns this was especially difficult and only the very lightest ordnance, the 'leather' guns, could be hauled up the defile.[22] It is possible that
the troops were harassed by Jacobite snipers – the terrain was certainly ideal
– but the Williamites emerged substantively unscathed. Mackay set up his
HQ at Urrard House and planned his deployment.

His left was to be held by a commanded body of shot led by Lieutenant
Colonel Landers, with the foot regiments of Balfour, Ramsay and Kenmure
in line stretching eastwards. He placed his horse in the centre with Leven's,
his own and Hastings's forming the right. Like a legendary host from a
distant, heroic past the clans came sweeping around the summit of Craig
Ealloch.

Seeing the Jacobites poised to occupy the higher ground Mackay moved
his line forward, in a quick scramble to gain a vantage. As the Williamites
reached the line of the Urrard Plateau, they found a dip to their front with
another rise beyond. Mackay considered his position adequate for defence,
though not a suitable platform for launching an attack of his own.

To conform to Dundee's perceived deployment the Williamite general
had to shunt or echelon his battalions to their right. The river, quite wide
and swift-flowing, lay at his men's backs; to retreat now would be difficult.
Landers's chosen men were still posted on the extreme left of the line, with
Hastings's exposed flank covered by a small tributary of the Garry.

As his line was stretched over the rim of the plateau he ordered the foot
to deploy in three rather than their customary six ranks. In practical terms
such a move offered better opportunities for telling volleys against the
rush of the Highland charge. However, the plan began to come unstuck
when Kenmure's in the centre failed, for whatever reason, to conform and

remained bunched in the denser formation. A gap of perhaps 150 yards now yawned between them and Leven's to their right.

Mackay's line comprised perhaps 3,500 foot, Dundee's a full thousand less. The MacLeods held the right; next came an Irish composite battalion under a Colonel Cannon. Then the MacDonald regiments – Clanranald, Glengarry and MacIan of Glencoe. To the right of Clan Donald, Grant of Glenmoriston with a small mounted squadron in the centre. The left comprised Lochiel, MacLean, MacDonald of Kintyre, MacNeil and MacDonald of Sleat. Dundee himself took station on the extreme left; his followers were most anxious he should curb the reckless rush of his own impetuous valour and stay out of the fight.

The strong summer sun was shining directly into the eyes of the clansmen and Dundee was not minded to attack whilst such a disadvantage obtained. The afternoon passed in a bickering of the light ordnance (which performed poorly) and sharpshooters. Lochiel dispatched a platoon of marksmen to occupy a bothy in the no-man's-land between the two armies and these opened a harassing fire. A company of Williamites led by Mackay's brother were sent forward to dislodge them.

At 8 p.m. the shadows began to lengthen, the fierce sun was calmed and Dundee chose the moment to launch his attack. His men were fewer and, like Mackay, he had been obliged to extend his line; to do so he had to increase the distance between each of the clan regiments. As it was he who was assuming the offensive this was less dangerous than the gap which had opened between Kenmure's, who were raw, and the steadier Leven's.

With their slogans ringing in the evening air the clans swept forward. Almost immediately the charge ran into difficulty: the nature of the ground caused the Camerons, who were targeted on Leven's, to move sharply to their left and bunch with the MacLeans and MacDonalds who were seeking to engage Mackays. Lochiel's men were winnowed by volleys from Leven's and Mackay sent his cavalry forward to exploit the hole in the Jacobite Line. They, in turn, were charged and held by Dundee's horse.

As they routed, the Williamite troopers careened into the ranks of Kenmure's, precipitating the disintegration of both this and several companies from Leven's Regiment. On Mackay's left, Balfour, commanding the battalions on that flank, saw only the collapse of the cavalry and Kenmure's. He assumed, too soon, that the day was lost and tried to withdraw in an orderly manner.

This proved a most dangerous manoeuvre. The difficult terrain and the wild charge of the MacLeans, supported by a formation of the Athollmen, swiftly turned retreat into rout and the hacking blades of the Highlanders took a fearful toll as the panicked men stumbled toward the formidable barrier of the Garry.[23]

In fact the position on Mackay's right was not yet hopeless. The charge had scattered several companies from his regiment but Hastings's and the remnant of Leven's held firm; they were able to fall back and form a defensive hedge around Urrard House. Mackay, who, even if he had lost his army, had not lost his nerve, was able to withdraw the survivors under cover of darkness.

Though they probably did not realise it, a volley from Leven's had claimed the life of James Graham. He had ridden forward with his troop of horse and now paid the price of glory. He had won the field but lost his life and, with his death, any hopes of a Jacobite victory in Scotland that year faded with the summer light.

Dundee was buried in the chapel at Blair, his body wrapped in a plaid, and he joined the pantheon of heroic failures. A romantic figure and clearly charismatic and competent, he left, however, no plan for succession – he was the fount and inspiration of the Jacobite army.

Killiecrankie must therefore rank as a pyrrhic victory. The government side undoubtedly came off far worse in terms of casualties though the clans, particularly Lochiel's Camerons, suffered heavily in the opening bout of musketry.[24] Deprived of their revered general the clans appointed Colonel Cannon to succeed, a neutral choice unclouded by partisan rivalries. If the Irishman was acceptable to the clans, he had none of the dead man's charisma.

With the declared object of taking Perth, the Jacobite army advanced down the line of the Tay as far as Dunkeld. It was here, by a fine twist of irony, that Dundee's former nemesis, William Cleland, was stationed in command to twelve hundred Cameronians, the cutting edge of Protestant fervour. On 21 August the Highlanders attempted to storm the town. This was not the kind of fighting they were used to: the Lowlanders had barricaded the streets, loopholed and fortified houses.

The streets resounded to the crack of musketry and the cries of men wounded and dying. Cleland had built a final redoubt enclosing the cathedral and Dunkeld House, two of the most prominent and substantial buildings. As fires spread through the houses and bothies, the clansmen stripped lead from the roofs to make good their dwindling supplies of shot. Time and again they came shrieking from the smoke to storm the barricades and every time they were thrown back. Shot in the liver and wounded in the head, Cleland dragged himself into Dunkeld House so his men would not lose heart as they saw him fall. It was an end Dundee would no doubt have applauded. Nor was his sacrifice in vain, for the grimed and exhausted defenders held on as the attack faltered and failed. Several hundred Jacobites had died in the fruitless assault.

Cannon withdrew to Lochaber so the clansmen could lick their wounds and plan for the next year's campaign. In April 1690 Major General Thomas Buchan arrived to take command and drum up fresh recruits. It was an uphill struggle; barely fifteen hundred could be mustered. Lochiel and the other chiefs, deprived of Dundee's inspirational leadership, began to look to themselves.

Early in May, at the Haughs of Cromdale, Buchan's fledgling army was surprised and scattered at the 'Rout of Cromdale'. This debacle marked the end of the rising, though it had been doomed to fail from the moment that unknown soldier in Leven's regiment fired his fatal shot.

4

DEATH OF NATIONHOOD –
THE ROAD TO UNION

To wanton me, to wanton me,
Ken ye what maist wad wanton me?
To see King James at Edinburgh Cross,
Wi fifty thousand foot and horse,
And the usurper forced to flee,
Oh, this is what maist wad wanton me!

Traditional Jacobite Song

Is it not strange that at a time when we have lost our Princes, our Parliament, our
independent Government… we are unhappy in our accent and… speak a very cor-
rupt Dialect of the Tongue which we make use of, is it not strange, I say, that in
these Circumstances, we shou'd really be the people most distinguished for Literature
in Europe?

David Hume[1]

Hume, as befits a historian of such standing in the Scottish Enlightenment, points to the dichotomy in Scottish intellectual development which the Jacobites represented. An increasingly archaic loyalty, harkening back to a past which was fast becoming unfashionable. It is unlikely that Hume and his contemporaries would have foreseen the nineteenth-century revival which would bring the wheel full circle.

While Dundee had been flying the Jacobite standard in Scotland, even weightier events had been unfolding across the Irish Sea. In March 1689 James had returned from France to Ireland to lead a great rally of his supporters and mount a serious challenge to the Williamites. The late Professor Hayes-McCoy has pointed out that Ireland was to be the base for a Jacobite recovery and Scotland the back door to England.[2] This is undoubtedly correct and war was to continue until the final defeat of these hopes after the Battle of Aughrim in 1691.

The key encounter has been identified as the Battle of the Boyne, fought the year before, when both sides recognised the strategic importance of Dublin. At that point James controlled the city, while William of Orange sought to wrest that control away. The battle was not a major tactical defeat for the Jacobites who, though worsted, did not incur crippling losses. James lost perhaps a thousand men from his substantial army, the Williamites as many, if not slightly more.[3]

Strategically the gains were significant: not only Dublin but the whole of Leinster and a fair portion of Munster fell. Though the Jacobites kept the field for a further year, their hopes, after the Boyne, began to wither. French troops, so vital to the continuance of the struggle, were largely withdrawn but the fighting persisted with a series of stubborn rearguard actions. However, with the final fall of Limerick in October 1691, hostilities in Ireland were effectively ended and James's hopes lay in ruins.

The surrender of Limerick and the rout of Cromdale between them sounded the death knell of the Jacobite cause. In retrospect this period was the best opportunity James, his son and his grandson were ever to experience in terms of a real prospect of success. The Jacobite movement as a political affiliation was only getting started but its heyday had already passed. Never again would the House of Stuart be able to raise such a major challenge.

As the fighting raged in Ireland, French and Anglo-Dutch forces also clashed at sea. In June 1690 the French admiral Tourville had beaten Torrington off Beachy Head. This might have been dangerous had a French army been poised to swoop from the Channel ports. Fortunately for the Williamites no such force was then in being and the moment passed – Tourville had to be content with a relatively minor spoiling raid on Teignmouth.

Rumours of an incipient invasion persisted and there were not enough troops available on the South Coast to serve as a viable deterrent. Jacobite sentiment was, however, muted in the extreme and the usual precautions were taken against recusant gentry. This was unfortunate for James, unlucky his cause had failed to prosper in either Scotland or Ireland, for this was a rare interval when the French Navy could command the Channel.[4]

Within a year this had changed. The English were putting more and more ships into the fight and the French reverted to privateering, avoiding fleet actions. Louis, in 1692, determined to try again to land an army in support of James. This, perhaps, though often overlooked, was a moment of great danger for the Williamites and one of real hope for James. In May the two fleets collided off Barfleur, and this time the Anglo-Dutch, under Russell, having achieved numerical superiority, bested Tourville.[5]

Four years later, after William had fought the French to a standstill in the Netherlands, Louis rediscovered his enthusiasm for the idea of invasion. Substantial forces were collected on land and made ready. There were various plans to have William assassinated by a cabal of disaffected officers but these, like the proposed landing, came to nothing. Security was lax and a formidable flotilla of English men o' war, assembled off Dunkirk, sufficed to frustrate the scheme.

Whilst securing the 'back door' in Ireland, King William sought to ensure the stepping-stone in the Highlands was also removed. The clans were now to be bound to the Crown by oath, a plan devised by Campbell of Breadalbane[6] after he had come to a compromise with the chiefs at Achallader.[7] The deadline for submission was to be 1 January 1692. Those who failed to swear faced the full wrath of the government, though the extremity of the sanction was not specified. It is unlikely that Campbell, however hostile to Clan Donald, anticipated just how draconian those consequences might be.

Glencoe, romantically if erroneously dubbed 'The Glen o' Weeping',[8] presents one of the most spectacular landscapes in the British Isles. Rearing above the almost primeval desolation of Rannoch Moor stands The Big Herdsman, Buachaille Etive Mor, and beyond it the rising crests crowd the skyline and hem in the valley floor where the Coe spills along the narrow ribbon.[9] In the seventeenth century the lower, more fertile reaches by the shores of Loch Leven were held by MacDonald of Glencoe, a small sept collected in huddled bothies at the settlements of Invercoe, Carnoch, Achnacone and Achtriochtan.

Alasdair MacIain of Glencoe, who at this time could muster perhaps 150 broadswords from a population of half a thousand, was a veteran of many scrapes and an enthusiastic scourge of the Campbells. His clansmen more than pulled their weight in terms of their propensity for fire and plunder. Despite his rough-and-ready image, MacIain, as a Highland chief, considered himself a man of propriety, and while he could see that the time had come to bend his knee to King William he first required absolution from James, a formal release from his earlier undertaking to the Stuarts. In due course this was obtained, and in the midst of a bitter December the chief arrived at Inverlochy, refurbished and garrisoned,[10] to take the oath. He was an impressive figure, sixty years old, and wearing a well worn buff coat that had survived the Commonwealth.

The fort's commander was also a Cromwellian survivor, Colonel Hill, a veteran driven back to the colours by the need to provide for his unmarried daughters. Hill, a decent man, undoubtedly had a soft spot for the old rogue and had striven to promote good relations with the clans. However, he could not in this instance oblige as MacIain had hoped. He was not authorised to take the oath, which would have to be sworn at Inveraray in the very heart of Campbell country.

As full of bravado as any MacDonald, this prospect nonetheless galled the old man. He had done sufficient hurts to Clan Campbell to be aware of what welcome he might enjoy. In this he was proved entirely correct. Having battled through the snows to reach Inveraray he was at first incarcerated, and did not secure either his relief or the administering of the oath until several days past the deadline.

Arguably this was a technicality but to Sir John Dalrymple, then Lord Advocate, the matter was quite clear. MacIain's submission was out of time and thus invalid; his people were thereby denied clemency. Sir John's purpose was quite simple: he intended that the entire sept should be exterminated, in what we would now refer to as an act of 'ethnic cleansing'. Whilst he might have had the letter of the law on his side, the Lord Advocate decided that such a murderous mission might prove unpalatable to Hill, who would very likely refuse the order.

The solution to this difficulty lay in the person of Major Duncanson, Hill's second-in-command, a ruthlessly ambitious officer, without scruple as to the means of his rise. To facilitate the plan the major called upon his subordinate Captain Robert Campbell of Glenlyon – a man driven, in late middle age, to seek a commission to service his debts, liabilities incurred as a result of Clan Donald's depredations.

On the night of 13 February, as a blizzard raged around the peaks and snow swirled in the valley, three columns of infantry were deployed to seal the trap prepared for MacIain. One of these, led by Duncanson, would march from Kinlochleven over the intervening high ground, known appropriately as the 'Devil's Staircase', to sweep down the glen whilst the other companies attacked from the mouth.

In the savagery that ensued a total of thirty-eight people were murdered including MacIain himself, shot down as he struggled to dress and greet what he imagined were guests, his last words a call for whisky for his visitors. Many men baulked at the task – the soldiers had previously been billeted with the very people they were expected to slaughter and for some, the idea of 'murder under trust' was intolerable. The foul weather helped many to flee, though the snows took a fearful toll of the sick and elderly, forced to take shelter in the high, hidden glens, such as the Coire Gabhail.[11]

The 'Macks' might be derided in the Lowlands but what amounted to genocide was a step too far. Once details of the atrocity were out and Glenlyon, who was less without conscience than his superior might fancy, was blabbing in his cups around Edinburgh, a clamour of unease arose. The government felt obliged to hold an enquiry and then a second; this did not report until June 1695 and only Dalrymple and Duncanson were censured, though neither was fully called to account.

Stair lived quietly for the rest of William's reign, keeping a low profile and avoiding public life. However, when Queen Anne succeeded he was fully rehabilitated and able to play his part in the Union. Breadalbane, though briefly incarcerated, also survived into a bitter old age, frustrated in his dream that his would become the senior branch of the clan, embittered enough to flirt with the Jacobites in 1715, though canny enough not to be too obvious.

Glenlyon died in Flanders, still debt-ridden, some four years after the Massacre. His heir, perhaps haunted by the 'curse' of Glencoe, came out for Mar in the '15 with 500 followers.[12] The MacDonalds received no compensation for the horror they had endured but endure they did and the clan survived. Such orgies of violence were far from uncommon during the Age of Forays and the sept could scarcely be surprised that their neighbours so disliked them.

The Massacre of Glencoe, apart from the murderous savagery of the act, was a great propaganda coup for the Jacobite cause. This was the justice the Highland clans could expect from a Williamite government, one that rated them no better than savages, to be slaughtered with impunity and with at least the tacit connivance of the administration. It was a nasty, bad and bloody business; if it spread disaffection, then this could hardly be wondered at.

Throughout his reign William's relationship with the Scottish Parliament was not altogether cordial. The overall position was complicated by the fact that a single monarch had two legislatures. The practical solution was simple – either the two realms must be somehow made wholly separate or the parliaments must be combined into one, and in the circumstances it would inevitably be the Scots who would cease to exist. The spectre of Glencoe haunted William, and after the Darien fiasco the Scots had a second grievance to add.

William's survival was, initially, by no means guaranteed, James, with French backing, appeared a potent threat, but defeat in both Ireland and Scotland, coupled in 1697 with the terms of the Treaty of Rijswijk, whereby Louis recognised William's legitimacy as King of England, severely dented the Jacobite cause. The Dutchman was by temperament an autocrat, and had little sympathy for popular government. Scotland did not interest him; his life's work lay in resisting French expansion as directed by Louis IV. Nonetheless, such a stance, coupled with his aversion to popery, won him some friends in Scotland.

Opposition came most obviously from the Jacobites, but also from the Episcopalians who resented William's acceptance of the Kirk, and, at the other end of the religious divide, the Cameronians, who had hoped for recognition of the Covenant of 1638 rather than that of the earlier and less extreme Presbyterian stance.

Until the peace with France, there was some unease in Scotland over the continuance of the war, based on a lingering sentiment for the Auld Alliance (although this had been defunct since the reformation.)[13] The Scots regiments had taken heavy loss in the seemingly endless round of bloody and inconclusive battles.[14] These grievances, however, collectively paled into insignificance compared to the Darien Disaster.

The Scots had not been idle in the swelling race for dominions. Despite legislative restrictions[15] they traded with the English colonies in North America and even planted some small colonies of their own. It was fashionable, and profitable, at this time to set up joint stock companies to exploit overseas business opportunities. In 1695 Scottish investors established a trading venture which, with the active backing of certain English interests, aimed to challenge the potent monopoly of the Honourable East India Company.

In terms of capital for the new concern some £300,000, a very substantial sum, was committed by both English and Scottish shareholders. William Paterson, a noted Scottish economist and founder of the Bank of England, suggested that the members should turn their attention to the isthmus of Darien where a trading colony would be able to straddle both east and west.

This appeared a sound notion; it was certainly threatening enough to cause ripples of alarm through the shareholders in the Honourable Company. Their considerable influence was brought to bear to frustrate the initiative. The English backers were scared off and sabres were rattled in the English Parliament.

By this time the venture had caught the imagination of an entire generation of Scottish investors who subscribed the whole cost of the project to the tune of some £400,000.[16] King William, anxious not to antagonise the Spanish, with whom he was in negotiations and who claimed Darien as theirs, became obstructive, demonstrably so.

Despite these difficulties the colony of New Edinburgh was established in October 1698. The founding was an unmitigated disaster; the adverse climate and English intransigence ruined the settlement, which was swiftly abandoned. The following year, undaunted by their losses, the shareholders tried again and reoccupied the township. The Spaniards came to the aid of the climate and, though they were initially seen off in a fight at Toubacanti, returned with greater force and the settlement finally capitulated on terms in March 1700.

Loss of life at around two thousand souls had been great, the financial penalties a hundred times worse. William wrote to the Scottish Parliament in October explaining why he had felt obliged to oppose the venture and providing vague assurances. As an attempt at appeasement this merely increased the ire of Scots. As a measure of this wrath an unfortunate English skipper, Captain Green, with two of his seamen, was hanged five years later on a rather thin charge of piracy against one of the Scottish Company's few surviving vessels.

To compound these injuries the English Parliament, in 1701, passed an Act of Settlement foreseeing that Queen Anne, who had succeeded her brother-in-law, might die childless.[17] The statute settled the succession upon the Electress Sophia of Hanover, a Protestant – it was also provided that the successor must be a communicant of the Church of England. The Scottish interest was simply overlooked.

James VII had died in 1701 and the torch of Jacobitism had passed to his son, to be known to Whigs as 'The Old Pretender'.[18] In their outrage against the English it was possible the Scots Parliament would refuse to be bound by the Act and offer the crown to their own nominee. If the Jacobite faction could seize the moment, it might even be James.

When King William, early in his reign, had first mooted the notion of uniting the two parliaments the Scots had responded with some interest and it had been the English who demurred. A bill proposed in the Lords was rejected by the Commons. William never lost sight of the concept and, immediately before his death, he was urging Parliament to reconsider.

Louis IV had already recognised James 'III' – Britain and France were again at odds in the War of the Spanish Succession, a conflict during which the Duke of Marlborough would win a series of dazzling victories that would shatter France's hegemony. Initially the war brought little hope for the Jacobites. The situation had changed since the days of the Nine Years War in the last decade of the preceding century. At sea the English were stronger than ever, the Jacobites no longer had armies in Ireland and Scotland and their residual support in England had been exposed as minimal.

In 1704 Marlborough utterly defeated the French at Blenheim and, within two years, Louis's armies had been chased both from Italy and the old Spanish Netherlands. With the war proving disastrous for French arms the appeal of an invasion to restore the Stuarts began to recover its lustre.

Queen Anne had the benefit of being free of the tarnish of Glencoe and Darien, and moreover she was a Tory, immured in a sea of Whigs. This did not, however, imply she could afford to dispense with the idea of union. England and France were presently at war, and Louis had recognised James, which necessitated continued antagonism to the Jacobite cause.

In November 1702, the first serious set of negotiations took place. Whilst some accord was possible, important differences, particularly concerning economic matters, could not be resolved. In Scotland the following year the Whigs clung to power. The Tories comprised the conservative 'Country' faction and the more radical Jacobites; diehards like Fletcher of Saltoun ranted against the concept of union. These opposition groups were widely disparate in their aims, united only by their dislike of England and the possibility of union.

Jacobite sympathisers were cheered by two statutes which the opposition did manage to steer through. The first provided that no monarch after Anne could declare a war in which Scots would be expected to serve without the concurrence of the Scots Parliament. The second allowed Parliament, within twenty days of the Queen's death (should, as was likely, she die without issue), to nominate a successor; this should be one who was both a Protestant and of the Stuart line.

With the war in the balance the English were obliged to tread warily; victory at Blenheim implied they could be more bullish. The Alien Act of 1705 was anything but conciliatory: if the Scots did not, within a deadline, accept the Hanoverian succession then dire economic consequences would ensue. This blustering facilitated the appointment of the current Duke of Argyll as commissioner.

The Campbell was not a seasoned politician. A dour man by temperament, he was a constant and skilled soldier. His Whig pedigree was unimpeachable; the integrity of the Kirk must go unchallenged but otherwise the negotiations could proceed on a constructive basis. The commissioners would hold their appointment directly from the Crown and all that was asked of the Queen was that she ensure the more confrontational provisions of the Alien Act were removed.[19]

When the commissioners, thirty-one from each realm, were empowered, Argyll stood back and, though convinced Jacobites were not excluded, both sides fielded a majority of Whigs. By July 1706 the bones of an accord had been hammered out. Pragmatism was the order of the day; the English wished, at all costs, not to have a hostile kingdom ruled by a Jacobite in their rear whilst at war with France.

The Scots would barter political independence for free trade. Though they had first held out for some form of federalism rather than a complete merger, the Scots themselves feared the Jacobite influence and a recurrence of civil strife. It would be a full and complete Act of Union.

This Act would bring into being the Kingdom of Great Britain, a common flag (the Union Jack), a common currency and a guarantee of the Hanoverian succession, this last a major blow to Jacobite hopes. As part of the complex financial settlement some element of compensation, by no means inconsiderable, was to be paid to the Scottish investors in the Darien Company.

The Scottish Parliament first debated the draft treaty in October 1706 and, once its terms were known, great howls of protest went up. In part this was orchestrated by the Jacobites and their Tory allies but there was undoubtedly a revulsion against the notion that the Scots commissioners had sold their independence to the English. Rioters took to the streets in Edinburgh, Glasgow and Dumfries.

There was protest too from the shires and even from some in the Kirk, but the die was effectively cast on 16 January 1707 when the Treaty was passed by a respectable majority in both divisions and the Scottish Parliament voted itself out of existence. Both bodies passed back-to-back legislation guaranteeing the Kirk and Church of England respectively.

As the Scottish Chancellor handed the final version, bearing the Royal Seal, to the clerk, he is said to have remarked: 'Now there's an end to ane old song'.[20] On 1 May the Parliament of Great Britain came formally into being. Though this dealt a fatal blow to any hopes the Jacobite faction may have entertained of some form of a constitutional restoration, in the short term the Act of Union provided a rallying point for Tory sentiment in Scotland and opposition to it became a prop of the Jacobite manifesto.

Resistance to the Act coincided with the nadir of French fortunes in the War of Spanish Succession. Now repeatedly hammered by Marlborough, Louis cast about for some fresh expedient and the notion of invasion was dusted off. He had received optimistic urgings from Jacobites in Scotland who had dispatched a 'Memorial' advising the King that an army 30,000 strong could be raised, not just from hardened sympathisers but embracing Highlanders, Lowlanders, Episcopalians and Catholics. France was exhorted to provide additional arms, a cadre of officers, sufficient regulars to overcome the 2,000 men of the Scottish military establishment – all the Earl of Leven, as Commander-in-Chief, could muster – and, of course, cash. It was presumed that northern England was replete with recusant gentry who would rise and, as in the Bishops' War of 1640, the Scottish Jacobite army could readily sustain itself in an occupation of the border shires.

On paper this might look very well; the North of England possessed few royal garrisons and the Scottish establishment was meagre. Nonetheless this was not 1640 and the Jacobites possessed virtually nothing that could compare with the formidable army of the Covenant. It is unlikely that Louis seriously believed James could topple England, but he was prepared to wager that the distraction could be serious enough to compel the recall of troops from Flanders. If so, this would suffice.

To complement the dispatch of James with 5,000 bayonets at his back, the French were fomenting civil unrest in Flanders; the extent of their preparations, however, put an undue strain on their security. Secrecy was obviously vital and once this was lost Admiral Byng swiftly appeared off Dunkirk to bottle up Forbin and the transport fleet. James, who certainly did not lack the courage of his ancestors, convinced the French admiral that the prize was worthy of the risk, and for once the elements obliged. In thick mist the French hoisted sail on 6 March 1708, and gave the English blockading squadron the slip. By 12 March the invasion force was in sight of the Forth with Byng in hot pursuit.

A brief landing of sorts took place about 100 miles north of the Forth, but no serious attempt was made; Forbin was more concerned about continuing to avoid the Royal Navy and slipped back to Dunkirk. The threat receded but the consternation and alarm in Whig circles did not. Leven had already pointed out that his slender forces were hopelessly inadequate: 'It vexes me sadly to think I must withdraw towards Berwick if the French land on this side of the Forth'.[21]

Certainly the danger had been great, and if the estimates of thirty thousand were wildly over-optimistic Scotland still contained many sympathisers, particularly amongst some of the gentry who could certainly have fielded a reasonable force. The Jacobite clans would have rallied and the

Whig administration in Scotland imperilled. Most of the royal fortresses were in poor repair and seriously undermanned.

The mood of nervousness was reflected in correspondence from the Whig Earl of Northesk, writing early in April:

> ...we have for some time been in great doubts and fears, if it end this way we have reason to be very thankful, for we were on the brink of being destroyed, we cannot doubt but the Queen who has shown so great a regard to this art of the island, shall lay down such methods, as may both secure us by sea and land, for it will be very odd if they leave this project, on so slender a repulse as they got. I'm very hopeful, however, it will appear there has not been such a disposition of rebelling in Scotland as the French have boasted of.[22]

These concerns were well founded, for Scotland's defences were in a parlous state. In Dundee's day Edinburgh Castle, under its recusant governor the Duke of Gordon, had defied the Williamites, and the failure of government arms at Killiecrankie illustrated how thin was the military establishment and how very slender its control over the western Highlands. Despite the weakness of the garrison, the siege of Edinburgh dragged on for three weary and dispiriting months.[23]

Some years earlier Mackay had successfully petitioned for the refurbishment of the old Cromwellian outpost at Inverlochy, so well sited for keeping a watchful eye on troublesome Lochaber:

> It is believed that it will be the sooner be more effectuate, by reason for some Remains of Fortification that yet continue there, since the time the English were in those Parts and made Inverness the chief garrison and head quarters in all those Highlands, which kept al the savage inhabitants in those countries in great awe and forc'd them to live regularly, as their Lowland neighbours used to do.[24]

At first the general clamoured in vain, but with the possibility of intervention from Ireland drawing closer, early in 1690 monies were found. Though he was not entirely satisfied with the siting of the old fort, Mackay had neither the time nor the resources to survey a fresh location and the new defences, in earth and timber, were thrown up as quickly as sweat and materials could oblige. Hill's initial garrison, which was forced to live in poor conditions within the rushed enceinte, often under canvas, comprised 1,200 foot and a dozen guns.

Despite the continuing threat, little had been done to strengthen 'North Britain'. After the scare of 1708 the need for an urgent review became accepted in part, and from the French perspective the plan had succeeded. Ten full battalions of foot were pulled from Flanders back to the Tyne and from there to Leith but swiftly returned to service under Marlborough, who trounced the French yet again at Oudenarde. 1708 is the forgotten landing, one that perhaps offered the best hopes for the Jacobites, for neither in 1715 nor thirty years later were substantial French forces actually embarked, and anger at the Act of Union was running high. Time and free trade would wither that resentment and local support would cool.

Glencoe and Darien were still fresh in people's minds, the Hanoverians distant, foreign and unknown, the Stuarts were the ancient kings of Scotland, whatever their differences with the Kirk and the Scottish Whigs, and James was to many a more attractive prospect.

The following year Louis half-heartedly considered a second attempt but his coffers were empty and Marlborough was pressing hard on the frontiers. Britain, too, was running out of steam, notwithstanding her general's brilliance. The Whigs suffered eclipse in 1710 and the Tories were minded to pay some attention to the exiled Stuarts. This was a slender advantage compared to the deterioration in James's prospects once the combatants began to explore terms.

As early as 1706 Louis had been prepared to cast his guest aside and recognise both Anne and the Hanoverian Succession. When, in September 1711, the provisional terms for peace were agreed, the exile lost his home. Like James II, his son had maintained a threadbare court at St Germain, outside Paris, an ideally located base. The English, however, refused to have anything to do with any foreign power that sheltered the Old Pretender and Louis, in his new desire for peace, obliged. James was to transfer to Lorraine.

In terms of his prospects in England, James diminished his appeal by his admirable if injudicious adherence to Rome. Had he been prepared to convert to the Church of England the Tories might have come to regard him as a very real competitor to the Hanoverians. Anne herself was of course a Stuart, though an Anglican one, and Hanoverian complaining that Britain had abandoned the war with France when the Treaty of Utrecht was finally signed in 1713 did little to endear them.

In Scotland the Act of Union had, if anything, become increasingly unpopular. This was not due so much to the drafting of the legislation or to its intent but rather to the high-handed condescension of the English who did, truly, appear to proceed on the basis that they had 'bought' Scotland. The inequality of the partnership particularly irked the Scots when so many of their countrymen were fighting for Marlborough: John Churchill's great victories were won at a very high price and the Scottish regiments made a full contribution.[25] Several officers, like Argyll and the Earl of Orkney, achieved both rank and fame.

Added to the cost in blood there was the groaning burden of the financial strain. As the lesser partner, Scotland should not, within the spirit of the Union, have been over-taxed, but in fact she found herself not only at a disadvantage in the free-for-all of the markets but carrying a significant tranche of the tax penalty. Constitutional inequalities also appeared and, to fan the fire of resentment, the Tories after 1710 were perceived as interfering with the supremacy of the Kirk.

By 1713 the Scottish peers had had enough, and a motion which they all supported was introduced into the Lords to repeal the Union. It was only very narrowly defeated. Nonetheless, when Anne died on 1 August 1714, the speed with which the Hanoverian succession proceeded must have astounded many Jacobites. George I's path was oiled by the Whigs of both nations, Argyll being particularly conspicuous in Scotland, and the 'wee, wee German lairdie' appeared to come seamlessly into his inheritance.

In the six years since the near invasion of 1708 the administration had been sufficiently alarmed to commit resources to the improvement of the principal strengths of Edinburgh and Stirling, as well as Fort William. The masons were on site at all of these within three months of the alarum, a measure perhaps of the government's uncertainty. Scotland had employed the services of a professional military engineer, John Slezer, for some decades and the improvements were overseen by his successor Captain Theodore Dury.[26]

Dury's plans for both Stirling and Edinburgh was considerable, though not all of the work was carried through. At Fort William, the enceinte had already been faced with masonry and now the interior buildings and accommodation were upgraded in stone. The barrack blocks were enlarged and extended, a new powder magazine was constructed and the capacity of the resident garrison expanded.

The apparent ease with which George, Elector of Hanover acceded to the throne was to prove misleading, and Whiggish complacency was to prove misplaced. A serious challenge was about to arise and, once again, this would come from the exiled House of Stuart.

5

THE TIME OF 'BOBBING JOHN'

There's some say that we wan,
Some say that they wan,
Some say that none wan at a', man;
But one thing I'm sure,
That at Sheriffmuir
A battle there was which I saw, man,
And we ran, and they ran
And they ran and we ran,
And we ran and they ran awa, man.

The Battle of Sheriffmuir[1]

These people will never fail to join with foreign Popish powers, to advance the inter-
ests they have espoused; so they have always been, and infallibly will be instruments
and tools in the hands of those who have a design to enslave or embroil the British
nation... notwithstanding the pains taken by the government to disarm them, they are
still well armed by supplies from abroad, sent them on purpose to put them in case to
encourage and support foreign invasions, which it is not possible to prevent by any naval
power, because of the wildness of their country, and the many convenient harbours and
landing places that are on their coasts.[2]

The Flying Post

The *Flying Post* extract above sums up the Whig view, echoing the prevailing fears that the Jacobites represented nothing more than the tools of
France and Spain – a slur the movement could never completely shake off.

Despite the apparently painless accession of George I in 1714, on 13
November the following year a Jacobite army faced government forces on
a cold heath in Perthshire. The odds, for once, heavily favoured the rebels
and it seemed, for that brief moment, James III might yet come into his
inheritance.

The dour German prince, speaking little or no English, was deficient in any semblance of charisma. The last ministry of Anne's reign had been headed by the Earl of Oxford and was, to all intents and purposes, a coalition. George favoured the Whigs as they supported the war with France. Oxford was arraigned for treason and the Tories systematically cut out of any role in government. The King sought to destroy the party altogether on the grounds the Treaty of Utrecht had been contrary to the national weal.

In this, he failed to grasp that Britain was tired of the unending war and his policy of emasculation alienated Tory sympathies throughout the shires. In terms of the propaganda battle the Jacobites, for their part accused of being Catholic and Pro-French, could now deride an openly pro-Hanoverian ruler, strongly influenced by Dutch advisers. From 1716 to 1731 Britain and France maintained reasonably cordial relations within the framework of an alliance. This made sound sense after the huge expense of the war but undermined the anti-Jacobite slur of their favouring France.

To the Tories it appeared that George and the Whiggish clique surrounding him were obsessed with the interests of Hanover rather than the greater good of England. Against such a background the Jacobite 'option' could be regarded as understandable rather than purely treasonable. Opposition to the Hanoverian regime provided an umbrella under which Jacobite sentiment could shelter and gain some aura of respectability.

A Jacobite pamphlet waxed voluble over the perceived shortcomings of the Hanoverian succession and the unfairness of the Williamite religious settlement in Scotland that had exalted Presbyterians above Anglicans:

> The partisans of Holland are very busy to cry up that people as Protestant states and Protestant allies, whereas nothing is more absurd, for it is well known religion is the least of their concern... if we are so fond of Dutch liberty I would gladly that my countrymen should know, wherein that liberty consists, and by the report of all travellers I have ever conversed with, I find the little finger of Holland to be heavier than the loins of any king I ever heard of... we see how your cruel German king thirsts after English blood. He resolved to cement the foundations of his reign by the blood of English nobles, to make room for German barons, and, and before he set foot on English soil sold the life of noble Ormonde to the Dutch States, contrary to the example and practice of English kings who begun their reigns with acts of clemency and amnesty, as if he would vie with the example of heathen Rome.[3]

Much of this is partisan rhetoric of course, and yet the general outrage would strike a chord with many Tories, disaffected by the King's continuing reliance on the Whigs. Within a year Jacobite support was becoming more widespread. Moreover, since the Hanoverian succession was now a fact, James's supporters could not entertain any hope of a peaceful, constitutional resolution; only force of arms would now suffice.

A three-pronged assault on the citadel of Hanoverian Britain was thus conceived. The main blow would fall upon the south-western shores of England, with two minor and diversionary risings in the Highlands and the eastern borderland. The English venture was by far the most ambitious, but faltered even before the first hurdle. Government spies and Jacobite incompetence foiled the venture before it began and only the lesser elements of the plan proceeded. In essence, therefore, the business was botched before it was begun!

'Bobbing John' was John Erskine, Earl of Mar, an accomplished, if slippery, politician, totally devoid of military experience. Prior to his 'coming out' in 1715, he had been notably short of Jacobite credentials, and his decision to throw in with the Pretender owed more to his chagrin at being excluded by King George.[4] His fluent tongue and glib assurance of major foreign intervention were powerful persuaders, however. Even if his master was doubtful of a successful outcome, Mar pre-empted him by unfurling the Stuart 'Restoration' standard at Braemar on 6 September.

Blind to the unfolding danger in Scotland the Earl, who had begun with barely 500 recruits, had by the end of the month brought in ten times that number and occupied Perth. Many of those who mustered were drawn from the Jacobite clans. If this was encouraging there was bad news from France where, on 1 September, Louis IV had finally died and with him the rebels' greatest potential ally. The regency council which followed was anxious not to upset the fragile accord with England and was willing to starve James of aid.

Having secured Perth Mar seemed to hesitate, devoid of a competent strategy, and this offered Argyll time to rally such troops as the Scottish establishment could muster. Numbering barely three thousand, these were nonetheless purposefully deployed beneath the great walls of Stirling Castle; the stop in the bottle.

In Northumberland the quixotic figure of the Earl of Derwentwater, a scion of the wealthy, recusant Radcliffe family had, perhaps with reluctance, emerged as the leader of the Jacobite faction, though Thomas Forster, a Protestant and an MP, was given actual command to avoid offending Anglican sensibilities. A worse choice would have been hard to imagine. With scarcely more support than their own tenantry could supply, the Jacobites failed at Newcastle and, after a rather aimless chevauchée through Northumberland, were glad to join forces with a Highland brigade under Mackintosh of Borlum at Kelso.

Bolstered by Mackintosh's weak brigade, much thinned by desertion, and by a handful of border lairds – Lords Kenmure, Nithsdale, Carnforth and Winton – Forster, now in overall command, decided on a bold attempt to sweep down the western side and link up with the perceived numbers of Jacobite sympathisers there. His command comprised perhaps 1,400 Lowlanders and 1,000 of Borlum's clansmen. On 1 November, with more and more deserters slipping away, the Jacobites entered Cumberland.

If they failed to rally support then neither did they inspire much opposition. Carlisle looked too strong a nut but Viscount Lonsdale, who had raised the local militia and sought to intercept the Jacobites by Penrith, was sadly disappointed by his levy's performance:

> The Posse Comitatus for the County of Cumberland was appointed to meet on Wednesday near Penrith, where I really believe there was near 13,000 men, who by the assistance of some broken officers of General Elliot's regiment (who were extremely diligent) were put in very tolerable order, but as soon as the news came that the rebels were marching towards them, they run off by hundreds, all the means that were possible were tried by several of the gentlemen for keeping the men together but was all to no purpose; when we found there was no possibility of engaging the rebels in the open field, the officers advised the drawing the men into town, to endeavour to defend that place which we accordingly did, but when we went to put the men upon guard to defend the avenues of the town, there were not a hundred men left, that could be of any defence (excepting two companies of Trained Bands). I don't know whether this revolt proceeded from fear or disaffection, what makes me imagine it was a thing designed is because most of the men came without any manner of arms, and though the rebels knew their number to be so great they did not alter their march at all, which I fancy they would have done, if they had not depended on a great many friends who did not show themselves. The posse for Westmorland was to have met yesterday, but the accounts of what happened in Cumberland the day before so terrified the people, that those who were coming to the place appointed for the rendezvous turned back

as soon as they heard the news, and the rest would not stir from home. The country is entirely without defence and I am very much afraid these rebels won't be stopped till they meet with a regular force.[5]

This content of this rather despairing letter from Lonsdale would tend to suggest that the Jacobites, if they lacked recruits, did not want for sympathisers or those who were, at best, indifferent. The Hanoverian government was distant, alien and aloof, not a regime to inspire loyalty. Forster's diminishing band advanced southwards by Appleby, Kirkby Lonsdale and Lancaster to Preston, which was reached on 9 November.

Preston held unpalatable memories for the Scots, recalling the disaster of 1648, nor were matters set to improve. General Wills, with three battalions of foot and five squadrons of horse, was hourly approaching and a further government detachment under General Carpenter was hurrying westwards from Newcastle. Forster suffered a crisis and retired to his bed leaving Derwentwater and the other Jacobite gentry to barricade the town as best they could.

During the afternoon of 12 November Wills launched a series of probing attacks, testing the rebels' defences but these were stoutly held and the assaults were seen off with loss.[6] Two key bastions, stout houses turned into strongpoints, were taken, Wills succeeded in blockading the town and, next day, was joined by Carpenter's reinforcements. Forster entered into negotiations for the surrender of the survivors, his best efforts reserved for saving his own neck, and the rebels capitulated.[7]

In Perthshire Mar had now succeeded in raising a force of some 10,000 men and controlled all Scotland north of the Tay. His strategy is not easy to determine but appears to have involved an attempted move south to link up with Forster, unaware of the difficulties the English Jacobites had encountered. He detached three battalion-strength groups to filter across by Stirling to keep Argyll guessing whilst he led the rest. At Auchterarder he was joined by Gordon of Doune who was given charge of the detached forces and tasked with securing Dunblane. Argyll had not been idle, nor was he as easily deceived. Calling in his outposts he marched swiftly to secure the town, beating the Jacobites by a narrow margin and obliging Doune to fall back smartly on the main body.

Mar was wrong-footed. His army was stalled at Kinbuch by the Allan water, to his front a stretch of high, waterlogged moor, used by the local militias as a training ground and known as Sheriffmuir. Next morning the

Earl treated his chilled regiments to a thoroughly rousing address, so impassioned as to arouse the approbation even of his enemies (who were many). He outnumbered Argyll by around three to one and appeared determined to fight. The Duke's 3,500 men were already drawn up in battle order.

With the wet ground hardened by frost, Argyll had strung his line over the icy plain, cavalry on the flanks and his foot regiments deployed in the centre, the bulk in the first line, a thin reserve behind. The lie of the ground confused both sides. Argyll kept getting glimpses of his enemy's approach, a glittering arc of steel over grey skies, but the extent of Mar's intended deployment was far from clear. The Jacobites were also drawn up in two lines, each comprising ten battalions of foot and horse to the flanks. The Highlanders, Clan Donald prominent, held the front with the Lowlanders in reserve.

Though barely 700 yards now separated the combatants, the extent of the dead ground masked the fact that the two forces were misaligned – each army's right wing overlapped the other's left. Mar was forced to frantically echelon battalions to extend his left, the first and second lines bunching into one mass. Argyll, commanding the right wing of his army, had already had to stretch his thin line thinner still. His left, where General Witham led, was already overstretched and could thin no more.

As the Jacobite right milled in confusion, Argyll seized the moment and threw forward all of his horse and five foot battalions. Though Mar's clansmen on that wing were hard pressed, they did not break but gave ground grudgingly, holding their ranks. The Duke now sent a commanded body of cavalry to essay their flank, but the Jacobites held their formations and their nerve, bending their embattled line back in an arc. For three grim hours the slogging match continued. Argyll, to his considerable credit, intervened to prevent the slaughter of an isolated company. This was commendable but he might have done well to consider how matters stood on the left of his line where Wightman's regiments has been broken by the Highland charge, though the victory was not gained without loss.[8] Once he became aware of the disaster which had engulfed his left, Argyll regrouped his victorious battalions on the right with those who had held firm in the centre.

Mar too drew off to consolidate his line. Had he renewed the assault Argyll, with scarcely 1,000 men left on the field, must have been swept away completely, but Bobbing John had had enough of generalship for the moment, as the survivors spent the remainder of that short winter's day glaring at each other through the freezing air. At nightfall both withdrew, the Jacobites toward Ardoch and the Hanoverians back to Dunblane.

Argyll had lost just under 300 men. Mar would only admit to sixty dead but, in all probability, his real losses were likely to have been very similar. When his patrols began probing across the moor next morning the Duke was surprised to find no trace of his foe; he had been convinced the darkness had brought only a respite. As he held the field he could rightly claim victory. And it was a victory: Mar would have needed to win decisively to eliminate the Hanoverian forces in Scotland, while Argyll had merely to prevent him from so doing. In this he had succeeded.

Mar had failed to win victory in the field but he still had a single trump card and this, in the person of James III, came ashore at Peterhead on 22 December. The Pretender did not much enjoy his stay in the ancestral kingdom; he had little hopes of success with the English rising stalled, and the climate made him ill. Undeterred, Mar had stage-managed the show of a coronation, appropriately at Scone, for 8 January 1716.

Most disobligingly, and substantially reinforced with 5,000 Dutch troops, Argyll was on the move. Immured, at Perth the Jacobites appeared strategically impotent whilst their supporters, such as Huntly, began to think of suggesting terms. In the short, winter days the rump of the rebel army fell back through Dundee toward Montrose, having thrown its guns into the Tay. Argyll remained unshakeably loyal to King George, even though he had suffered the humiliation of being superseded as Commander-in-Chief.

On 4 February, James, together with Mar, the Earl of Melfort and Lord Drummond, fled the realm. Neither the Old Pretender nor 'Bobbing John' would return. What remained of the army continued its retreat into the Highlands where it melted back into the hills. The '15 was over.

A shrewd observer had noted, on the death of Louis IV, that 'if the old gentleman is going, that will extinguish the hopes of the Pretender better than any of our acts of Parliament'.[9] The British ambassador to Madrid was moved to comment: 'I am surprised to see so large a body of nobility engaged in so foul a case. I do not know how far it may be a mark of their bravery, but sure it is none of their judgement to have chosen the present season to show themselves.'[10]

Though the French were too much overcome with anxiety for the treaty with England to openly side with James, a great deal of residual sympathy remained. Nullifying any shred of encouragement from France became a prime objective in negotiations, and the French were informed that the Pretender must be driven beyond their borders.

In the wake of the '15 the desire to emasculate the Jacobites loomed large in Hanoverian policy. Though the rebellion had failed, the threat posed by the formidable army which Mar had disposed could not be underestimated. That it had failed was as much due to Bobbing John's ineptness as to the government's state of preparedness. A more able commander would have swept Argyll's meagre detachments aside and marched, unopposed, on Edinburgh.

On 28 November, an alliance between England and France was finally concluded at The Hague. If this gave George I and his Whig advisors any comfort, their equilibrium was still disturbed by regular alarums: In July 1716 there had been fears over a possible amphibious descent on Portsmouth and Whig peers were still fretting over residual Jacobite sentiment. In the spring of 1718 there were fresh reports of sedition in Northumberland, where the Tory gentry were not subdued, even after the debacle at Preston. George Liddell wrote that there were murmurings on the streets of Newcastle, a city previously regarded as solidly Whig:

> It is the opinion of all the judicious well affected people both in the county and Northumberland that we shall have another rebellion and that very speedily unless some more than ordinary care be taken by the government... You may depend upon it we shall, in a very little time have another insurrection in Northumberland if not... prevented by the governments sending a regiment or two of dragoons into Northumberland and a regiment of foot to Newcastle.[11]

The domestic and foreign policies of George I did little to endear him to the Tory survivors or even to the more moderate Whigs. Throughout his reign the King was primarily concerned to secure the interests of Hanover, which won him few friends on the continent. In general the British, and the English in particular, saw France as the traditional enemy, and even if the late King William's confrontational and warlike policy had been costly, bloody and irksome, it was at least understandable.

Sweden, in the early eighteenth century, was the leading power in the Baltic region. Her military capabilities had been brought to prominence by King Gustavus Adolphus during the Thirty Years War. Her young and exceedingly martial sovereign, Charles XII, had embarked on an extended conflict which would be remembered as the Great Northern War.[12] George I, as Elector, had previously sought to grab some of the Swedish territories in North Germany, thus making a powerful enemy of Charles.

At the start of the century Charles XII had been prepared to look favourably on James II and this fostered the hope that Sweden would lend

arms and men in support of the late rebellion. Happily for the administration, the Swedish King was too much embroiled in his own, unending
war. Undeterred, the Jacobites, in 1716, entered into correspondence with
Count Gyllenborg, the Swedish ambassador. These letters were intercepted
and deciphered through efforts by the government's admirable espionage
network, but the evidence showed that a possibility of Swedish intervention
might have substance.

Despite the unravelling of the potential plot, Jacobite activists continued
to hope for aid from Charles XII. A Whig member, Robert Molesworth,
ranted: 'There is scarce a Jacobite school boy, or poor tradesman's wife about
our streets, who has not been instructed how conveniently Norway lies to
Scotland, and how much it was for their master's interests that the brave
King of Sweden should succeed in his undertakings.'[13]

It is most probable the Jacobites were deluded in their hopes of Sweden.
Charles XII needed cash more than anything, to maintain the great burden
of the lengthy war. He would only be minded to divert scarce resources
towards Britain if he could perceive a clear reward. His death from a sniper's
ball in 1718 ended the debate.

In that year another war broke out, this time between England and Spain,
and in the early stages a Spanish fleet was badly mauled off Cape Passaro by
Admiral Byng. The humiliation prompted Cardinal Alberoni, First Minister
to Philip V and Spain's *éminence grise*, to look afresh at Jacobite prospects. As a
result he began a correspondence with James Butler, 2nd Duke of Ormonde
and a leading Jacobite.[14] The Cardinal was encouraged by the notion of
widespread disaffection in England, but he was hard-headed enough not to
underestimate the risks attached to any form of amphibious undertaking:

> In order to prevent a landing it is necessary to have ships and they take time
> to arm… when we have talked of the project [an invasion] we have laid a
> great stress on speedy expedition but we can't command the winds, we have
> been constantly assured of the good dispositions of the British and they will
> rise when Spain sends you 5,000 regulars and arms… the British coast is too
> long to defend effectively… great enterprises cannot be attempted without
> major difficulties and only courage and firmness can vanquish them.[15]

Alberoni was canny enough to appreciate that England needed to be the
prime target. He did not favour Scotland, too remote, too difficult to supply
and with any amphibious operations vulnerable to a strong naval riposte. If

he overestimated Jacobite support in England he was aware how serious the consequences of another failure would be for James: 'if he misses this occasion that poor prince is lost and he should no longer think of the throne of England' – a pretty fair analysis, all in all.

In the course of further letters to Ormonde in the early spring of 1719, the Cardinal expressed a view that intervention from Spain could only work if the tide of domestic support was running high enough, and herein lay the tricky paradox for James. Only if sufficient sympathisers in England could be raised would the Spanish sail; conversely, it would be difficult to garner support at home unless foreign aid was certain. Ironically the Hanoverians discovered they had had active allies in the French, who passed on vital intelligence. Spain was no friend to France and fear of Spanish designs outweighed any sentiment for the deposed Stuarts.

The Scottish sideshow was to be led by George Keith, 10th Earl Marischal, who was to recruit a cadre of exiles including the Marquis of Tullibardine and his younger brother Lord George Murray. The main invasion force under Ormonde sailed from Cadiz in March with 5,000 troops and a further 30,000 of arms. The weather, in this instance, proved staunchly pro-Hanoverian and the fleet was dispersed in a violent storm off Finisterre before it even reached Corunna, where the Duke was based.

Keith, whose slender forces could be accommodated in two frigates and with only a very weak battalion of 307 Spanish regulars, set sail on 8 March and first made landfall at Stornoway. By 2 April the rebels had arrived on the mainland, by Eilean Donan castle at the mouth of Loch Duich. Despite their precarious position, the two senior figures soon fell to quarrelling. Tullibardine disputed Keith's right to overall command and insisted that the land forces, such as they were, be led by him. So bitter was the row that the handful of invaders were soon occupying separate camps!

Two of the chiefs, Lochiel and Clanranald, ventured into the hills to drum up recruits, though these proved very hard to find. The news of Ormonde's failure caused any residue of morale to plummet; it would not be long before the Royal Navy was snapping at their heels. The Duke sent encouraging messages instructing them to press on, a foolish exhortation in the circumstances. The Whig Duke of Montrose succinctly summed up their prospects when he observed, 'they must soon starve or be ruined'.[16]

As April passed into May, the Jacobites struck their camps and moved inland, establishing a further base at the Crow of Kintail. Eilean Donan, which had been left as a depot for munitions, was wrecked by naval bombardment.[17] The rebels now marched in two columns toward Glenshiel and, at the start of June, their numbers were swelled by, at best, 1,000 clansmen. Scouts swiftly confirmed that General Wightman had advanced from Fort Augustus to Glen Moriston and, by 9 June, reached the head of Loch Cluanie. It was now time to run or fight.

Wightman's forces were no greater than those of his opponents: less than a thousand foot, some of whom were Dutch, two detached companies of grenadiers, some dragoons, 100 or so broadswords from the Whig clans and six Coehorn mortars.[18] The ground was mountainous and favoured the defence. As his first command, Murray was tasked to hold the right, south of the Shiel, whilst the rest of the line stretched uphill. This comprised the Spaniards, Lochiel, the famous rascal Rob Roy MacGregor with forty odd of his clan, the Mackenzies, a contingent of Campbells,[19] Mackintosh of Borlum and then, on the extreme left, Seaforth.

The government battalions were drawn up in conformity, with the Mackays facing Seaforth and dragoons bunched across the drove. The Coehorns, with Clayton's and Munro's, stood south of the river. The two sides watched each other for much of the warm spring afternoon, the calm punctured only by the popping of carbines and long-range sniping. Once the mortars began lobbing shell at Murray's men, these were obliged to withdraw, allowing the gunners to shift their aim toward the Spanish. In all probability the projectiles inflicted few casualties, but the thump and crash of the explosions frayed morale and scattered sparks onto the dry heather.

Now Mackay's Highlanders were probing around the flank of Seaforth's men and, though the fight did not come to contact, the Earl Marischal collected a ball in the arm and the Jacobites on the left now also fell back. With both flanks driven in, the centre began to waver and a general retreat ensued. Though worsted, the Jacobites were far from routed and fell back through the cleft by the base of Sgurr na Ciste Duibhe. Several of their officers, including both Murray and Seaforth, suffered wounds, but fatal casualties were light on both sides, perhaps a score or less for each.

The clans could simply melt back into the hills in their traditional manner, but not so the Spanish, who had no choice but to lay down their arms. The rebellion was over, a profitless exercise for the Jacobites, Glenshiel a mere skirmish in an irrelevant sideshow. Even if Keith could have brushed Wightman aside, it is difficult to imagine what more could have been accomplished. With the projected invasion of England wrecked, the Scottish diversion was stillborn.

Despite these failures, there was a perception that Jacobite sentiment remained rife in England, and a spate of disturbances which spread through certain cities (Bristol, Manchester, Newcastle and Norwich) was blamed on the Pretender's faction. Even if this were true, which is questionable, Spain was in serious difficulties, facing a formidable coalition of Britain, France and the Empire, and the Royal Navy, notwithstanding its other commitments, remained unshakeable.

Whilst James skulked in Rome, the current refuge for his truncated court, his hopes for Spanish aid withered. A sympathetic newsletter from London pointed out the stagnation of Jacobite hopes unless substantive foreign aid could be procured:

> After the total disappointment of the invasion intended from Spain last Spring his Majesty's friends in England seemed to have nothing to do but to wait events and in the meantime to keep up the spirit of the party and to prevent desertion and it must be owned to their honour no persons of any figure or consideration seemed the least disposed to enter into an opposite interest. Neither are the commonality grown better affected than formerly to the present government or less desirous of a thorough change.[20]

Some degree of patient fortitude was to be required. By 1720 Alberoni was in disfavour and his master suing for peace. A year later, the seemingly interminable Great Northern War finally spluttered out and the palpable tension between Britain and Russia dissipated.[21] With his hopes in Spain slipping, though by no means abandoned, James sought to reignite the flame of French support. Despite his best endeavours and however sympathetic the French court might appear, the administration was firmly committed to maintaining the amity of England. In the spring of 1721 James was writing to the Earl of Orrey:

> The Duke of Ormonde in Spain and Dillon in France never cease representing the present favourable disposition of England, nor soliciting that help which can alone enable us to profit of it, but till Abbe Dubois be gained of which I see little prospect or till he be removed which I think less unlikely to happen, on account of the universal hatred he has acquired, I see little hopes of our receiving much favour from that government, although I have so many and so considerable friends in France that I should not think it altogether impossible to gain our end by them alone, this particular is not neglected but what success it can or will have, is more than I can yet tell, our hopes from Spain are much more solid.[22]

The early 1720s were a time of political uncertainty in England. The rifts between the Whig factions had been papered over but the economic crisis engendered by the bursting of the South Sea Bubble[23] further compromised the administration, whose role in that sorry business was far from above reproach. The Jacobites drew heart from the government's discomfort, and foresaw a swelling wave of discontent that might yet open the gates at home without the need for overseas aid.

In these rather desperate circumstances, the Earl of Sunderland, one of the chief pillars of the crumbling administration, fearing his rival Robert Walpole would achieve a landslide in the elections planned for 1722 and equally fearful of the disfavour of the Prince of Wales, connived at an unholy alliance of Tories and Jacobites. The plot called for a rising facilitated by the Irish Regiments in French service, the 'Wild Geese',[24] supported by Ormonde from Spain.[25] Their plan was to seize key centres in London including the Tower, the Royal Exchange and the Bank of England by a *coup de main* to be orchestrated by Lord North, leading Tory elements from the Guards regiments and Jacobite sympathisers from the City. It was then intended to mobilise more widespread support from like-minded elements amongst the commons. With London safe, disaffected gentry in the shires would rise, bolstered by Ormonde's forces disembarking at Bristol and those of Lord Lansdowne landing in Cornwall.

As an exercise in theory this was all very threatening, but the reality was that the grumblers would grumble regardless, and any real sympathy with the exiled Stuarts stayed within the ale houses and coffee shops. Tangible support from men willing to hazard their lives and property on so chancy a throw was much harder to find. As one of the Under Secretaries noted in correspondence from the capital, penned during March:

> The Jacobites abroad were in firm expectation of the great event, and doubted not if the foreign powers would only stand neuter to carry their point. Ormonde and others were beginning to put themselves in motion, and they seemed to depend that it was 'un coup seur', but for my life I can't reason as they do; nor because the mob is poisoned, women and parsons rail, and the grumblers put about libels and ballads, that therefore the whole nation will join and take up arms in favour of the Pretender... But such are the hopes hot and jealous people encourage one another to.[26]

Any serious prospect of a rising died with Sunderland, who succumbed to pleurisy on 19 April. From France, Orleans sent timely intelligence and Walpole was able to cement his grip on power, thereby assuring the continuance of the Whig supremacy. Troops were brought in and bivouacked in Hyde Park; reinforcements from Holland were requested. Orleans cooperated fully by pulling his battalions back from proximity to the Channel coast, the Spanish were warned off, and the Imperialists pledged support. Known Jacobites were closely watched; all mail from abroad was scrutinised.

By the autumn, William Stanhope, British envoy in Madrid, was observing that 'if any truth is to be given to the most solemn repeated protestations and assurances, together with all other possible appearances of sincerity, this court cannot be engaged in any measures in favour of the Pretender. These assurances the King of Spain has often given me himself.'[27] Though Stanhope had no high estimation of the Spaniards' integrity he was still correct in visualising real support for a further attempt as minimal.

The Bishop of Rochester, Francis Atterbury, was arrested when a relatively minor tool of the conspirators, the clergyman Philip Neynoe, was taken and persuaded to disclose details of the leadership. Walpole was content to leave some of the gentry, such as North, unmolested, though lesser fry, like the Norfolk advocate Christopher Layer, suffered the full rigour of the law.[28] His horrible fate would serve as a timely lesson to the rest; Atterbury was lucky to escape with exile.

For James, this was yet another in a growing list of disappointments, a string of 'what might have beens'. He bore these reverses stoically and with his habitual, unfailing courtesy. The failure of the Atterbury conspiracy convinced those diehards in England that only large-scale foreign intervention could secure a restoration.

Whig opinion, as exemplified by *The Flying Post*, remained perturbed by the perceived continuing disaffection of the Highland clans. As the feature which appeared on 7 March 1723 pointed out, the ragged and remote coastline was impossible to police effectively from the sea and the Highlanders were a martial people, ready armed and undisturbed by any meaningful military presence. *The Flying Post* went on, echoing Whig sentiment, that it was time these remote fastnesses were brought within the full orbit of the Crown. New industry and education were needed if this historic threat was to be defused, and what were required to facilitate this plan for constructive change was roads. A new network, driven over the remote moors and dipping glens, that could service a network of garrison outposts and bring civilisation to the benighted clans.

6

ROADS, REDCOATS AND REBELS

Had you seen these roads before they were made,
You would hold up your hands and bless General Wade.

Traditional doggerel

What is properly called the Highlands of Scotland is that large tract of mountainous
Ground to the Northwest of the Forth and the Tay, where the natives speak the Irish
language. The inhabitants stick close to their antient and idle way of life; retain their
barbarous customs and maxims; depend generally on their Chiefs as their Sovereign
Lords and masters; and being accustomed to the use of Arms, and inured to hard living,
are dangerous to the public peace; and must continue to be so until, being deprived of
arms for some years, they forget the use of them.[1]

The usual habit of both sexes is the plaid... the men wear theirs after another man-
ner... it is loose and flowing like the mantles our painters give their heroes. Their thighs
are bare with brawny muscles. Nature has drawn all her strokes bold and masterly.
What is covered is only adapted to necessity, a thin brogue on the foot, a short buskin
of various colours on the legs, tied above the calf with a large shot pouch on each side
of which hangs a pistol and a dagger... a round target on their backs... in one hand a
broadsword and a musket in the other.[2]

The two quotes above sum up the southerner's view of the Highlands, a barbarous tract of primeval waste somewhere north of Edinburgh. The eighteenth century was not an age that admired wilderness; that would have to wait for the Romantics. It favoured order, the taming of nature, and polite landscaping, with anything truly rustic kept at a discreet distance.

Silence, total silence, is an elusive commodity in the modern world. We are surrounded now by noise, man-made sound, omnipresent, insistent, frequently irritating; mobile telephones, vehicle alarms, traffic noise, power tools, aircraft. To understand the Highlands in the eighteenth century it is necessary to imagine a time devoid of this shrill, pointless cacophony. It is perhaps ironic that there are few better places to comprehend such a world than the surviving stretches of Wade's Roads, the network of highways built by Marshal Wade and his successors, for the prime purpose of policing the trackless glens.

The battered surface stretches over the wide expanse of moor, with only the haunting lament of the curlew to pierce the absolute calm, still passable on foot and perhaps by the brave adventurer in a Land Rover. The clansmen lived their lives in relative silence and the sounds that punctuated their days were those of nature; roads themselves were a novelty and an unwelcome novelty at that. They belonged to an era when the passage of armies, any army, friend or foe, was a terrifying experience, a monstrous, tramping, all-devouring invasion that consumed everything in its path, usually without compensation.

A surviving section of Wade's Roads heads north-west from Fort Augustus and skirts the shoulder of Druim a' Chathair.[3] To understand the world of the clansmen this is probably an essential experience, an eloquent testimony both to that quiet world and to the Hanoverian government's attempt to dominate it.

The Highlands of Scotland constitute the most remote and inaccessible part of mainland Britain, their inhabitants separated from their fellow Scots and English not just by the inconveniences of topography but by perceived race, culture, language, custom, dress and religion. The land north of the Highland Line and the Great Glen offers the most dramatic of landscapes: masses of ancient, hunched, rock-strewn peaks and lunar pinnacles, a coast-line slashed with the long fjords of sea lochs and a chain of islands that scatter out into the vast emptiness of the Atlantic, as far to the west as the tiny, mystical St Kilda.

In the extreme north-west of Sutherland, where the waves batter distant Cape Wrath and the long sweep of Sandwood Bay, the Mackays held sway, staunchly pro-Hanoverian. South and across to Skye and Lewis, the MacLeods, a sept of Clan Donald, lived around Loch Broom and what is now the pleasant fishing town of Ullapool. MacDonalds (Clanranald) held Uist and Moidart, the MacLeans Mull, Clan Cameron claimed Lochaber whilst Argyll to the south was the fief of Clan Campbell.

It was a wild land, untamed by major roads or highways, largely devoid of government outposts; those that did exist were decayed and undermanned. The sea and inland lochs provided the most natural arteries of communication. The soil was too poor to encourage arable farming, and the mainstay of what was at best a subsistence economy were the shaggy black cattle. Highlanders acquired these as often through foray as through commerce.

George Wade was of Anglo-Irish stock, a career soldier whose commission, into the 10th Regiment of Foot, dates from 1690. By 1714 he had risen, largely through merit, to the exalted rank of Major General. He did the House of Hanover good service and was active in sniffing out the 'Swedish' plot of 1717. As a senior commander, his first whiff of action was against the mob in Bath, said to be a Jacobite heartland.[4] Prior to this he had, in the words of the song, fought Queen Anne's enemies 'through Flanders, Portugal and Spain'.

The events of the '15 and the '19 should have served sufficient notice on the administration to be wary of the disaffected clans. A timely reminder from Simon Fraser, Lord Lovat, which was submitted to King George in 1724, was sufficient for Wade to be entrusted with a mission to

> narrowly to inspect the present situation of the Highlanders, their manners, customs and the state of the country in regard to the depredations said to be committed in that part of his Majesty's dominions; to make strict enquiry into the allegations that the effect of the last Disarming Act[5] had been to leave the loyal party in the Highlands naked and defenceless at the mercy of the disloyal; to report how far Lovat's memorandum was founded on fact, and whether his proposed remedies might properly be applied; and to suggest to the King such other remedies as may conduce to the quiet of his Majesty's faithful subjects and the good settlement of that part of the Kingdom.[6]

Wade moved with haste and reported that of an estimated 22,000 Highlanders capable of bearing arms more than half were disaffected:'10,000 are well affected to the Government, the remainder have been engaged in Rebellion against Your Majesty, and are ready, whenever encouraged by their Superiors or Chiefs of Clans to create new Troubles and rise in Arms in favour of the Pretender.'[7] This can scarcely have afforded King George any measure of comfort, nor is there any reason to doubt Wade's estimates.

His survey was not, however, merely a warning, he had practical recommendations to make concerning the policing and control of the dark glens north of the Highland line. Firstly, he advised that it would be prudent to raise independent companies of loyal Highlanders to enforce the royal writ on their disaffected neighbours, to disarm the malefactors, to enforce law and order, and to bring troublemakers to book. In essence this was nothing new in concept but had, thus far, failed in application. Secondly, a fort was to be built at Inverness to police the upper end of the Great Glen, and the existing works at Kiliwhimen should be extended or moved to bring the defences down to the shoreline of Loch Ness; both these suggestions were entirely logical. Thirdly, in order to better patrol the Glen and maintain communication between the outposts, he advocated stationing a sloop on the loch 'sufficient to carry a Party of 60 or 80 soldiers and Provisions for the garrison'.[8]

The findings were submitted early in December 1724 and by Christmas Wade was appointed Commander-in-Chief of North Britain. In the following spring he requested funds to the tune of £10,000 to be made available over a two-year building programme. Included in the schedule of works, and in addition to the new forts, was a list of major repairs at both Edinburgh and Fort William. In the interim he had rethought the situation at Kiliwhimen and decided that the existing fort was unsuitable. He now proposed that a decent communications network be established to link the outposts: Wade's Roads.

In practical terms, although Wade was the instigator of the road building programme it was his successor Major William Caulfeild who oversaw the greater part of the work. In the earlier part of his extensive career Wade had witnessed the difference a viable transport system could make in securing the rapid deployment of troops and guns. He perceived how acute was this need in the Highlands, where the harsh, trackless terrain, abetted by the wetness of the climate, suited the indigenous and highly mobile insurgents while presenting a major obstacle to regular troops, burdened by the need to transport their guns, stores and impedimenta. It was not that roads did not exist at all; this perception, like that of raising the independent companies, was not innovation, more the repetition and development of previous common sense ideas. Such links as did exist were few in number and invariably in serious disrepair. What is unique about Wade's overview was that he was thorough, comprehensive and, due to the administration's high state of alarm, listened to. He was heard to the extent that funding, previously highly elusive, was found.

During his tenure four main arterial routes were created or developed: Fort William to Inverness, Dunkeld to Inverness, Crieff to Dalnacardoch, and Dalwhinnie to Kiliwhimen (now to be the new Fort Augustus). The General proved to be a highly efficient and dedicated military engineer. Often he carried out the requisite location surveys personally, leading a small team, usually consisting of a non-commissioned officer and, say, half a dozen infantry.[9]

In terms of technique, Wade preferred the straight clean lines that any Roman would have applauded, with series of hairpin bends built to tame steep gradients, the most epic of which surmount the Corrieyairack Pass which links Ruthven and Fort Augustus. This magnificent stretch of road survives, traversing some of the wildest and most unspoilt country in Europe west of the Carpathians.[10] Like the Romans, Wade used his soldiers as engineers and labourers, perhaps 500 to each section of road; he described these working parties, with more than a hint of irony, as 'Highwaymen'.[11] The actual work was mainly conducted in the summer months with long hours of daylight and, hopefully, the mosses dried by the warming sun. The men spent the long winter months in barracks and lived, like nomads, in hutted encampments whilst working.

Wade had provided a general specification, though this could vary according to geological and topographical constraints. Some of his works, particularly certain of the bridges, most impressively that over the Tay at Abefeldy,[12] are a triumph of elegant functionalism.

The General's intention to station an armed vessel on Loch Ness was based on a Cromwellian precedent; he built a thirty-ton sloop that could carry a full company of infantry and mounted eight guns. Wade himself experienced the full rigours of the harsh upland climate when, in 1728, the boat was tossed for thirteen hours in a most violent storm, with all onboard expecting their final hour had come.

His preoccupation with road building did not deflect him from his parallel intention to construct strong new forts in the Glen. Inverness had possessed a castle since the Middle Ages. A Commonwealth Citadel had been built and abandoned, while Mackay had opted to turn a tower house on the old castle motte into an ad hoc fort, which had itself now fallen into disrepair. Consequently, Wade's architect, Captain John Romer of the Board of Ordnance, repaired and extended the tower and added additional barrack piles and a magazine. The new garrison outpost was to be known as Fort George, tactfully named after Wade's new employer, George II.

This was a relatively modest plan compared to the proposed replacement for the fort at Kiliwhimen. Wade had toyed with upgrading the original, but opted for an ambitious new design on the loch shore. This was to be named Fort Augustus after the new King's third son.[13] This was planned on the grand scale and was to be headquarters and linchpin of the Highland garrisons. A quartet of substantial bastions was linked by sections of curtain wall, screened by outworks, with elegant barrack piles, completed in fashionable detail. It was at once a declaration of intent and a statement of style, an illustration to the rude clansmen of Hanoverian power, wealth and taste.[14] The garrison was to include the Governor, his full HQ staff, logistics personnel and around 300 soldiers. If the Jacobites thought policing the Highlands was just another manifestation of transitory intervention that would soon wither, the very substance of Fort Augustus indicated quite the contrary: Wade was out to impress.

Throughout his tenure additional work was being carried out at Fort William and a new barracks was erected at Ruthven,[15] again utilising the old medieval site. Another had earlier sprung up at Bernera,[16] by the hamlet of Glenelg, which was intended to guard the approaches from the Inner Hebrides. The defence of the Lowlands was not neglected; substantive improvements and modernisation was undertaken at Edinburgh[17] and Dumbarton. Prior to Wade's improvements a substantial and impressive new barracks had been built at Berwick-upon-Tweed within the Elizabethan enceinte.[18]

As his chief surveyor Wade may have had Edward Burt, who left us a memoir in the form of a compilation of correspondence published as *Letters from a Gentleman in the North of Scotland*.[19] He was by no means enamoured of his Highland hosts, nor for that matter their Lowland contemporaries. However, his were perhaps the first general observations that many in England would have encountered:

> The Highlands are but little known, even to the inhabitants of the low country of Scotland... to the people of England... the Highlands are hardly known at all; for there has been less than I know of written upon the subject than of either of the Indies...[20]

In this observation he was, undoubtedly, likely to be correct. He noted, with perhaps a Whig bias, that the chiefs still enjoyed too much power for his liking:

> The heritable power of pit and gallows, as they call it, which is still exercised by some within their proper district, is, I think, too much for any particular subject to be entrusted with.[21]

He went on to expound, speaking of one of the chiefs:

I have heard say of him, by a very credible person, that a Highlander of a neighbouring clan, with whom he had long been at variance, being brought before him, he declared upon the accusation, before he had seen the party accused, that his very name should hang him.[22]

As a good Whig he deplored the hereditary powers of the magnates, whose power over their subjects, from 'the mere accident of birth', exceeded that of any peer in England over his tenants. He was, however, no more impressed by those fervent sons of the Kirk, members of the 'Society for the Propagation of Christian Knowledge', who were striving to bring the fuller appreciation of their dour brand of Calvinism to the glens. Burt noted that their task, in part, was to separate the Highlanders from their ancient, heathen tongue, though of course the radical ministers had to learn it themselves so they could communicate with their proposed congregations.

The majority of these missions failed miserably, though some stalwart preachers like the Herculean Aeneas Sage enjoyed success, winning through sheer indomitable persistence.[23] In addition to their feudal adherence, the clansmen's pride in their name confounded Burt, a southerner's view, with no attempt made to penetrate his subject's different understanding:

This kind of vanity… in people of no fortune, makes them ridiculous… thus you see a gentleman may be a mercenary piper, or keep a little ale-house where he brews his drink in a kettle; but to be of any working trade would be a disgrace to him, his present relations and his ancestry.[24]

He was equally dismissive of the bagpipes, the butt of many a Lowland joke since, though this disdain was entirely founded in ignorance.[25]

There is a view, expressed by certain writers, that clan society was moulded from the mists of time and not subject to change. This was by no means true, for the Highland way of life was constantly evolving. We have already seen how the chiefs, in the years between the end of the Civil Wars and the Glorious Revolution of 1688, adapted away from reliance on their swords to settle disputes. They found the hire of lawyers more cost effective than the maintenance of caterans. In the seventeenth century, although the existence of Gaeldom as a cultural entity appeared imperilled by external factors, the Gaels proved resilient and their literature and verse enjoyed a significant renaissance.[26] The 'Clan' was still the basis of the social framework. The clans of the seventeenth century were not Celtic survivals from the age of heroes, and their origin can more properly be traced back to the fourteenth century. The chiefs might originally have held their lands without the benefit of feudal charter, but feudal tenure gradually became more commonplace.[27]

Scotland, as a nation, was plagued by a succession of minority kingships during the late medieval and renaissance periods, with the inevitably factional feuding this entailed.[28] If the King, as tenant-in-chief, could not provide for his subjects or vassals then they would find they had to make shift for themselves. This they did, and the more aggressive increased their share at the expense of the weaker. Increasing power necessitated additional followers. This process could be cloaked or ratified in law by the lesser tenant agreeing to hold his land now from the greater, and the Crown's acquiescence sealed by deed or charter. As an alternative or as part of this process, the head of a family group or affinity could establish superiority over the lesser septs or branches. Lastly, men could enter into bonds or contracts whereby they pledged friendship and loyalty to each other. Where such an agreement was contracted between those of unequal standing, the lesser party bound himself and his affinity to obey the greater, the consideration being shelter under the great man's banner.

Feudalism, kinship and bonding ('manrent')[29] became the cement that bound the fabric of society. It is from this backdrop that the clan system emerges, a response to the lack of effective royal authority. 'Clan' means children – so there is a presumption all members spring from a common stock, a concept that the chiefs encouraged with their lengthy and often fantastical pedigrees, stretching their line back to Gaelic heroes of a distant past.

In the glens of the West the idea of loyalty to a chief gained favour as royal power waned. This was a reversal to previous precedents which had themselves declined when the Crown waxed strong. Many of these magnates were of Anglo-Norman descent and had obtained their lands through feudal charter, their authority thus a mix of Gaelic and purely feudal custom. In such hybrid form did many of the clans develop their later identities.

Throughout the period to 1745 the clans could not be distinguished by tartans or even by surnames. The former were a later creation, and until the eighteenth century many Highlanders did not possess a surname.[30] By the time of the first Jacobite rebellions this had begun to change and those who followed a certain chief would adopt his name. By this means they would claim affinity with the chief though they were not necessarily blood relations in any degree.

By the time Bobbing John was raising the Stuart colours at Braemar in 1715, the formation of the clan could comprise a number of disparate groups, welded by their obedience to the chief: the senior grayne, who could claim consanguinity with him, and the lesser septs, who were still blood relatives. Below them in the hierarchy, men of other names who owed allegiance through feudal or other ties and, lastly, a smattering of caterans or outlaws whose loyalty was dictated largely by expediency. Grafted on to the body of the clan proper was the corpus of retained individuals who served the chief as officials, bodyguards, doctors, lawyers, harpists or pipers.

Caterans had been present as an element in the fabric of Highland society since the late fourteenth century at least. Both sides who fought at Harlaw in 1411, Donald of the Isles and Alexander Earl of Mar, employed caterans as mercenaries. The name probably derives from the Irish 'cearnach' or soldier. They have been likened to Irish 'kerns' or 'buannacht'. In terms of quality they could range from a hardened and reliable elite to something akin to armed robbers. Traditionally chiefs employed caterans to carry out cattle raids and attend to the more dangerous enterprises. Lowland magnates with estates in the North, such as the Earl of Mar or his notorious father the Earl of Buchan, more colourfully known as 'The Wolf of Badenoch', employed caterans as a rough-and-ready police force, much resented by those on whom they were habitually billeted or who suffered generally from their depredations.

The clan, therefore, was a social organisation whose members were bound by a common loyalty but whose kinship, status and motivation might vary considerably. Clans were not so much built around blood relationships as upon a common obedience – loyalty to the chief as 'father'. As time passed this common affinity would become the norm and the ties that bonded the disparate elements would mesh and sometimes blur. If a chief claimed this paternal relationship to those who were in effect his subjects, he offered them a status higher that mere vassalage and implied a level of mutual obligation that might ordinarily apply only to those related by blood. In a violent and uncertain world, such as obtained during the Age of Forays, a man needed to belong somewhere and be able to call upon the shield of one far mightier than himself. Expediency, properly nurtured, could breed pride in the name and a willingness to identify closely with the chief, and this could in turn lead to a very considerable degree of personal loyalty. Obviously, as the generations passed and those of the blood married into those of lesser claim, the net of kinship was cast wider.

Those of the senior branch and the senior members of cadet branches formed the gentry of the clan. In the earlier stages these held their lands as of right and through heredity, but latterly it became the custom of many chiefs to grant formal leases or 'tacks'. In time of strife these tenants or tacksmen formed the officer cadre of the clan regiment. Their leases were usually heritable and military service a condition of tenure.

Though the chief enjoyed great power this was not, initially at least, without limitation or constraint. His position was not inexpugnable; he was expected to consult with a council of advisors and tacksmen. His successor was chosen from amongst a class of his immediate family, harking back to the old Celtic practice of tanistry. By the eighteenth century, however, the chief's position had developed into something more authoritarian and sometimes aloof, with the concept of primogeniture firmly established. This may sound retrograde, but the uncertainty of tanistry had sparked many a feud.

Differences between various clan groupings were frequently exacerbated by a weak, or inefficient, royal authority. Lands were sometimes separately granted to different claimants, who could then cite not only traditional tenure of long usage but a viable feudal charter. A pernicious situation could arise where men living on a certain portion of land could find themselves obliged by charter to one feudal superior whilst owing traditional allegiance to another. The Campbells were particularly skilled in what could be termed 'aggressive' feudalism.[31]

In many ways this pattern did not differ overly from that established in the Lowlands. Change and the widening gulf was gradually spurred on, after the mid-sixteenth century, by the impetus of the reformed church, which drew the line between Calvinist Lowlands and the Recusant or Episcopalian Highlands. The pace of cultural change began to gather noticeably south of the Great Glen as church lands were parcelled out and the burgeoning middle classes created a more market-based economy, with land and property being dealt in as commodities.

As the cultural gap widened it was exacerbated to a significant degree by the lack of a common language. The ancient, guttural tongue of the Gael, melodic as it can sound to those suitably attuned, grated as harsh, barbaric and backward to those who looked more often to the south than north and west. Gaelic culture was heartily despised by the Lowlanders, who had no feel for its subtlety or tradition, and by those who saw learning as the province of formal schooling and university cloisters. Differences of language were compounded by marked variations in dress and by the Highlander's equally hubristic clinging to his own way.

Unsurprisingly the spectacle of everyday life in the Highlands failed to impress Edward Burt, solidly wedded to the virtues of regular industry. He found the cramped, earthy conditions in their bothies primitive in the extreme. This revulsion at the primitive conditions endured by the clansmen informs the writings of most of those southerners (few as they were) who visited.

Their world seemed utterly at variance with the burgeoning cultural, commercial and artistic life of the Lowlands. The great age of the Scottish enlightenment, the time of Adam Smith, David Hume and a generation of Scots whose achievement was to turn Edinburgh and the Lowlands into the intellectual powerhouse of Europe, was just around the corner.

This soaring upsurge was expected to coexist with backward Highlanders who appeared to have no more in common with their Lowland contemporaries than the native tribes of North America. What labour there was seemed to be undertaken by the females, whilst the men idled their time around in the smoky glow of peat fires, apparently with nothing resembling gainful employment to occupy them.

> Many are supported by the bounty of their acquaintances or friends and relations, others get their living by levying blackmail[32] and the rest by stealing.[33]

This may be a southerner's pejorative view of a society he was unable and unwilling to understand. Such reports would only fuel the government's alarm at the likely menace posed by these hardy mountaineers who, if they were nothing else, were natural fighters, hardened by their climate, their martial tradition, the practices of cattle raiding and the feud or vendetta.[34]

One who knew them better than Burt was Duncan Forbes of Culloden, Lord President of the Court of Session.[35] He was a staunch Hanoverian but had spent his life amongst the chiefs and was able to offer the government the benefit of his accumulated wisdom:

> A Highland Clan is a set of men all bearing the same sirname, and believing themselves to be related, the one to the other, and to be descended from the same common stock. In each clan there are several subaltern tribes, who owe their dependence on their own immediate chiefs but al agree in owing allegiance to the Supreme Chief of the Clan or Kindred and look upon it to be their duty to support him in all adventures.[36]

Forbes explained why the Crown had, to a large degree, perpetuated the power of the chiefs, largely through an exercise of expediency:

> It has been for a great many years impracticable (and hardly thought safe to try it) to give the Law its course among the mountains. It required no small degree of Courage, and a greater degree of power than men are generally possessed of, to arrest an offender or debtor in the midst of his Clan. And for this reason it was that the Crown in former times was obliged to put Sheriffships and other Jurisdictions in the hands of powerful families in the Highlands, who by their respective Clans and following could give execution to the Laws within their several territories, and frequently did so at the expense of considerable bloodshed.[37]

In his efforts to provide informed enlightenment to the government in London the Lord President calculated the likely total of fighting men available to the chiefs as a whole and arrived at a figure of 31,930. Not all of these were, of course, disaffected; Whig clans such as the Campbells, who could muster 4,000 broadswords, accounted for a fair proportion. But the warning was clear: if a few thousand of the Tory clans could shake loose Scotland, get the better of Crown forces in two major and several minor engagements then march, unchecked, as far as Derby, the threat from the whole was potent indeed.

There is a view that, by 1745, the Highland way of life was again in transition and that the power of the chiefs was waning. It is this factor that is cited as the reason why men of rank and estate such as Cameron of Lochiel and MacDonald of Keppoch would throw in with Prince Charles Edward, the desperate throw of gamblers who know the tide of fortune is rising inexorably against them.

Wade's roads had certainly had an impact in opening the glens to a degree never possible nor envisaged before. By the time the Prince landed it had been thirty years since the last major rising, discounting the fiasco of the '19, and residual enthusiasm for the Jacobite cause was sluggish. There is also evidence to suggest that at least some of those brought out by their chiefs were in no great hurry to oblige and that coercion was necessary. Where such recalcitrance obtained, the usual remedy was a threat to burn the clansman's roof over his head should he fail to reconsider. This was a powerful incentive, and Lord Lewis Gordon, for one, appears to have placed reliance on the threat whilst drumming up recruits from Speyside.[38]

After the smoke from Culloden had dissipated, the Reverend James Robertson of Lochbroom begged relief for those of his parishioners held captive as rebels. He advised that MacDonald of Keppoch, as chief, had, in March 1746, carried out a forced levy, dragging unwilling men from hearth and plough:

> One I did myself see overtaken, and when he declared he would rather die than be carried to rebellion, was knocked to the ground by the butt of a musket and carried away all blood.[39]

This testimony is uncorroborated, yet carries an undeniable ring of truth. Another clergyman, Mr Gordon of Alvie, offered a similar account of events amongst his flock. Of the forty-three who joined the Prince, he averred that only three were willing and the remainder had been terrorised by thatch burning, damage to livestock and physical violence. Lochiel's tacksmen raised recruits in Rannoch, not by beat of drum by through threats. Dr Archibald Cameron,[40] brother to Lochiel, was said to have been active in a similar vein, 'declaring to all men of the chief's name that if they did not come off directly he would burn their houses and cut them in pieces'.[41]

When they did muster, the clothing, habit and arms of these Highlanders marked them utterly apart from their Lowland contemporaries. Edward Burt, as might be anticipated, found their manner of dress outlandish:

> The common habit of the Highlander is far from being acceptable to the eye. With them a small part of the plaid, which is not so large as the former, is set in folds and girt round the waist to make of it a short petticoat that reaches halfway down the thigh, the rest is brought over the shoulders and fastened before, below the neck often with a fork, and sometimes with a bodkin or sharpened piece of stick, so that they make pretty nearly the appearance of the poor women in London when they bring their gowns over their heads to shelter themselves from the rain. This dress is called the quelt, and for the most part they wear the petticoat so very short that in a windy day, going up a hill, or stooping the indecency of it is plainly discovered.[42]

In battle the plaid was customarily shrugged off before the charge bit home and the warrior came to contact with only his long, saffron shirt to preserve his modesty. Uniforms were unknown, everyday wear continuing during hostilities. In some areas breeches were as common as the plaid.[43] Shoes,

should the wearer possess them, were usually soft leather brogues and every-
one usually sported a woollen bonnet. The 'philabeg', or kilt, probably came
into use during the early eighteenth century and its creation is customarily
attributed to an Englishman called Rawlinson.[44] The gentry wore fine hose
or 'truibhs' (trews) which were essentially close-fitting leggings akin to
medieval hose, cut to favour the shapely thigh and calf of the wearer.

The clansmen's arms were as distinctive as his dress. During the earlier
period the rank and file had relied on the bow spears and axes. The 'Lochaber'
axe does not make its first recorded appearance until the sixteenth century.
In its matured form this was a long-handled polearm featuring a curved
axe blade, elliptical in shape and finished with a hook set in the head of the
shaft.[45]

Swords were normally reserved for gentlemen; a decent quality blade was
an expensive and prized item. Highland swords, in the sixteenth century,
were characterised by the development of the double-hander or *claidheamh
mor*. This was a broad double-edged blade, the crossguard finished with
distinctive drooping quillons terminating in pierced quatrefoils. Whether
any survivors of this type featured in the '45 is questionable but they may
well have been wielded in the course of the earlier rebellions.[46]

By the mid-eighteenth century the design and construction of basket-
hilted broadswords had reached its full, fine flowering. The double-edged
blades were mainly imported from Europe, many bearing the cypher
'Andrea Ferrara', but the hilts were fashioned locally. By the 1730s two
major schools of design, at Glasgow and Stirling, were flourishing. The
original simple framework of defensive bars, which had defined the earlier
'Irish' hilts, was transformed into a rectangular framework decorated with
circles, diamonds and clubs – the Allan family of Stirling were particularly
noted. These weapons remain some of the finest produced by British crafts-
men. Variants included a single-edged version or 'backsword'[47] and some
with curved blades.[48]

Descended from the medieval 'ballock' knife and later 'dudgeon' dagger,
the Highland Dirk, fancifully named the 'widowmaker', was a long-
bladed dagger that was traditionally carried in the left hand, held behind
the shield or target, for parrying. The blades, habitually the length of the
owner's forearm, were sometimes salvaged from cut-down sword blades
but otherwise tended to be single-edged and tapering, perhaps mounted
with brass.[49] Bog-oak or myrtle were favoured for the stubby, pot-
bellied handles, the pommel disc shaped and the whole hilt finished with

a filigree of silver or brass. These are elegant, yet functional weapons, used like the medieval rondel dagger as an everyday tool as well as a means of dispatching foes.

The target was a round timber shield or buckler which was constructed from two layers of oak or perhaps fir, a couple of feet across, the grain opposing and covered in supple hide. The basic product was decorated with brass studs and intricate tooling and with a centrally mounted boss that could be drilled to accommodate a projecting spike, a useful device for parrying.

Firearms were a relative rarity in the Highlands. A bemused citizen of Edinburgh, after its occupation in 1745, commented, somewhat sourly, on the paucity and inferior nature of the clansmen's long guns:

> I observed their arms they were guns of diferent syses, and some of innormowos length, some with butts turned up likk a heren, some typed with puck thread to the stock, some without locks and some matchlocks, some had swords over ther shoulder instead of guns, one or two had pitchforks, and some bits of sythes upon poles with a cleek some [had] old Lochaber axes.[50]

Some of these venerable pieces were undoubtedly matchlocks from the era of the Civil Wars. There would also be surviving Spanish escopetas from the arms supplied for the '19. The rout of the government forces at Prestonpans would, from the spoil, produce a fine haul of muskets.

Distinctive Scottish and Highland firearms did exist, both pistols and long guns, though perhaps never in significant numbers, while the latter were reserved for the gentry. These pistols, or 'daggs', were distinguished by their all-steel finish, with no wooden stock or grips. Early examples were fired by the wheel lock mechanism and latterly by the snaphaunce.[51] Their design was also characterised by a lack of the conventional trigger guard, a short stubby trigger with the distinctive 'fish tail' or 'lemon' butts. Latterly the flintlock assumed dominance and the weapons were carried in pairs, fitted with belt hooks rather than being slung in holsters.[52]

For the true Highlander war was an affair of honour, with individual pride in feats of arms the paramount aim. A man standing in his clan regiment would be judged by his kin and by his following. His was a martial society where the Homeric spectacle of the duel of champions was kept fresh by the bards, and the rant from the pipes called for individual feats of arms to rival the deeds of distant heroes:

O Children of Conn of the Hundred Battles
Now is the time for you to win recognition,
O raging whelps,
O sturdy bears,
O most sprightly lions,
O battle-loving warriors,
O brave, heroic firebrands,
The children of Conn of the Hundred Battles,
O children of Conn remember
Hardihood in time of battle.[53]

When the charge struck home it did so with fearful effect. A man standing in the front rank armed with broadsword and target, facing an opponent equipped with musket and bayonet, would use his target and the dirk, held behind in the left hand, to sweep aside the point of the infantryman's bayonet and deliver a sweeping cut to the neck or head – a killing blow. The razor-sharp edge of the blade would slice through tissue and smash bones, biting into the flesh and severing arteries. Blood loss from the wound would be catastrophic, the fight over in seconds.[54]

Duncan Forbes, in his assessment of the fighting strength of the clans, did not grade the worth of the combatants. It would be false to suggest that every able-bodied clansman was a warrior; most were not. Prowess in arms was generally reserved for gentlemen and professional fighters, caterans. They had the choice weapons, the training and motivation. The average commoner would be ill armed and without much in the way of military kit.

General Henry Hawley, who had fought at Sheriffmuir and would command the government army at Falkirk, earned, perhaps unjustly, the reputation of being a martinet. He had little sympathy for the clans and wrote somewhat dismissively of their tactics in battle:

They commonly form the Front rank of what they call their best men or True Highlanders, the number of which being always but few, when they form in battalions they commonly form four deep, & these Highlanders form the front of the four, the rest being Lowlanders & arrant scum. When these battalions come within a large musket shott or three score yards this front rank gives their fire, and immediately throw down their firelocks and come down in a cluster with their swords and targets, making a noise and endeavouring to pierce the body or battalion before them – becoming twelve or fourteen deep by the time they come up to the people they attack.[55]

Hawley was to find these 'Highlanders' and indeed the 'arrant scum' sufficient opponents at Falkirk! When mustering for a raid or foray the numbers involved would be likely to be quite small. When, however, the clan was called to battle then the organisational system employed was fairly conventional, with the commons being mustered in companies. The gentry would naturally form the officers whilst the caterans might supply the sergeants. Colonel Sullivan[56] noted that when the clans first responded to the Prince's summons at Glenfinnan in August 1745 individual units varied greatly in size and, like some Royalist formations during the Civil Wars, were burdened with a surfeit of officers.

Where it did not prove necessary to resort to physical violence and threats of burnings to stimulate recruitment, the traditional means of assembly was the fiery cross – two lengths of timber lashed together with a strip of (in theory at least) blood-soaked linen attached. This device was passed, smouldering, from hand to hand through the chief's domain, the talisman of war.[57] The muster assumed a ritual significance, ringed with superstition. If the company met an armed man, this was a good omen. Any game that darted across the way had to be killed else ill fortune would ensue. Should a barefoot female be encountered then a drop of blood must be pricked from her forehead. The clan was distinguished, not by tartan, but by its badge or emblem, a plant or herb, and by the slogan, the wild summons to slaughter, joy in the fight.

In terms of tactics the clans were feared for the Highland Charge. This was not merely a wild rush upon the enemy, a desire to come to hand strokes as quickly as possible. Obviously, any force that relies essentially upon the individual fighting prowess of its component members and is generally deficient in firearms would seek to come to contact as quickly as possible. A drawn-out advance, in the teeth of enemy fire, would winnow the ranks and, as the best armed men were to the fore, the casualties would be inordinately damaging to the unit's cohesion and fighting capacity.

Based on heroic tradition, the well-armed gentleman or cateran was the cutting edge, while the followers or 'ghillies' were cast very much in a supporting role. In true Homeric fashion, in the course of earlier, smaller-scale encounters these may have stood back whilst the respective paladins slogged it out. During Montrose's campaigns the ghillies provided, on a rather ad hoc basis, the missile arm, using their bows. Alasdair MacColla is credited with developing the wild rush of the Gael into a sound military tactic, deploying then men either in column or, sometimes, in a wedge-shaped formation.[58]

With the advent of firearms the role of the missile arm changed. As relatively few of the clansmen possessed long guns, and those that did were mainly gentry, the single volley was fired from extreme range before the charge crashed home. The ghillies would not, therefore, have had any kind of fire support role, as before. The swiftness of the advance, essential to cover ground and maintain momentum, did not permit reloading.

Let us return to Colonel Sullivan who, though he has not enjoyed a good press amongst historians, was capable of some trenchant remarks. He observed, prior to Culloden and as a criticism of the ground favoured by Lord George Murray, that:

> Any man yt ever served with the Highlanders, knows yt they fire but one shot & abandon their firelocks after. If there be any obstruction yt hinders them of going on the enemy all is lost; they don't like to be exposed to the enemy's fire, nor can they resist it, not being trained to charge [load] as fast as regular troops, especially the English wch are the troops in the world yt fires best.[59]

In this assertion the Irish officer was undoubtedly correct. It would not be possible to expect from Highlanders the level of drill and the rate of fire which a regular battalion might deliver. Their tradition of war and their lack of firepower both mitigated heavily against it. This is not to say, however, that they were without discipline, and those authors who regard the Jacobite army as a 'rabble' fall into the same trap as Edward Burt.

Tactically the commander of Highland troops had to choose his field with care. Level ground was to be preferred, with perhaps a slight downward angle, dry and not impeded by obstacles such as standing timber, walls or gullies. If the Highland formation could approach in dead ground (that is, out of sight of the enemy), and then charge home over a short distance, the prospects for victory were much improved.

At Killiecrankie and Prestonpans, apart from Montrose's earlier victories, the Highland charge shattered government armies. In the former battle the government troops on Mackay's left were swept from the field with loss. This is not to say the deployment of the clan regiments was perfectly executed: we have seen how the Camerons, instead of advancing directly upon

Leven's, echeloned to their left and suffered fearfully from volleys poured into their exposed flank.

A dry analysis of the fight fails to convey the impression which the charging clans clearly made upon raw troops. They came on, throwing off their plaids, as a body of men who knew their business and at a rapid rate of advance, a far swifter pace than regular formations could attain. With the screaming rant of the pipes and the wild scream of the slogan, their onrush must have been fearful. Psychology in war is all important, if underrated and difficult to fathom. These thundering clansmen, a steel tipped avalanche, with their great swords raised and the grinning blades of Lochaber axes swung by the commons, would be fierce enough to test the mettle of any young Lowlander recruited from an apprentice's bench.

Cohesion, in the clan regiment, came from a long martial tradition, pride in the name and a consciousness of fighting under the gaze of your peers. Those men with whom the Highlander charged were men he knew, some of them from his immediate family, others from the wider affinity. The clan regiment was bound together by its loyalty to the chief, by its long history, real and romanced, by the songs of the bards and by the rant of the pipes.

The men knew their weapons from long usage, they were physically fleet and hardy, inured, as Forbes observed, to hardship and therefore able to function with far less supply. For all of their shortcomings, these men marched as far as Derby as shook the House of Hanover to its core.

7

WILDERNESS YEARS

[The] Pretender is an unhappy fugitive, driven in his infancy from his country, and by consequence without any personal interest; that he is supported by the charity of a prince whose name is hated almost by every inhabitant of the kingdom; that he has neither sovereignty or money, nor alliances, nor reputation in war, nor skill in policy; that all his actions are watched by British spies... What could a wise man conceive of a nation held in continual alarms by an enemy like this; of a nation always watchful against an invasion from a man who has neither dominions to supply, nor money to hire a single regiment; from a man whose title all the neighbouring princes disown, and who is at such a distance from them, that he cannot be assisted by them without open preparations, of which we cannot fail of having intelligence, and which may be defeated without danger, by the vessels regularly stationed on our coasts.

William Pulteney (leader of the Whig opposition in the Commons)[1]

This description of James and his prospects was penned late in 1740 by the leader of the opposition Whigs, William Pulteney. It is no more than the truth and the prospects for a Jacobite restoration appeared, since the collapse of the Atterbury Plot, to be very dim indeed. The situation in Britain and within Europe had not favoured the Stuart faction and, inevitably, as time went on, any popular support for the cause began to wither.

Despite the outbreak of hostilities at various times with France, Austria and Spain, none of these was willing to hazard the risk of amphibious operations, especially at a time when the strength of the Royal Navy was continuing to grow. Notwithstanding international tensions which swelled like the ebb and flow of the tides, there was a distinct move away from the confrontational policies of George I. The guiding genius in this was undoubtedly that of Sir Robert Walpole, who enjoyed a long and influential tenure as, effectively, 'prime' minister, through the 1720s and 1730s until his final eclipse in 1742.

At home, also, Walpole steered a more moderate course. He abandoned the movement to enfranchise Dissenters, which pleased both church and country. His ministry might have been tainted by corruption but he was able to reduce levels of taxation, a sure-fire method of winning general approbation!

James, in waning exile, constantly hoped, like Mr Micawber, that 'something would turn up', that some shift in the uneasy relationships between the leading continental powers would open the door to a further attempt. None came. Many former Jacobites, bereft of their estates, began inevitably to think of coming to terms with the Hanoverian administration to salvage whatever could be salvaged from the wrack of their fortunes.[2]

British ambassadors reported dismissively from the courts of Paris and Madrid. Horatio Walpole, the prime minister's younger brother, wrote from the French capital: 'there is not the least reason to suspect at present any design in this court in favour of the Pretender; but that there is and always will be in this nation among the Catholics an inclination towards him, there is no manner of doubt'.[3] These sentiments were echoed by the Duke of Newcastle, Secretary of State for the Southern Department,[4] who opined that both houses were united in their support for the Hanoverian dynasty and no window of opportunity remained for the Jacobites to exploit.

A brief flowering of optimism flourished in 1725 when France and Spain once again fell into dispute, friction that resulted in a new understanding between Madrid and Vienna, traditionally so long at odds. There was some suggestion that the resulting Treaty of Vienna made some favourable mention of Stuart hopes, and the tone of the Pretender's correspondence brightens accordingly. Horatio Walpole was expressing concern over rather vague threats and suggestions by Bishop Fleury that vigilance in the Channel needed to be stepped up.

This sudden tension between France and Spain worked in Walpole's favour as the French felt the need to consolidate their accord with Britain. In the late summer of 1725 a tripartite alliance of Britain, France and Prussia came into being as a counter to the Treaty of Vienna. Any hopes James might have entertained of some form of Catholic League against the English Protestants vanished in the haze.

Undeterred, the Pretender concentrated on winning over the Austrians and Spaniards. He no longer clung to the hope that he might be restored by a domestic coup, recognising that nothing could be achieved without substantive foreign intermeddling. At this time the person the Jacobites would have to convince was none other than Prince Eugene of Savoy, Marlborough's favourite ally, a distinguished and hard-headed commander, who was clearly unconvinced by assertions that a force of soldiers no greater than 6,000 in number would suffice to spark a successful rebellion.

A whole raft of optimistic expectations – the proximity of Ostend,[5] the certainty of surprise, the absence of British men o' war, the fact the invaders could rely, for the short crossing, on a motley of craft – all failed to win over the sceptical Prince. He was quite right to be sceptical. Though relations with Austria might be less cordial than hitherto there was no outright breach and Britain, for once, stayed aloof as the continental powers squared up for the War of Polish Succession, which raged for two years between 1733 and 1735.

The Spaniards made an attempt on Gibraltar[6] but the Royal Navy controlled the seas. There was little comfort for James, and even the death of George I in the spring of 1727 failed to stimulate any upsurge in Jacobite sentiment. He entertained hopes of support from France and Austria; both, however, demurred. Vienna would not stir unless the Pretender could show he enjoyed the support of a substantial domestic faction, and of this there was little sign.

Many Tories hoped that the new King, George II, might be less opposed than his father, but in this they were to be largely disappointed and the Whig supremacy remained unaffected. The Tories might have been disheartened but showed no inclination to resort to arms – plainly there would be no repeat of the '15. Even in Ireland there was quiet; the substantial British military presence and the loss, through emigration, of so many supporters had stripped the country of potential. Riots in Scotland[7] and a whiff of suspicion over Russian intentions[8] proved no more fruitful. The flame of the White Cockade appeared to be guttering toward extinction.

Whig commentators became increasingly dismissive. At home the opposition found it impossible to dislodge Walpole who, though his position appeared inexpugnable, did not have matters go entirely his own way. The spectre of Jacobitism was always a useful weapon in the Whig arsenal that could be dragged into service, either to stimulate alarm over moves from abroad or to discredit the opposition. Walpole was a canny politician and would play the Pretender's card to suit his purposes. This does not, of course, mean that no genuine concerns existed. James and his faction would always be a tool that foreign powers could employ to destabilise Britain, and every Whig would, at the back of his mind, harbour a residual doubt as to the true level of latent sympathy that continued to persist.

In 1731, the difficulties with Austria were resolved and an alliance, the second Treaty of Vienna, concluded. This, in turn, undermined the prevailing accord with France, to whom certain aspects of the treaty were unsupportable. The Emperor, lacking a male heir, had decided ('The Pragmatic Solution') on settling the succession on his daughter Maria Theresa. This was accepted by Britain but viewed by the French as an opportunity. This falling-out provoked fresh concerns over Jacobite plans and British Intelligence sources recorded an increase in activity.[9]

Britain naturally feared the French would use the Pretender as a card in the diplomatic game, a pawn thrown onto the board to undermine the new understanding with Austria. In these changed circumstances James could no longer be written off: 'It is certain the Jacobites begin to conceive hopes of France and therefore the greatest attention should be given to that'.[10]

At this time the truncated Stuart court was skulking in Rome having, through British pressure, been expelled firstly from Lorraine and then from Avignon. A coincidental increase in the tempo of Anglo-French naval activity exacerbated this web of fears, and the tension did not drain away until the smoke had finally cleared from Culloden Moor. Military preparations were also stepped up, with troops being diverted to the South Coast, requests for assistance transmitted to Vienna and The Hague, and reinforcements drafted in from Ireland.

Despite this revival of hope there appears little evidence that the French were actively preparing to assist in a Stuart restoration. The twin factors that had hampered a Jacobite resurgence in the past still prevailed. No foreign power would commit until it could be shown that a powerful faction existed at home and was willing to rise. Conversely, Jacobites in England and Scotland, were, understandably, unwilling to hazard their lives and fortunes unless they could be assured of decisive intervention.

When the war in Poland broke out, James would have hoped that Britain would be drawn in through the alliance with Austria, but the Whigs were not overly impressed by their ally's conduct to date and demurred. Choosing the diplomatic option, the government of George II offered its skills and impartiality as a mediator whilst, at the same time, ensuring it maintained naval supremacy in the Channel and drafting in troops from Ireland to strengthen garrisons in both England and Scotland.

The fact that French armies had been turned eastwards to confront Austria lessened the prospects for any dash over the narrow waters. Reporting in 1734, the Earl of Chesterfield advised the Upper House that:

We are certainly in greater danger of being suddenly invaded by our neighbours, when they have their troops unemployed and quartered upon the sea coasts, than when all their troops are marched many hundred miles from their sea coast, and employed against another enemy; and surely they may more suddenly fit out a fleet proper for that purpose, when none of their ships of war are employed elsewhere, than when they were obliged to keep many of them in seas very distant from this island.[11]

Walpole had domestic difficulties of his own and there was a swelling chorus of opposition against his economic policy.[12] All of this might have served to keep Jacobite spirits high, but there was nothing to be gained for the French in opening a war on two fronts. The Pretender was a rogue card in the diplomatic deck, to be played or discarded as might be expedient. James certainly had his supporters within the French polity but Fleury remained cautious. Walpole, meanwhile, not only survived the fiscal crisis but won the next election; the Whig supremacy remained intact.

In England Walpole's grip seemed unshakeable. The opposition had foundered in its efforts to establish a common platform, and though both King and Prime Minister were advancing in years[13] there was little encouragement for the Pretender's faction. Time was not on his side, for the plain fact was that the longer the Hanoverian government continued, the more the population would become accustomed to it. The exclusion of the Tories and the other factors which might have afforded some hope to James would be progressively diluted by time and long habit; people would simply forget.

From the end of the 1730s, however, the Whigs began to appear less strong and Walpole's grip less sure. Again, the Jacobite card was played as a bogeyman to unite the Whigs and discredit the Tories. What actual, residual influence the Pretender's supporters were able to exercise within the fragmented opposition is not clear; the Tories consistently stressed their underlying loyalty to the House of Hanover. Any taint of Jacobitism stood to undermine their credibility so, with the Whig opposition, they were quick to downplay any influence. Toward the end of 1739 the Earl of Winchelsea, anxious to show a united front between Tories and dissenting Whigs, stressed to his peers that 'the Jacobite party is now... entirely broke'.[14]

Nonetheless, in 1738, Gordon of Glenbucket[15] had journeyed to Rome, ostensibly on behalf of a majority of the Tory clans, to urge James to attempt a landing in Scotland. Support was plentiful and this could be used as a springboard for the greater enterprise of England. This rather jars with the lukewarm reception Charles Edward would initially receive in the Highlands some seven years later, and the report sent back by the Pretender's agent

James Hay was considerably more cautious in tone. The steadier counsels in James's camp warned that a rising in Scotland would be met by the usual rounding up of sympathisers in England, and a concerted military effort thereafter would overwhelm the clans.

Relations between Britain and Spain had deteriorated through maritime rivalries, and the celebrated incident involving Captain Jenkins's severed ear escalated tensions to the point of hostilities, notwithstanding a serious attempt at compromise.[16] This raised fresh hopes, though earlier Jacobite attempts to interest Spain, in 1737 and 1738, had produced nothing. A series of alarums followed. Ormonde was ordered to take command of a supposed invasion force assembling at Corunna at the start of 1740, and concerns were expressed over possible landings in Galway or Mayo, but all these fears and aspirations proved illusory.

Ormonde sought to interest the Spanish war minister, the Duke of Montemar, in the idea of an invasion, adding the twin lures of disaffection in England and a reservoir of armed support in the Highlands. Spain, however, had other immediate priorities;[17] the Pretender was just another card in their deck, more for show than substance. James, perhaps, continually clutching at straws, saw tangible support where in fact there was only bluster. For any foreign power, a useful pawn that could keep English ships locked in the Channel and troops mustered on the South Coast was worth its hire if nothing more.

If Spain alone could not, or would not, undertake a landing, there was hope that the French might be persuaded, even though no state of war existed with Britain at this time. Her agents were active – one discreetly hiked from the capital to the South Coast, becoming convinced that an amphibious attack could secure a foothold in the Thames Estuary.[18] Fleury was too canny to be drawn into hostilities. He did not want to see Spain stripped of her imperial, overseas jewels through British aggression, but not to the point of declaring war. The French minister might demonstrate against Hanover by shifting troops threateningly, or even appear to menace the West Indies, but he had no interest in proceeding past bluster.

Arthur Villettes, Britain's emissary in Turin, wrote cogently to his opposite number in Florence concerning Charles Edward:

> I am persuaded as you are that a journey was really intended or rather that this
> family is a tool in the hands of some people and made to believe great things
> in agitation in their behalf, when those or the like bruits can serve their ends.
> I am still of the opinion that unless another power should join with Spain in

the present war against us, little or nothing is to be apprehended from that side, however one cannot be too cautious in the present circumstances, and the trusting to outward appearances and one's own conjectures in a matter of this importance is what no prudent man and truly zealous in the service of his prince could forgive himself should things turn out contrary to his surmises.[19]

Fleury had no particular reason to invest much trust in Spain. He had concluded, almost certainly correctly, that if France openly espoused the Stuart cause this would have no effect other than to unite the British polity. He remained dubious over the actual level of domestic support and chose the agent sent to make an assessment with care, one who would err on the side of scepticism. He did offer James general assurances, promising arms for the Jacobite clans and the Irish regiments to be got ready but there was no serious intent.

In spite of the apparent feebleness of his cause, support from James still had a value and the opposition, Whigs and Tories, canvassed for just this to help bring about Walpole's defeat in February 1742. His fall brought a change to the political landscape – for so long he had bestridden the Commons like a colossus. Whether James had foreseen that Walpole's eclipse would open the way for a notably anti-French policy thereafter cannot be certain, but the new ministry antagonised Paris to a degree that resulted in far more serious consideration being given to the exiled Stuarts, who came to be viewed as a potential alternative rather than simply a useful nuisance.

The new government remained Whiggish; even if a sprinkling of opponents now gained high office, the Tories continued to be excluded. In the manner of the times those Whigs who now accepted appointments appeared willing to compromise on their previous stances. This volte-face, a triumph of expediency over principle, did not serve to endear the new administration.

Internationally, the death of Charles VI of Austria in 1740 had spurred Frederick II of Prussia to mount an attack on Maria Theresa's Habsburg patrimony. Bavaria, Spain and, importantly, France now joined in the free-for-all. At the outset Britain's response had been solidly pro-Austrian and pro-Maria Theresa, but a French feint at Hanover panicked George II who hastened, with perhaps an indecent celerity, to confirm his support for France's puppet, Charles Albert of Bavaria.

The government, though it might attempt to maintain a rather precious distinction between British and Hanoverian policy in the matter, suffered a blow to its credibility. George's timidity encouraged the more optimistic Jacobites: the notion of a French seizure of Hanover, which would only be evacuated when George returned the throne of England to it rightful owners, had been mooted for some time. Again, these hopes were to prove groundless. Fleury could easily exert such pressure as he chose on George by threatening Hanover, and French armies were better deployed gainfully in continental Europe than maintaining a hopeful and likely fruitless watch by the Channel.

French aspirations against Austria began to come unstuck in 1742. Walpole's removal ensured a far more aggressive response and, in the following year, British troops were being ferried to Flanders. France was now directly threatened, the spectre of Marlborough raised. George II became, on 16–17 June 1743, the last British monarch to personally lead forces in battle when he defeated the French at Dettingen.[20]

The army which George II deployed onto the field at Dettingen – which would fight again under his son at Fontenoy two years later and which would, under the same general, stand at Culloden – was not, in the main, a popular institution. British forces had swelled dramatically during Marlborough's wars and, despite the many laurels, opinions varied. The Tories feared the military as an instrument of intimidation and repression under the Whigs and George I.

During this period the military establishment comprised two separate forces, that controlled from England and that which served in Ireland and was controlled by Dublin. Though the latter was the smaller it was less vulnerable to the politician's axe. This arrangement was provided for by statute in 1699 and the initial Irish division was some 12,000 strong. These troops could, of course, be used as a pool of reinforcements when emergency threatened the mainland.

Marlborough's victories had been dearly bought in cost of blood and treasure. The fiscal burden of the military establishment was resented almost as much as the fact of its existence. The Whig opposition and Tories found the concept of the rising power of the state backed by the armed forces an anathema:

> There was nothing so odious [as Lord Hervey averred to George II] to men of all ranks and classes in this country as troops; that people who had not sense enough to count up to twenty, or to articulate ten words altogether on other subjects had their lessons so well to heart that they could talk like

Ciceros on this topic and never to an audience that did not chime in with
their arguments.[21]

That level of fear generated by the '15 had witnessed Oxford being leaguered by a regiment of foot and one of horse, on the rather fantastical
assumption that the scholars therein were all rampant Jacobites![22] The strong
military presence imposed across the capital during the dangerous days of
the Atterbury Plot fed Tory fears over Whig intentions and the will to support these with brute force. There was, at this time, no police as such and the
redcoats were regularly called upon to deal with rioters and smugglers.[23]

Each annual Army (previously Mutiny) Act was sure to have a rough ride at
the hands of the opposition. The shade of Cromwell, as tyrant, was regularly
alluded to, and in order to get the legislation through the administration had
to fuse parsimony with dissembling. The prevailing system abetted this practice, as in some ways the army resembled a form of private enterprise with
advancement, in the main, being secured by purchase, a system regarded as
archaic even as far back as 1688.

A colonel was provided with funds from the public purse to raise, equip,
feed and clothe his men, subject to the normal audit procedures, usually
undertaken externally, and with inspections from within the establishment
undertaken by senior officers. At this time the War Office was but a small
department and much of the day-to-day administration was undertaken by
the regimental agents, essentially civilian contractors. Britain (apart from
the creaking militia) did not suffer any form of conscription, so recruitment
into the ranks depended on the zeal of the colonel, the depths of his pockets
and the wiles of the recruiting sergeant.

Military life in the eighteenth century is portrayed as the last resort of
the desperate, or a dumping ground for felons. This is, however, unfair;
agricultural unemployment, the lure of adventure, or the need to escape
domestic entanglements might equally serve to motivate recruits. Work on
the land might be both seasonal and uncertain. Instructions on the matter
of recruiting forbade the inclusion of Catholics, foreigners, and those too
young, too old, or too feeble in mind or body. As ever, though, expediency
proved a great leveller. The magistrates were also happy to provide recruits,
whose choice in the matter was strictly curtailed.

At this time there was no fixed period of service: a man would remain
wedded to the colours 'for life' or until age, wounds or disability compelled

their discharge. It would be fair to assert that the majority of those who came in were young men aged between seventeen and twenty-five (though more than a sprinkling were older), and that unemployment was the single prime motivator.

The success of the Jacobites in 1745 produced a panicked response from the government, which hastened to enact statutes which provided, in effect, for a manner of conscription, the forced enlistment of:

> [all] able-bodied men who do not follow or exercise any lawful calling or employment... all such able-bodied, idle and disorderly persons who cannot upon examination prove themselves to exercise and industriously follow some lawful trade or employment, or to have substance sufficient for their support or maintenance.[24]

Each recruit this impressed earned his parish a pound, with three more put aside into the vestry account for the upkeep of the man's dependents. Any man feeling he might be caught in this particular trap could pre-empt the situation by volunteering, whereby he received the whole of the four pounds. These 'vestry' men were, in reality, no great asset: their service was limited to six months or the duration of the disturbances, and their military value was at best highly questionable.

The officers might regard their men as a commodity, yet many belied the image of the hard drinking, flogging variety, though corporal punishment was still considered necessary for discipline and the lash freely administered. Marlborough's battles had justified an innate sense of superiority in the British soldier: he was a volunteer, even if compelled occasionally by desperation. He could load and fire his musket faster and to far greater effect than his continental adversaries.

His remuneration was modest in the extreme and subject to stoppages for necessaries, so many soldiers maintained additional part-time employment. The defeat at Fontenoy and the rout of Prestonpans briefly focused the administration's collective mind on the state of the armed forces, but the impetus for reform waned after the seeming deliverance at Culloden. It would require the loss of America to refocus political will more sharply.

In the person of George II the army had a stalwart supporter. His German origins led him towards an over-fondness for the rigidly formal Hanoverian model; his British troops, in contrast, often appeared sartorially defective. Royal intermeddling had restricted the market in the sale of commissions

in 1720 and again, two years later, regulations were introduced to set standards for the clothing provided to the men. Abuses such as fictitious soldiers
('dead pays') appearing on the muster roll were curtailed. A professional
standards authority, the Board of General Officers, set up late in 1714, did
much to improve current practices. The Board provided the monarch with
military counsel and undertook annual, spring inspections, power, from
1716, being delegated by the monarch to high-ranking officers.

Marlborough had introduced a drill manual, *New Exercise of Firelocks and
Bayonets*, in 1708, updated only three years later. A new volume of Regulations
appeared in 1726 and continued, virtually unaltered, for the next two decades.
The army, however, did not require its young officers to exhibit any level of
academic qualification or professional competence, apart from the specialist
units such as artillery or engineers.[25] This is not to say that leadership skills
were lacking, quite the opposite – most officers learnt their profession well,
and purchase did not cancel out merit. It has been estimated that, in 1740,
most foot captains had served for nearly twenty years before taking command
of a company.[26] Since the days of Edward I in the late thirteenth century, campaigning in Scotland held little lustre. English officers in the mid-eighteenth
century would far rather do their service in Flanders, fighting conventional
foes in a war of massed battalions, than endure the cold, misery and outpost
skirmishing that 'frontier' warfare in the Highlands might entail.

Britain was primarily a naval and maritime power, and once peace was
declared new regiments raised for the recent war were disbanded and the
older survivors reduced, often to the bone. This meant that drill mainly consisted of a basic exercise of arms, the grander movements by brigades could
not be attempted, and even battalion-sized manoeuvres only occurred once
a year in the course of the spring review.

This notwithstanding, the British army enjoyed a formidable reputation
for the killing power of its shot. In line the battalion would deploy not by
companies but by platoons, at this time a rather artificial formation, perhaps
twenty-five or thirty men strong, devised to maximise firepower on the
field. The platoons were detailed into three 'firings' and these stood in a
three-deep line of shot in a chequerboard formation. Each firing shot or
'gave fire' in a strict numerical sequence – the effect was a continuous pattern of rolling fire by volleys. This was not an aimed fire but a general volley,
effective against a massed target.

Some years after Culloden, at the fight for Quebec on the Plains of
Abraham in September 1759, General Wolfe's[27] diminutive British army

advanced steadily on the French. Each man's weapon was 'double shotted', [28] and at 100 yards they opened fire. Marching on to close the gap to less than half that distance, they delivered a perfect, crashing volley. The French who had earlier rushed out incontinently to meet them were put to rout and the battle effectively ended.

Writing of the earlier battle at Dettingen, an anonymous correspondent, serving with the Royal Welch Fusiliers, [29] describes the action:

> Our men were eager to come to action, and did not at all like the 'long bul-
> lets' (as they term'd them), for indeed they swept off ranks and files. However
> when we came to the small ones, they held them in such contempt that they
> really kept the same order as at any other time.
>
> Our army gave such shouts before we were engaged, when we were about
> one hundred paces apart before the action began, that we hear by deserters
> it brought a pannick amongst them. We attacked the Regiment of Navarre,
> one of their prime regiments. Our people imitated their predecessors in the
> last war gloriously, marching in close order, as firm as a wall, and did not fire
> till we came within sixty paces, and still kept advancing; for, when the smoak
> blew off a little, instead of being amongst their living we found the dead in
> heaps by us; and the second fire turn'd them to the right about, and upon
> along trot. We engaged two other regiments afterwards, one after the other,
> who stood but one fire each; and their Blue French Guards made the best of
> their way [off] without firing a shot. [30]

Despite this fine showing and a resultant British victory, the lack of battle experience in the years since Malplaquet was clearly evident. Lieutenant-Colonel Russell of the 1 Guards [31] found little good to say of the higher command:

> excepting three or four of our generals, the rest of 'em were of little service;...
> our men and their regimental officers gained the day; not in the manner of
> Hide park discipline, but our foot almost kneeled down by whole ranks, and
> fired upon 'em a constant running fire, making almost every ball take place;
> but for ten or twelve minutes 'twas doubtful which should succeed as they
> overpowered us so much, and the bravery of their maison du roy coming
> upon us eight or nine ranks deep; yet our troops were not seen to retreat, but
> to bend back only, I mean our foot, and that only when they fresh loaded;
> then of their own accord [they] marched boldly up to 'em , gave 'em such

a smash with loud huzzas every time they saw them retire, that they were at
once put to flight; that had our horse been of any service, and those of our
mercenaries we should, as it was [have] made a much greater slaughter.[32]

Another eyewitness was James Wolfe, a sixteen-year-old experiencing his
first battle, whose impression of the effectiveness of the British cavalry was
scarcely more favourable that that of Lt. Col. Russell:

> The horse fired their pistols, which if they had let alone, and attacked the
> French with their swords being so much stronger and heavier, they would
> certainly have beat them. Their excuse for retreating – they could not make
> their horses stand the fire!
>
> The third and last attack was made by the foot on both sides. We advanced
> towards one another; our men in high spirits, and very impatient for fight-
> ing, being elated with beating the French horse, part of which advanced
> toward us; whilst the rest attacked our horse, but were soon driven back by
> the great fire we gave them. The Major and I (for we had neither colonel
> nor Lieutenant Colonel) before they came near, were employing in begging
> and ordering the men not to fire at too great a distance, but to keep it till the
> enemy should come near us; but to little purpose. The whole of them fired
> when they thought they could reach them which had like to have ruined us.
> We did very little execution with it. As soon as the French saw we presented,
> they all fell down, and when we had fired they all got up and marched close
> to us in tolerable good order and gave us a brisk fire, which put us into some
> disorder and made us give way a little, particularly our and two or three more
> regiments, who were in the hottest of it. However, we soon rallied again and
> attacked them with great fury, which gained us a complete victory...[33]

Wolfe was not a great admirer of the quality of the rank and file he was
called upon to command. He deprecated their lack of discipline, their want
of valour, and their apparent willingness to murder their officers. (Such
instances might indeed happen but could also be attributed to the perils of
what we now, rather oddly, term 'friendly fire'.)

These accounts, though highly informative, do not give a full picture of
the horrors of battle in the mid-eighteenth century. Black powder (gunpowder), the propellant for both artillery and small arms, is a particularly
noxious mixture, which when discharged gives off vast clouds of cloying,
sulphurous smoke, blinding the combatants after the first volley. The men,

who were obliged to bite off the paper cartridges they carried, dribble powder into the pan of their muskets and then charge the barrel, would quickly be blackened and begrimed by the greasy residue. To add to this they could expect to be maddened by thirst, blinded by smoke and deafened by the hurricane of noise.

Round shot from the great guns, bouncing or 'grazing' before impact, would punch through files, knocking men over like skittles, shearing limbs, spreading a noisome mess of entrails, fragments of bone, brain tissue and great gouts of blood. The soft lead musket balls, flattening on impact, would inflict gaping wounds, driving cloth and fabric into the cavity, the cloying stench of black powder competing with the stink of blood and ordure. Many men opened their bowels or emptied bladders as the fight began. It is unlikely that recruits had earlier been apprised of any of these elements by the recruiting party!

British fire superiority, created by these long rippling volleys, was effective against slow-moving regular formations and against the French whose Gallic élan frequently triumphed over discipline. Against fast-moving Highlanders they were less effective: the fire, though steady, was not sufficiently intense to mow down the attackers before they closed to contact. Consequently, the practice against Highlanders was often to fire massed battalion volleys for maximum effect, and the front rank would, after discharging their muskets, kneel with fixed bayonets to present a steel-tipped hedge.

The principal weapon of the infantryman was the famous 'Brown Bess' flintlock musket. At the time of Culloden the foot were armed with the 'long' land pattern which had a 46-inch barrel and wooden ramrod[34] of .75-inch calibre (12 bore), around fifteen pounds in weight, and which fired a 1¼-ounce ball from 4½ drams of black powder. The musket was loaded by biting off the end of the paper cartridge, as described above, and, after priming the pan, tipping the balance of the powder down the barrel. This was followed by rolling in the ball and compressing the load with the remains of the cartridge, used as wadding and tamped down with the ramrod. The recoil was fierce and got fiercer as firing continued, the residue of powder progressively fouling the barrel.

Though slow to load and vulnerable to damp and wind, Brown Bess was durable and functional. Each man was, to a degree, his own armourer, carrying spare flints (a flint would be worn out after thirty or so rounds) and other replacement parts. His cartridges, ready made up in their paper cases, were carried in leather container, the 'cartouche' or cartridge box, with the individual rounds slotted into a drilled wooden 'magazine' within.

A socket bayonet with a triangular 17-inch blade was fitted, and drill, at this time, more resembled the more stately moves of the pike than the now more familiar practice which was later introduced and based more on the Prussian model. On the command 'charge your bayonet', the barrel and stock were grasped in the left hand, in front of the lock, and the right hand placed behind the brass butt plate, with the weapon then thrust forward on the next command, 'push your bayonet'. As this was now a socket bayonet and not the dagger-like plug variety, which had served Mackay so badly at Killiecrankie, the musket could still be loaded and fired with the blade attached. It was not ideal, however, as the length and the angle of the socket made loading and ramming considerably more difficult.

Conventional bayonet drill was also of limited effect against clansmen. The superiority of their seemingly archaic arms at close quarters, and their long familiarity in the use of them, could see them batter and hew their way through a line of bayonets with horrifying speed and fearful execution. To combat this, the Duke of Cumberland, prior to the Battle of Culloden, instigated a new form of drill. This required that the infantryman did not receive the foe bearing directly down upon him, but engaged the man attacking his comrade on his right, thrusting directly toward the undefended flank as he raised his sword arm for the decisive cut. This technique negated the value of the target in deflecting the bayonet point and substantially evened the odds in the melee.

Prior to 1742 regiments had been distinguished by the name of their colonel, a system that would have been instantly recognisable to the combatants of the Civil Wars a century earlier. Thereafter, however, they were to be numbered. In the period from 1743–1748, the duration of the War of the Austrian Succession, and which, obviously, included the events of the '45, the army list contained some seventy-nine listed regiments. Those from number 67 upwards were raised specifically as a consequence of the Jacobite threat; these were quickly demobilised as soon as the threat had passed, and another seventeen were likewise disbanded when the larger war ended.

This disbandment was usually carried out strictly on account of seniority. Cumberland, as Commander-in-Chief, did interfere in this blanket practice to try and root out notoriously bad regiments and save certain good ones, but he was only partially successful.[35] The majority of foot regiments comprised only a single battalion of ten companies,[36] though unless the ranks were bolstered by the lure of active service, some units, in the long, dull years of peace, could barely muster eight.

Of these companies, three were led by field officers, though it was increasingly rare to see a full colonel commanding on campaign.[37] Usually it was the lieutenant colonel that commanded in the field. The third officer, the major, assisted by the adjutant, was responsible for drill and training. The remaining companies were all led by captains.[38] These, in turn, were assisted by a lieutenant and an ensign. This differed in the case of the two elite flank or 'grenadier'[39] companies, which had no ensigns but a second lieutenant. The regiment would also field a quartet of specialist officers – the adjutant, quartermaster, surgeon and chaplain.[40] Each company held (at full strength) some seventy soldiers, three sergeants, the same number of corporals and a brace of drummers.

For the rank and file, life beneath the colours was by no means an entirely attractive occupation. As a rule the men were accommodated in the damp and cold of canvas encampments or billeted out in inns, taverns or on hapless civilians who much resented the practice. Purpose-built barracks were still a relative rarity. The private man's pay was meagre, and subject to the usual deductions for clothing. Ale and spirits, together with cards and dice, were likely to be his principal diversions.

Many soldiers were married, and the 'army women' were not necessarily the cohort of harlots that they were frequently portrayed as. The women in fact performed a whole series of vital functions, as cooks, laundresses, sutlers, and, in an age before the establishment of army medial services, nurses.

The soldier's clothing consisted of a greatcoat, with coloured cuffs and facings, worn over a sleeved, woollen doublet or waistcoat with breeches and dark coloured gaiters; there was little concession to seasonal variations. The ordinary or 'hatmen' companies wore the tricorne, while the elite grenadiers sported the more ornate and distinctive mitre cap. By way of equipment he was furnished with his cartridge box, worn from a stiff leather belt slung over the left shoulder. Around his waist was another broad buff leather belt from which was suspended his bayonet, together with a short sword or hanger. To complete his marching kit he would carry a form of knapsack, a linen bread bag and a tin canteen.

Though many officers were humane and exhibited a genuine concern for the welfare of their men, discipline was both strict and punitive. The lash was considered the fittest remedy for a whole range of offences, and the number of strokes awarded might be considerable, 1,500 for certain offences. These would be administered in batches to allow the recipient some chance for recuperation. For lesser offences a man might be sentenced to solitary confinement in 'the black hole' on a bread and water diet.

Despite the severity of the regime, desertion was by no means uncommon. The bullying of unscrupulous sergeants, the poor diet, bad accommodation and the sheer, grinding tedium of garrison duty all undermined a soldier's will to continue. The more enterprising officers and men cultivated diverse interests and 'business' activities, to ease both the financial strain and the tedium.

Officers were usually, in the broad sense, 'gentlemen' of good if not necessarily wealthy stock. Most would be younger sons or otherwise impoverished men. Following family tradition was common, but the burgeoning professional classes and the clergy contributed their sons. Increasingly, as the eighteenth century progressed, the percentage of officers coming from Scottish or Anglo-Irish families increased. Despite this, promotion from the ranks was by no means unheard of, such promotion having been earned through ability and good service.

For most, the vehicle for entry was purchase. Even though the practice had, to an extent, been regulated after 1720, the acquisition of a commission was a financial investment. It inevitably cost more to buy into a fashionable regiment and price was influenced by the unit's proximity to London. When an officer was moving up he could sometimes effectively trade in his existing commission against the higher rank and supply the difference in cash; alternatively he could sell his present commission and pay the full rate for the other. Should an officer fall in battle or be cashiered then the nearest below him in seniority would be made up at no cost. (Such a 'free' commission, however, held no residual 'trade-in' value.)

Obviously the modern world views such a system, with its implications of elitism and privilege, with disdain. To the politicians of the day, however, it had the considerable recommendation of being self-financing and it implied that control of the armed forces at battalion level remained in the hands of men of property. The outbreak of hostilities in 1743 and the consequent expansion of land forces served to quicken the pace of advancement, which otherwise tended rather to stagnate in peacetime.

The expediency of wartime also prompted the practice of giving commissions to any who could, subject to the right level of patronage, deliver a set number of recruits – free enterprise in action! The fiscal risk attached to the raising of volunteers naturally fell on the officer concerned, and he might even be forced to buy in recruits from an agent or 'crimp'. This practice could be expanded to involve the raising of whole regiments – a dozen foot battalions and two of horse were recruited by enterprising individuals to combat the Jacobites in 1745.[41] When he retired the officer could sell his commission to create a pension fund or he could go onto the Half Pay List.[42]

For the mounted arm the Duke of Cumberland would, at Culloden, be able to deploy two regiments of dragoons[43] and one of light horse. The former had begun as mounted infantry: they rode to the field but fought on foot and, as such, during the Civil War had a distinctly varied role from the cavalry proper. By 1745 the distinction had blurred very considerably and dragoons now represented the mounted arm. In terms of dress and accoutrement they closely resembled the foot, save that their coats were devoid of facings and they wore heavy, thigh-length horseman's boots.

Carried in holsters on his saddle the trooper bore a brace of flint pistols and, for combat on foot, a shorter version of the infantryman's Brown Bess with a 42 inch barrel. His edged weapon was a basket-hilted broadsword, usually of only munition quality, similar in appearance if not in finish to the Highland broadsword. Light cavalry, such as Kingston's Horse, carried swords curved slightly like a sabre and had carbines rather than muskets, shorter in length and lighter in calibre.

During the course of the '45 the government cavalry generally performed rather poorly; discipline and moral were clearly both lacking. The horse were organised in troops, with perhaps fifty men with three troops forming a squadron, and three squadrons a regiment, commanded, as with the foot, by a colonel.

The artillery to be deployed on the field of Culloden (in addition to Coehorn mortars) were three-pounder battalion guns, small but relatively easy to move in comparison to their larger brethren. We are indebted to the great eighteenth-century artillerist John Muller[44] who has left a detailed listing of the artillery train commanded by [then] General Belford in the continental campaign of 1747. The handy three-pounders needed only four draught horses each – the twelve-pounders required fifteen! In addition to the guns and mortars themselves, the artillery train would require ammunition carts, pioneer tools, forges and replacement parts, spare carriages, pontoons, and limbers, the latter needing an extra horse apiece. In addition to the gunners and matrosses, the train would usually require the services of pioneers to ease progress over uncertain country.[45]

Ammunition was generally comprised of made-up cartridges, and some 70 per cent of the projectiles would be round shot – as the name implies, solid, round iron balls. The shot was habitually fastened to a 'sabot', a timber disc, usually elm, intended to seal the bore on loading. Round shot are fired over a flat trajectory and intended to bounce or graze before striking. Men under fire in this era could often see the balls skipping toward them, seemingly innocuous, as though they could easily be stopped by an outstretched foot. Those who tried this would invariably be shorn of the limb!

Normally each piece, when deployed for action, would be served by a team of half a dozen and could expect to commence firing at a distance of 600–700 yards. Frederick the Great advocated holding fire until the enemy was closer, to maximise both the impact of the shot and the psychological effect of the screaming rounds. Canister or case shot, which spewed lead bullets like a giant shotgun cartridge, was generally reserved for ranges of a few hundred paces or less; the effect of this fire on charging infantry formations could be utterly devastating.

Normally, the first target would be the enemy guns, counter-battery fire, the object being to smash the pieces and kill the crews. Once this was achieved, the victorious gunners would be free to concentrate on the foot, or, if they attacked first, the horse. Frederick also pressed the advantages of mortars deployed on the field. These could lob explosive shells in a high trajectory. The fuse, by mid-century, was constructed using a beechwood tube with a length of quick match wound around in a series of rings; this was inserted into an aperture in the iron shell casing. Cutting the fuse to the required length determined the moment of detonation.

This was the army of the Georges which would be called upon to deal with any armed attempt by the Jacobites. The clash between conventional regiments – some, it must be said, of very indifferent quality – and the Highland clans would be dramatic and, for the government, a source of great concern almost verging on hysteria. For the Stuart cause was not dead, its most dramatic hour was still to arrive, along with its most charismatic and controversial paladin, Prince Charles Edward – the 'Bonnie Prince Charlie' of romantic lore.

8

RAISING THE STANDARD

We are, in this instant, alarmed with the old ministerial cry of France and the Pretender; of armies and transports, incog. at Dunkirk; of invincible armadas from Brest… either true or false. If true; how will our all sufficient statesman excuse himself from having treated France as a contemptible power, from which so little was to be feared, that we had nothing to do, but to draw the sword, and carve out his dominions into what shreds and fritters we pleased? Where was the intelligence which ought to be the fruit of all those mighty sums, which are said to be annually expended in secret service? How can he keep himself in countenance for having embroiled us in his rash and ridiculous measures abroad and thereby draw upon us this shocking insult at home? That the French were able to put a formidable squadron of ships to sea is now self-evident; that till the very instant, almost of their sailing, we were ignorant alike of their strength and their preparations, seems to be highly probable… the affair of Dettingen might have convinced us that she would not stand upon ceremonies when revenge was in her power.

Old England *(the opposition London newspaper)*[1]

This extract from the anti-Whig paper *Old England* reflects a reaction to the crisis of 1744, calling for the recall of British troops from Flanders. The Jacobite bogeyman, as the foil of France, continued to exert considerable influence. The final, flawed champion of the cause was poised in the wings, ready to make his dramatic entrance.

Charles Edward Louis John Casimir Silvester Severino Maria Stuart was born, amidst rejoicing, in Rome on 31 December 1720, and grew to young manhood in those dry, despairing years of arid exile. His mother, Clementina Sobieski, was descended from the great John Sobieski, whose magnificent Polish Winged Hussars had driven off the Turkish besiegers of Vienna in 1683. It was said that, on the night of his birth, a new bright star appeared in the firmament, and certainly the guns of Fort St Angelo roared a celebratory cannonade.

However threadbare the Jacobite cause seemed in the 1720s and 1730s, the birth of an heir was a significant and, from the Hanoverian viewpoint, worrying occasion. The boy grew up to be markedly handsome, with a good carriage, excelling at sports, if less distinguished in the classroom, certainly less academic than his younger brother Henry.[2]

When only fourteen, at the invitation of his cousin the Duke of Liria,[3] he took part in the siege of Gaeta, where the Spaniards sought to wrest control of the city from an Austrian garrison within. Charles fell romantically in love with the military life, showing a casual disregard for danger that both impressed and rather worried his cousin, who was responsible for his safety.

His mother died young, at only thirty-three, and was buried in St Peter's, where her tomb became something of a shrine. The Prince had been brought up in the sure conviction that he was, after his father, the rightful King of both England and Scotland, but the empty years gave little hint of any prospect of restoration. Instead, Charles hunted and enjoyed the mindless social round of a shadow court, surrounded by toadies and with British agents, like Baron von Stosch, watching his every move.

It did rather seem, at first, that 1744 might be the time in which the Stuarts' long years of exile finally ended. Given the scale and intent of the French preparations that year, the events of the '45 in some ways appear anticlimactic. Had Charles Edward, whilst his army was marching down the western spine of England the following year, received succour from across the Channel on the scale then envisaged, his efforts might very well have been crowned with success. History would then have taken a very different view of him. Success can make heroes out of the most flawed personalities, and Charles was singularly flawed.

The defeat at Dettingen had humiliated Louis XV to the degree that he was prepared to dust off the faded relic of Jacobitism and reconsider its worth as a medium of revenge. Fleury, that paragon of caution, had died and reports from French spies appeared to be encouraging.[4] By November, the King was writing to both James and Philip V of Spain advising of his renewed support.[5] In this he appeared most serious; the expedition was to be commanded by no lesser general than Marshal de Saxe, who would lead just over 10,000 bayonets. The invasion would target the South Coast (Maldon was the preferred landing), and march directly on London.

Initially, the English Jacobites requested a second, lesser expedition to bolster the Tory clans, who would rise simultaneously. This element did not proceed, but Saxe's 10,000, should they succeed in crossing the Channel, would almost have parity of numbers with the troops the Hanoverians could muster in the South of England. The Scottish establishment, at under 3,000 strong, was minuscule. There was a suggestion[6] that the invaders rely on small boats, but the Marshal wanted men o' war as ushers for his vulnerable transports.

The Naval aspect would involve the Brest squadron taking station by the Isle of Wight, to block the inevitable British riposte. Sir John Norris commanded the home squadron, at anchor in Spithead. If he got past their blockade, the French were to engage whilst a handful of warships shepherded the transports toward the Thames Estuary. Winter weather delayed the fleet's embarkation during January 1744 and it was not until early the following month that the ships raised anchor.

By now, British Intelligence had divined that Charles Edward had slipped out of Italy and was believed to be in France. The threat of imminent invasion hung in the air and yet the government was clearly confident that the Royal Navy could see off any attempt. Nonetheless, a further six thousand Dutch troops were to be put on standby.

Some confusion now arose as the destination of the supposed invasion fleet. Was there to be an attempt on Ireland? Charles Edward had arrived safely in Paris, despite the Navy's best efforts, by 8 February – his intervention was, at this stage, in fact unsolicited, perhaps even unwelcome. The French were aware that his presence would only serve as a banner advertisement for the forthcoming attempt.

British agents had meanwhile disbursed a hefty bribe to gain sight of the French plans, and the additional army units from Holland were now requested. The upshot of the security leak was that the French blamed the failure on Charles Edward for his precipitate action, which served to ensure that they would think twice before involving him too deeply in their counsels.

Parliament was quick to affirm its members' undying loyalty to George, and the old spectre of Popish Plot and rising was paraded. Despite this, there was no vast outpouring of pro-Hanoverian sentiment in the country but the usual haul of known sympathisers was rounded up, including prominent figures such as Lord Barrymore and Colonel Cecil. Regiments were recalled from Ireland and Flanders. Norris was instructed to put to sea and seek out the French. To this extent the threat of invasion had already worked in France's favour, insofar as it had diverted British resources and attention away from the cockpit of the wider war.

By late February the two fleets were in sight of each other off Dungeness, but strong winds scattered both before battle could be joined and the French tacked back toward Brest. More bad weather struck at Dunkirk, damaging transports and ruining supplies. Saxe began to fret, as he had neither warships nor pilots (the latter promised by the English sympathisers). Once again, the weather showed a strongly Hanoverian shift. Early in March a further great storm did yet more damage to the transports riding at Dunkirk. Saxe now wrote to Charles advising him that the invasion had been cancelled. The '44 was over before it began and the government in Britain sensed a deliverance.

Deliverance indeed: the intelligence failures had been lamentable, the preparation tardy and possibly inadequate. Happily, Britain's defences were not put to the test and the moment, always fleeting, passed. For such a brittle and excitable disposition as Charles's this was intolerable.

The failure undoubtedly worked on him and led him to consider a more desperate avenue, a rising in Scotland with or without French assistance. If this was not forthcoming at the outset then success coming from the Highlands would serve to stimulate the appropriate enthusiasm. This was a highly dangerous course which, in the spiral of its unravelling, would lead directly to the slaughter on Culloden Moor. This should perhaps be called the Romantic Solution, and many men would die at its bloody denouement.

Largely forgotten by his French hosts after the abandonment of the expedition, Charles had resided for a while in Gravelines, maintained if ignored by Louis XV, who would not grant him an audience. In the spring he moved to the outskirts of Paris, from where he wrote to his father:

> The situation I am in is very particular, for nobody nose where I am or what is become of me, so that I am entirely burried as to the publick, and can't but say that it is a very great constrent upon me, for I am obliged very often not to stur out of my room for fier of some bodys noing my face. I very often think that you would laugh very hartily if you saw me going about with a single servant bying fish and other things and squabling for a peney more or less. I hope your Majesty will be thoroughly persuaded, that no constrent or trouble whatsoever either of minde or body, wil ever stoppe me in going on with my duty, in doing any thing that I think can tend to your service or your Glory.[7]

It is only natural that such a frustrating relegation to pensioner status on the sidelines would jibe with a young man of dash and fire, especially when he has been keyed up for great events. Charles certainly had charm and charisma, physical courage and stamina. He lacked experience, any real knowledge of the military art, and the ability to cope with adversity. In this he was the opposite of his father, who had borne his many reverses with unfailing courtesy. Charles could appear able to inspire men but was ultimately too shallow to lead them. As his life progressed, his fondness for the bottle, already noticeable in 1745, and amongst company where copious imbibing was scarcely unusual, became his solace. It was to be a sad waste of his life and the lives of those who were to die in his cause.

If the projected invasion had proved a fiasco, this did not diminish its value to France in terms of diverting British attention from the European theatre and creating a scare that might promote a redistribution of resources. In the bigger game the '44 thereby served a purpose. This was of no value to the Jacobites, though a definite gain for France and her allies. Robert Trevor, British ambassador at The Hague, felt that

> perhaps this uneasiness is all that France at present aims at; and that if she could augment it enough to make us weaken Flanders, she would strike a home blow on that side... I have no idea of an invasion, though the news from Dunkirk and all along that coast are suspicious.[8]

It is perhaps questionable what advantage France gained from the business in practical terms. In the wake of the earlier tempest, Norris's squadron was weakened, as ships were diverted to reinforce that which was operating in the Mediterranean. Once again it is necessary to consider that the Jacobite cause was just one of a series of options available to belligerent eighteenth-century powers. War and diplomacy were clearly linked. France wished to strike at Britain as Spain had during the earlier war. Philip V had seen better and riper pickings in Italy.[9]

France, too, needed to be aware of a Protestant backlash if she interfered too pointedly in British domestic affairs. George II was far more assailable in Europe; Hanover was his Achilles heel. Louis XV was surrounded by an influential clique of 'German' advisors, who were in favour of progressing the war by a demonstration against Hanover, abandoning Charles Edward. He was to be sent back to Italy, like a rejected bride, and there, presumably, left to moulder, the faded aspirations of his affinity slowly dissolving in the dust of obscurity.

It is questionable whether the invasion scare strengthened support for George II at home, though some contemporary observers, such as Trevor, felt that it did. He felt that the French intermeddling

> gives the flat lie to the boasted moderation and innocence of her views; and must convince every subject of the Republic [the Dutch] as well as of England, that not only the possessions of the House of Austria and the balance of power, but even our own liberties and religion, are struck at by that ambitious power.[10]

In some quarters there was a burst of patriotic fervour. The Northumbrian gentry, whose natural inclinations might have been suspect based on the evidence of the '15, rushed, in gushing terms, to reaffirm their undying loyalty. Contemporary correspondence relates the zeal with which the county had responded in enforcing the provisions operating against recusants.

For the French, it could be argued that their success in diverting British attention allowed them to seize, and thereafter to retain, the strategic initiative in Flanders. This they did not relinquish for the remainder of the war and their gains placed them in a strong position when the time came to negotiate peace terms. Most eighteenth-century military operations tended to be relatively limited in their objectives, often confined to key towns and fortresses. France was not at home with the hazards of amphibious operations, and as the century progressed it would be the British who became masters of the combined operation. Her involvement with the Jacobites, therefore, could be viewed as both cynical and opportunistic. However, the shades of Jacobite hopes for an actual landing would inform thinking during the '45, would influence the decisions of men of large estate in throwing in their lot with Charles Edward and would lead to their utter ruin in his cause.

Having given England a thorough scare, the French were left freer to concentrate on making gains in Flanders. This was, of course, of equal concern to Britain. The loss to Austria of Ostend would be seen as a major threat, an available springboard and a growing hegemony that threatened British command of the Channel. Throughout that troubled spring and summer, the administration remained nervous. There were fresh alarums in late June. In July, Charles Edward was writing to Louis XV, arguing that with more troops being sent to Flanders, England was again vulnerable. In the autumn the English Jacobites were pressing in a similar vein.

Charles's ideas about a single rising in Scotland were met with some alarm. Such an action would, came the oft-rehearsed argument, isolate the English sympathisers, who would swiftly be rounded up and neutralised, leaving the Hanoverians in control of London and the South-East. Notwithstanding the fact that his father was equally opposed to a Scottish attempt, Charles found the notion increasingly attractive. He was not a strong enough character to accept good advice which clashed with his own concept, preferring to see jealousy and spite where there was none.

Louis, certainly, was not impressed. The Prince's request for 3,000 foot to support a bid for Scotland, lodged in October 1744, produced no response. Undeterred he went ahead, seeking to finance his war chest from private sources. In this he enjoyed some success. He was able to tap into the web of finance and banking contacts managed by a band of Scottish and Irish expatriate entrepreneurs. Some of these had shipping interests in Nantes and St Malo.[11] Their willingness was not entirely philanthropic – obviously if the great gamble now being planned came off, the rewards would be substantial, and the risk if, as seemed likely, it failed, relatively modest.

In the spring and summer of 1745 Britain faced a growing crisis in Flanders. On 11 May Saxe defeated Cumberland in the long, bloody duel of Fontenoy,[12] Ghent and Bruges were lost in July and Ostend capitulated on 23 August. This was very bad indeed and distracted British attention away from the plans of Charles Edward, who appeared to be a very small player in the midst of such grand manoeuvres. However, on 22 June the Prince went aboard the frigate *Du Teillay* and sailed from St Nazaire. He was about to take centre stage.

Nearly three weeks before his departure the Prince had written to Louis XV, whom he addressed as 'uncle', intimating that he had resolved to make himself known by his deeds, and single handed. To embark on an enterprise to which even a very moderate amount of help would ensure success, and being so bold as to think that the King of France would not refuse this:

I would certainly not have come to France if the expedition which was planned to take place last year [1744] had not shewn me that your Majesty wished me well… and so I go to seek my destiny which, apart from being in the hands of God, is in those of your Majesty.[13]

This would clearly seem to indicate that Charles had confidence in the certainty of French aid, once his expedition should be seen to stimulate results.

What he had not taken into account was the fact that Fontenoy and the gains in Flanders had conferred the strategic initiative on France. There was no real need for any sideshow, other than that it might sow further confusion.

Certainly the French could not pretend they were unaware of what was afoot. One of the vessels the Prince's entrepreneurial friends had chartered was the sixty-four gun *L'Elisabeth*.[14] It was quite customary for the French Navy to grant charters with letters of marque to enterprising merchant raiders, who might seek a profit from the wars. It appears unlikely that *L'Elisabeth* could have been hired for the expedition to Scotland without the direct authority of the minister concerned.[15] The ship carried a naval complement and large stores of arms, accoutrement, powder and shot had been amassed, which required ministerial authorisation. From the French perspective the expedition was a low-cost extension to the war which had the potential to increase the pressure on Britain, with whom France was tentatively seeking to negotiate.

 Charles had, on 12 June, written to his father to explain the desperate venture on which, without James's commission, he was about to embark:

Sir,
I believe your Majesty little expected a courier at this time, and much less from me; to tell you a thing that will be a great surprise to you. I have been, above six months ago, invited by our friends to go to Scotland, and to carry what money and arms I could conveniently get; this being, they are fully persuaded, the only way of restoring you to the Crown, and them to their liberties... After such scandalous usage as I have received from the French Court, had I not given my word to do so, or got so many encouragements from time to time as I have had, I should have been obliged, in honour and for my own reputation, to have flung myself into the arms of my friends, and die with them, rather than live longer in such a miserable way here, or be obliged to return to Rome, which would be just giving up all hopes... Your Majesty cannot disapprove a son's following the example of his father. You yourself did the like in the year '15; but the circumstances now are indeed very different, by being much more encouraging, there being a certainty of succeeding with the least help... I have tried all possible means and stratagems to get access to the King of France, or his Minister, without the least effect... Now I have been obliged to steal off, without letting the King of France so much as suspect it for which I make a proper excuse in my letter to him; by saying it was a great mortification to me never to have been able to speak and open

my heart to him. Let what will happen, the stroke is struck, and I have taken a firm resolution to conquer or to die...[16]

Brave words, appropriate in the romantic, if not the pragmatic, sense. Charles, in this apologia to his father, suggests that he has been drawn to the Scottish venture by the assurance and entreaty of sympathisers there; his reception in the Highlands would indicate otherwise. On the other hand the expedition may be seen to represent the final throw of the despairing gambler, determined to risk all on a last roll of the dice. The fact that the fount of overt French support had dried up should have indicated to a wiser man how the land lay in that direction; hubris is a poor reason for campaigning without some more substantive bedfellows.

On 2 July the sleek *Du Teillay* was joined by the heavier and ageing *L'Elisabeth* off Belle Isle and the pair sailed north-west until, with typical misfortune, they ran foul of HMS *Lyon* (fifty-eight guns). The English man o' war, if under-gunned, was faster, having just been refitted; Captain Dan of *L'Elisabeth* ran out his guns to make a fight of it. The French ship cleared for action, exchanged a token shot, and hoisted her colours, the Englishman gave chase and presently the two warships were exchanging broadsides. There was no subtlety here but a grinding, yardarm to yardarm attrition of screaming round shot.

At one point in the action Lyon was able to rake her opponent,[17] causing fearful loss, yet she certainly did not have matters all her own way, and the Frenchman shot away her rigging and partly dismasted her. The battle raged until darkness when *L'Elisabeth* limped back toward Brest with fifty-seven dead, including her gallant skipper and nearly twice as many wounded.[18] Though she survived, her priceless cargo of supplies and quota of volunteers was lost to Charles Edward. The diminutive *Du Teillay*, with the Prince's equally modest entourage on board, sailed on alone.

Despite the continued vigilance of the Royal Navy, Captain Durbe steered his ship north and west, around the treacherous coast, past the bastion of Cape Wrath and, on 23 July, sighted the Outer Hebrides. The vessel made landfall off Barra, where the steep hills crowd down to the anchorage. The Highlander turned financier, Aeneas MacDonald, went ashore to establish contact with his brother-in-law and staunch Jacobite, Macneil of Barra. The '45 had begun.

It did not begin particularly well for the Prince. Macneil was away and it was feared the government had rumbled the whole affair. Undeterred,

Charles was for pressing on. There was a further fright when what appeared to be a large man o' war was sighted and *Du Teillay* took shelter amongst the necklace of islands. More alarums followed, and Charles and his tiny band received a taste of the fury of a West Coast summer storm. The laird of Boisdale was the first man of consequence the Prince spoke to on the barren strand of Eriskay. His advice was as harsh as the wind but the Jacobite counsels were disturbed by the renewed attentions of supposed British warships.[19]

Charles had further dispatched Aeneas MacDonald to locate his older brother MacDonald of Kinlochmoidart. He, with other MacDonalds, stepped aboard the frigate to meet the Prince and one of that party left a vivid memoir of the incident:

> We called for the ships boat and were immediately carried on board, and our hearts were overjoyed to find ourselves so near our long wished for Prince. We found a large tent erected with poles on the ships decks covered and well furnished with variety of wines and spirits… there entered the tent a tall youth of most agreeable aspect in plain black coat with a plain shirt not very clean and a cambrick stock fixed with a plain silver buckle, a fair round wig out of the buckle, a plain hatt with a canvas string having one end fixed to one of his coat buttons, he had black stockins and brass buckles on his shoes; at his first appearance I found my heart swell to my very throat… he saluted none of us and we only made a low bow at a distance. I chanced to be one of those who were standing when he came in, and he took his seat near me but immediately started up again and caused me sitt down by him upon a chest, I at this time taking him to be only a passenger or some clergyman, presumed to speak to him with too much familiarity yet still retained some suspicion that he might be one of more note than he was said to be. He asked me if I was not cold in that habite [Highland dress] I answered I was so habituated to it that I would rather be so if I was to change my dress for any other. At this he laughed heartily and next enquired how I lay with it at night, which I explained to him; he said that my wraping myself so close in my plaid I would be unprepared for any sudden defence in the case of a surprise. I answered that in such times of danger or during a war we had a different method of using the plaid, that with one spring I could start to my feet with drawn sword and cock'd pistol in my hand without being in the least incumber'd with my bedcloaths. Several such questions he put to me; then rising quickly from his seat he calls for a dram, when the same person whisper'd me a second time to pledge the stranger but not to drink to him, by which seasonable hint I was

confirm'd in my suspicion who he was. Having taken a glass of wine in his hand he drank to us all round, and soon after left us.[20]

On 25 July the swift French frigate nosed into Loch nan Uamh and the Prince, with his tiny entourage, stepped ashore at Arisaig.[21] Charles was now upon his native land, the arms and stores were unloaded and local gentlemen consulted. Having re-victualled, *Du Teillay* made ready to put out to sea. If Prince Charles Edward was having any second thoughts, now was definitely the time. If he lacked wisdom and judgement he lacked for neither courage nor energy. Durbe and Walsh, who had accompanied the voyage, said their farewells, the latter departing with a letter of commendation from the Prince in his pocket. It was time for business.

At first MacDonald of Boisdale's strongly uttered words of caution hung heavy in the air. His nephew Clanranald was reluctant to commit but Charles's charisma won him over, as did bland assurances that once the Highlands had risen, France would be swift to lend support. MacDonald of Scotus was also won over and his voice influenced Glengarry, Keppoch and Glencoe. Both MacDonald of Sleat and the MacLeod[22] refused, however, to be drawn in. Clan Cameron, led by Lochiel,[23] came out and the recruitment of such a powerful and respected chief was a great inducement. Charles could afford to be free with his promises. He was a landless exile of no estate; true, he was hazarding his liberty, perhaps even his neck, but as for property and land, he had none to lose.

MacDonald of Kinlochmoidart, won over to the cause, chanced, while rowing over the glassy waters of Loch Lochy, to meet another boat bearing Bishop Hugh MacDonald. He was astonished at Kinlochmoidart's news, astonished and horrified. His recusant ministry had succeeded so well because of its essentially covert nature, and the bishop had proceeded without causing a stir – stealth over confrontation. The arrival of the Prince could spell disaster and bring the full weight of the government's repression down on the clans.

Having failed to dissuade Kinlochmoidart the bishop pushed on to Arisaig to meet with and, hopefully, persuade the Prince to depart whence he had come. In this he was unsuccessful. Charles riposted with scorn on the doubters:

He did not chuse to owe the restoration of his father to foreigners, but to his own friends to whom he was now come to put it in their power to have the glory of that event... As to returning to France foreigners should never have it say that he had thrown himself upon his friends, that they turned their backs on him and that he had been forced to return from them to foreign parts. In a word, if he could get but six trusty fellows to join him he would chose far rather to skulk with them in the mountains of Scotland than return to France.[24]

Whether the Prince had the intellectual wherewithal to contemplate the wider European picture must remain doubtful; that he first allowed himself to be deceived before proceeding, in turn, to deceive others may be quite likely. The '45, therefore, was born out of false optimism and launched on pious hopes, presented as sure. In short it was founded on an entirely false premise that the Highlands had but to show the white cockade and the French would be sufficiently enthused to intervene, as had been so tantalisingly close the previous year. None of those chiefs, seduced by the Prince's easy charm and charisma, which would hold only as long as he was seen to be winning, seriously envisaged that the clans must bear the weight of the whole campaign unaided.

For every laird who was prepared to follow the Prince's standard more refused, temporised, or declared for the government, which could count on the Whig clans, Campbells, Mackays, Munros and Sutherlands. Even those who did lend support continued to hedge their bets by sending detachments led by the chief's kin or tacksmen, avoiding an all-or-nothing commitment – lesser mortals whose actions could be later 'denied' or denounced as the mood of the times dictated.

This is not to be wondered at; Charles and his entourage had barely an acre between them. If the affair went badly they could hope for the return of the *Du Teillay*, or some other swift vessel to lift them clear of peril and safely back to France, beyond the redcoats' wrath. The Highlanders had no such comfort. Consequently, the Prince was left with relatively few recruits and delayed raising his standard in the glens. From Borrodale on 8 August he wrote an open letter to the recalcitrant chiefs:

Having been well informed of yr Principles and Loyalty, I cannot but express at this juncture, that I am come with a firm resolution to restore the King, my father, or perish in ye attempt. I know the interest you have amongst those of yr name and depend upon you to report it to ye utmost of yr Power... I intend to set up the Royal Standard at Glenfinnan on Monday ye 19th instant and shou'd be very glad to see you on that occasion. If time does not allow it, I still depend upon your joyning me with all convenient speed. In ye meantime, you may be assured of the particular esteem and friendship I have for you.[25]

Stewart of Ardshiel had by now declared for the Prince. Simon Fraser, Lord Lovat, by now an old man (he was born in 1667) and thoroughly untrustworthy, gave vague, indirect assurances of support whilst also writing in enthusiastic terms to General Guest, commander of the Edinburgh garrison. James Drummond, Duke of Perth, a sickly young man and an ardent Jacobite, was already on the run from government agents at this time, having been incriminated in captured correspondence; it would be September before he could join the Prince's nascent army.

Charles now moved his HQ to Kinlochmoidart House at the head of Loch Moidart. His supporters, mustering in bands throughout the West, successfully captured Captain Swetenham of Guise's Regiment, an engineer, who was carried off from his post on the Corrieyairack Pass. A couple of days later a brace of commanded bodies of clansmen, relatively few in numbers, surprised two companies of the Royal Scots attempting to march from Perth to Fort William. The Jacobites launched an impromptu ambush by the inn at Highbridge on the river Spean. After a running fight in which the rebels sustained no losses, Captain Scott was captured along with some three score or so of his men. Three soldiers were killed in the skirmish and Scott himself was wounded. First blood to the Jacobites. The captives were certainly not ill-treated; Scott was tended by Lady Lochiel herself at Achnacarry and eventually released on parole.

Monday 19 August, St Oswin's Eve,[26] saw the Prince with his following at Glenfinnan, where the high hills crowd the loch. Apart from a pair of local shepherds, the tranquillity was undisturbed by the tramp of marching feet. After what must have been an increasingly anxious wait, a small MacDonald contingent of no more than 150 broadswords came in, and with them James Mor MacGregor, son of the celebrated Rob Roy and as much a rogue.[27] It was not until around four in the afternoon that Lochiel finally made an appearance, bringing in perhaps 700 of his affinity, to be followed by Keppoch with, at best, half as many. It was scarcely an army, hardly sufficient for two weak battalions. In his report to the Lord Advocate MacGregor described the scene. Evaluating the worth of the Pretender's recruits, he observed:

that most of them appeared to be good men, but some Young and Raw and some Old that had been at Sheriffmuir. That he believed 600 or so of Lochiel's men were very good…That most of Lochiel's men had no arms, supposing that they were to have been provided when they came to the camp, and accordingly they went… to Kenlochmoydart's house, or somewhere thereabouts and came back with arms… that he saw 22 Field Pieces about the size of one's leg, that were brought in a boat from Kenlochmoydart's house up Loch Shiel to Glenfinnan, with a number of Barrells of Powder and ball and about 150 pair of Pistolls… That he observed many of the guns Lochiel's men got were in great Disorder, some of them with their Locks broken and others with Broken Stocks, and many of them wanted ramrods, and the men were complaining they were in great want of Smiths, Lochiel having but one… That he did not see above 20 Saddle Horses in the Camp but there were a number of Country Horses for carrying Baggage.[28]

The Jacobites were short of just about everything necessary to wage war. The Prince was about to embark on a bid to win the thrones of both kingdoms, with perhaps 1,200 under-equipped clansmen, with a dearth of regular and experienced officers, deficient in small arms and artillery and without cavalry.

These shortcomings were overlooked in the ceremony of raising the standard which followed. Blessed (no doubt reluctantly) by Bishop Hugh MacDonald, the banner of 'white, blue and red silk' was unfurled and spread in the warm evening air, and a declaration of war upon the House of Hanover was read out. There could be no going back.

9

ADVANCE – THE INVASION OF ENGLAND

From France and pretender
Great Britain defend her,
Foes let them fall;
From foreign slavery,
Priests and their knavery,
And Popish reverie,
God save us all.

Additional verse added to the British National Anthem[1]

The Pretender's son is in Scotland with near 3,000 rebels with new arms and French
louis dors. We have not above 1,500 men under Sir John Cope, and not a clan has risen
to join him though he has marched two thirds of the kingdom… I confess this affair in
Scotland taken by itself gives me no great terror, but when I look upon it only as a branch
of a more extensive and pernicious project, connected with the Spanish embarkation from
Ferrol and contrived by France, who now has it in her power to invade us, void of troops
and defense at present, from Ostend, Dunkirk, Brest and where not, I cannot but wish
for the return of the Duke of Cumberland and the forces, at least 10,000 under his com-
mand, without which I am certain we do not sleep in whole skins.

Our danger is near and immediate, all our defence at a distance. You cannot well
imagine the concern all people are in… I am thoroughly convinced we shall be invaded
from Flanders. And the 6,000 Dutch that are to come over will do nothing without
10,000 of our own people to fight our own battles. I bewilder myself in scenes of misery to
come, unless providentially prevented.[2]

Thus Benjamin Keene, a diplomat, in correspondence from London, reveals
the popular conception that the rising in Scotland must be the curtain-
raiser for a more substantial intervention. He, like most contemporaries,
would not have thought that the clans would seriously contemplate 'going
it alone'.

The skirl of the pipes and the fine panoply of the standard could not disguise the fact that Prince Charles Edward had very few supporters. What is remarkable in the story of the '45 is not that it ended as bloodily on Culloden Moor, but that it ever proceeded so far in the first place.

If, however, the Prince had no grounds for undue optimism, the government's Commander-in-Chief for North Britain, Sir John Cope, had every reason for concern.

His brigade marched from Stirling on 20 August, bound for Fort Augustus by way of Crieff and Tay Bridge. He could muster no more than 1,500 bayonets. These comprised Murray's regiment, five companies of Lee's, and two companies of the Black Watch. The next day at Cullen, he was joined by eight companies from Lascelles's.

In terms of ordnance he had only four small 1½-pounder guns, the same number of Coehorn mortars and a thousand stand of arms with which to equip the loyal clansmen who were expected to rally to the government cause. As his march was intended to be a rallying call to the Whig clans, Cope had decided that a 'show' of artillery would suffice, and the train was provided by the master gunner of Edinburgh Castle, Eaglesfield Griffith. No trained gunners were to be found. The train was commanded by a Lieutenant Colonel Whitefoord of Cochran's Marines, serving as an attached volunteer. Two regiments of dragoons, Gardiner's and Hamilton's, were left behind at Stirling.

In terms of the strategy, Cope had consulted with Duncan Forbes and the plan was to nip rebellion in the bud and rely primarily on the Whig clans. This anticipated support proved to be something of a chimera, and most of the muskets had to be sent back as there were so few takers. Neither the Duke of Atholl nor Lord Glenorchy came in and the latter wrote an apologia to the Marquess of Tweedale, Secretary for State, blaming adverse economic conditions amongst his people. Even Argyll sat on the fence, piously claiming that arming his clansmen would contravene the provisions of the Disarming Acts.

It was a poor pass indeed when even mighty Clan Campbell would not raise a hand to defend the Whig faction. With this helpful advice the Duke decamped to his London house. Cope was both furious and impotent. Had he been aware of how lukewarm the King's friends in the Highlands would prove, he would have done better, like Argyll in the '15, to have stayed safe behind Stirling's fortifications. Here his position would have been inexpugnable and he could have controlled all access to the Lowlands.

The Black Watch companies were plagued by frequent desertions, though a further, weak company from Loudon's joined the column at Aberfeldy. By 25 August Cope had reached Dalnacardoch where Captain Swetenham, released on parole, appeared. He estimated (wrongly) the rebels numbers at close on 3,000 and worse, they had taken up positions across the dizzying ascent of the Corrieyairack. The general, heeding this intelligence, decided against trying to force the pass and debated whether he should now simply fall back toward Stirling or try and concentrate around Dalwhinnie.

Neither option at this stage appealed; he felt that to retreat at all would only serve to push the waverers toward the Prince's cause. Better to march eastwards to Inverness, as this would help secure the isolated garrison at Fort Augustus and discourage the rebels from trying to march south with the Hanoverian army poised in their rear. Besides, supplies were short and Inverness offered the best prospect for replenishment.

The high ground was ablaze with saffron and plaid; the Jacobites looking forward to disputing the pass. Some of the light swivel guns brought ashore from the *Du Teillay* were carefully sited to cover the seventeen hairpins. Since quitting the rallying ground at Glenfinnan on 21 August, the Prince's numbers had been swelled by more MacDonalds and Grants and with Stewart of Appin's people, though his army was still far short of the numbers Captain Swetenham had calculated.

To confuse the Jacobites, Cope pressed on to Correy but then swung eastwards, just short of Garva Bridge. He continued to Ruthven, where he left only a nominal garrison, and entered Inverness on the evening of 29 August. For General Cope the Highland capital proved a serious disappointment, and he found little evidence of cooperation. The horses he needed to pull his baggage carts were not forthcoming, and supplies were scanty. If he retreated overland, by the way he had come, he risked being outflanked and ambushed by the faster moving rebels. His position was an unenviable one but he had definitely surrendered the initiative. In so doing he left the road to the Lowlands wide open and the Jacobites marched boldly on.

By 4 September Cope was also marching, rather belatedly, south to Aberdeen, where he proposed to embark his men on transports for the cruise back to the Lothians. At Inverness he had withdrawn a garrison company of Guise's and left some of his mercurial Black Watch. He further acquired another brace of 1½-pounders and Coehorns. The task of collecting the transports and getting men and equipment aboard was not completed until 16 September.

Charles had sagely elected not to pursue Cope and bring on a battle. His Highlanders would have been on ideal ground on the high moor of the Corrieyairack but they would have been significantly disadvantaged if forced to attack regulars in entrenchments. Ruthven Barracks had been briefly leaguered, but the stout leadership of Sergeant Molloy had stiffened the resolve of the few defenders and the attack was abandoned.

By 31 August the rebels reached Blair Castle, and three days later they were in Dunkeld. Duncan Forbes had already written to Tweeddale, intimating that Cope's defection had left the Lowlands totally exposed. On 4 September the Prince entered Perth, the ancient seat of Scottish Kings, where his father's return to the ancestral throne was proclaimed.

He was now joined by both James Drummond[3] and Lord George Murray.[4] This was a momentous meeting. Murray had kept his head down since the debacle at Glenshiel and the swift unravelling of the '19. He was to display real ability as a leader of irregular forces but his blunt, authoritarian disposition grated, particularly with O'Sullivan and others of Charles's Irish cronies. His relationship with the Prince was based on Charles's bland assertions of the sureness of French support and this would steadily deteriorate as the campaign progressed and the promises failed to materialise.

As his aide-de-camp, Lord George retained the Chevalier de Johnstone, who left an invaluable record of both the campaign and the Battle of Culloden. Johnstone was from an influential family of Edinburgh bourgeoisie, well connected to various gentry, as the 'Chevalier' likes to remind his readers. His early youth was spent, or perhaps wasted, in sensual pleasures; he was then sent to Russia, where his uncles were in business, to imbibe some sense of responsibility. The experiment was not a success. His affinity with the Jacobite cause may, to a degree, have been romantic but he secured an introduction to Lord George. He clearly had a very high regard for his commander, but equally he was not blind to his faults:

> Lord George Murray, who had charge of all the details of our army and the sole direction of it, possessed a natural genius for military operations, and was indeed a man of surprising talents, which, had they been cultivated by the study of military tactics, would unquestionably have rendered him one of the greatest generals of the age. He was tall and robust, and brave in the highest degree, conducting the Highlanders in the most heroic manner, being always the first to rush, sword in hand into the midst of the enemy. He used to say when we advanced to the charge, 'I do not ask you, my lads, to go before, but

merely to follow me' – a very energetic harangue, admirably calculated to
excite the ardour of the Highlanders… He slept little, was continually occupied with all manner of details, and was altogether most indefatigable, for he
alone had the planning and directing of all our operations… However, with
an infinity of good qualities, he was not without his defects; proud, haughty,
blunt and imperious, he wished to have the exclusive disposal of everything
and, feeling his superiority, would listen to no advice.[5]

By 11 September the Jacobite army was again upon the march. Their
advance, free from resistance or interception by government forces, sparked
a panic in the capital. Cope was still upon the seas and there were no troops
available; the walls, long neglected, were indefensible. The rebels, with their
colours proudly aloft, marched past Stirling, whilst a token cannonade from
the fortress's guns hailed their advance. By the 15th Charles had reached
Linlithgow, site of the Renaissance palace of his ancestors.

Next day the rebels advanced as far as Corstorphine, barely three miles
distant. On the following day Cope's laden transports finally made landfall
at Dunbar and this comfort sufficed to stiffen the resolve of the magistrates
to resist. The example set by Gardiner's Horse was scarcely encouraging,
no opportunity for retreat had been overlooked and the cavalry screen
had simply melted away as the Jacobites continued their advance. The city
fathers wavered.

When Cope marched from Stirling he had left his two regiments of dragoons, Gardiner's and Hamilton's, the former actually at Stirling and the
latter in the capital, both of which were now under the nominal command
of Edinburgh's venerable castellan, General Joshua Guest. Colonel James
Gardiner had been a distinguished and dashing officer in his youth. He had,
however, subsequently undergone what was either a religious conversion or
nervous breakdown and was by now of a melancholy and fatalistic disposition,
and his mental health was clearly such that he was unfitted for command.[6]
The zeal displayed by both units, which could have hung upon the flanks of
the advancing Jacobites like prowling jackals, was singularly lacking.

It was considered wise to keep Hamilton's to hand in Edinburgh,
where the sympathies of the populace were open to question. Gardiner
fell back before the advance of the rebel army, firstly upon Falkirk, and
then to Linlithgow and finally as far as Corstorphine, where he was joined
by Hamilton's and a motley of local volunteers. Brigadier Thomas Fowke,
sent from England to have charge of the dragoons, had reviewed his new

command in camp at Edinburgh. He was not impressed: Gardiner's bearing and dress were distinctly unsoldierly, the rest were worse, some half disabled, others totally exhausted; their mounts were also in very poor shape. The colonel clearly had no confidence in his command:

> [He] represented to the Brigadier very strongly, and repeated many times... the bad Condition his Regiment was in; in particular being harass'd and fatigued for eleven days and eleven Nights, little or no Provision for the Men, nor Forage for the Horses... and that if they stay'd another Night on that Ground, it was to be feared his Majesty would lose two regiments of Dragoons; But added, the Brigadier might do as he pleased; for his Part he had not long to live.[7]

Both regiments were packed off to Leith, there to await Cope. A rearguard at Corstorphine was thrown into a total panic by the appearance of Jacobite scouts. After some popping of pistols the English horse turned tail and fled, galloping in disorder down the line of what would later become Prince's Street, in an episode which became known as 'the Coltbrig Canter'. Leith proved unsatisfactory, owing to the paucity of decent forage, and they moved, firstly to Musselburgh and then on to Prestonpans, adjoining Gardiner's pleasant estate at Bankton.

That same day, 17 September, the rebels seized the city gates by a *coup de main* and, by dusk, the great city was theirs, all bar the castle which stood inviolate upon its outcrop, unassailable yet impotent. The garrison was comprised mainly of invalids, along with the spry, octogenarian governor, who remained resolute in his defiance. The citizens accepted the presence of their occupiers with a kind of sullen shock and resentment.

To the citizens of a place that was undergoing transformation from a medieval warren of streets into one of the great cultural centres of Europe, a beacon of the Age of Reason, such a thing seemed impossible. This was a city poised on the brink of an intellectual and creative fervour which would inform thinking throughout the civilised world. That an ill-armed body of recusants, sprung from a Celtic twilight, could take and hold the nation's capital without, as it appeared, any interference from government, was against all reason and order. Yet, here they were, these wild, tattered men from the glens, as alien to the population of their nation's capital as a Zulu Impi. The Prince himself, however, provoked a different reaction. Even the most ardent Whigs would confess he was a fine looking young man, and the ladies in particular were impressed. Despite this easy success, the rebels' position remained as insecure as ever. The city contained few available arms, and those that did exist were safely under lock and key in the bowels of the great fortress, looming like a malevolent giant. Recruits were equally sparse.

As Charles Stuart rode in triumph into Scotland's capital and took up residence, appropriately, in Holyrood House, the Union Jack still flew defiantly from the castle. Cope, now at Dunbar, soon learnt he had lost the race but was determined to make good the delay and offer battle as soon as possible. Like Fowke, he was unimpressed by the state of his mounted regiments and particularly by the mental state of their commander. The Commander-in-Chief chose not to take any immediate action, and indeed there was little that could be done. Gardiner, veering from melancholy to garrulous excitement, was less inhibited. He found a ready listener in Lord Mark Kerr, a former rival of Cope's, recently disappointed of his opportunity to take office as commander of Edinburgh castle:

> Upon my getting there [Dunbar], I met with Coll: Gardiner who complain'd much of the retreat, I may say run away, of the two Regts. of Dragoons from the nieghbourhood of Edinburgh, which he said had ruin'd his Regt. were his words. An in conversation with my old Acquaintance he said that there has been the oddest proceedings and Blunders that were ever heard of, these were his Words. I ask'd him what he believed would be their operations now; he said he believed Sir Jn. Cope would fight to retrieve what had been passed, upon which I shak'd my Head, but don't really remember what I said, but Coll. Gardiner added he believed they should beat them. I had no sooner sshifted than I found Sir Jn. Cope standing by me, he complained that the rebels would get both Arms and Ammunition by being in possession of Edinburgh. He communicated nothing more to me, and I having no Power to Command bid God bless him and set out.[8]

This rather smacks of the politicking of a disappointed subordinate. By the time an enquiry was convened to examine Cope's subsequent defeat, Gardiner was dead and the army dispersed in rout. Cope was in fact exonerated, and rightly so – he had been forced to make difficult decisions and let down by the disinterest of the Whig clans. He was to be further let down by the fighting quality of his troops.

The rebels had secured only some 1,200 muskets from private hands in Edinburgh, and the quality of the requisitioned arms also varied immensely.

Whilst there might have been citizens who had some sympathy for the cause, most were hostile. Rapid manoeuvre might confound the government forces, success in the field might follow, but hearts and minds would not. For Lowland, Presbyterian Whigs, anything that come from the Highlands, reeking of Popery, was an anathema. Charles might yet win Scotland by the sword but that would not make his people love him.

Cope's failure to date had so alarmed the government that orders had been sent to Flanders to recall ten seasoned foot battalions under Sir John Ligonier, and these disembarked at Gravesend on 3 September. The usual range of preventative sanctions were enforced against Catholics and known sympathisers; these were ordered away from the capital and any who failed to swear an oath of allegiance were to suffer forfeiture of arms and horses. The Duke of Newcastle wrote, in urgent terms, to Viscount Lonsdale, the Lord Lieutenant of Cumberland:

> …it will give them great hold in Scotland and encourage the French and Spaniards to make attempts in favour of the Pretender, which undoubtedly they must have engaged to do, when the Pretenders' son came to Scotland. We had an account last Tuesday that there are at present thirty ships at Dunkirk, capable of bringing over 7 or 8,000 men, and some men-of-war, that the Irish regiments and officers are all quartered upon the coast, that their seamen are all sent to Dunkirk, that there is an embargo laid on the ships in the River Charente, and we all have reason to think for some time that there are French and Spanish men-of-war of the line near thirty at Ferrol and in the western ports of France. All these circumstances make it much to be apprehended that we shall soon have some attempt from abroad. I wish we were in a better condition to oppose it, that I am afraid we are. However, we have a very considerable squadron of great and small ships in the Downs under the command of Admiral Vernon, and Admiral Martin will have fourteen or fifteen sail, I think of the line, with him cruising off the Lizard to watch the ships from Brest etc. Last night orders were sent to the Duke of Cumberland to send over hither with the utmost expedition ten of the best regiments of foot from his army and Sir John Ligonier to come over with them. The Dutch are sending hither 6,000 men… as we have hardly any regular force between Berwick and London, it has been thought proper to direct the Lord Lieutenants of the four northern counties to have the militia in readiness. I hope we may send some northwards, if there is occasion, but at present, by what I understand, there are not in all England of all kinds 6,000 men, guards included. I must

own I have been for some time under great apprehensions, I think people begin now to be alarmed, I heartily wish they had been so a little sooner.[9]

It would, therefore, appear likely that it was not only Charles Edward who believed in the certainty of French or Spanish interference. The logic being that there could be no other purpose for the Scottish expedition, unless it was to be the curtain raiser for a larger undertaking from across the Channel. This may go some way to explaining how it was that the Jacobite army eventually penetrated as far south as Derby: Ligonier, and to a lesser extent Cumberland, must have been in the entirely reasonable belief that this was a diversion, not the main, and indeed only, event. Conversely, there was also a faction within the English polity that saw the Jacobites as nothing more than a distraction, a local disturbance, that should not serve to divert attention away from Flanders.

Rumours abounded that French landings were imminent or had indeed already taken place.[10] There were fears that the Jacobites, having out-manoeuvred Cope seemingly without effort, might now simply ignore his forces and march straight over the border into England. Cumberland's battalions and the Dutch Brigade[11] were to be pushed northwards as quickly as possible, augmented, somewhat optimistically, by detachments of militia.

Edinburgh's fall removed any question over whether the rebellion was a serious threat or merely a local disturbance. Two Dutch regiments were dispatched to Newcastle and Whigs in the North began to consider flight. Perhaps the loudly voiced Hanoverian support from the Northumbrian gentry was mere puff after all, just a smokescreen, and at the first sight of the White Cockade they would revert.

With this small rebel army now having moved, on 19 September, from King's Park to Duddington, a mile south-east of Edinburgh, a further body of foot came in, Athollmen and MacLachlans, together with a weak mounted company under Lords Elcho and Balmerino. Charles now commanded perhaps 2,500 foot, with barely half a hundred horse. Having marshalled his forces Cope marched out of Dunbar on 19 September. To recover the initiative and, as he hoped, crush the rebels it was necessary to bring about a general engagement. That evening the government troops bivouacked just to the west of Haddington.

By the 19th, and with Murray leading with van, the Jacobites too were on the march, the two armies in marked contrast. Cope's battalions, tramping beneath the colours, a long column of scarlet, the jumbled baggage following on; the Prince's Highlanders loping easily across the level ground, with a noticeable lack of both formality and impedimenta. Beat of drum and skirl of pipes.

Cope was warned by Loudon's[12] scouts that the rebels were drawing close to Preston. The general decided he would hold his ground, and presently his forces were arrayed on a flat, level plain between the villages of Preston and Seton. The hamlet of Prestonpans stood to his right, as did a number of thick-walled stone enclosures. On his left flank the plain deteriorated into a morass, draining into a pond behind the houses. His front was protected by another mire, complete with ditch and hedge. Cockenzie lay to his rear and, beyond the village, the dark waters of the Firth.

Jacobite forces were now crowding the slopes of Fawside Hill,[13] to the west of Cope's army. Murray divined the strength of his opponent's position, though he believed the government forces (barely 2,000) to be stronger than they were; a frontal attack was clearly out of the question. The waning day witnessed some further shuffling and manoeuvre but little changed. At a council of war that evening the Jacobites debated their options, which appeared to be somewhat limited.

One of the relatively few Lowland recruits to be seduced by the lure of the Prince's standard was one Robert Anderson; he had hunted snipe through these very wetlands and knew of paths through the mire. Before the sun tilted the horizon next morning, the fleet Highlanders, in bunched files, followed Anderson's lead, threading a damp passage over the fens. A skein of mist shrouded the wet ground and, though challenged by a mounted picquet, Perth, leading the van, skirted the steading at Riggonhead without any general alarm being raised and debouched onto the flank of the government line. The rest followed.

The shift from column into line was momentarily clouded by a dispute between Clan Donald and Clan Cameron as to who should have the honour of the right.[14] Clan Donald won the argument and Lochiel's men, with poor grace, formed on the left. From the right the rebel front line thus comprised Clanranald, Glengarry, Keppoch, Macgregor, Perth's contingent, Appin men and Camerons. Behind them, and also from the right, Athollmen, Robertsons and MacLachlans, with the horse on the left flank. The Prince commanded this second line, in front, Perth the right division and Murray the left.

Cope now found himself outmanoeuvred and outflanked. To conform to the new and threatening Jacobite deployment, he must swing his whole force to the left. His raw troops were already shaken and, sensing the tremor, the General treated his battalions to a rousing address, designed to stiffen their resolve and dismissing their enemy as 'a parcel of rabble, a parcel of brutes'.[15] The ground to his re-formed front was a level plain; the harvest had been got in and the dull ochre of stubble covered the ground. Directly in front of his line ran a timber colliery waggonway. This had the potential to disrupt a charge and would certainly represent an element of industrial technology totally unfamiliar to Highlanders.

Having posted dragoons on both flanks and as reserves, he placed his foot battalions, from left to right: Murray's, Lascelles's, two companies from Guise's, and a half battalion of Lee's. Had Cope been able to repose more confidence in his cavalry he might have sent them forward to exploit a noticeable gap which now yawned between the two front-line divisions opposite him. Perth, totally inexperienced, had allowed his deployment to drift too far to the north, his overview obscured by dead ground.

Colonel Whitefoord manfully strove to sight the government ordnance, light guns and mortars, hampered by untrained crews who promptly bolted as the Highlanders charged. Undeterred, the gallant Colonel stayed and discharged five out of six guns and all the mortars. The rounds fell amongst the advancing Camerons and certainly caused them some loss.

The blast from the guns appears to have discomfited the wobbly troopers of Gardiner's Horse, which were stationed to the rear and somewhat to the left of the ordnance. The men now wavered; Gardiner, despite a conviction that this fight would be his last, strove to rally his men, but they broke and the Colonel was left alone. He did not flee, however, but fought on until the fearful swing of a Lochaber axe cut him from the saddle.[16]

Chevalier Johnstone describes the action:

Lord George, at the head of the first line, did not give the English time to recover from their surprise. He advanced with such rapidity that General Cope had hardly time to form his troops in order of battle, before the Highlanders rushed upon them sword in hand. They had been frequently enjoined to aim at the noses of the horses with their swords, without minding the riders, as the natural movement of a horse, wounded in the face, is to wheel round, and a few horses wounded in that manner are sufficient to throw a whole squadron into such disorder that it is impossible afterwards to rally it. They followed this advice most implicitly, and the English cavalry were instantly thrown into confusion.

Macgregor's company did great execution with their scythes. They cut the legs of the horses in two, and their riders through the middle of their bodies. Macgregor was brave and intrepid, but, at the same time, altogether whimsical and singular. When advancing to the charge with his company, he received five wounds, two of them from balls that pierced his body through and through. Stretched on the ground, with his head resting on his hand, he called out to the Highlanders of his company, 'My lads, I am not dead! By G—, I shall see if any of you does not do his duty.'[17]

Cope's foot managed only a single volley before the panic gripped and they, too, bolted. The poor deployment of the Jacobite divisions had, in fact, worked in their favour. By striking and scattering the dragoons rather than rushing directly at the foot, they came in now from the flanks and simply rolled up Cope's line. The hacking broadswords, shearing through bone and tissue, completed the rout. Cope's disordered, wavering ranks simply collapsed into an avalanche of fleeing men, the stricken field strewn with abandoned gear. The melee lasted but a few minutes but the ground was 'covered with heads, legs and arms, and mutilated bodies'.[18]

The panic-terror of the English surpassed all imagination. They threw down their arms that they might run with more speed, thus depriving themselves by their fears of the only means of arresting the vengeance of the Highlanders. Of so many men in a condition, from their numbers, to preserve order in their retreat, not one thought of defending himself. Terror had taken entire possession of their minds.[19]

The Chevalier goes on to describe the valour and accomplishment of one youthful prodigy of the Highland army, no more than fourteen, who had tallied a score of English dead, equal to his years, a feat of bloodletting that earned the Prince's commendation. The Highlanders, in their hour of victory, were becoming the victims of their own legend, invincible, unstoppable, almost superhuman. This sweeping triumph would lead the Prince to grossly overestimate his clansmen's ability to trounce regular troops regardless of ground. Now, at Prestonpans, the fleeing soldiers had found themselves fatally hemmed in by the solid park walls at Preston, with no escape from the relentless blades.

There was an attempt, short lived, to rally the horse, but the men refused to stand and galloped off in disarray, heading for Dalkeith, leaving the field to the jubilant rebels. Cope, who was by no means the poltroon of the popular Jacobite doggerel, mopped up what remnant he could, barely 200, and with his officers, Loudon, Drummore, Home and the motley of stragglers, fell back towards Coldstream. The Jacobites, who christened the field Gladsmuir, lost less than half a hundred dead, perhaps twice that number injured.

By 16 October the local broadsheet circulating in Newcastle acknowledged the swift and apparently irresistible rush of the clans:

> Poor Sm—h was apprehended and imprisoned yesterday, for saying, over a bottle, that the Dutch auxiliaries here would find an infinite odds between pluffing at the petit Maitres before Tournay or Fontenoy, and encountering with the desperate Highlander's trusty broadsword and targe, headed by a person who can lie on straw, eat a dry crust, dine in five minutes and gain a battle in four.[20]

Some 300 men had fallen from the government side and five times that number taken prisoner. Most of those who were slain or wounded suffered their wounds in the rout, the infantry had fired no more than a single volley and no clansman had been impaled upon their virgin bayonets. Loss amongst the horse, apart from Gardiner himself, was trifling. All of Cope's ordnance, small arms, baggage and treasure formed the prize. No longer would the rebels be starved of arms, powder and shot nor, for that matter, of cash. The rebels treated their captives well; for all their vaunted ferocity, the clansmen had spared those who laid down their arms:

> Never was more quarter given with more humanity by the Highlanders even in the heat of battle… the wounded (who were mainly of the enemy) were taken as great a care of as possible.[21]

On the government side, most of the opprobrium, of which there was, inevitably, an abundance, fell upon the soldiers themselves, both foot and horse, who were roundly accused of cowardice. A subsequent observer, writing from Berwick, noted:

> …the action or rather the rout… The officers in the general condemn the soldiers and in particular manner the dragoons who they say did not strike one blow before they fled and neither they nor the foot could be prevailed upon to rally. We think this accounts for the defeat without any other reason

either the attacks being early in the morning or the bravery or number of the Highlanders.

One thing is certain that this defeat will make it a dangerous experiment for his Majesty's troops to engage the rebels a second time without a visible superiority. This has raised their contempt of the regular troops and I own I have a great doubt but that his majesty's troops will have a diffidence of one another especially of their leaders though they have come safe off in this action.[22]

This criticism of the private men is, to a degree, unfair. The regiments comprised mainly raw and untrained recruits, and their drill and tactics did not really allow for this type of fighting. The swiftness of the clans and their resolute charge would be truly terrifying, giving no chance for the stately, rolling platoon volleys that might winnow more sedate adversaries. Opinion in England also saw fit to transfer some of the blame on the Lowland Scots who, it was opined, had been less than zealous in resisting the Pretender's son. Quite how the Lowlanders, without any military establishment, were supposed to resist was not spelt out!

Any doubt as to whether it was necessary to withdraw troops from Flanders was settled by the outcome at Prestonpans. Untried troops would simply not suffice: the obvious precedent was Montrose's 'Year of Miracles' a century earlier, when inexperienced, local levies had been pitched into battle against clansmen and veteran Irish. The defeat convinced many in England that a more widespread insurrection south of the border might now erupt despite the usual precautions – lingering fears of the Jacobite bogeyman still persisted.

For Charles this was a famous victory. Recent apologists have tried to minimise the scale of the disaster. It is true the numbers involved on both sides were modest, and casualties relatively light. The troops were raw, and both sides made tactical errors – the gap which Perth's injudicious deployment created could have been decisively exploited by a more resolute enemy. Nonetheless, the Jacobite army, which did not exist a couple of months before, had effectively cleared Scotland of government forces, trounced a regular army and made itself master of the northern realm. For a young man of Charles's disposition it was a very fine thing indeed; let all who had ignored him or sniggered behind his back in Rome or Paris take heed. He had seemingly achieved when all before him had failed; the land of his ancestors was, once more, in their keeping.

For those who still sought to reverse the Act of Union then it was done, and for most this would have been enough. Prestonpans was a victory which led the Prince deeper into the illusion that his Highland army was invincible and that his cause could prosper even without French aid. Of course, he had no intention of being content with Scotland, even if he could hold it; his sights were firmly fixed on the greater prize to be found in London, the Enterprise of England.

The rebels had yet to subdue the Hanoverian garrisons in Edinburgh, Stirling, Fort William, Fort Augustus and the outposts. These were each a significant obstacle, particularly for an army that possessed no siege train, nor skilled gunners nor engineers. In the modern context the Jacobite force was a guerrilla army which, through boldness and an element of good fortune, had bested a regular opponent.

Chevalier Johnstone was in no doubt as to what should have been done:

The victory at Prestonpans, however unimportant it at first seemed, made the Prince the entire master of Scotland, where the only English troops which remained were the garrisons of the castles of Edinburgh and Stirling. As the whole of the towns of Scotland had been obliged to recognise the Prince as regent of the kingdom in the absence of his father King James, all that he had to do now was to retain possession of it. His chief object ought to have been to endeavour, by every possible means, to secure himself in the government of his ancient kingdom, and to defend himself against English armies (which could not fail to be sent against him) without attempting, for the present, to extend his views to England.[23]

An immediate gulf opened between the aims of Charles and those of his supporters, particularly the more articulate Murray and Lochiel, who were opposed to an advance into England whilst the Jacobite grip on Scotland was still insecure. The Prince was confident, despite the paucity of recruits in the Scottish Lowlands, that a popular swell would greet his passage through England. Based on the experience of the '15 this was clearly delusional. If the English had not flocked to the standard three decades past, they were unlikely to do so now. For the chiefs, the business of England could only proceed if the French were able to land men and arms in the South.

For a full six weeks the Jacobites remained in and around the Scottish capital. The winds freshened and blew the ochre leaves from the trees, the autumnal breezes keening through the narrow wynds of the old town,

the shortening days enlivened by the Prince's social calendar and the odd
stray ball from the garrison. The victory did not produce above a trickle of
recruits from the Lothians though fresh detachments were still coming in
from the north and east.

The government, meanwhile, had not been idle. Cope's debacle had
certainly concentrated minds and there was a feverish mustering of forces
from hardened regulars to the despised 'vestry' men. The venerable Marshal
Wade was stationed at Newcastle, with forces at his disposal. More were
being mustered in the Midlands and the South-East. In a burst of patriotic
fervour, spurred by the old demon of the Popish horde, volunteer units
sprang up across the nation. On 19 October, Cumberland was appointed as
Commander-in-Chief.

For the Duke, who was convinced of the need to maintain a strong presence in Flanders, this appeared as an unwelcome distraction. To draw off
troops at a time when the French enjoyed a tactical and strategic supremacy
must weaken the overall allied position in Europe. Such an action might
encourage Austria, already at war with Prussia, to side with France and
those amongst the Dutch who favoured an accommodation might acquire
a louder voice. Cumberland was, however, to make a major contribution by
taking charge of the military response. His united command, with a clear set
of objectives – put simply, the elimination of the Jacobite field army and the
recovery of Scotland – imbued the government cause with both purpose
and method.

At the Jacobite council session on 30 September Charles was all for a
swift descent through Northumberland, the East Coast route, to try conclusions with Wade before the ageing Marshal was reinforced or superseded by
a more youthful replacement. There was some logic in this: it is obviously
better to defeat your enemies in detail while they are still scattered. The
problem was Berwick, a formidable fortress whose sixteenth-century walls
remained strong. The small Jacobite army had not the men, the resources,
nor the skills necessary to undertake siege operations, besides which such a
course would have been pointless, granting the government a reprieve and
time to organise.

The situation with Edinburgh Castle demonstrated the clansmen's inability to cope with fortresses. No attempt was made to storm the place, General
Guest is said to have refused a bribe and his small garrison of greybeards and
invalids stuck to their battlements. A blockade was attempted but Guest
responded by opening fire on the city with his great guns and mounting

several energetic sallies. The Prince could not afford to have civilians being killed by stray round shot so the sanction was withdrawn.

A lack of cavalry was a singular defect in an eighteenth-century army, and yet the fact the Jacobites could move, in late autumn, without having to consider the need for forage, was a form of advantage. Most armies of the day retired into winter quarters but the Highlanders were used to moving over difficult ground in all seasons, and the onset of winter would perhaps assist rather than hinder.

Council meetings were apt to prove contentious; the Prince did not care for opposition, and could usually count on the support of his Irish friends. The chiefs and Lord George were less accommodating. Murray's manner was equally abrasive and his arguments were delivered with force rather than diplomacy. The chiefs were alarmed at the prospect of the English adventure and advocated the complete reverse, a withdrawal to the Highlands to mop up all remaining centres of resistance and to consolidate.

The army was receiving fresh drafts, though none of these was from the Lowlands. Lord Ogilvy brought in 300 foot from Angus, old Glenbucket as many from Aberdeenshire, and 120 Mackinnons arrived from Skye led by their chieftain. A further 300 broadswords marched in under MacPherson of Cluny, who had previously been offered a commission in Lord Loudon's regiment. The Duke of Gordon's younger brother Lord Lewis Gordon was drumming up recruits, willing or otherwise, and new detachments were swelling the existing regiments.

Cavalry were still scarce but Lord Elcho had raised a troop of mounted gentlemen as Life Guards: 'Completed it all of gentlemen of familly and fortune... their uniform blew and reed, and all extremely well mounted'.[24] Lord Pitsligo led a further mounted company, while Murray of Broughton led a troop of hussars who sported plaid waistcoats and distinctive furred headgear. Lastly Lord Kilmarnock, one of the few Lowlanders to come out, raised a further, diminutive troop.

October had also brought some welcome aid from France. On the 3rd of the month three swift vessels ran the gauntlet of the Royal Navy's patrols to land stores and munitions at Montrose and Stonehaven. These included half a dozen battalion guns of Swedish manufacture, twice as many gunners with a skilled artillerist, Lieutenant Colonel Grant, and an emissary, the Marquis d'Eguilles.

Conversely, slippery old Lovat was still prevaricating whilst MacLeod and Sir Alexander MacDonald had declared for Hanover. Charles also faced the hostility of the northern clans, Mackay, Sutherland and Munro, all Whigs, who were openly hostile. Other names such as Mackintosh, Gordon and Grant were divided. Duncan Forbes, cannily, played on divided loyalties by offering inducements: he had commands of twenty independent companies to offer.

If there had to be an invasion then Murray certainly did not like the Prince's idea of a descent down the eastern flank, and had devised a more cautious plan. The North-West was undefended: let the army cross by Carlisle and advance through Cumberland into Lancashire, keeping the formidable barrier of the Pennines between them and Wade. Moreover, it was supposed that Lancashire was awash with willing sympathisers, whose swelling numbers would open the road to London.

It is quite likely Lord George believed no such thing. Neither he nor Lochiel, both men of experience, could have much faith in an English rising. Murray may have been motivated in suggesting the western route by the idea that it would be far easier to retreat from this side than the east, with Wade's garrison between them and Scotland. If this was indeed his underlying supposition then events would certainly serve to vindicate his choice.

In England the government was not in any doubt. The Whigs saw quite clearly that Charles must surely invade and that this would be a thrust aimed at the heart of the Hanoverian administration, not merely a cross-border incursion, a chevauchée, in the old style. It was assumed that such a move would, in some manner, be conducted as part of a wider strategy involving French intervention. Given the events of the previous year this seemed eminently logical. The Hanoverians, like Charles's supporters, saw French participation as crucial; for the government it was inconceivable that the Prince would march his small army into the jaws of the lion, unless he was confident of help.

How best then to respond, that was the nub of the dilemma. If too weak a garrison was left along the South Coast, might this not be the very consequence the French were seeking and provide them with their opportunity? On the other hand, not to mass against the Jacobite army might embolden sympathisers in the North and add to the weight of the incursion. Prestonpans showed quite clearly that locally raised forces – the militia, if any could be found, and if they could be brought to the field – would be swiftly overcome. Action there had to be, for the series of disasters in the North had shaken confidence and initiated a run on the Bank of England. The government's grip was becoming precarious.

Jacobite successes had been as much of a shock to the French as the Hanoverians. Plans for an invasion to consolidate these achievements was sanctioned by mid-October, but no such undertaking could be mounted at a moment's notice. Had the French been ready then matters might very well have turned out differently. When Charles was to argue, in the heated council at Derby, that French support was imminent, he was closer to the truth than he knew. French unpreparedness gave the government the time it needed to recover its breath and its nerve, to redeploy forces from Flanders and to draw up a plan of campaign to contain, and then defeat, the invasion.

On 1 November, the Jacobite army marched out of Edinburgh to attempt the conquest of all England. There was no real intimation of any major French intervention, nor was there any particular cause for optimism in terms of local support. With the exception of the recruits who had come in from the Lowlands, this was still very much a Highland army, about to attempt what no purely Highland force had ever done. The men were, however, now well armed and equipped, with adequate supplies, buoyed by their victory, and ably led by Lord George Murray who had not wasted the intervening weeks.

Thirteen clan regiments, five from the Lowlands, two troops of Horse Guards, one troop of Life Guards under Lord Elcho and a train of a thirteen assorted pieces: in all, there were some 5,000 foot and 500 horse. Murray's plan involved a march in two columns, one of which would feint to the east, as though by Wooler, to perplex Wade whilst the second proceeded directly westwards, via Peebles and Moffat. The marching columns would reunite at Carlisle.

In this, the geography and topography of northern England greatly assisted the rebels. The left-hand column was led by William Murray, Duke of Atholl and by the Duke of Perth. Lord George and the Prince took the right, which marched by Lauder to Kelso and on to Jedburgh, then veering westwards down the length of Liddesdale, haunt, in the sixteenth century, of the notorious riding names: Armstrongs, Elliots, Bells and Crosers. What was noticeable on the march through the borders was that very few recruits came in — even the old riding names could not be tempted. Lord Strathallan had been left behind at Perth to muster additional Highland companies still coming in.

The spinal cord of the Pennines split the land into east and west; to advance northward by either route meant leaving the other uncovered. In the past Scottish incursions from the Lothians traditionally opted for the eastern flank through Northumberland. When Wade had mustered at Doncaster he had to choose which approach seemed the most likely.

His choice of the Great North Road to Newcastle was a fortuitous error for the Jacobites. For other reasons the eastern side seemed the safer option as it was obviously much easier to land reinforcements from Flanders in the east coast ports. Wade's force would be 10,000 strong, well furnished with ordnance, and at Newcastle would draw in Cope's remnants from Berwick.

What remained of the dragoons, with General Cope, were eventually instructed to hold fast at Berwick, which would, as ever, be the front-line bastion in the event the Scots attacked from that direction. Ironically, the delay in the departure of the Highland army from Edinburgh worked in Murray's favour, for the government spent the intervening weeks building up strength in the east and virtually ignoring the west.

The great red sandstone citadel of Carlisle had regularly defied the Scots since the Normans first decided to draw the line here. Many attempts had been made but none had succeeded.[25] Captain Durand was in charge of the defences, 580 citizen volunteers had been mustered, Lord Lonsdale had managed to enthuse some 200 of the militia and there was a regular garrison of 83 invalids, supplemented by 38 stragglers from Cope's army. The captain had requisitioned ten pieces of ordnance from Whitehaven and was determined to make a fight of it.

On 11 November, Charles had drawn off most of his forces to move eastwards toward Brampton, there to offer battle to Wade whose arrival was thought imminent. When the Field Marshal failed to appear, the Jacobites once again returned to manning their entrenchments. The magistrates, pinning all their hopes on Wade and with the volunteers deserting wholesale, sought terms, but Durand withdrew to the castle when, on 14 November, the city capitulated. Deserted by his remaining garrison, Durand followed suit a day later. Before striking his colours, he managed to spike some of the great guns, but the rebels still secured further supplies of arms and powder.

Wade, realising he had been humbugged, had begun the march westwards on 16 November, striking his encampment on Newcastle's Town Moor. His battalions struggled over vile roads in dismal weather, the ground at Hexham was too ironbound to pitch tents, men froze to death at their posts, dysentery was rife. When he heard that Carlisle was already lost, he turned his force around again and marched back to Newcastle, which he attained on the 22nd.

Murray's assessment of the Marshal had been correct. A younger man might have kept advancing regardless, which could then have placed a large body of troops astride the rebels' line of retreat; in the circumstances of the following month's events, this might have been disastrous. Wade, rightly famous for his roads, was never truly a fighting general. Born in 1673, he had had his first battlefield command in Europe only the previous year, and by 1745 he lacked both the heart and the stamina for operations in the field.

Carlisle, however, again proved a prize of only limited value in terms of fresh recruits; certainly there was no stampede to fall in behind the Prince's standard. It was too much to hope that even the aged Wade would remain immured at Newcastle for the duration of the campaign. At the conclusion of the siege Lord George threw a memorable tantrum in front of the Prince, alleging his opinions were not being sought, and he offered to surrender his commission and remain in the ranks as a gentleman volunteer. This was mainly posturing, and the affable Perth poured oil on the troubled waters by resigning his own position in favour of Murray. The Prince bore this unseemly outburst with outward calm but he was doubtless left seething. Charles may have respected Murray's abilities but he did not trust him; Murray had been inactive for too many seemingly quiet years and the Prince, with his coterie, could not forget that his first reaction had been to offer his sword to the Crown.

On 21 November the march south began once more, with only a token garrison of 100 men left behind in Carlisle, the army proceeding in two corps to minimise the difficulties of billeting in the hard uplands of Westmorland and Lancashire. The tensions between the Prince and his senior officer were bubbling away beneath the surface. Murray was not an easy subordinate, and his swagger undoubtedly caused friction. He was sceptical of Charles's assurances of support – rightly so, as none existed – whilst the Prince remained suspect of his loyalties and had a tendency to see disagreement as treasonable, his temperament unsuited to rigorous debate.

Sir John Ligonier was known to be mustering a sizeable force in the Midlands, while behind them the Glasgow garrison, with a smattering of loyalist militia, had concentrated on Stirling, with the potential to pose a significant threat in rear. The chiefs remained uneasy, and began to talk in terms of withdrawal. Charles, as ever, was having none of it – it was onward, deeper into the trap of England. However, the rebels still had the government perplexed. Obviously if they kept to the western side they would have to deal with Ligonier, but the hardy Highlanders could traverse the backbone of the Pennines, having left Wade immured at Newcastle, and then strike down the exposed eastern flank.

In Lancaster, the magistrates decided that the militia was totally unreliable and disbanded those who had come in on 21 November. They also abandoned the idea of trying to hold the castle and the Jacobite army entered the city unopposed on the 24th. By 27 November the rebels had reached Preston, of dismal memory, where two previous Scottish armies had come to grief. If this was a hotbed of Jacobite sympathisers then there were few who cared to step forward. The Highlanders were greeted with a species of bemused indifference, almost as though they represented an army of Ottomans or Hottentots, an alien race.

Charles's optimism had not been entirely unfounded. The Northumbrian gentry had come out during the '15 and the government certainly regarded the North-West as a hotbed of Jacobitism. The intervening three decades had eroded that tendency, however, as the Prince was to find, and support, the whole time the army was in England, never reached beyond lukewarm.

It was clear to most of the county magnates that the militia were at best unreliable, and there was an argument for giving out commissions to the gentry to raise volunteer regiments. This would provide loyalists with an opportunity to express their fervour and would, as it was hoped, produce local forces which might be counted on to stand. How steady these might prove if confronted was uncertain; the response from the militia in the North-West was scarcely encouraging. If the French could land troops in the South-West it was felt that this would act as a catalyst to galvanise Jacobite support there.

Wade had finally lurched out of his cantonment at Newcastle and set his army on the road south on the 26th. Two days later Cumberland reached Lichfield and took over command from Sir John Ligonier. The Duke did not think it likely that Wade's army would be able to join forces with his before he engaged the Prince's, and he was confident his regulars could deal with the Jacobites unaided. Despite their success at Prestonpans, the Hanoverian Commander-in-Chief did not have a high regard for the Highlanders.

After snatching a day's much-needed respite at Preston and, still marching steadily south, without any interference from the government, the rebel army came next towards Manchester. In his company Johnstone had an engaging renegade, sergeant Dickson, who had joined the Jacobites after being taken at Prestonpans. Fancying himself a recruiter, Dickson had been disappointed by the poor response to his blandishments at Preston and begged leave to make a dash for Manchester to get ahead of his fellow sergeants.

He then disappeared with Johnstone's horse and blunderbuss, taking with him a camp follower and a drummer. His efforts in the city were at first attended by peril as the mob proved hostile. The blunderbuss proved a handy deterrent and Dickson won over some 180 recruits. These were not, it has to be said, of the better sort and most had been ready to join whichever army pitched up first, unemployment and lack of prospects being a common denominator. Johnstone estimated the cost of this initiative at around three guineas, a fairly modest investment.[26]

Once converted, the Mancunians lit bonfires and rang church bells to welcome the Prince's army but, aside from Dickson's complement, there was an ominous dearth of volunteers. The Prince was sufficiently enthused to begin planning an appropriate wardrobe for his triumphal entry into England's capital, having assured his subordinates that the French fleet would sail on 9 December. His officers, even O'Sullivan, were less sanguine; 'we expected at least 1500 men would joyned us here', the Irishman observed.[27]

To confuse Cumberland, Murray now set in motion another ruse, a further feint to the west to convince the Duke that the rebels intended to make for Wales. In fact the army sidestepped the Hanoverians and, on 4 December, entered Derby. Cumberland had deployed his men for battle a day earlier at Stone, thinking he must be attacked. Wade had, by this time, not passed further south than Boroughbridge.

For the Jacobites, London was scarcely more that several days' march. Both armies were tired and adequate supplies of suitable footwear were a problem for each. Cumberland quickly appreciated the fact that he, like Wade before, had been humbugged, but he remained a good deal more decisive, deciding to position his forces around Northampton to bar the rebels' advance on London. It seemed that the decisive battle would now be fought there.

From the unpromising days of July, when the Prince, without means or supporters, had first cruised through the Western Isles, he had raised an army, brought men of repute and estate under his banner, traversed the length of Scotland, secured the capital, and destroyed the Hanoverian forces in Scotland. He had crossed into England, reduced Carlisle, and now penetrated as far south as Derby. It was a remarkable achievement. Chevalier Johnstone describes the panic that had infected London:

Our arrival at Derby was known at London on the 5 of December, and the following Monday, called by the English Black Monday, the intelligence was known throughout the whole city, which was filled with terror and conster-

nation. Many of the inhabitants fled to the country with their most precious
effects, and all the shops were shut. People thronged to the Bank [of England]
to obtain payments of its notes, and it only escaped bankruptcy by a strata-
gem… they dreaded to see our army enter London in triumph in two or
three days. King George ordered his yachts, in which he had embarked all
his most precious effects, to remain at the Tower Quay, in readiness to sail at a
moment's warning.[28]

For Murray and the chiefs it was quite far enough. The plain facts were that
no significant flow of recruits had come in, nor was there any sign of aid
from France. The government forces were massing and Cumberland must
soon realise his mistake. The Duke was not such a ditherer as Marshal Wade
and might be expected to seek conclusions without delay. One of those
on whose opinion the council relied was an apparent sympathiser, Dudley
Bradstreet, who warned the Jacobite officers of the weight of forces that lay
between them and the capital. In this they were misled, as Bradstreet was in
fact a government spy, one who certainly earned his pay.

Lord George was now convinced that no less than 30,000 troops stood
between the rebel army and London. Even allowing for Bradstreet's exaggera-
tion, the odds were still formidable, impossibly so. If the army were defeated, so
deep into England, then clearly there could be no escape; they would be anni-
hilated. On the face of it his caution seems entirely logical, and to retreat was
thus the only viable option. The Prince, when put to the question, could not
produce any correspondence from English Jacobites, nor could he guarantee
the French were on the seas. His lies now returned to haunt him and greatly
diminished his credibility with his subordinates. When pressed he became
truculent, accusing his officers of betraying his cause; it was not impressive.

To his fury and chagrin, the Prince was overruled. His brand of excitable
optimism had remained undiminished by the unfavourable strategic realities, and he persisted in the belief that the capital and the throne were his
simply for the taking. But it was to be retreat and, on 6 December, the army
turned about and began the long march north, back up the western spine of
England, the weather deteriorating and their enemies gathering strength.

With hindsight it is possible to argue that Charles was right to wish to
press on. Had the army successfully entered London he could very possibly
have achieved the dream and history would have judged him a hero rather
than a fool, a strategist rather than a gambler. To retreat was in fact a poor
option: there was no avoiding battle at some stage and, had the Jacobites

defeated Cumberland or bypassed his forces to occupy the capital, the Hanoverian cause might very well have foundered. The hastily raised forces around the city would most likely not have stood, and Wade was too far away and too enfeebled to intervene.

It could be said that the defeat of the Jacobite army actually occurred at Derby and that 6 December, 'Black Friday', marked the ruin of their hopes – Culloden was merely the postscript, a tying of loose ends. For all of Lord George's considerable tactical talent, he had underestimated the nature of the government's response. The army had come so close to toppling the house of Hanover that the measure of retribution would be commensurate. This could not be the almost gentlemanly business that had followed the '15. Moreover, Cumberland was a scion of the ruling house; this was, for him, a very personal fight. He was by nature a hard man, though respected by his troops, and if no butcher, he was not inclined to show clemency. The majority of Whigs wholeheartedly supported him.

For Charles, such a setback was beyond the compass of his emotional capacity, his personality too shallow to surmount what he saw, with mounting bitterness, as the ruin of his hopes. It was easier to blame timid and disloyal subordinates and the rift with Lord George Murray, whom he chose to condemn for the decision, began to widen. In time it would become an unbridgeable chasm.

Charles no longer displayed any semblance of leadership, preferring to sulk, seemingly indifferent to the welfare of his men, with whom his stock plummeted. This perhaps is the real cause of failure: Charles ultimately lacked the quality of leadership necessary to retain the unquestioning loyalty of his men. Had the Jacobites at Derby been led by a Montrose, or Dundee, then they might have taken the final, giant gamble. Charles simply was not of the right calibre, and the real failure was want of leadership on his part. He had not the charisma and genius that would unite his officers as a brotherhood and his abilities with the rank and file only obtained whilst matters stood in his favour.

Lord George was moved to comment on the Prince's changed demeanour:

We were commonly very late before the rear got to their quarters… His Royal Highness, in marching forwards, had always been the first up in the morning, and had the men in motion before break of day, and commonly marched himself afoot; but in the retreat he was much longer of leaving his quarters, so that, though the rest of the army were all on their march, the rear could not move till he went, and then rode straight on, and got to the quarters with the van.[29]

The English locals in the North-West, sensing the mood, became hostile, and discipline in the Highland army, hitherto admirable, faltered. Lochiel and Murray rose to the occasion, the latter assuming the role of chief of staff. The retreat now began, a race against time, before the government troops either caught up or were able to place themselves across the line of march. Either could be fatal, for there was no room for manoeuvre to the east, the gaunt barrier of the Pennines shrouded in mist and the early winter snows.

From Scotland there was some good news. The French had finally landed at Montrose, under Perth's brother Lord John Drummond. Not, it is true, an army, merely a single battalion of foot, the Royal Ecossois, and a weak battalion of Irish Picquets, half a hundred men drawn from each of the six regiments which comprised the Irish Brigade. These new arrivals were bolstered by more recruits which Lord Strathallan had managed to raise. In his communication, Drummond did stress that he believed the Irish Brigade and several French regiments were already aboard transports and awaiting favourable tides. With the local reinforcements, Drummond could now muster perhaps 3,000 men.

This good news from the north actually added weight to the chiefs' arguments for a withdrawal, for it was surely folly to fight now against the odds when, with Drummond's brigade added, the rebels would at least have parity with Cumberland and their choice of ground. It is probable that the Prince had, as one of his heroes and exemplars, Charles XII of Sweden. One of the great captains, the Swedish King had won great victories in his youth, often against considerable odds, and these had been won by bold and daring offensives. The difference was that Charles's force of Highlanders, however brave and hardy, could scarcely hope to emulate the achievements of a large, well-equipped field army, superbly drilled, well armed, and supported by formidable cavalry and artillery.

Once he realised that the rebels were retreating, Cumberland was swift to react. He based his strategy on the notion it would be preferable to bring the Jacobite army to battle as soon as possible and whilst still on English soil. If the matter could be decided quickly then any further campaigning in Scotland would be essentially a mopping-up operation and the regular battalions could be returned to Flanders to prop up the alliance. On 8 December the Duke sent orders to Wade, presently at Wetherby, to begin a movement westwards to seal off the route north through Lancashire. The aged Marshal attempted to conform; if he could place his 6,000 men across the rebels' line of retreat then this would be potentially catastrophic for Charles and the Jacobite army.

Once again, Wade moved very slowly; by the 10th he was no nearer than Wakefield. Here he began to fret over the security of Newcastle and considered he had little prospect anyway of reaching Manchester before the Prince. He did, however, detach Major-General James Oglethorpe with 500 horse, who were to cross the hills and shadow the rebels. He was correct insofar as he would not win the race for Manchester, which the Jacobites entered, once again, on the 9th. On the same day Cumberland set off in hot pursuit northwards, taking only his cavalry and 1,000 mounted foot.

The Pretender's army, footsore and weary, regained Preston on 11 December. Charles was for making a stand, maintaining the bridgehead in England so that the French would not lose interest. Murray again would have none of it. Preston had been indefensible in 1715, a trap, and he had no wish to repeat the experiment. Besides, as he argued, the army needed a respite to replenish supplies and gather strength.

The French, however, appeared to be on their way. As far back as 13 October Louis XV had decided to send an invasion force 6,000 strong to assist the Prince, and news of his successes had galvanised opinion. By mid-November the ubiquitous Walsh had received instructions to begin gathering available transports. The Irish were moved up to Dunkirk, and a commanding general, the Duc de Richlieu, appointed. Lack of guns and adverse winds caused delays, and the conditions were unlikely to be favourable before 20 December. The Royal Navy was not best placed to counter the threat; more men of war would be needed in the Downs. A descent on one of the ports on the South Coast seemed the likeliest option, though a landing in the South-West, where Jacobite sympathies flourished, could not be ruled out.

On 10 December, the febrile mood in the South erupted in fresh panic when it was rumoured that the French had actually landed at Pevensey. A gang of smugglers plying their illicit trade off Beachy Head were also mistaken for a vanguard. Richlieu was, however, beset by difficulties and a series of cutting-out raids by British frigates resulted in the loss of some thirty ships.

By 13 December Oglethorpe's troopers were scrapping with Jacobite outposts between Lancaster and Garstang. Charles toyed with the notion of making a stand but on the 15th the slow march northwards began again, and Oglethorpe's clattered into the streets behind. Cumberland sensed that he might be able to bring about a general engagement but was now ordered south to foil the chimera of the French invasion, orders which irritated him to a great degree, so engaged was he in the close pursuit of the retreating rebels. Next day the orders were countermanded and the chase was on again.

News of the retreat caused some consternation amongst the French, but tidings of the successful rearguard action subsequently fought at Clifton raised hopes again – the skirmish was inflated into a major engagement. But, whilst Richlieu prevaricated, blaming shortages, the Royal Navy was steadily building up its strength in the Downs. By the end of the year the invasion force had still not moved. Louis XV appeared to be still resolute and chivvied his increasingly reluctant general.

On 2 January the Irish Brigade was ordered to be ready for the passage to Rye, but the moment was slipping. It had seemed so tantalisingly close; a smaller expedition aimed at Scotland was mooted but nothing was done, and even the further victory at Falkirk failed to put fresh impetus into the venture. This was the supreme irony of the '45 – all the Prince's assertions over French assistance had been on the very point of becoming a reality. Had he progressed south on 6 December it seems inevitable that the French must have sailed.

Cumberland had followed Oglethorpe into Lancaster on 16 December by which time the Jacobites were slogging up the long incline to Shap, deluged in cold, relentless downpours, that added soaking misery and liquid mud to the fatigues of the march. The Duke was anxious to fight before the rebels reached Carlisle: his supplies would not permit any pursuit across the border.

By 17 December, as the weather continued to deteriorate, the footsore Jacobites reached Penrith. Charles would not abandon the guns and baggage, which greatly slowed the army's progress and made very heavy going of steep gradients. Murray had on a couple of occasions sought to requisition lighter, two wheeled carts but this was not actioned, even though there were plenty to be had. By the time the vanguard had made the town, the supply train was still lumbering up the long incline of Shap, a good ten miles behind.

> On the 16th our army passed the night at Shap, but our artillery remained at a distance of a league and a half from Kendal, some ammunition waggons having broken down, so that we were obliged to pass the whole night on the high road, exposed to a dreadful storm of wind and rain. On the 17th the Prince, with the army, arrived at Penrith; but the artillery, with Lord George, and the regiment of the MacDonalds of Glengarry, consisting of five hundred men who remained with us to strengthen our ordinary escort, could only reach Shap, and that with great difficulty, at night fall.[30]

Murray was personally in command of the rearguard, a few companies from Glengarry's Regiment. Aware that the hounds were closing in, he sent forward a request for reinforcements and the Prince detached John Roy Stewart's Edinburgh battalion.

As the column had struggled up Thrimby Hill, perhaps five miles north of Shap, a detachment of dragoons appeared — they were drawn from Bland's Regiment and were intent in pouncing on the rearguard as it emerged. Two companies of Perth's, commanded by a Lieutenant Brown of Lally's Regiment, formed the cutting edge of the van; these drew swords and launched themselves at the dragoons, who rode off without serious contact. Johnstone took part in the charge:

> We stopped a moment at the foot of the hill, everybody believing it was the English army, from the great number of trumpets and kettle drums. In this seemingly desperate conjuncture, we immediately adopted the opinion of Mr Brown, and resolved to rush upon the enemy sword in hand and open a passage to our army at Penrith, or perish in the attempt. Thus, without informing Lord George of our resolution, we darted forward with great swiftness, running up the hill as fast as our legs could carry us. Lord George, who was in the rear, seeing our manoeuvre at the head of the column, and being unable to pass the waggons in the deep roads confined by hedges in which we then were, immediately ordered the Highlanders to proceed across the enclosure, and ascend the hill from another quarter. They ran so fast that they reached the summit of the hill almost as soon as those who were at the head of the column. We were agreeably surprised when we reached the top to find, instead of the English army, only three hundred light horse and chasseurs, who immediately fled in disorder. We were only able to come up with one man who had been thrown from his horse and whom we wished to make prisoner to obtain some intelligence from him. But it was impossible to save him from the fury of the Highlanders, who cut him to pieces in an instant.[31]

Such an incidence of savagery, the butchery of a helpless prisoner, was undoubtedly an isolated occurrence, but the hewing in pieces of one of his troopers was precisely the type of action which would give substance to Cumberland's assertions of ruthless brutality. It was fuel for propaganda that would be employed to justify far more murderous retribution.

Around 1 p.m. on 18 December the army was moving at a virtual snail's pace, hopelessly encumbered by the baggage train, sacrificing that swift and agile movement of which the Highlanders were capable. Dragoons, like circling wolves, were appearing in ever greater numbers, ready to snap at the flanks and rear.

Within an hour the horse, stiffened by some local volunteers, were increasing the pressure on the rearguard, sweeping and circling, becoming emboldened and charging. Glengarry's men kept their nerve and their order, meeting each advance with a flourishing riposte. The sight of these ragged Highlanders, pale winter light catching the edge of the sword, was sufficient deterrent. After an hour and a half of this cat-and-mouse the Jacobites attained the village of Clifton, the winter's daylight already thickening.

Had Colonel Oglethorpe not overslept the horse might have been able to concentrate their efforts, but by 4 p.m. Cumberland himself was on the scene having given the unfortunate Oglethorpe a severe rebuke.[32] Light was fading and the ground difficult; Pitsligo's Horse attempted an ambush but were flushed out upon the cold reaches of Clifton Moor. Musketry rattled in the darkening air as the outposts bickered.

Charles had now detached Perth with the Atholl Brigade, while Stewart of Ardshiel brought up the MacPhersons and the Appin men. Perth, who now conferred with Murray, might have entertained the notion of making a stand and trying to turn Cumberland's flank, but the Prince had given clear orders that nothing more than a rearguard action was to be attempted. Cumberland had dismounted his dragoons and deployed them in skirmish order: two lines, the first comprising Bland's, Lord Mark Kerr's and Cobham's with Lord Montague's and Kingston's in support. A commanded party was detailed to cover the Appleby Road.

Murray, meanwhile, was attempting yet another ruse, the time-honoured trick of marching his few men up and down the single village street to suggest they were more numerous than they were. To meet the threatened advance of Cumberland's dragoons he now posted his MacDonald broadswords on the right, amongst hedges fronting the expanse of moor just west of Clifton. The line stretched obliquely toward Lowther, with the Appin men in the centre, Cluny's MacPhersons taking the left, more hedges to their front, while John Roy Stewart's Lowlanders were kept in reserve.

An eerie, rather fumbling fight began to develop. The encroaching darkness and uncertain ground confusing both sides, the scene lit from time to time by moonlight, then plunged into near obscurity by scudding clouds, the crack and flash of musketry creating bright bursts of blinding brilliance.

Bland's men began to penetrate the hedges on the Jacobite left, to be met with volleys from the MacPhersons. A firefight developed until Cluny's men drew swords and surged forward, skipping over the dykes and hedges like deadly wraiths, broadswords clanging against musket barrels. The work proved too hot for the dragoons, who retired, their commander Colonel Honeywood amongst the injured.

On the other flank Cobham's were attempting to feel their way around the western extremity of the MacDonalds' position, while Kerr's troopers advanced by the road. Too far as it transpired, for an ambush party of Clan Donald sharpshooters poured enfilade fire into their ranks at virtually point-blank range. Lord George had taken station with the MacDonalds on this western flank and, having seen off these probing attacks, began, true to his orders, to disengage. The Edinburgh men to the rear fell back first, followed by the Appin men, Cluny and then Clan Donald. Lord George Murray was the last man to quit the field.

All in all it was a skilful little action, credited as the last 'battle' on English soil. The attack had cost Cumberland perhaps forty dead and more wounded, the Jacobites considerably less. The Duke claimed the affair as a victory as he took the field, but it was a field empty of an enemy who had successfully blunted his pursuit. The honours, therefore, must go to Murray.

Cumberland, however, makes mention in his report of allegations that the Highlanders had slashed and hacked several already wounded officers who had tried to surrender. To him this was further evidence that he was fighting against savages, men who, besides being rebels, engaged in atrocities. Men such as these could not expect clemency.

20 December marked Charles Edward's twenty-fifth birthday and the day the army marched into Longtown. All that now barred their return to Scottish soil was the formidable river barrier of the Esk. Johnstone recalls how the army accomplished the difficult task of crossing the dark, swollen waters on that afternoon:

Nothing could be better arranged than the passage of the river. Our cavalry formed in the river, to break the force of the current, about twenty-five paces above that part of the ford where our infantry were to pass: The Highlanders formed themselves into ranks of ten or twelve abreast, with their arms locked in such a manner as to support one another against the rapidity of the river, leaving sufficient intervals between their ranks for the passage of the water. Cavalry were likewise stationed in the river, below the ford to pick up and save those who might be carried away by the violence of the current. The interval between the cavalry appeared like a paved street through the river, the heads of the Highlanders being all that was seen above the water. By means of this contrivance our army passed the Esk in an hour's time without losing a single man.[33]

Several young women, following sweethearts in the army, appear to have attempted the crossing to remain with their lovers but were swept away and drowned. Once safely across the men lit fires to dry their sodden plaids and danced reels in the dank greyness of a winter's afternoon, partly to energise the blood flow in wet, frozen limbs and partly to celebrate their return to their native land. Perhaps they now believed themselves safe. If so, they would have been quite wrong.

Not all Jacobite forces had left England: Charles had expressed the intention to leave a garrison of some 300 and more in Carlisle, to demonstrate his intention to return. This unhappy company included the Manchester Regiment under Colonel Francis Towneley, who, like his men, no doubt wished they had stayed and joined Cumberland instead. The Mancunians comprised perhaps a quarter of the garrison, the rest being drafted from Perth's, Ogivly's, Glenbucket's and John Roy Stewart's regiments.

Their task was a hopeless one. Cumberland, who reached the city on 21 January, was in no mood for any form of compromise and he set about the siege of Carlisle with energy and drive. Heavy guns were dragged over from Whitehaven, and construction of the batteries was completed by the 27th:

A battery of six eighteen-pounders was perfected the 27th at night, and on Saturday was fixed with good success, but the shot failed a little so that the fire was slacker on Sunday, however this little loss of time was of no consequence as a suply is received which will be continued as fast as there is occasion; and the battery was augmented that night. Overtures for a surrender were made Saturday night and again on Sunday night, but his R.H. would not hearken to anything.[34]

There was little the defenders could do but pitifully seek terms, but none were offered and no assurance given other than that they would not all be executed on the spot. On 30 December Carlisle surrendered; those found in the Jacobite ranks who had turned their coats after Prestonpans were hanged without fuss, and the Duke considered dealing with the rump in a similar manner. Rebels can expect no quarter.

10

RETREAT – THE RETURN TO SCOTLAND AND THE BATTLE OF FALKIRK

The terror of the English was truly inconceivable, and in many cases they seemed quite bereft of their senses. One evening as Mr. Cameron of Lochiel entered the lodgings assigned to him, his landlady, an old woman, threw herself at his feet and, with uplifted hands and tears in her eyes, supplicated him to take her life but to spare her two little children. He asked her if she was in her senses, and told her to explain herself. She answered that everybody said the Highlanders ate children, and made them their common food.

The Chevalier Johnstone[1]

Britons, behold the Royal Youth, 'tis he
Who fights your Battles, sets your Country free,
The Rebels hear, and tremble at his Name,
And Ch—s with Envy, eyes his rising Fame.
See there the Highlanders, in fearful plight,
On carrion Horses make a hasty Flight.
Satan has caught 'em in his Net, and see
He drags 'em onward to the triple Tree.[2]

In the first of the above extracts Chevalier Johnstone describes the fears of the English, their terror of the perceived demonic natures of the Highlanders. The irony in this is that the army appears to have behaved itself with complete propriety throughout, in an age when the passage of armies was commonly, and understandably, a matter of dread.

After reducing Carlisle the Duke of Cumberland retired into winter quarters. He had seen the rebels off English soil but the problem of the northern kingdom would have to wait for the spring. In terms of his prime objective of bringing the Jacobites to a decisive engagement prior to their safely crossing the Esk, he had failed. Field command in North Britain was delegated to General Hawley.[3] The appointment had, largely for the sake of form, been offered to Wade who, pleading infirmity, had declined.

Cope had been succeeded at Berwick by Lieutenant-General Roger Handasyde, who had scraped sufficient remnants from Price's and Ligonier's, plus what remained of the dragoon regiments, to march to the relief of Edinburgh. Lord Loudon, his own companies augmented by those Forbes had succeeded in raising, held the Highland capital. The Argyllshire militia were being drilled by Major-General John Campbell of Mamore. With the Jacobites advancing down the spine of England, the government position in Scotland had to an extent rallied. Despite the reverse at Inverurie, Stirling was still firmly in hand, as was Inverness and the garrison outposts.

Lord Strathallan, holding Perth for the Jacobites, could now muster a detachment of Frasers, under the Master of Lovat, the Earl of Cromarty's Mackenzies, Farquharsons and a Mackintosh regiment raised by 'Colonel Anne' Mackintosh of Moy Hall.[4] These recruits were now joined by the Franco-Irish troops under Lord John Drummond. The arrival of the French had precluded the further commitment of the Dutch battalions who, under the terms of their parole, were constrained to withdraw from the campaign.

The propaganda campaign, orchestrated by the English press, was continuing to portray the rebel army as a horde of fiends, bent solely upon destruction:

> They affirmed in the newspapers of London, that we had dogs in our army trained to fight, that we were indebted for our victory at Prestonpans to these dogs, who darted with fury on the English army. They represented the Highlanders as monsters, with claws instead of hands...[5]

Merely because the army was now returned to Scotland did not wholly imply that they were amongst friends. Whig sentiment in south-west Scotland was manifest to the point of fanaticism:

> As soon as we had passed the river, the Prince formed our army into two columns, one of which took the road by Ecclefechan, conducted by the Prince in person, and the other, under the orders of Lord George Murray, took the road that leads to Annan. Lord Elcho, with the cavalry, went straight to Dumfries, a considerable town, full of fanatical Calvinists, who had seized some of our ammunition waggons when we entered England. We punished the inhabitants by levying a considerable fine on them.[6]

1 Facsimile Lochaber axe from the sixteenth century with facsimile target.

Right: 2 A pair of brass-barrelled flintlock officer's pistols from Hudson of London (*c.* 1740).

Below left: 3 Detail of a fine eighteenth-century broadsword hilt. Facsimile by kind permission of Armourclass.

Below right: 4 The cutting edge. Facsimile by kind permission of Armourclass.

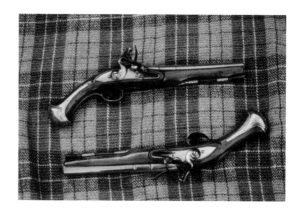

Above and below: 5 & 6 The original medieval castle of Inverlochy built in the fourteenth century by the powerful Comyn family, also lords of Badenoch. Ruthven barracks sits on the motte of their former hold. The Red Comyns held Lochaber, and their successors in title occupied the castle until the seventeenth century; it featured in the battle of 1645.

Above: 7 A view looking westwards along the Great Glen, Loch Ness in the foreground and Castle Urquhart glimpsed in the distance.

Below: 8 Kilchurn Castle on Loch Awe.

9 The Coire Gabhail, Glencoe.

10 Mingary Castle on the Ardnamurchan Peninsula.

11 Glencoe: approach to the Coire Gabhail.

12 Glencoe: the old road.

13 Ardvreck in Sutherland, 'The Deadly Refuge'.

Above and opposite above: 14 & 15 Ruthven barracks, now roofless but well conserved by Historic Scotland. It was built after the '15, with stables added in 1734. Sergeant Molloy resisted the Jacobite attempt in 1745 with only a dozen men, but was obliged to capitulate after the rebels returned with artillery in the following year. It was here that the survivors of Culloden briefly rallied before dispersing.

16 Inverness: the nineteenth-century courts complex stands on the site of the medieval castle, subsequently the original Fort George. Part of the medieval wall survives.

Above left: 17 Fort George: a view along a length of the outer curtain.

Above right: 18 Fort George: the inner drawbridge.

Left: 19 Glencoe: the cairn upon which it is said the MacDonald chieftains of the sept were installed.

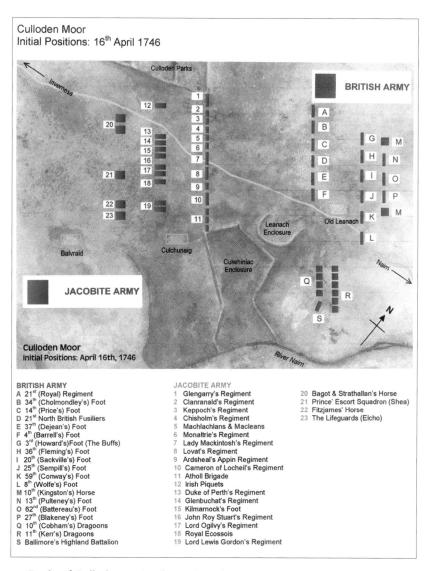

Culloden Moor
Initial Positions: 16th April 1746

BRITISH ARMY

JACOBITE ARMY

Culloden Moor
Initial Positions: April 16th, 1746

BRITISH ARMY
A 21st (Royal) Regiment
B 34th (Cholmondley's) Foot
C 14th (Price's) Foot
D 21st North British Fusiliers
E 37th (Dejean's) Foot
F 4th (Barrell's) Foot
G 3rd (Howard's)Foot (The Buffs)
H 36th (Fleming's) Foot
I 20th (Sackville's) Foot
J 25th (Sempill's) Foot
K 59th (Conway's) Foot
L 8th (Wolfe's) Foot
M 10th (Kingston's) Horse
N 13th (Pulteney's) Foot
O 62nd (Battereau's) Foot
P 27th (Blakeney's) Foot
Q 10th (Cobham's) Dragoons
R 11th (Kerr's) Dragoons
S Ballimore's Highland Battalion

JACOBITE ARMY
1 Glengarry's Regiment
2 Clanranald's Regiment
3 Keppoch's Regiment
4 Chisholm's Regiment
5 Machlachlans & Macleans
6 Monaltrie's Regiment
7 Lady Mackintosh's Regiment
8 Lovat's Regiment
9 Ardsheal's Appin Regiment
10 Cameron of Locheil's Regiment
11 Atholl Brigade
12 Irish Piquets
13 Duke of Perth's Regiment
14 Glenbuchat's Regiment
15 Kilmarnock's Foot
16 John Roy Stuart's Regiment
17 Lord Ogilvy's Regiment
18 Royal Ecossois
19 Lord Lewis Gordon's Regiment

20 Bagot & Strathallan's Horse
21 Prince' Escort Squadron (Shea)
22 Fitzjames' Horse
23 The Lifeguards (Elcho)

20 Battle of Culloden, 16 April 1746: initial positions.

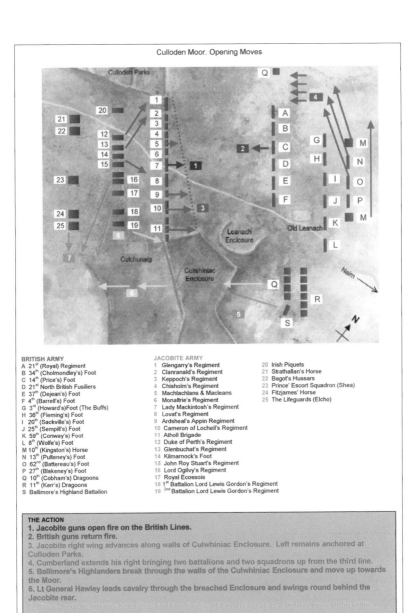

Culloden Moor. Opening Moves

BRITISH ARMY
A 21st (Royal) Regiment
B 34th (Cholmondley's) Foot
C 14th (Price's) Foot
D 21st North British Fusiliers
E 37th (Dejean's) Foot
F 4th (Barrell's) Foot
G 3rd (Howard's)Foot (The Buffs)
H 36th (Fleming's) Foot
I 20th (Sackville's) Foot
J 25th (Sempill's) Foot
K 59th (Conway's) Foot
L 8th (Wolfe's) Foot
M 10th (Kingston's) Horse
N 13th (Pulteney's) Foot
O 62nd (Battereau's) Foot
P 27th (Blakeney's) Foot
Q 10th (Cobham's) Dragoons
R 11th (Kerr's) Dragoons
S Ballimore's Highland Battalion

JACOBITE ARMY
1 Glengarry's Regiment
2 Clanranald's Regiment
3 Keppoch's Regiment
4 Chisholm's Regiment
5 Machlachlans & Macleans
6 Monaltrie's Regiment
7 Lady Mackintosh's Regiment
8 Lovat's Regiment
9 Ardsheal's Appin Regiment
10 Cameron of Locheil's Regiment
11 Atholl Brigade
12 Duke of Perth's Regiment
13 Glenbuchat's Regiment
14 Kilmarnock's Foot
15 John Roy Stuart's Regiment
16 Royal Ecossois
17 Royal Ecossois
18 1st Battalion Lord Lewis Gordon's Regiment
19 2nd Battalion Lord Lewis Gordon's Regiment

20 Irish Piquets
21 Strathallan's Horse
22 Bagot's Hussars
23 Prince' Escort Squadron (Shea)
24 Fitzjames' Horse
25 The Lifeguards (Elcho)

THE ACTION
1. Jacobite guns open fire on the British Lines.
2. British guns return fire.
3. Jacobite right wing advances along walls of Culwhiniac Enclosure. Left remains anchored at Culloden Parks.
4. Cumberland extends his right bringing two battalions and two squadrons up from the third line.
5. Ballimore's Highlanders break through the walls of the Culwhiniac Enclosure and move up towards the Moor.
6. Lt General Hawley leads cavalry through the breached Enclosure and swings round behind the Jacobite rear.

21 Battle of Culloden: opening moves.

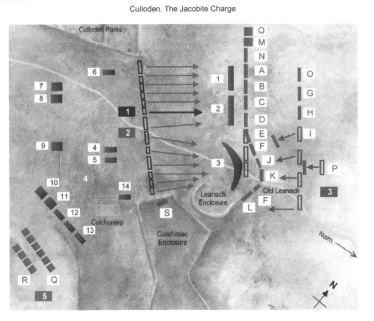

Culloden. The Jacobite Charge

BRITISH ARMY
A 21st (Royal) Regiment
B 34th (Cholmondley's) Foot
C 14th (Price's) Foot
D 21st North British Fusiliers
E 37th (Dejean's) Foot
F 4th (Barrell's) Foot
G 3rd (Howard's)Foot (The Buffs)
H 36th (Fleming's) Foot
I 20th (Sackville's) Foot
J 25th (Sempill's) Foot
K 59th (Conway's) Foot
L 8th (Wolfe's) Foot
M 10th (Kingston's) Horse
N 13th (Pulteney's) Foot
O 62nd (Battereau's) Foot
P 27th (Blakeney's) Foot
Q 10th (Cobham's) Dragoons
R 11th (Kerr's) Dragoons
S Ballimore's Highland Battalion

JACOBITE ARMY
1 Duke of Perth's Regiment
2 John Roy Stuart's Regiment
3 Lord George Murray
4 Kilmarnock's Foot
5 Royal Ecossois
6 Irish Piquets
7 Strathallan's Horse
8 Bagot's Hussars
9 Prince' Escort Squadron (Shea)
10 Fitzjames' Horse
11 The Lifeguards (Elcho)Atholl Brigade
12 Lord Ogilvy's Regiment
13 1st Battalion Lord Lewis Gordon's Regiment
14 2nd Battalion Lord Lewis Gordon's Regiment

THE ACTION
1. Lady Mackintosh's Regiment moves forward before formal orders are received. This triggers the Jacobite charge.
2. The Jacobite front line advances in a disorderly charge, forming a three-pronged attack. The largest group is pressed together in a bottle-neck around the the Leanach Enclosure and rams into the British left.
3. British forces from the second line move forward on their left front to counter-attack at the Leanach Enclosure.
4. Jacobite re-enforcements move to support the defensive line at the rear.
5. Hawley waits for news of the battle on the Moor.

22 Battle of Culloden: the crisis.

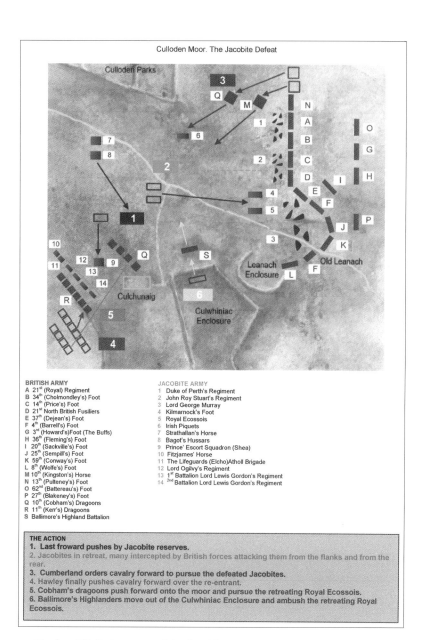

Culloden Moor. The Jacobite Defeat

BRITISH ARMY
A 21st (Royal) Regiment
B 34th (Cholmondley's) Foot
C 14th (Price's) Foot
D 21st North British Fusiliers
E 37th (Dejean's) Foot
F 4th (Barrell's) Foot
G 3rd (Howard's)Foot (The Buffs)
H 36th (Fleming's) Foot
I 20th (Sackville's) Foot
J 25th (Sempill's) Foot
K 59th (Conway's) Foot
L 8th (Wolfe's) Foot
M 10th (Kingston's) Horse
N 13th (Pulteney's) Foot
O 62nd (Battereau's) Foot
P 27th (Blakeney's) Foot
Q 10th (Cobham's) Dragoons
R 11th (Kerr's) Dragoons
S Ballimore's Highland Battalion

JACOBITE ARMY
1 Duke of Perth's Regiment
2 John Roy Stuart's Regiment
3 Lord George Murray
4 Kilmarnock's Foot
5 Royal Ecossois
6 Irish Piquets
7 Strathallan's Horse
8 Bagot's Hussars
9 Prince' Escort Squadron (Shea)
10 Fitzjames' Horse
11 The Lifeguards (Elcho)Atholl Brigade
12 Lord Ogilvy's Regiment
13 1st Battalion Lord Lewis Gordon's Regiment
14 2nd Battalion Lord Lewis Gordon's Regiment

THE ACTION
1. **Last froward pushes by Jacobite reserves.**
2. Jacobites in retreat, many intercepted by British forces attacking them from the flanks and from the rear.
3. **Cumberland orders cavalry forward to pursue the defeated Jacobites.**
4. Hawley finally pushes cavalry forward over the re-entrant.
5. **Cobham's dragoons push forward onto the moor and pursue the retreating Royal Ecossois.**
6. Ballimore's Highlanders move out of the Culwhiniac Enclosure and ambush the retreating Royal Ecossois.

23 Battle of Culloden: rout of the Jacobite army.

24 Culloden: Old Leanach Cottage. Despite its venerable appearance this is not the building that stood here in 1746 but a subsequent rebuilding. The original may have been used by Cumberland's surgeons as a dressing station, and it is said that one of the barns was set on fire with thirty-odd wounded rebels immured within.

25 Culloden: the clan graves. A road was driven through the ground occupied by the grave pits in 1835. The headstones were erected by Duncan Forbes in 1881, though there are inevitably questions as to their authenticity: Cumberland's burial details were unlikely to have sorted the dead into clan affiliation, even if such a process with naked, stiffening corpses had been possible.

26 Culloden: towards the Jacobite right in the vicinity of the Leanach Enclosure.

27 Culloden: a restored fragment of the Leanach Enclosure.

28 Culloden: the Athollmen's view towards the Government left. The Leanach Enclosure would have been in the middle foreground; the memorial can be glimpsed on the left.

29 Culloden: a view from the Jacobite left, with the present road on the far left of the picture. The walls of Culloden Park would have been some way left again of the B9006. The original road ran in a similar direction to the present one, coming from Inverness but veering diagonally across the field toward Barrel's position on the extreme left of Cumberland's line.

30 Culloden: the view south-west toward Culchunaig, from the approximate ground taken by Ballimore's Campbells.

31 Culloden: the view south-east over the area of the Culwhiniac Enclosure.

32 Culloden: the view from Clan Donald's position on the Jacobite left. The breadth of ground they were obliged to cover can be appreciated. The terrain is now far firmer and drier that at the time of the battle, when their advance was slowed by knee-deep ooze and standing water.

Left: 33 Culloden: the Clan Donald Stone, with the rear elevation of the memorial cairn glimpsed looking eastwards.

Below: 34 Sunset in the Highlands, Loch Maree.

Glasgow, which the reunited columns entered on 26 December,[7] proved no more welcoming, a Whig citadel which did not take kindly to the Prince's demands for clothing and shoes to be provided for his army. Home's regiment, largely raised in the city, was serving with Handasyde in Edinburgh.

On 3 January, the Prince's army marched out of Glasgow, again split into two columns. Charles led the first of these through Kilsyth to Bannockburn – both sites of famous Scottish battles – whilst Lord George took the other by Cumbernauld towards Falkirk. The strategic aim was for the marching columns to reunite before the walls of Stirling and reduce the great fortress, stubbornly held for the Crown by another lively, septuagenarian castellan, Major-General Blakeney. Two days later Cumberland had returned to London, where the unfortunate Towneley, with a dozen others, was executed.

The Jacobite muster now totalled some 9,000, the high water mark for numbers. Stirling town was easily forced into capitulation but the castle was an altogether more formidable proposition. Drummond had also brought a mixed battery of guns,[8] to give the besiegers some teeth, though moving the heavier ordnance from Perth put a considerable strain on the rebels' logistical capacity. Siege operations were directed not by the capable Colonel Grant but by a French officer, recently arrived, Mirabel de Gordon. Despite an apparently impressive record and achievement, he proved less than efficient, earning the scorn of Johnstone and other Jacobite officers:

> It was supposed that a French engineer, of a certain age and decorated with an order, must necessarily be a person of experience, talents and capacity; but it was unfortunately discovered, when too late, that his knowledge as an engineer was extremely limited, and that he was totally destitute of judgement, discernment and common sense.[9]

Some three days after the rebels marched from Glasgow, Hawley's commission was confirmed, but the movement of Wade's former command from Newcastle, via the east coast route to Edinburgh, had already begun. By 2 January the first Hanoverian regiments had entered the city. The battalions had marched in pairs and within a week a dozen had been assembled, these reinforcements comprising 2nd battalion Royal Scots, Howard's,[10] Barrel's, Wolfe's, Pulteney's, Blakeney's, Cholmondeley's, Fleming's, Monro's and Battereau's. The citizens of Edinburgh were enthusiastic:

...the first division of the troops viz a battalion of the Royal and Battereau's regiment arrived here this evening from Dunbar twenty long miles in one day, but were carried all that way on our country horses and entertained at the expense of the country... They were received into Edinburgh betwixt five and six this night with huzzas, illuminations etc to the great mortification of the Jacobites, and now I have the pleasure to tell you that this place is in no apprehension from the rebels and we hope to send them soon back to starve in the mountains, they threaten to besiege Stirling Castle.[11]

Though most of these were seasoned units, withdrawn from Flanders, the ranks were, in some cases, filled with raw recruits and most were under strength. Much fatigued by their recent marches, Hawley did not yet consider this to be an army fit to take the field. He had, however, enjoyed the consolation of erecting two sets of gallows, just in case the townspeople should be in doubt as to his seriousness of intent![12]

The General could also muster Home's volunteers, a Glasgow regiment of 'enthusiasts' as he described them, and the 'Yorkshire Blues' raised by William Thornton, a gentleman of that county.[13] Neither of his two dragoon regiments imbued him with any confidence: these were reduced to under 200 men apiece, and their standard of conduct was abysmal. Cobham's, coming as reinforcement, and who had fought at Clifton, were felt to be made of sterner stuff. He had now a dozen battalions of foot, a total of some 5,488 officers and men, 800 horse and perhaps 1,500 volunteers.[14]

Hawley, who had reached Edinburgh on 6 January, was soon fretting about a dearth of ready cash, forage, supply in general, the lack of skilled gunners and the disconcerting presence of Highlanders in the government army. His primary concern in taking personal command of the forces marshalled at Edinburgh was to repulse any attempt by the Jacobites to retake the Scottish capital. His wider role called for a government offensive to stamp out the rebellion once and for all. The government was determined to finally put an end to the whole business. Newcastle had written to Cumberland on 28 December in terms that left no room for misapprehension:

...it is of the utmost importance that a speedy end should be put to it; that the public credit may soon revive, and the peace of the country be restored, which, during the continuance of the rebellion, does, and must, so necessarily suffer, for this reason his Majesty destined for that purpose, as great a force, as could be collected, from the troops now in the North; leaving always sufficient garrisons

for Berwick, and Carlisle, and for the security of the town of Newcastle. And as
the rebels may possibly form two parties, the one of the Highlanders returned
from England; the other of those now assembling at Perth under Lord John
Drummond; it is very possible, Mr Hawley may be obliged to divide his force,
and to have two armies also; which makes it necessary to have a number sufficient to enable him to do so, if there should be occasion.[15]

The royal artillery train, a major element in the general's stock of worries, was
also rather poorly served, the guns stationary at Newcastle for want of horses and
a remarkable dearth of professional gunners.[16] Hawley possessed one asset in the
form of his second in command, Major-General John 'Daddy' Huske.[17] Despite
his low opinion of Highlanders, Hawley was not unaware of the potential of the
charge to overwhelm regular foot through speed, aggression and sheer terror:

> The sure way to demolish them is a 3 deep to fire by ranks diagonaly to the
> Centre where they come, the rear rank first, and even that rank not to fire till
> they are within 10 or 12 paces but if the fire is given at a distance you prob-
> ably will be broke for you never get time to load a second cartridge, & if you
> give way you may give your foot for dead, for they being without a firelock
> or any load, no man with his arms, accoutrements &c. can escape them, and
> they give no Quarters, but if you will but observe the above directions, they
> are the most despicable Enemy that are.[18]

His views as to the efficiency of Highlanders in battle inevitably clashed
with those of the Chevalier de Johnstone, whose regard for the clansmen,
not unsurprisingly, was much greater:

> The importance commonly attached to artillery, their supposed utility, or rather
> the absolute necessity for them on all occasions, are greatly over rated, and I do
> not doubt but that, in the course of time, an army will think itself lost, if it has
> not these enormous masses to drag after it, the cause of so much embarrass-
> ment, just in the same manner as infantry have been taught to tremble for their
> safety, unless they have cavalry to protect their flanks. The Highlanders, how-
> ever, entertain a sovereign contempt for cavalry, from the facility with which
> they have always defeated them, throwing them into disorder in an instant by
> striking at the heads of the horses in the manner I have already mentioned…
>
> If we had remained firing at a certain distance instead of rushing impet-
> uously upon the enemy, two thousand regular troops, regularly trained to

fire and unaccustomed to the sword, would have beaten four thousand Highlanders with ease. Their manner of fighting is adapted for brave but undisciplined men. They advance with rapidity, discharge their pieces when within musket shot of the enemy, and then, throwing them down, draw their swords, and holding a dirk in their left hand with their target, dart with fury on the enemy through the smoke of their fire. When within reach of the enemy's bayonets, bending their left knee, they cover their bodies with their targets, which receive the thrusts of the bayonets, while at the same time they raise their sword-arm and strike their adversary. Having once got within the bayonets and into the ranks of the enemy, the soldiers have no longer any means of defending themselves, the fate of the battle is decided in an instant, and the carnage follows – the Highlanders bringing down two men at a time, one with their dirk, in the left hand, and another with the sword.[19]

By 13 January Hawley had dispatched Huske on a reconnaissance in force toward Stirling, taking five battalions of foot, both regiments of horse and the Glasgow militia. Some forces were detached beforehand but Huske pushed on to Linlithgow with the rump, and on the next day he was reinforced by a further three battalions. Jacobite scouts had detected Huske's probing and Murray concluded that a battle must be in the offing.

From his perspective it was logical to deal with Hawley before he was further reinforced, so Lord George began to concentrate his forces around Bannockburn leaving 1,200 or so behind to man the trenches and mask the garrison.[20] His immediate intention was probably to 'beat up' the government forces around Linlithgow and relieve them of stores and supplies.

At Linlithgow, Lord George sent Elcho off with the horse to scout ahead. Contact came quite soon thereafter as the Jacobites prepared to contest the passage of the river Avon, Murray perhaps hoping to replicate Wallace's feat and attack whilst the government troops were but half across. It was the dragoons who appeared first but limited their engagement to volleys of insults, irritating perhaps but scarcely threatening. There was little point in lingering and Lord George pulled back to Bannockburn.

By now most of the reinforcements from the north had come in, and spirits were high. Johnstone considered that had the Prince delayed his invasion of England until this entire force had been assembled then the decision to retreat from Derby need never have been taken, for with such a host at his back, London could so easily have been his.

Hawley had not marched until the 15th, the delay being occasioned by the need to wait for the ordnance. The train was escorted by the remainder of the foot whilst the general rode out next day with Cobham's. By nightfall the royal army was encamped on level ground, just west of Falkirk, within the enceinte of an ancient Roman camp. Here, Lieutenant-Colonel John Campbell brought in three companies of Loudon's, one from the Black Watch and a dozen more of the Argyll Militia.

Murray had deployed for battle on the Plean Muir on the 15th and again the next day. By the 17th he was proposing to seize the initiative with an advance to the hill of Falkirk, a moorland rim that overlooked Hawley's lines on the plain below. The intervening ground did not favour the Hanoverians, a steep and straggling ascent, slashed by a ravine, difficult for foot and horse alike.

By noon, in the cold east wind of a Scottish winter, the lines of rebel battalions were moving forward in column, saffron and plaid, a fat, sinuous snake of clansmen. Lord John Drummond was sent off with a commanded party to feint toward the government lines;[21] his advance would be clearly visible. Murray had the inestimable advantage of acute familiarity with the ground and led the main body on from Plean Muir, where the Stuart Standard was left as a further touch to the deception, in a wide arc, under the shelter of Torwood and across the river Carron at Dunipace.

Our army marched across the fields, and by bye-roads, to Dunipace, leaving the highway from Stirling to Falkirk at a considerable distance to our left, and making a great circuit to conceal our movement from the enemy. Having passed through the village of Dunipace, which is about three and a half miles from Falkirk, at two o'clock in the afternoon, we suddenly found ourselves on the heights above the town, in sight of the English army and within nine hundred yards of their camp, before General Hawley knew of our departure from Bannockburn. Their surprise on seeing us may easily be conceived. They immediately flew to arms, and, with great precipitation, ascended to a part of the height between us and the town of Falkirk. There was a high wind, accompanied by a heavy rain, which the Highlanders, by their position, had in their back, whilst it was full in the face of the English who were blinded by it.[22]

Murray had now humbugged Hawley who, having ridden the terrain during the morning, had concluded no attack was likely. He had, therefore, accepted an invitation to dine with the beguiling Lady Kilmarnock, wife of the rebel peer, upon whom he was billeted. It has been suggested that the lady's charms, and the conviviality of a long and vinous luncheon, sapped the General's awareness, though this is probably apocryphal; Hawley was too old a hand to be distracted by a pretty face and a full glass. However, the afternoon was to prove a deal more eventful.

The Jacobite plan had nearly foundered when Murray and O'Sullivan fell into a wrangle. The Irishman apparently felt it unwise to expose the troops as they crossed the river and suggested a halt until night. Lord George, and we may imagine his tone, protested: the crossing place was well screened from the government army and the passage could be accomplished swiftly. O'Sullivan was ignored and retired. Having reported directly to the Prince (and we may imagine the tenor of his report), it was Charles himself who next appeared to moot the idea of a halt. Again, Murray prevailed and the advance continued.

A patrol of volunteers had meanwhile informed Huske of the Jacobites' proximity and their likely intentions. Valuable time was now lost as the commanding General could not be found and 'Daddy' Huske would not move without orders. Soon, however, the commander of government forces in North Britain was riding pell mell and wigless from Callendar House. One correspondent described his appearance as that of one who had enjoyed the pleasures of a groaning table and ample cellar!

Now, however, Hawley was fully alerted to his peril. He sent his dragoons, the three regiments commanded by Colonel Francis Ligonier, to seize a toehold on the high ground, whilst he marshalled the foot. For once the weather favoured the Stuart cause: a lashing barrage of rain and sleet deluged the government troops, soaking heavy woollen cloth and spoiling powder.

Civilian contractors had been engaged to haul the guns and these swiftly became mired at the base of the hill. As Hawley floundered the Jacobites were deploying into line of battle, the rain at their backs, powder dry.

Clan Donald again claimed its ancient privilege of the right, their exposed flank beyond covered by miry ground. Left of Keppoch, Clanranald and Glengarry stood Farquharson, Mackenzie, Mackintosh and Cluny's MacPhersons. Holding the left of the line were Frasers, Camerons and Stewart of Appin – this flank abutted the cleft. Forming the second line, the Atholl Brigade, Ogilvy's, and Lord Lewis Gordon's MacLachlans. Drummond's commanded party, having achieved their mission of deception, now formed the reserve.

Despite his careful advance, Murray mistook the situation when he placed himself on the right, thinking Lord John Drummond would command the left. This was not so, as His Lordship was stationed to the rear, where the Prince commanded the French, Irish Picquets and the horse. The left was, in fact, leaderless. Murray was distracted by some further helpful advice from the irrepressible O'Sullivan, who criticised His Lordship's dispositions and suggested a forward movement. To this Murray acquiesced, but he demurred, no doubt sharply, when the Irish officer suggested that the Atholl brigade be brought up to cover his flank.

A dismal curtain of squalls cast a veil between the two armies as the government troops scrambled for position. Hawley placed the Royal Scots on the right of his first line, flanked by Ligonier's, Price's, Pulteney's, Cholmondeley's and then Wolfe's. His second line, again from right to left, comprised Barrells, Battereau's, Fleming's, Munro's and Blakeney's. Howard's were left in reserve.

Captain Cuningham, struggling to bring up the guns, found the going very heavy indeed, and his heavier pieces stuck fast as the marching columns plodded by. His efforts to bring up the lighter guns fared little better and Hawley was effectively without artillery support. The Jacobite ordnance was equally distant, however, and would also play no part in the coming engagement.

The foul blanket of showers and the topography colluded to create a situation where the government right outflanked the Jacobite left, the latter hemmed in by the widening rift of the ravine. On the other flank, however, exactly the reverse obtained. Here Hawley had placed his dragoons, Cobham's, Ligonier's[23] and Hamilton's. Several companies of Loudon's loyalist Highlanders were set upon the extreme right of the government line, while a further, loose battalion of Glasgow Volunteers were struggling up the hill toward the Hanoverian left.

To open the fight the General detached two squadrons from each flank of his horse regiments. Quite why he chose to do so is uncertain; his subordinates could not discern a sound tactical gambit, and the troopers themselves showed little sign of enthusiasm. It is possible that Hawley hoped to create an effective cavalry screen that might discourage the Highlanders from launching a precipitate charge whilst he ensured his foot were made fully ready to receive them. He seems to have maintained his belief that the Highlanders would not stand against cavalry:

The English began the attack with a body of about eleven hundred cavalry, who advanced very slowly against the right of our army, and did not halt till they were within twenty paces of our first line, to induce us to fire. The Highlanders who had been particularly enjoined not to fire till the army was within musket length of them, discharged their muskets the moment the cavalry halted and killed about eighty men, each of them having aimed at a rider.[24]

Lord George led the MacDonalds steadily on and, at barely twelve paces, the clansmen discharged their firearms and fell to with blades. The dragoons milled in uncertainty, saddles already empty. The Highlanders darted like salamanders, their dirks eviscerating terrified mounts and making short work of the riders, who tumbled screaming. Johnstone, who fought in the action, described the fury of the melee as Clanranald's men fought hand to hand with the dragoons:

> The most singular and extraordinary combat immediately followed. The Highlanders, stretched on the ground, thrust their dirks into the bellies of the horses. Some seized the riders by their clothes, dragged them down, and stabbed them with their dirks; several again used their pistols; but few of them had sufficient space to handle their swords. Macdonald of Clanranald... assured me that whilst he was lying upon the ground, under a dead horse, which had fallen upon him, without the power of extricating himself, he saw a dismounted horseman struggling with a Highlander: fortunately for him, the Highlander, being the strongest, threw his antagonist, and having killed him with his dirk, he came to his assistance, and drew him with difficulty from under his horse.[25]

Ligonier's and Cobham's swerved aside after this sudden and vicious contact. Some of the latter did manage to penetrate as far as the Jacobite second line, getting through or past some of the MacDonalds and disordering Ogilvy's. Hamilton's showed no such enthusiasm and bolted downhill. In their rout they collided with the Glasgow Militia, disordering and riding down some of the volunteers who replied with an angry volley!

Cobham's pressed on, riding between the ranks toward the Jacobite left where they were raked by a rolling but largely ineffectual volley, a few dead and wounded spilling from bloodied saddles, though the musketry was probably more loud than deadly. Nonetheless, by firing precipitately at the cavalry the clansmen had loosed their only volley, and the lashing rain made reloading almost impossible.

With this, their single volley discharged, the clan regiments could do no more than draw steel and charge their opponents. The Appin men, Camerons and Frasers drove into the line. Wet powder spoiled many muskets and the government troops began to give ground. Four of Hawley's half dozen front line battalions — Wolfe's, Blakeney's, Pulteney's and Munro's — gave way. Their panic infected the line behind so that only Barrel's still kept a fighting formation. This sudden depletion came so swiftly that the Jacobite officers perceived a ruse, a 'Parthian' retreat, to draw their regiments into an ambush. This hesitation saved the fleeing soldiers from slaughter, their general carried away in the rout.

Huske was left to salvage what he could from the debacle. Ligonier's and Price's, shielded by the cleft, held their ground, Barrel's moved up and the three battalions advanced uphill, echeloning to the left. With Huske and Brigadier-General James Cholmondeley keeping tight rein they discharged several well-directed volleys into the flanks of the Jacobite regiments. The pursuit had turned to confusion with officers calling the men back. As the clansmen milled about under fire, some even thought it was they who had been bested and now fled in turn. O'Sullivan observed:

> …the cursed hollow square came up, took our left in flanc & obliged then to reture in disorder. There was no remedy or succor to be given them. The second ligne, yt HRHs counted upon, went off past the river & some of them even went to Bannockburn & Sterling, where they gave out yt we lost the day.[26]

Thus the situation on the flanks was almost reversed, with the rebels beginning to give way in the teeth of a well-directed fire. This sudden reverse on the Jacobite left may have been the incident which convinced their officers that the apparent rout of the other Hanoverian battalions was a mere feint and that Huske's rally was a reality. A planned ambush:

> Mr. John Roy Stuart, an officer in the service of France, afraid lest this might be an ambuscade laid for us by the English, called out to the Highlanders to stop their pursuit, and the cry of stop flew immediately from rank to rank and threw the whole army into disorder. However, the enemy continued their retreat, and the three regiments at the foot of the hill followed the rest, but

with the difference that they retreated always in order, acting as a rear-guard of the English army, and continued a fire of platoons on us till their entrance into the town of Falkirk.[27]

Lord George Murray had been left with only that remnant of Keppoch's MacDonalds which he had managed to keep in check. The rest had pelted after the fleeing horse and foot, pausing only to strip the dead or garner loot and captives. He brought up his three battalions of Athollmen and organised an orderly and disciplined advance down the hill.

Cobham's dragoons, meanwhile, having retained their martial vigour, slipped past the Athollmen, attempting to wheel and fall on the MacDonalds' rear. The Prince, spotting the danger, sent his Irishmen forward and the dragoons withdrew, not, however, in rout. The nature of the ground and the confusion in the Jacobite command structure had served to ensure that the left- and right-hand divisions completely failed to coordinate.

The dragoons were able to reinforce the three regiments while still holding ground, and the whole now formed an effective rearguard, which retired in textbook manner toward Falkirk. Far from being disheartened, Barrel's tough veterans even managed to salvage some of the abandoned guns, man-handling one of the pieces and subsequently recovering others.

Murray had barely 700 broadswords under his immediate command and a further advance seemed impractical, besides which the light was failing. Lord Kilmarnock had scouted ahead and advised that the whole of the Hanoverian army was in full retreat toward Linlithgow. The Jacobites took possession of Falkirk, where the Prince and his officers enjoyed the choice foodstuffs and liquor that their enemy had abandoned in his haste to be away. By way of bonus, a quantity of arms, ammunition, wagons, tents, colours and impedimenta were also secured.

Falkirk was clearly a victory for the rebels, though by no means a disaster for the government. Hawley, submitting his report, observed a degree of economy with the evident realities when he preferred to describe the engagement as a draw. The fight had cost him perhaps 300 dead and almost as many prisoners; the Jacobites had lost perhaps half a hundred. Many of the captives were officers and, as O'Sullivan laconically noted, 'gold watches were at a cheap rate'.[28] For the government wounded, hacked and bleeding, left on the field, the night brought the despairing death of the small hours, numbed by cold, weakened by exsanguination or sliced by the looter's casual dispatch.

Johnstone recounts that, in the immediate aftermath of the fight, the Jacobite army was in as great a degree of confusion as their beaten opponents:

> The Highlanders were in complete disorder, dispersed here and there with the different clans mingled pell-mell together, whilst the obscurity of the night added greatly to the confusion. Many of them had even retired from the field of battle, either thinking it lost or intending to seek a shelter from the dreadful weather.[29]

The cull amongst Hawley's officers had been particularly high. Sir Robert Munro had fallen at the head of his regiment[30] as had his lieutenant-colonel, Ligonier's had lost Lieutenant-Colonel Whitney, and Ligonier himself fell ill soon after from the soaking he had received and presently expired. Lieutenant-Colonel Powell of Cholmondeley's had also died on the field.

More rumours circulated amongst the Hanoverians that many of their men had been cut down in cold blood, either when injured or surrendering, and that 'no quarter' was the Jacobite cry. There is no real evidence for this; in the heat of battle the stroke is given without the matter being thought through, but there is no tangible proof that the Highlanders were unwilling to offer quarter.

Hawley's earlier reflections on these 'arrant scum' must by now have been modified. Observers noted that he seemed dazed by the defeat, as wretched as Cope after Prestonpans. His dispatch to Cumberland reflects this anguish even if he does, tactfully, seek to minimise the scale of the reverse:

> Sir, My heart is broke. I can't say we are quite beat today, But our Left is beat, and Their Left is beat. We had enough to beat them for we had Two Thousand Men more than They. But suche scandalous Cowardice I never saw before. The whole second line of foot ran away without firing a Shot. Three squadrons did well; The others as usual…[31]

Later, when the battered army had limped back into Edinburgh, Hawley dealt with his troops in the manner he appeared to understand best, with the firing squad and hangman busily engaged. A number of officers, including the unfortunate Cuningham, lost their commissions to save what remained of their General's tattered reputation.

The plain fact of the matter was that nobody had performed well at Falkirk. Hawley had been negligent in not perceiving the developing threat and tardy in his reactions. He had placed reliance on his cavalry, which was beyond its capacity to perform, and had grossly underestimated the capabilities of his opponent. Cholmondeley, writing of the affair, was decidedly of the opinion that the Hanoverians had been bested for want of offensive spirit:

> …they [the dragoons] began the attack with spirit which did not last long, nevertheless they broke a considerable body of the Highlanders, but another body coming upon our left flank, our foot gave a feint fire, and then faced to the right about, as regularly as if they had been at the word of command, and could not be rallied, 'till they got a very considerable distance, altho' I do not think they were pursued by two hundred men.[32]

Another eyewitness account of the battle was written by one of Hawley's staff, James Stuart Mackenzie:

> …as I acted in the capacity of Aide-de-Camp to the general I had occasion to be in every part of the line, during the action… We lay there till midday… when there was an alarm given that the rebels were in full march towards us, upon which the whole army was drawn up in the front of our camp, which was a very strong one by the natural situation of the place; advice was brought us that the rebels were not advancing directly towards our camp but were marching up on some high grounds which were to our left, and about 1½ miles from us, so the general who was reconnoitring those high grounds sent me to order the cavalry to move that way immediately and the infantry and artillery to follow them as fast as possible, he being afraid the rebels might get by us on the left, and perhaps cut off our communications with Edinburgh, or, at least, get away from us, which was the thing we were most afraid of. As soon as the troops could come up we were formed into two lines, with all our cavalry (which consisted of six squadrons) on our left on the summit of the hill; as the general imagined the enemy was more afraid of horse than foot, he ordered the dragoons to begin the attack, which they did very briskly, but the Highlanders, making all their efforts against them, and giving them a sharp fire, Hamilton's Dragoons most scandalously gave way, which soon put the other squadrons into confusion. They again, coming in upon the foot broke them, this caused a general panic, many of them threw down their arms and ran away, whole platoons on the left of the first line went off, and by that means broke the second line; what hindered the rebels from pursuing our left God knows

if they had, they must have cut almost the whole left wing to pieces. Two or three battalions on our right kept their ground, and even obliged the left of the rebels to retreat, so that we were a matter of half an hour on the field of battle after all firing ceased, but night coming on, and there having been during the whole time of the action a violent storm of hail rain and wind, our ammunition was so wet, that not one in twenty muskets would go off, upon which it was judged proper to retire to our camp, where we drew up expecting the Highlanders would come down upon us. By this time numbers of our foot rallied, and some of the dragoons; so when we had remained about half an hour under arms and found the rebels did not care to attack us a second time, we were ordered to burn the tents, and march to Lithgow directly, but the tents were too wet to burn, so most of them fell into the enemy hands, who came to Falkirk about an hour after we had left the camp… our ammunition was entirely spoilt with the rain, so that it would have been impossible for us to have remained in our camp that night. We were obliged to leave seven pieces of cannon on the field of battle, for some of our runaways had carried off the horses belonging to the train… our artillery did not come up time enough to do us any service, which was a great disadvantage to us, especially as we had to do with the Highlanders, who don't at all love cannon… this unfortunate affair which does us very little honour, for they were inferior to us in numbers, had no artillery, and made but very little use of their broadswords, which is the weapon they rely most upon, and yet notwithstanding all this, if the victory was to be given to either side, it certainly was theirs… we have long expected the Hessians with great impatience, their hussars would be of great service to us at present, as well as their regular troops to animate our men, who seem to have lost all spirit, and sense of honour.[33]

Murray's performance, equally, was far from perfect. The clansmen had shown a lamentable want of discipline and cohesion, which in the face of a more determined enemy could have proved fatal. Their left wing was left leaderless and communications between the divisions woefully inadequate. The battle had been won but the victory was imperfect. Murray, the arch-pragmatist, did not share the Prince's blind faith in the invincibility of the Highlanders, a view he seems to have shared with the majority of the officers under his command:

…the best of the Highland officers, whilst they remained at Falkirk after the battle, talking of the affair, were absolutely convinced, that, except they could

attack the enemy at very considerable advantage, either by surprise or by
some strong situation of ground, or a narrow pass, they could not expect any
great success, especially if their numbers were in no ways equal, and that a
body of regular troops was absolutely necessary to support them, when they
should at any time go in, sword in hand; for they were sensible, that without
more leisure and time than they could expect to have to discipline their own
men, it would not be possible to make them keep their ranks, or rally soon
enough upon any sudden emergency, so that any small number of the enemy,
either keeping in a body when they were in confusion, or rallying, would
deprive them of a victory, even after they had done their best.[34]

Counsels amongst the rebels were now divided. The bolder spirits were for
pursuing Hawley and seeking to destroy his battered army, others pressed
for the continuance of the siege. This latter course was really a distraction;
the possession of the castle, as Johnstone observed, was of no great matter,
while to defeat the government troops in the field was a far more logical tactical option, especially as the Highland regiments were constantly
plagued by desertions.

Blakeney had been summoned to surrender after the rebuff of Hawley's
army but maintained his defiance, short of ammunition but not wanting
in spirit. Undoubtedly this tough old soldier was not impressed by the
buffoonish Mirabel ('Mr Admirable')[35] and his works. In fact, as he almost
certainly realised, Blakeney was doing good service just by pinning the rebel
army beneath Stirling's great walls. Though Hawley's campaign had failed
utterly in its objective of relieving Stirling, and Edinburgh was, once again,
imperilled, the rebels, equally, had failed to win a real advantage.

On 29 January the enthusiastic Mr Admirable at last completed his
batteries and opened fire. The results were not encouraging, however,
for counter-battery fire quickly knocked out most of the Jacobite guns.
Meanwhile Hawley had been reinforced by the rest of the government
artillery with a corps of professional gunners, together with the Royal Scots
Fusiliers, Sempill's and three squadrons of Lord Mark Kerr's Dragoons.

The services of the Glasgow Militia could now be dispensed with, as could
those of Ligonier's and Hamilton's regiments, both of which had maintained
their record of sustained incompetence throughout. Perhaps of even greater
significance, on 30 January Hawley was superseded by Cumberland as
Commander-in-Chief. The ageing martinet escaped without a court martial,
but there could be no question of his exercising further command in the field.

Prince Charles Edward had problems of his own. Despite the advantage of Falkirk, the initiative was slipping away. On 28 January, Murray and the chiefs had presented their Prince with an 'Address' – little more, in practical terms, than an ultimatum. Murray was of the view that, weakened by desertions, the army could not face another round, one that was almost sure to prove decisive. Better to retreat to the relative fastness of the Highlands, there to consolidate, gather fresh recruits and clear the remaining government outposts. The artillery was problematic and it was conceded that some of the heavier pieces might have to be abandoned or spiked.

To Charles this smacked of more defeatism. He argued, not without reason, that a further withdrawal would destroy any hopes of large-scale French intervention (in reality all but dead already). The delay would serve only to further dissipate the rebels' strength whilst the Duke's army grew in size and confidence. It is difficult not to see the wisdom of this, but the plain fact was the Prince's cause was stalling, slipping into irreversible decline; the decision at Derby continued to determine events. He acquiesced to his officers' demands – he could do little else – but, not untypically, disowned all responsibility for the consequences. The die was cast.

Equally, it is difficult to see what real alternative remained. The Highland army was ill-suited to siege work and desertions would increase with tedium. If the army could get into winter quarters and, having beaten up or eliminated the remaining garrisons, recruit fresh drafts to the colours, there was a chance they might meet Cumberland or more or less equal terms in the spring.

On 1 February the long retreat began. Cumberland had already advanced to Linlithgow as Murray withdrew toward Bannockburn, leaving a cavalry screen to mask the manoeuvre. Plans for an orderly continuance of the evacuation were given but, due to error or poor staff work, communications broke down and the retreat began to assume the appearance of a disorderly escape. Worse, mishandling of ammunition and powder stores resulted in the blowing up of the village church in St Ninians. That night the army straggled into its billets in Doune and Dunblane.

While the Highland division pushed on to Crieff, the Lowland regiments entered Perth. The council meeting which ensued was highly charged and beset by unseemly squabbling. At length it was resolved that the southrons would press on to Inverness by the coast road, shielded by the cavalry, whilst the clan regiments took the shorter if more arduous overland route. The former would be led by Murray, the latter by the Prince. Neither would be unduly pained at the parting.

By 6 February Cumberland's army entered Perth. The Duke was faced not only with deteriorating weather conditions but with uncertainty as to the rebel intentions. It might be that the clan regiments would simply melt away into the hills as they had done thirty years earlier, in which case he would face a guerrilla-style campaign. His army was meanwhile augmented by the disembarkation of six battalions of superbly drilled Hessians, a modest cavalry arm and a light train. These would make good the loss of the Dutch regiments.[36]

These newcomers would effectively be deployed as garrison troops to hold Stirling and Perth, maintaining the army's lines of communication and supply whilst the main body proceeded as far as Aberdeen. The capital would be held by a mix of loyalists and five companies of Lee's drawn from Berwick.[37]

The hunt was now on.

11

DECISION – THE WITHDRAWAL TO INVERNESS: CHOOSING GROUND

As soon as the rebels passed the Forth, the men deserted fast, so that they were not above 3,000 when they went through Crieff; they marched in a great hurry to Perth, but did not enter it with their main body, only detached 1,000 who spiked up twenty pieces of cannon which were left there, and threw all the ammunition into the river. The inhabitants of Perth as soon as the Highlanders were gone rung the bells, and took up arms, and seized about twenty men that had loitered behind.

Anonymous letter describing the retreat of the Highland army[1]

This anonymous letter describes the grim realities of the retreat. Highland armies were not accustomed to being kept in the field for long periods, no withdrawal is ever good for morale, and when an army begins spiking its own guns, things may be seen to be going very badly indeed.

The arrival of the Duke of Cumberland in Edinburgh had been greeted with renewed enthusiasm by the Whigs in the city, further cheered by the retreat of the Highland army. It seemed perhaps that the rebels would now simply disperse and melt away into the hills as they had done thirty years before. Anyone, however, who assumed that the end of the business was in sight would have mistaken His Royal Highness's intentions. The Jacobites had come so uncomfortably near to shaking his father's throne that repeating the previous pattern of half measures simply would not serve.

For the moment, the atrocious winter weather was hampering any notion of an immediate pursuit. Lieutenant-Colonel Joseph Yorke, a member of that elite cadre of senior officers who surrounded the Duke, wrote from Crieff, which the army had reached on 5 February:

The only difficulty will be subsistence, which is bare already, but when beyond Perth will be much worse, for they have destroyed all they could in their flight... Every step we take here grows worse and worse, and ever since we left Stirling, we have gone up hill, and I see nothing but snowy mountains above us.[2]

Cumberland might acknowledge the limitations imposed by winter but he had no intention of abandoning his campaign; quite the reverse, it was time to put an end to the Jacobite menace. His was not to be a punitive expedition but a war of annihilation. Yorke understood this completely, and his view was undoubtedly indicative of the mood of the officer corps in general. It was time for a military solution to the Jacobite threat, sure, ruthless and relentless, to be undertaken speedily whilst control lay in the military rather than the political sphere:

> The want of several necessaries has obliged us to stop here… but I hope soon we shall be able to move forward and extirpate the race if we are not *stopt by lenity* [author's italics], as has been the case on former occasions… I hope we may not be deprived of the power to revenge the nation on the beggarly wretches… the thing must be put an end so effectually now, that it will never be able to break out again, otherwise you may depend on having it again in a very short time… I don't doubt soon but we shall have shut 'em up within the Lochs, where it will be at least a summer's work to clear those parts of 'em and to destroy their clannism, but it must be gone thro' with.[3]

There have been a number of attempts to suggest that Hanoverian policy in the aftermath of Culloden was less savage and draconian that previously portrayed, yet here there is clear evidence of a deliberate intent to do away with an entire way of life by the ruthless application of force. It was not the fact that the Jacobites failed which damned them, it was the thought they came so close to sucess. The rising, however ill timed in certain respects, had seriously diverted attention from the war in Flanders. This proved a significant boon for the French who would, in the course of 1746, garner considerable gains from what had been a most modest investment of manpower and treasure.

Though the rebels might be falling steadily back, with desertion rife, the army still had teeth. The gallant Sergeant Molloy had been obliged to surrender Ruthven Barracks[4] and the Prince spent the night of 16 February at Moy Hall in the congenial company of 'Colonel Anne'. Lord Loudon's loyalists, well informed and perhaps 1,500 strong, attempted a daring night raid.

His Lordship had, on hearing of the Prince's arrival at Moy, thrown a tight security cordon around Inverness and prepared to march with a commanded body of picked men. An alert young woman, serving in one of the taverns, overhead the plans being discussed and, slipping past the sentries, ran all the way to Moy to raise the alarm. Though the Prince prudently withdrew, the loyalist column was seen off in unseemly haste by a handful of local sympathisers led by the bold blacksmith of Moy. Such was the speed of their withdrawal that the affair was christened 'the Rout of Moy'. Lord Loudon was a capable administrator and had done the government good service simply by keeping the loyalist cause alive in the North-East. He was not, however, at his best in a tactical role.[5]

It was not until 20 February that the Jacobite army struggled into Inverness, the Highland capital.[6] The weather, on their dismal retreat, had been foul, heavy snow piling on demoralisation. A couple of days beforehand Loudon had decided to evacuate the town, his morale shaken by the business at Moy and his shrinking forces much plagued by desertion, leaving two companies of his regiment, well provisioned, to hold Fort George. The governor at first breathed defiance, yet within hours of the besiegers digging their first line of entrenchments he suffered a change of heart and capitulated. As Johnstone observed:

> The governor of the castle, who was in a situation to stand a siege, at first refused to comply with the summons of the Prince, but two hours after the trenched were opened, he surrendered himself with his garrison which consisted of two companies of Lord Loudon's regiment. The Prince immediately gave orders to raze the fortifications and blow up the bastions. Monsieur L'Epine, a sergeant in the French artillery, who was charged with the operation, lost his life on the occasion. This unfortunate individual, believing the match extinguished, approached to examine it, when the mine sprung, which blew him into the air, with the stones of the bastion, to an immense height.[7]

Whilst Charles occupied Inverness, substantive elements of the Lowland division had been posted further south to block any crossing of the Spey. Loudon was at first pursued by the Earl of Cromarty, whose leadership was soon shown to be defective. The loyalists had initially withdrawn only as far as the Black Isle. Loudon's conduct was subjected to a deal of criticism but he pleaded that he had only received weapons and cash on 9 February, and it is difficult to see how he could, with such slender forces, their confidence already badly shaken, be realistically expected to challenge the whole Jacobite army.

If Cumberland had imagined that he was confronted by a mere mopping-up exercise then the fall of Inverness came as something of a shock: the rebels were neither defeated nor dispersed and he still had a fight on his hands. This realisation came at a time when the absence of British troops from Flanders was encouraging French efforts against the allies. This was exacerbated by the need to replace the Dutch, obliged under the terms of their parole to refrain from further hostilities, with Hessians, thus further diminishing the Alliance's military resources.

As the year progressed, French gains continued to multiply: the plum of Antwerp in the spring, then Charleroi and Namur. The campaigning season saw virtually the whole of the Austrian Netherlands in their hands. Charles Edward had served his allies well; though his rebellion was doomed, his French stakeholders had reaped considerable advantage. The withdrawal of the British army units from Flanders had caused alarm and consternation in The Hague and, as the Allies' troubles continued to multiply, the Dutch were muttering about re-considering their position toward France![8] Robert Trevor, British envoy at The Hague, wrote in February 1746 that

> our measures for crushing the rebellion are taxed here with having been disproportionate and ill-placed; our dread of a French invasion to have been by some even affected, but by all to have been over hasty, and unsupported by any rational and certain intelligence; the promises which I made by order upon every notification of the recall of our national troops, of their being to return as soon as possible, are now reclaimed; and the total silence now observed on that head in my last notification is attributed in great measure to a want of zeal and a disgust in our military gentry themselves to their own trade... I was told in so many words by the First Deputy 'that, if every time France pleased to send over a single battalion to Scotland she could operate a diversion of 30,000 men in England's quota to the combined army, England was not an ally for the Republic.'[9]

Cumberland's uncompromising attitude toward the rebels therefore has to be assessed not only in the light of the immediate threat to his family dynasty that they had posed in late 1745 but now, in the following late winter and early spring, the very real risk that the anti-French alliance would splinter as a consequence of the British withdrawals. This implied that the Jacobite menace was both a domestic and an international problem. To crush the rebellion in the most forceful manner would be a clear demonstration to Britain's allies of the value she placed on the alliance.

That the Duke was mistaken in his earlier assessments of failing Jacobite strength was amply proven when, far from dispersing, the rebels now began a local campaign to reduce the government outposts in the Great Glen. The mere presence of large insurgent forces, undefeated in the field, contributed to economic disruption.[10] Further success was achieved with the early reduction of Fort Augustus. Wade's great statement of Hanoverian might crumbled remarkably swiftly and capitulated after barely two days. In one of those bizarre chances of war a lucky round from the attackers ignited the magazine and demolished a section of curtain wall.[11]

Murray's policy of clearing the outposts was by no means random. With the Highland army now having its back to the mountains it could maintain a quasi-guerrilla campaign more or less indefinitely; the earlier example of Montrose was clearly an encouraging one. It would be one thing for Cumberland's army to harry a dispersed foe at will but a commanded body of clansmen under arms was a very different matter. There was, as Lord George undoubtedly perceived, no need to fight a major battle for Inverness; the loss of the Highland capital of itself was of little consequence. If his army remained potent for the whole of 1746 and beyond then the Hanoverians, under mounting pressure from their allies, must surely be forced into a negotiating position.

By taking the offensive in the Great Glen, harrying Loudon, and foraying into Perthshire Lord George was keeping the morale of the Highlanders up, activity and the prospect of spoil being sure-fire incentives. At the same time he was denying Cumberland the full strategic initiative; he might have hoped that it could still be possible to maintain some form of conduit to France.

Both the Camerons and MacDonalds had pressed for an attempt on Fort William. Lochiel was particularly anxious to have this intrusion onto his territory removed,[12] but here the garrison resisted stoutly. The castellan, Captain Caroline Scott, was a name the Jacobites would have cause to remember. Colonel Grant, who was in charge of the siege lines, was injured by a spent round shot; command passed once again to the fatuous Mr Admirable and, to no one's surprise, very little progress made thereafter.

Scott mounted a bold sally on 31 March which slighted the besiegers' works and, by 3 April, the attempt was abandoned.[13]

In the course of its previous successes the Highland army had taken a sizeable number of prisoners, and these local actions constantly added to the score. It was a far more difficult exercise to effectively control this embarrassing train of captives, many if not most of whom escaped. Johnstone refers to 500 officers alone as prisoners, most of who were released on parole, effective for eighteen months from the date thereof.[14]

Lord Loudon, meanwhile, had withdrawn to Tain in Ross-shire. He had not been idle and had taken pains to secure all the available craft to effect a juncture with Cumberland at Banff, originally planned for 10 March. He found, however, that many of his local recruits were unwilling to serve beyond their own country. Nonetheless, his initiative in seizing boats had left Cromarty powerless to move effectively against him, being obliged to march his men around the head of the Cromarty Firth. Loudon took advantage of the interval to ferry his troops over to Dornoch.

Perth, who took over local command from the ineffective Earl, marshalled a flotilla of fishing smacks from Findhorn. Their movement cloaked by a thick mist that hid them from the men o' war blockading Inverness, the Jacobites landed a force on the north flank of the Dornoch Firth on 20 March. Possibly as many as 200 of Loudon's unwilling heroes laid down their arms, though His Lordship with Forbes and the Earl of Sutherland withdrew unmolested. The survivors marched westwards toward the relative sanctuary of the Inner Hebrides. Perth's neat little action had effectively denied the Duke any of those local forces the Whigs had raised:

> The Duke took with him about eighteen hundred men, and a very thick fog which came on in the morning, having greatly favoured the enterprise, he landed his detachment very near the enemy, who did not perceive our troops till they were within fifty paces of them, advancing rapidly sword in hand. The enemy were so much confounded on seeing the Highlanders ready to fall on them, that the greater part threw down their arms and surrendered themselves prisoners of war.[15]

Murray also had an eye to the government outposts established in his native Atholl. The Hanoverian grip on Perthshire raised the possibility of a two-pronged assault from there and Aberdeen in the east. The garrison troops comprised mainly Argyll Militia, though it was considered likely that these might be reinforced by detachments of the formidable Hessians. By mid-March Lord George was advancing in the area with a commanded party, perhaps of weak battalion strength. Moving with speed and striking effectively, they mopped up the smaller posts with ease and gained control of the Pass of Killiecrankie — the last Jacobite army moving over the same ground as the first.

Johnstone leaves the impression that the Hanoverians had been brutal in their treatment of locals and that retribution was therefore both swift and, in many cases, final:

> Having planned his march so as to arrive at Atholl in the beginning of the night, the detachment separated, dividing itself into small parties, every gentleman taking the shortest road to his own house, and in this manner all the English were surprised in their sleep. Those who found their wives and daughters violated by the brutality of these monsters, and their families dying from hunger and the inclemency of the season, made no prisoners. All the English received, while they slept, the punishment which their inhumanity merited. Thus they were all either put to the sword or made prisoners...[16]

By 17 March he was before the still formidable walls of Blair Castle. This could not fall to either ruse or escalade and the puny four-pounders Murray had with him could make no dent in the enceinte. The initiative so affrighted Frederick of Hesse and the Earl of Crawford at Perth that they advocated a retreat to Stirling. Cumberland, however, would have none of it — the abandonment of Perth would seriously jeopardise the Duke's overland supply.

Frederick, the veteran of several campaigns, advanced cautiously toward Pitlochry. To advance beyond the town would, however, mean forcing the Pass of Killiecrankie. Whether he was concerned at the unfortunate precedent of Mackay's army or too much attached to his baggage train, he ventured no further. It did, for a fleeting moment, appear as though a battle might be imminent, but Frederick's caution and haggling over prisoner protocols[17] denied any further impetus. A party of Hessian-mounted skirmishers did penetrate as far as the Jacobite lines but were seen off, with loss, by the Highlanders.[18]

Charles, who was unwell at the time and fearful of Cumberland, had declined to send a reinforcement to Murray, and further alarums suggesting

the Duke was already on the march prompted Lord George to withdraw his force toward Inverness. Blair Castle was thus delivered, but the
raid had achieved a purpose insofar as it appears to have neutralised the
Hessians. Cumberland, certainly, was unimpressed by his brother-in-law's
performance.

Cumberland was fully aware of the need to take the field and deal the
rebels a crushing blow as soon as conditions would permit. At Perth, in
early February, he began amassing the stores needed to facilitate his further
advance. Cash to purchase materiel and pay the men, a problem that had
confounded Hawley, was resolved when the Duke arranged for taxation
income from the northern shires of England to be disbursed directly to
Edinburgh. Hitherto, these monies had been routed through the Treasury,
where the dead hand of bureaucracy slowed matters interminably.

A sufficiency of bread was another difficulty he had to overcome: grain
was short and, especially with the arrival of the Hessians, he had many
mouths to feed. By 27 February, matters had progressed sufficiently to allow
the army to march north and east to Aberdeen. Garrison outposts were left
at Blair Castle and Castle Menzies to interdict any attempt by the rebels to
outflank the Hanoverian army and slip southwards, much as they had done
with Cope.

With Cumberland firmly in control of the East Coast ports he could
now be supplied from the sea and, at the same time, deny the French any
gateway for further aid. Prince Charles Edward had adopted an indifferent
stance, passing his time in such pleasures as the Highland capital had to offer,
and when Murray of Broughton became ill the rest of the coterie took over
administration, to dire effect.

Cumberland detached a commanded party to secure a quantity of Spanish
arms and ammunition, held in Corgarff Castle.[19] The Duke and Hawley,
now relegated to a subordinate capacity, lived well and at free quarters;
Hawley managed to filch a quantity of his hostess's chattels![20] Though the
necessity of remaining at Aberdeen was irksome, given the need to make a
speedy end and return the troops to Flanders, the delay was put to good use
in terms of both recuperation and training. Many of the men were debilitated by the winter marches Wade had undertaken, shaken by the reverse
at Falkirk. Aberdeen gave the Duke time to weld his army into a cohesive
and well-honed instrument of war. Part of their drill was the new bayonet
tactics, intended to minimise the advantage of broadsword and target in
hand-to-hand combat.

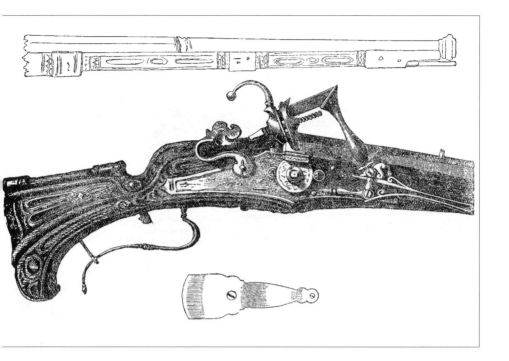

Above: 35 Musket from
c. 1620, equipped with
both wheel lock and
matchlock mechanisms.

Right: 36 A musketeer's
bandolier of the Civil
War era, with cords,
rings, bullet bag and
primer.

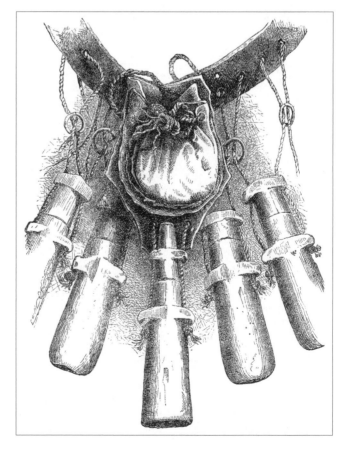

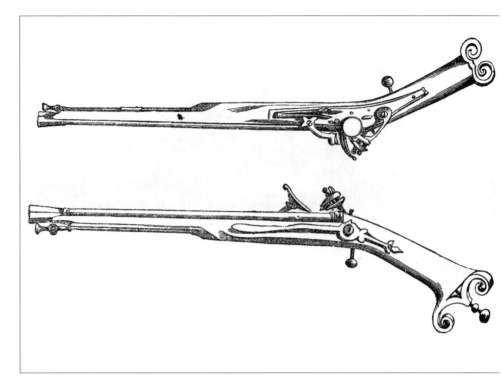

37 Scottish steel pistols or daggs, snaphaunce, *c.* 1630.

Opposite: 38 Highland target, from Warwick Castle.

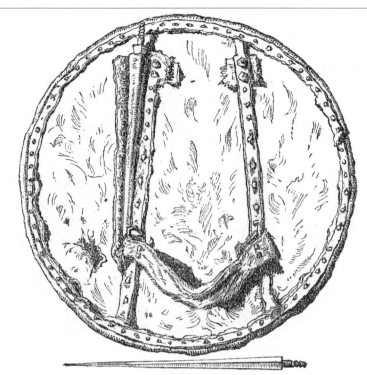

.PRO : REGE : : ET : : PATRIA .

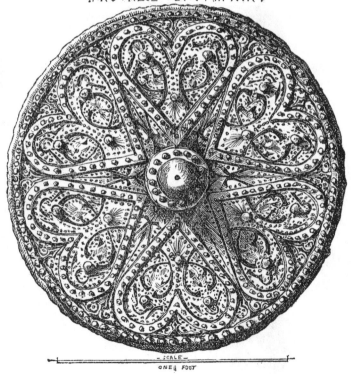

– SCALE –
ONE ½ FOOT

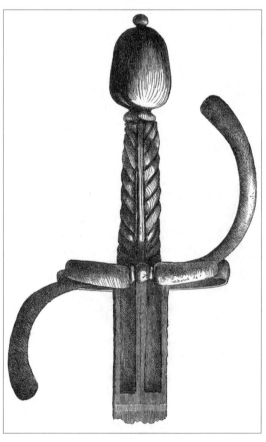

Above: 42 General Tam Dalyell rides into Edinburgh at the end of the Pentland Rising, 1666.

Opposite above: 39 The charge of Sir Hector MacLean's regiment at the Battle of Inverkeithing, 1650.

Opposite left: 40 Musketeer's sword (detail of hilt and ricasso) from the Civil War period.

Opposite right: 41 A Civil War pikeman.

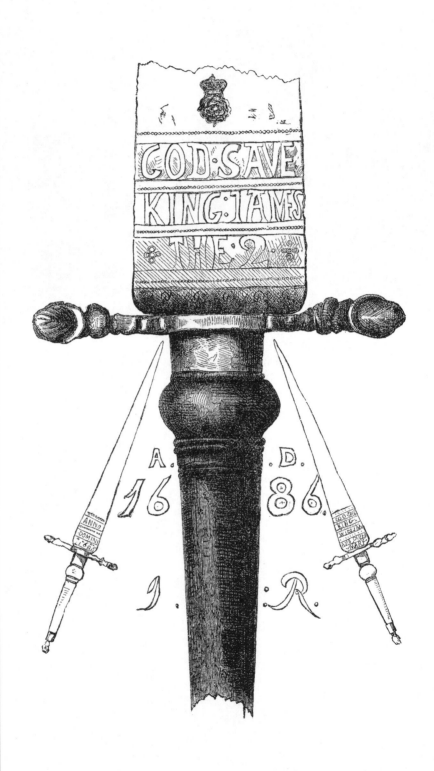

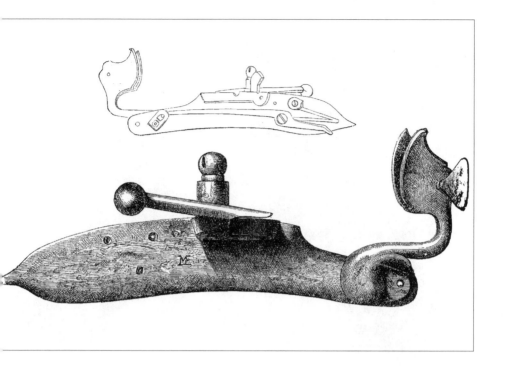

Above: 44 Matchlock
mechanism from the reign of
William III.

Right: 45 James Graham
of Claverhouse, Viscount
Dundee ('Bluidy
Clavers'/'Bonny Dundee').

Opposite: 43 Detail of a plug
bayonet from the reign of
James II, *c.* 1686.

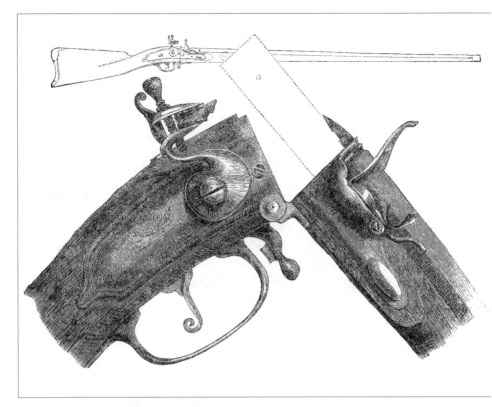

46 Breech-loading flintlock fusil, *c.* 1700.

47 The Earl of Mar's Council, 1715.

48 James III, 'The Old Pretender', Chevalier St George.

49 The Battle of Glenshiel, 1719.

50 Musketry exercise, early eighteenth century.

Opposite below: 52 The Battle of Culloden 1746, from a contemporary print.

51 The Highland advance at Prestonpans, 1745.

53 Charles Edward being sheltered by the Highlanders after Culloden.

54 James Graham,
Marquis of Montrose,
King Charles's paladin in
Scotland, genius of 'The
Year of Miracles'.

55 James II of England,
VII of Scotland.

56 William III of England, James's son-in-law.

57 Mary, daughter of James II, Consort of William III.

58 Simon Fraser, Lord Lovat, the slippery fox.

59 Prince Charles Edward as a
young man, unbowed by adversity
and dipsomania.

60 Prince Charles Edward in his later
years, dissolute and defeated.

As March wore on, the impetus for action increased; the Duke's army was consequently formed into two corps and a reserve division. On 16 March Major-General Humphrey Bland[21] proceeded westwards into Strathbogie, with the reserve to hand at Old Meldrum. The General caught John Roy Stewart[22] with a Jacobite detachment, perhaps 1,000 strong, and obliged him to withdraw in haste to Keith. Here, four days later, Stuart had better luck, launching a night raid and taking a government detachment of some Argyll Militia and troopers from Kingston's horse prisoner. Bland now fell back upon Strathbogie and the Jacobites held Keith against the next advance.

After the reverse at Keith, the Duke had dispatched more troops toward the forward outpost and detailed the Earl of Albemarle to assume overall command. The Earl would have two cavalry regiments and two brigades of foot; his orders were to remain in position at Huntly to act as the army's vanguard whilst the rest began its general advance. On the day following Bland's encounter with Stewart, Albemarle had written from Aberdeen to the Duke of Newcastle:

> You, happy Londoners may be surprised at our long stay here, but the deep snow, bad weather and consequently bad roads, and above all these difficulties contrary winds keeping our provisions and necessarys coming from Keith has obliged His Royal Highness, against his will, to it, but now that the aspect of the sky seems more favourably inclined I believe we shall march soon, Bland with four battalions, Kingston's Horse and Cobham's Dragoons moved from hence last Wednesday to Inveraray [Inverurie], Old Meldrum, and places adjacent, this day Mordaunt with four more battalions and cannon, marched from hence to those quarters, and Bland from thence to Strathbogie in order to attack a large detachment of the Rebels commanded by Roy Stewart, if they keep their post, and he thinks himself much inferior to them, he will encamp and send for Mordaunt to join him and attack them with their whole force, in which case we shall hear of our success by tomorrow evening, for I don't doubt wherever they stand of beating of them. These Highlanders (notwithstanding the way of thinking of some) are sad cowardly rascals.[23]

Despite Albemarle's contempt for the Jacobites, misplaced given the level of aggressive action they were mounting, there was mounting political pressure on the Duke to bring the whole business to a speedy end. The ministers in London were in no doubt that the rebels still had teeth but it was imperative to free the troops for an early return to Flanders, where the flagging allied cause was in need of urgent support.

Mordaunt had, on 23 March, led the 5th infantry brigade toward Old Meldrum with four pieces of ordnance. By 8 April the Duke was on the march with the main body, Mordaunt moved up to Turriff and Cumberland entered his former quarters at Old Meldrum. The rearguard, under Lord Sempill, was at Inverurie. Next day, the 9th, both Mordaunt and the Duke pressed on to Banff, joining Bland at Cullen on the 11th. By the following morning the army was poised to attempt the Spey crossing, between the mouth of the river and Fochabers, currently garrisoned by the rebels under Lord John Drummond.

It had been confidently predicted that such a vital river barrier would be defended, but the speed of the Duke's advance combined with the pernicious effects of poor staff work had ensured that the available forces comprised only the Lowland brigade, the available cavalry and roughly half the French Regulars. The crossing was difficult, complicated by the depth of the water and strong currents, the gravel base an uncertain footing for horse and man.[24] However, no serious opposition was encountered and the cold waters broached in three places with only trifling loss.[25]

Joseph Yorke, though his predictions had misfired concerning the likelihood of the rebels dispersing and the ability of Fort Augustus to hold out, correctly assessed that the Jacobites would not seriously contest the crossing of the Spey:

> With all these detachments out, they would fain persuade us that they will dispute the passage of the Spey. Whether they imagine we are fools and will believe this or are really fools themselves and will attempt it, I cant tell; but to convince the world that there is a good deal of difference between regular and irregular troops on these occasions, I must confess I would fain flatter myself it is their intention. These people have no tents nor can they, by their own confession, encamp if they had. Firing across a river would not suit with their constitutions, since they pretend to nothing further than a coup de main; and lastly, within the space of ten miles, there are upward of forty fords… it does not seem probable to me they will be so civil as to play the ball thus into our hands.[26]

Despite the condescending tone of Yorke's correspondence, he is of course quite right, on two counts. Firstly, the Jacobite army was ill suited to a regular military undertaking of this nature, and secondly, the sheer number of available crossing places meant that it was impossible to adequately defend them all. Given that the Highlanders' sole tactic was the charge, a contested river passage afforded little opportunity for its deployment; firepower, an area in which the rebels were seriously deficient, would be a major factor in any such encounter. Lack of resources was also a limiting factor, as Yorke touched upon as he continued his account:

> If the rebels had defended this river, we should have found some difficulty to have passed so cheap; for I never saw a stronger post in my life by nature, and a very little art would have rendered it very strong and tenable. The rebels here, who were chiefly the Lowlanders, complain bitterly of the Pretender and the clans for not coming down to them which, joined to the entire want of money, renders them mutinous and fearful. The greater part of the Macintoshes left them some days ago and the men desert in droves... Our men are in high spirits and showed the utmost alacrity in fording the river, though up to their waists.[27]

Despite the advantages in numbers of horse, foot and guns which the government army enjoyed, the fact that no serious attempt was made to hold the line of the Spey reflects the deep malaise within the Jacobite ranks. Whatever energy and initiative Murray and Perth might exhibit, there was no escaping the fact that the army was without true leadership. Charles Edward had been tested and found wanting, unable to provide the mainspring the continued cohesion of the army so desperately needed.

As Drummond's unwilling defenders fell back from the north bank of the Spey, Lord Lewis Gordon's regiment provided a rearguard whilst they retired, firstly on Elgin and then on to Nairn. By the time O'Sullivan bestirred himself to ride out and investigate, two days later on the 14th, he discovered that Perth, who had joined his brother, was also preparing to abandon Nairn.

As Charles idled away his time, admittedly afflicted by a severe chill he had contracted as a consequence of his precipitate night flight from Moy, his cause was unravelling around him. Cash was scarce, supplies and fodder if anything scarcer. The Prince's stock with his lieutenants had plummeted to new depths. In this last winter of the White Cockade, all of the Prince's shortcomings were magnified. At a time when dynamic leadership could have rallied support and achieved the miracle of keeping the army together and ensuring an adequacy of supply, Charles and his Irish cronies retreated into a fantasy of alcohol-fuelled optimism.[28]

O'Sullivan, at Nairn, was now aware that the Highland division's situation at Inverness was imperilled by the Duke's rapid advance and his successful forcing of the Spey crossing. It was too late to establish any form of blocking position in the town so, while the remnant of the Lowland division withdrew across the single bridge, he threw out a weak cavalry screen. This comprised the Life Guards, under Balmerino, a single squadron of Fitzjames's Horse, led by a Captain O'Shea, with Bagot's Hussars, strung out in an uncomfortably thin line. The foot had formed on the far bank, with the idea that the whole force could thus fall back in an orderly manner. However, when the horse retreated to the bridge, the infantry simply formed column and marched off!

An under-strength platoon from Berwick's regiment was all that stayed to lend support whilst the Hanoverian cavalry maintained a steady if somewhat desultory pursuit before breaking off and returning to Nairn. Cumberland proceeded to establish his HQ in the town, with the foot brigades setting up their encampment at Balblair to the west and the horse being quartered by Auldearn, scene of Montrose's great victory a century before, to the southeast. By now the Duke must have been aware that the rebels intended to stand and fight and, whilst he could be criticised for not immediately leading his men on toward Inverness, he would be right in assuming that the initiative still rested with him. The decisive battle was now imminent; his forces would be ready, rested and fully concentrated. His royal cousin could scarcely say the same.

In Inverness Lord John's poor showing caused deep unrest. It had been expected that he would entrench and make the Hanoverians fight:

> Relying on the resistance of Lord John, who, he supposed, would have recourse to every device to defend the ford and who, if he could not render it altogether impassable, would at least, by fortifying it with strong entrenchments, retard the approach of the Duke of Cumberland, the Prince expected to have had sufficient time to assemble his whole army, of which nearly the half had gone home to see their families, along with the chiefs who intended to order out every vassal capable of bearing arms. Besides, the excessive scarcity of provisions at Inverness was an additional motive for permitting them to return home, as the Prince was convinced they would cheerfully rejoin his army the moment they received orders for that purpose.
>
> The astonishment which prevailed at Inverness, when the information came upon us like a clap of thunder that the Duke of Cumberland had forded

the river Spey without experiencing the least opposition, may be easily conceived.[29]

More bad news followed. As Charles sent out summonses to the absent chiefs, he learnt that Cromarty, with his son Lord MacLeod, had been surprised and taken by the Mackays whilst at the home of the Countess of Sutherland, thus depriving the Jacobites of most of the Mackenzies.

Some additional French support, in penny packets, had filtered through. In part the attempt had been foiled by the vigilance of the Royal Navy, but one vessel, subsequently run aground by British frigates, did manage to disembark supplies at Peterhead. This provided Charles with a slender supplement to his empty war chest, but the thousand reinforcements, in the other transports, were harried back to Dunkirk. A brave attempt by the fast sloop *Hazard*[30] to run the British blockade with coin and arms was intercepted and frustrated with the loss of the ship, its crew and cargo, all of which were captured by a detachment of Loudon's men.

This chronic shortage of cash was to be a factor in persuading the Prince that a battle was inevitable and that, should matters continue, his army would inevitably disperse for want of wages. This played neatly into Cumberland's hands. It was his intention to advance upon Inverness, uncertain if the Jacobites would oblige by offering battle. A long-drawn-out guerrilla campaign against a dynamic foe was the very worst of alternatives. It is likely that the Duke shared Murray's view that if the rebels kept the field and avoided a major engagement they could tie down the government forces indefinitely. The consequences of this upon the fragile Alliance could be catastrophic and might make negotiated settlement unavoidable.

Even before Cumberland's most recent advance, Murray had been detailed to examine the lie of the ground to the east of Inverness, across the supposed route of the Hanoverian army. Consequently, he had ridden over the area with Colonel Ker and a Major Kennedy,[31] lately come from France, and had come upon what they judged to be a sound defensive position near Dalcross Castle. O'Sullivan, sent to pass judgement on this terrain, pronounced it unsuitable:

…it was the worst that could be chosen for the Highlanders & the most advantagiouse for the enemy… There is a Ravin or hollow yt is very deep & large yt goes in zig zag, formed by a stream yt runs there… I aske yu now yt knows the Highlanders whither a field of battle, where there is such an

impediment as yt Ravin was, wch is impractical for man or horse, was proper
for Highlanders whose way of fighting is to go directly sword in hand on the
enemy? Any man yt ever served with the Highlanders, knows yt they fire
but one shot & abandon their flintlocks after. If there be any obstruction yt
hinders them of going on the enemy all is lost; they don't like being exposed
to the enemy's fire, nor can they resist it, not being trained to charge [i.e. load]
as fast as regular troops, especially the English wch are the troops in the world
yt fires best. If I was to chuse a field of battle for the English, or if they were to
chuse it themselves they could not chuse a better, for there are no troops in
the world but what they overcome in fireing, if yu don't go in sword in hand,
or the bayonet among them.[32]

The Irishman preferred an area of level moorland a mile or so south-east of
Culloden House, where, as he opined, wet ground would secure the Jacobite
left. Lord George was scandalised and dismissed the Irishman's choice of
a suitable field with characteristic bluntness: 'Not one single souldier but
would have been against such a ffeeld had their advice been askt… A plain
moor where regular troops had… full use of their Cannon so as to anoy the
Highlanders prodigiously before they could possibly make an attack'.[33]

Despite these reservations, it was upon this stretch of ground that the
Jacobite army, the last ever to take the field, deployed in the cold dawn
light on 15 April. Murray, with whom tact was never a priority, chose the
moment to insist that the Atholl Brigade should occupy the coveted place
on the right – this was apparently in response to suggestions that he had
been guilty of keeping his own men out of danger in the past. Obviously,
this offended MacDonald sensibilities and yet another row erupted.

Exasperated by Lord George's intransigence, 'Clanranald, Keppoch and I
[Lochgarry] begged he [the Prince] would give us our former right, but he
intreated us for his sake we would not dispute it as he had already agreed to
give it to Lord George and his Atholl men'.[34] As there was yet no sign of the
enemy the men were stood down. By now they were hungry and becoming hungrier. Charles's current secretary, John Hay, was responsible for the
commissariat and this had now broken down completely. All that the men
would get that day was a single biscuit. Needless to say, Lord George was
furious, his rage at the incompetent staff work boiling over:

The misfortune of a total want of provisions was intirly owing to misman-
agement. Non of the Principle Officers of the Army were allowed to know

any thing with regard to so absolutly and Necessary an article... That there was above ten days provisions in Inverness is certain & a vast deal of Bread had been Bak'd, but wither it was an ill-timed occonomie or that in the Confusion for two days before the battle they had neglected to provide horse to bring out the provisions trow it is there was non to be gott when most wanted... Had provisions been dist[r]ibut as they ought to have been, there would have been no obligation to have given as a reason a presipitat Batle when two thousand men more would have joined in a day or two... But I do not scruple to say that the Prince was made believe by those most in his Confidence that the Highlanders would not fight except they were obliged to do it for want of provisions; these people dreaded a summer campaign in the mountains.[35]

This is a serious accusation — Murray clearly believed that the Prince's entourage was more concerned with creature comfort than a satisfactory outcome, or, possibly, they were so deluded as to imagine the army could triumph whatever the odds. Clearly Lord George had an axe to grind where O'Sullivan and the Irish cadre were concerned, but he was now more convinced than ever that the choice of ground at Culloden was fatally flawed. He detailed Brigadier Stapleton and Colonel Ker to examine the terrain south of the river Nairn, where he discovered ground more to his liking:

The Ground which Ld George Murray sent Brigadier Stapleton & Coll. Car to vew was a very strong Ground, & tho not so inaccessible as some other posts that might be choise at a greater distance, yet it was such as the Highlanders, would have liked very well, & would have thought themselves in a fair way of Victory had the Duke of Cumberland ventur'd to have passt the water of [N]eirn in their Sight & atact them there; Lord George Murray had formerly vewd that Ground & upon Brigadier Stapleton and Coll: Cars report he was confirmed in the opinion that it was infinitely more proper Ground for the Highlanders then where they were, or where they fought nixt day.[36]

Prince Charles, together with his Irish advisors (and these were by now the real governing council of the army, for the Prince's distrust of his local subordinates had informed his decision to exclude them), now began to canvas an altogether more daring and desperate remedy. It was proposed to mount a night attack upon the Hanoverian army's encampment at Balblair. The officers were, at first, reluctant to agree to such a plan, especially with the

army so dispersed. Murray, too, was sceptical, but during the day some additional troops came in from Lochaber under Keppoch, and Elcho's scouts
reported a lack of activity amongst the Duke's lines. Perhaps Lord George
came around simply on the basis that this was potentially a less dangerous
expedient than a stand on the ground O'Sullivan had chosen. As he now
advised his fellow officers:

> His opinion was that they should march at dusk of that evening so that the
> Duke should not be apprised of it. He should march about the town of Nairn
> and attack them in their rear with the right wing of the first line, while the
> Duke of Perth with the left should attack them in front, and the Prince
> should support the Duke of Perth's attack with the second line. Everybody
> agreed to Lord George's opinion. It was only objected to him that, as he did
> not propose to march from Culloden until the dusk of the evening, and as
> Culloden was eight miles from Nairn, it was to be feared the army would not
> accomplish that march before the daylight.[37]

This was a highly risky operation. Every officer is aware of the difficulty
attaching to night marches, even with the benefit of modern communications. To move a large body of men over unfamiliar country for a distance of
some miles and to fall upon the enemy camp from both flanks was a highly
ambitious plan; in no small measure it smacks of desperation. Surprise was
clearly of the essence so the majority was left in ignorance. Fires would be left
to deceive the enemy scouts and a picked body of two Mackintosh officers
and thirty men, possessed of sound local knowledge, would act as a corps of
pathfinders for the first division of the army, with more to guide the second.

Secrecy, whilst on the one hand essential, meant that, as the men were
not privy to the plan, large numbers wandered off in search of food; perhaps
as many as a third disappeared to forage. Mounted officers went out after
these scattered stragglers but many were truculent, worn down by gnawing hunger, and could not be cajoled to return to the ranks. The plan was
already running into difficulties. The Jacobite army which set out to ambush
Cumberland was barely 4,500 strong. Many of the officers now protested
the scheme was harebrained and should be abandoned, but Charles was
determined and Murray, perhaps too weary now to care, supported him.

It was Lord George who led the first column and Lord John Drummond
the second; Charles and the French brought up the rear. The plan was to
cross the river some two miles short of the town of Nairn, skirt along the

south bank to avoid any outlying picquets, then traverse the water again a mile or so downstream. This would facilitate an attack from the south-east upon the cavalry lines. Drummond would march straight at the Hanoverian camp, bearing to the left just before contact, then, forming up, fall upon the foot. As the day marked the Duke of Cumberland's twenty-fifth birthday it was hoped the men might be in their cups and insensible.

On paper this appeared feasible, but theory did not allow for the difficulty of the march, in the pitch dark, over unfamiliar and most uneven ground. The men blundered into obstacles, sank, sometimes nearly to their waists, in the treacherous mosses, and were only able to advance in single file. The Highlanders were, in large part, inured to such hardships but the French regulars, groaning under the weight of their heavy uniforms, accoutrement and packs, began, not surprisingly, to fall behind.

To try and preserve order, the Prince sent forward a request that Murray should slacken his pace. But Lord George was already giving commands, through Colonel Ker, that no muskets should be discharged and that the attack should be pressed home with cold steel only, the men to strike through the canvas at the forms within. His message to the Prince was that the latter should form his rearguard into the second line for the attack, to ensure full impact whilst maintaining cohesion. Charles's reply was that his general should simply strike with those troops he had in hand without waiting for the rest to arrive.

Such an order was bound to frustrate the entire operation, already dangerously behind schedule. Murray's 2,000 broadswords had been progressively thinned as men dropped out through a mix of hunger and exhaustion. With a mood of despair only to be guessed at he passed word back, through Lochiel, that the situation was hopeless and that the attack could not possibly proceed with such reduced numbers. Charles, whose optimism remained invincible, despite the weight of practicalities, reiterated his instructions that Murray must continue as planned.

Presently, as the vanguard struggled by Knockbuie, perhaps a mile short of the designated river crossing, Lord John and O'Sullivan both came up. Drummond confirmed that a sizeable gap had now opened behind Murray's division and the men could not be induced to hurry forward. The plan was stalled and time was running out. Daylight was already filtering from the east, the grey, creeping light of a dreary morning. A party of Life Guards, with cavalier élan, was enthusiastic for pressing on, regardless of the fact the column would now be visible for a full two miles before contact.

O'Sullivan shared their sentiments, for entirely the wrong reasons, and John Hay, arriving belatedly, added his voice to the chorus. For Murray and his officers this was too much. The delays had come from the rear and it was this failure that rendered the plan unserviceable. Surprise had always been the key and this required the cloak of darkness; both were now lost, and there was simply no point in continuing. Ominously, a drum could be heard beating in the distant camp, sounding the death knell for the planned assault. There was nothing left but to order a withdrawal. The exhausted, hungry Highlanders must trek back over those wet, wearisome miles to arrive precisely where they had begun, with the added certainty the Duke's army would soon be on their trail and that a battle must surely now be inevitable.

Perth and his brother returned to the second of the two columns with the instructions to face about. John Hay, however, had gone hurrying back to the Prince, who now rode up brimming with indignation. In the confusion of that pallid dawn, neither Perth nor Lord George could be located, and even O'Sullivan had vanished. Charles, distracted, pleaded with Perth to try and turn the men around, firm in his conviction that a famous victory was slipping from his grasp. The Duke endeavoured to instil some reason into the Prince and was soon supported by Lochiel, who stressed that with daylight the opportunity had gone.

Johnstone, no friend of the Prince's Irish coterie, acknowledged that Murray, in withdrawing his column, had acted without orders, and this, at best, was intemperate:

> I do not mean to justify the conduct of Lord George in retiring with the first column, contrary to the express orders of the Prince, and without informing him of it. Had he waited at the entrance into the meadow for the arrival of the whole army, he might have insisted on the absolute necessity of forming in order of battle in order to begin the attack like people in their senses, and have convinced the Prince of the absurdity of acting otherwise. The Irishmen, whom the Price had adopted as his only counsellors upon all occasions, and who were men of the most limited capacities, endeavoured, by all manner of clandestine reports, to cause it to be believed that, in acting as he did on this occasion, Lord George had betrayed the Prince. But, knowing him perhaps better than any other person, I can only attribute his disobedience of the Prince's orders to the violence and impetuosity of his character.[38]

With bad grace Charles was forced to concur. His over-excited mind, spurred by the mutterings of his cabal, was convinced that he had been betrayed and that Lord George Murray was the principal betrayer, that it was his contagion which had infected Lochiel and the others. It is said he even detailed a group of Irish to keep close watch upon Murray for signs of incipient treachery! This was the young man who would be king.

The night march, bold as it was in concept, had foundered in the attempt. This was caused neither by treachery nor folly. The task was simply too great, the plan too complex and dependent upon a whole range of factors, particularly timing, frustrated by distance and the nature of the ground. The plain fact was that the Jacobite army was now desperately hungry, physically exhausted and demoralised. The Prince had failed to display any qualities of leadership and preferred to retreat into the closed world of his Irish toadies. He appears to have been almost incapable of dealing with realities, steering the foundering vessel of his cause onto the rocks of blind optimism.

Charles's conduct during the abortive night march would clearly suggest that he continued to believe in the myth of his Highland warriors' invincibility. True, they had bested Hanoverian forces at least four times in the field (if the action at Inverurie is to be included). But the Prince had completely failed to appreciate that the force Cumberland was now preparing to bring against him was of an altogether different stamp.

It was now dawn on 16 April, the curtain of uncertain light rising on what was to be the last act of the Jacobite saga. For Charles Edward, the chiefs and the clansmen around him, this day would mark the end of their era. They now faced a strong and implacable foe, determined, as never before, to root out this anachronistic phenomenon of 'clannism'. The association of the Highland Tory clans with the House of Stuart, which the Prince's grandfather had, almost unintentionally, fostered, was about to be irrevocably severed. From this day that was dawning, things would never be the same again, and the transition would be largely written in blood. The Battle of Culloden was about to begin.

12

BATTLE – CULLODEN MOOR

16 APRIL, MORNING AND EARLY AFTERNOON, UNTIL 2 P.M.

All is going to pot!

Colonel John William O'Sullivan

Tis mine and everybody's opinion, no history can brag of so singular a victory.

Trooper Enoch Bradshaw, Cobham's Horse

I never saw a field thicker of dead.

Fusilier Edward Linn

Had Prince Charles slept during the whole of the expedition, and allowed Lord George to act for him, according to his own judgement, there is every reason for supposing he would have found the crown of great Britain on his head when he awoke.

Chevalier de Johnstone

The exhausted Jacobites straggled, wet, hungry, and with even the most jocular spirits quiet, towards Culloden. The day was not ended, the curtain was, in fact, just rising on the final act of their particular tragedy. Johnstone was amongst those whose only immediate thought was for rest:

> Exhausted with hunger and worn out with the excessive fatigue of the last three nights, as soon as we reached Culloden I turned off as fast as I could to Inverness, where, eager to recruit my strength by a little sleep, I tore off my clothes, half asleep all the while. But when I had already one leg in the bed and was on the point of stretching myself between the sheets, what was my surprise to hear the drum beat to arms and the trumpets of the picket of Fitzjames sounding the call to boot and saddle.[1]

Dragging on damp kit and stumbling toward his horse, Johnstone rode back the way he had come to gain the high by the rim of Culloden Moor. Here he found whatever could be mustered of the Jacobite army and, some two miles eastwards, the standards and drums of the advancing Hanoverians.

The ground upon which the armies were now to fight actually formed part of Duncan Forbes's estate of Culloden, and the stone walls encircling his parkland were to play a role in the battle. The distance from Inverness is roughly five miles, and the spur of higher ground runs from east to west. At the time, as indeed now, the area was exceedingly wet; 'The ground in the hollow, between the Castle of Culloden and an enclosure on our right, being marshy and covered with water which reached half-way up the leg, was well chosen to protect us from the cavalry of the enemy.'[2]

Despite being dotted with small pools the ground is roughly level with a fall of some ten yards from Lord George Murray's position, on the right of the Jacobite line, to the extreme left of the government front rank. A more noticeable drop, of perhaps twice this, occurs along the spread of the rebel deployment, toward their left and by the walls of the Culloden Parks; so that the MacDonalds, on that wing, would charge over ground that was virtually flat.

To the north and west, the land falls gradually toward the shore of the Moray Firth, where the sailors of the blockading squadron enjoyed a grand-stand view of the unfolding action. On the opposite flank the drop is far more marked, beyond the Jacobite right, a sharp decline toward the defile of the River Nairn. On this flank the tactical position was further complicated by the presence of some additional walled enclosures, referred to as the Culwhiniac Enclosures.

The contemporary stone walls which encircled these have now vanished but the line running eastwards from the ferm-toun[3] at Culchunaig ran across the field and a further earthwork, the Leanach enclosure, lay between the Jacobite right and the government left. This was a semicircular horseshoe-shaped feature, with tumbled rubble or turf walls. Between its western flank and the more substantial wall of the park ran a lane which marks the parish boundary. Southwards from the Jacobite right, the line of the Culwhiniac wall bore sharply south-east and then almost due southwards down the hillside, the whole forming a rather irregular pentagon.

Perhaps the most famous view of the battle, and one which is certainly the most contemporary, was drawn by Thomas Sandby. The field is viewed from the north, with the artist standing more or less midway between the Jacobite left and the government right with the corner of Culloden Park in the right foreground. Sandby has added a few romantic figures for dramatic effect but he clearly shows the cone-shaped effect of the two armies' alignment, with the gap narrowing toward the southern flank. A number of ferm-touns are also indicated: Leanach, which lies to the south-east behind the government left; Culwhiniac; Culchunaig, located as mentioned just behind the Jacobite right and the south-west angle of the Culwhiniac Parks; and lastly Balvraid, which stood a thousand yards or so further west.

A number of small watercourses also bisect the moor and one of these, which drains into the Nairn, runs from behind Culchunaig, arcing south-wards. Another ran from due west to east along the flank of the government right. A lane or sunken way ran from the buildings at Culchunaig and followed the edge of the enclosure wall down toward the river. The present B9006 roughly follows the line of the then unmetalled highway from Nairn to Inverness. The road ran along the southern flank of Old Leanach, past the extreme left of Cumberland's line, then proceeded diagonally across the field to bisect the centre of the rebel position before angling northwards to run parallel to the wall of Culloden Parks.

When O'Sullivan had first decided upon the ground, he had expected that the army would be able to muster far nearer its full complement than was now the case. As it was the Jacobites could field under 4,000 men:

> The Prince, on his return to Culloden, enraged against Lord George Murray, publicly declared that no one in future should command his army but himself. As soon as the English army began to appear, the Prince, who was always eager to give battle without reflecting on the consequences, was told that, as the Highlanders were exhausted with fatigue, dispersed, and buried in deep sleep in the neighbouring hamlets and enclosures, many could not possibly be present in the battle from the difficulty of finding them. Besides, what could be expected from men in their situation; they were not pos-sessed of supernatural strength… The Prince, however, would listen to no advice, and resolved on giving battle, let the consequences be what they might.[4]

Matters, having begun badly, swiftly deteriorated into the old wran-gle about which unit should have the honour of standing on the right. Johnstone makes no mention of this but O'Sullivan points to his difficulties in dealing with Lord George Murray's intemperate behaviour. Whilst His Lordship's genius cannot be denied, he was clearly not given to tact and had allowed the relationship between himself and the Prince's Irish coterie to degenerate into open hostility. In large part this was undoubtedly motivated by petty jealousy on their part, but Murray's short fuse and intellectual arrogance served only to exacerbate a tense situation. O'Sullivan expresses a most pejorative view, obviously highly partisan, but one which cannot be discounted:

> Ld George comes up and tells Sullivan who had the honr to be near the Prince, yt he must change the order of battle, yt his Regiment had the right yesterday. 'But My Ld,' says Sullivan, 'there was no battle yesterday, besides it is no time to change the order of battle in the enemy's presence.' 'Laid up the men then, it's your businesse to set them in battle.' 'Yt I will My Ld,' says Sullivan 'if you'll be so good as to make them follow in their ranks, yt there may be more confusion, for there is nothing more dangerouse then to change regiments from one ground to another in the presence of the enemy. The Prince caress'd Ld George, pray'd him to laid the men & yt he and Sullivan would make them follow in their ranks. 'Gad Sr,' says Ld George swearing 'it is very hard yt my Regimt must have the right two days running' when it is he himself wou'd have it so absolutely, but 'Sr' says he again, 'the ground is not reconnoitred' 'I ask pardon,' says Sullivan 'here is as good a position as yu cou'd desir. Yu see yt Park before yu wch continues to the river with a wall six foot high, & them houses near it, wch yu can fill with men, & pierce the walls, yt it is on your right. Yu see this Park here is to be our left, & both in a direct ligne. If there be not ground enough, we'l mak use of the Parks & I warrant yu My Ld' says Sullivan 'the horse wont come to yu there.' He went off grumbling.[5]

This did not please the MacDonalds who again protested that the coveted right was theirs. The Prince apparently assured the MacDonald officers that Murray had, in effect, bullied him into it but that he was now committed to allowing the Athollmen to hold that flank. Whatever the precise detail of the squabble, such unseemly wrangling could do nothing to improve the battered morale of the tired, hungry, dirty men upon the moor on that cold morning in early spring.

With the simmering dispute over priority temporarily abated, if not resolved, the Athollmen formed by the wall of the Culwhiniac Enclosure just in front of the steading of Culchunaig.[6] Lord George commanded three weak battalions, perhaps 500 broadswords all told. These were his own people and comprised groups from a smattering of smaller clans: Robertson of Struan, Menzies of Shian, Murrays of course, and perhaps some of the wily MacGregors.

Next to them came some 650 of Lochiel's Camerons, then 150 of the Appin men under Stewart of Ardshiel. Lochiel himself was not present, the name led by his son Donald, and the officers drawn from the gentry of the clan. This regiment, like others, was a family affair. Whatever else was lacking, generations of pride and the honour of their tribe welded these men into a cohesive military unit.

The Stewarts of Appin were said to have been primarily motivated by their intense hatred of Clan Campbell; they came from the pleasant country around Loch Linnhe, and with them stood their Balquhidder allies the MacLarens. Again, many of these Appin men were minor gentry; desertion had thinned the other ranks rather than the officers, so many regiment had a surfeit of gentlemen beneath their banners. The remaining commons comprised McColls, Carmichaels, Livingstones and MacLeays.

This whole right-hand division came under Murray's direction. The centre was led by Lord John Drummond, notwithstanding his poor showing earlier. The 500 Frasers were led by Fraser of Inverallochy. Lord Lovat was too foxy to be seen anywhere near the field and his regiment was nominally commanded by his young son, though he too appears to have been absent.

To the left of the Frasers stood roughly the same number of Colonel Anne's Mackintoshes, MacGillvrays and MacBeans: these were together known by the name of their ancient alliance, Clan Chattan, 'the Clan of the Cats'. Their pretty colonel was not on the field, the regiment being led by MacGillvray of Dunmaglass, a giant of a man, who though handsome was almost effeminate in appearance.[7]

Left again was Farquharson of Monaltrie, with 150 men from Deeside (Farquharsons were also a part of Clan Chattan). Next to them, MacLeans and MacLachlans, their combined strength amounting to no more that 180 clansmen. The MacLachlans were an ancient tribe from Argyll, led by their chief Lachlan; MacLean of Drimmin served as his immediate subordinate and MacLean gentry formed the officer cadre of the joint regiment. Their long feud with Clan Campbell added a particular urgency to the decision to fight. Some of those soon to stand opposite would have had a hand in the harrying of Morven, Ardgour and Mull, 'taken up' by Campbell militia, whilst the menfolk followed the Prince. Such matters rankled.

Beyond them, a hundred of the Chisholms, stout recusants, with their priest in attendance; despite this, two of the chief's five sons were serving under Cumberland with commissions in the Royal Scots. The youngest son, Roderick Og, led the regiment. The clan piper, Ian Beg, had with him the clan's Black Chanter, a silver-bound affair that was believed to be imbued with mystical powers. If this was indeed so then it would be sorely needed.

The amiable Perth commanded the MacDonald regiments on the left: Keppoch (200), Clanranald (200) and Glengarry (500). Amongst the MacDonalds may have been a sprinkling of MacLeods and Grants. Clan Donald was still the backbone of the Tory clans, the descendents of Somerled. The right of the line had been their reward from Robert the Bruce, and it was well earned; they had done the King good service and the privilege had been jealously guarded ever since. Today's slight at the hands of Murray was a gross insult to the honour of their name and to men of such ticklish sensibilities this was a very grave matter indeed.

Ranald MacDonald, the eldest son of Clanranald himself, led the regiment; he had been one of the very first to pledge his allegiance to the Prince's cause. As with the other clan regiments the officers were drawn from the chief's kin and tacksmen. One of Ranald's captains was Macdonald of Drimindarach, another Hector who is said to have battered in the gates of Carlisle with a sledgehammer! Keppoch, at the head of his reduced regiment, was a veteran of the '15; he concurred with Murray that this was not fit ground for Highlanders.

Glengarry was another absentee, the regiment led by two sons of different wives, one of whom had been accidentally killed earlier in the campaign.[8] The other, James, now colonel, was only eighteen. The Macdonalds of Glencoe, the tiny sept that had suffered in the massacre of 1692, stood with Keppoch, Macdonald of Kinloch Moidart and Morar brigaded with Clanranald, whilst Coll Macdonald of Barisdale was attached to Glengarry. Though by right belonging in the second line with Perth's, Johnstone had taken station with Clan Donald, beside his friend Macdonald of Scotus, serving with Glengarry.

Some 3,832 men thus stood in the front rank, which comprised a frontage of perhaps a thousand yards.[9] As all the available fighting troops were spread so thinly, there was no possibility of a strong second line. Rather, the remaining units were deployed in three very thin brigades, marshalled in column and standing roughly a hundred yards behind the first.

On the left, behind the MacDonald regiments, stood the Irish Picquets (302). These were drawn from Dillon's, Ruth's and Lally's regiments in the French service but were mainly of Irish descent, 'Wild Geese'. In the centre John Roy Stuart was in charge of a loose formation of Perth's Regiment (300), mainly raised from the Duke's own estates and containing some Robertsons as well, possibly another handful of Macgregors, with the added mix of some English deserters. These men would have no illusions as to their fate, should the day go badly. He also commanded Gordon of Glenbucket's regiment (200), his own (200), Kilmarnock's Footguards (200) and Ogilvy's double battalion regiment (500).

Next, moving to the right, came the Royal Ecossois (350), commanded by Lord Lewis Drummond, who was the son of the attainted Earl of Melfort. Most of the rank and file were Scottish exiles, or descendants of earlier emigrants. In their blue coats and red facings these French regulars could at least count upon receiving the civilities of war in defeat.

On the extreme right was posted the double battalion of Lord Lewis Gordon's regiment, once a lieutenant in the Royal Navy and Huntly's third son. These comprised Stonywood's, 200 Aberdonians and a hundred more from Strathbogie, led by Gordon of Avochie. A final weak battalion of foot, barely above company strength, Bannerman's 120-odd men from the Mearns may, though it is not clear, have been brigaded with the Gordon regiments.[10] Lieutenant-Colonel Stapleton of Berwick's regiment was in overall charge of this second line. He had voiced considerable doubts about the steadiness of the clans, should matters go badly.[11]

Prince Charles's army was dreadfully deficient in cavalry, and the two small squadrons he could muster, Lord Strathallan's Perthshire riders and Bagot's Hussars, were posted behind the reserve line. Bagot's was on the left and Strathallan's perhaps on the right, though these may also, at least for a time, have taken station on the left and the Hussars moved, at some point, to the centre. Many of the mounts were in poor shape, and a number of troopers had no horses at all.

What remained of Fitzjames's Horse, with Elcho's Life Guards, led by Captains Bagot and Brennan were on the right, whilst Captain O'Shea commanded the Prince's slender personal escort, less than a score in numbers. Again, there is some confusion as to the deployment of Balmerino's Horse, which may have been placed with Strathallan's, or, at least in part, have formed a section of the Prince's Lifeguard. D'Eguiles gives a grand total of 131 mounted troopers in the Prince's army – this is scarcely impressive!

Exactly how the dozen Jacobite guns were posted is again subject to controversy. Sandby[12] shows them placed at intervals along the length of the first line – three on the right, five in the centre and another three on the left – and this is very likely correct. The last gun, a four-pounder, only appears to have been dragged up by the French after the battle had begun and was emplaced on the extreme left of the rebel line.[13] There was a very distinct lack of professional gunners, the pieces indifferently served by some of the French and a gaggle of volunteers.

This then was the last Jacobite army. Pitifully few, without food, tired, wet, cold and, in the case of the MacDonalds, truculent, their resentment against Murray still rancorous. Their line was a riot of saffron and plaid, the men armed with a motley of captured flintlocks and their traditional edged weapons, the dull gleam of morning light catching on a burnished blade. Nothing about these men shone but their arms, to all intents and purposes little changed in the century since Montrose.

Each man wore his blue bonnet, wherein he carried the ancient badge of his name and, in many cases, the distinctive white cockade. This was a ribbon or band of knotted linen or silk, which bore a laurel wreath and the motto: 'With Charles our brave and merciful P.R. we'll greatly fall or nobly save our country'. The army must have appeared almost medieval in its dress and accoutrement. This was not the type of foe the redcoated battalions drawing up opposite would have recognised, being more used to the sartorially superior lines of French, Dutch, Austrian and Germanic forces.

This was the last clan army ever to muster, and whilst it is not possible to assert that the clan system as it obtained in 1746 was of great antiquity, the tribal spirit which drove these men was unaltered over centuries. Pride of name, the warrior ethos of the Norse-Gael, driven by pride of blood, fuelled by the rant of the pipes, these were the legacy of Somerled and back, long before him, to Finn MacCool and the paladins of legend. Given the odds which now confronted them, their desperate hunger, utter exhaustion and the failures of command, it is not to be wondered at that they were beaten; it is to be marvelled at that they fought at all.

Orders issued by the Prince, two days previously, when battle had appeared imminent had specified that:

Each indevidual in the Armie as well officer as souldier keeps their posts that shall b allotted to them, and if any man turn his back to run away the next

behind such a man is to shoot him. No body on Pain of Death to Strip the
Slain or Plunder till the Battle be over. The Highlanders all to be in kilts...[14]

A farmer heard the Jacobites singing the words of the Twentieth Psalm
as they mustered on the wet ground that morning. The army was ragged
and despondent, and some in the ranks were very young, barely into their
teens.[15] Some, even younger, were crouched amongst the heather, playing
truant from school in Inverness, to watch the far more exciting prospect of
a battle.

There were women too, the wives and sweethearts of clansmen, on or
close to the field. The womenfolk of Clan Chattan were huddled by the
stream of Creagan Glas, across the Nairn. Others, devoid of standing and
affiliation, scavengers drawn by the scent of plunder and pickings, were
already circling the margins of the field like prowling jackals, in the certainty that, whoever won, their time would come. These lawless Bacaudae,
comprised of locals, tinkers, deserters and outlaws, were a feature of every
contemporary battlefield, the crows that gathered to pick the carcasses of
the fallen clean.

As this deployment was being concluded, Lord George became increasingly worried about the Leanach enclosure which stood in front of the
extreme right of his brigade. He decided to advance some distance and
re-form his regiments in column (i.e. from three ranks deep to six), at
the same time angling the line of attack more toward the north. In itself
this was a reasoned response to a tactical problem, as it would enable his
men to charge unimpeded by the obstacle, and as the fall of ground was
increasing to the north, this might also provide further impetus. Whether
he now intended that the entire line should conform or whether he simply
saw this as a local move is unclear. However, he certainly does not seem
to have informed Perth, who, viewing this 'changement', attempted to
conform.

This proposal immediately ran into objections from the truculent
MacDonalds who were minded neither to oblige Lord George further,
nor advance beyond the sheltering wall of Culloden Park which guarded
their exposed flank so completely. Such an extension of the line caused
even greater gaps to appear between the clan regiments, already stretched
desperately thin. The cry of 'close up, close up' had been heard all morning and now reached a veritable crescendo. The attenuated line now ran at
an angle from about halfway down the wall of the Culwhiniac enclosure,

where the gap between the two armies equalled 600 yards, back to the wall of Culloden Park, by which point it had increased by a further 200 yards.

O'Sullivan now decided that the shortfall in front-line manpower could only be made up by pushing in reserves from the second. He was later to recall that he had moved up Perth's and Strathallan's but the latter was a cavalry unit, though it is possible some dismounted troopers were used as unwilling infantry. In fact it was Perth's and Glenbucket's he sent forward and these were now deployed on the extreme left, allowing the MacDonald regiments, no doubt equally unwilling, to echelon to the right. To complete the redeployment he moved John Roy Stuart's regiment up beside that of Stewart of Ardshiel.

> ...we saw the English army at the distance of about two miles from us. They appeared at first disposed to encamp in the position where they then were, many of their tents being already erected; but all at once their tents disappeared and we immediately perceived them in movement toward us. The view of our army making preparations for battle probably induced the Duke of Cumberland to change his plan. Indeed he must have been blind in the extreme to have delayed attacking us instantly in the deplorable situation in which we were, worn out with hunger and fatigue, especially when he perceived from our manoeuvre that we were impatient to give battle under every possible disadvantage, and well disposed to facilitate our own destruction.[16]

The Hanoverian army had, in fact, begun its march from Nairn at around five o'clock that morning. If the men had toasted the Duke's health on the occasion of his birthday, they were certainly not befuddled. The regiments were already responding to the General Call to Arms as the dazed Jacobites were reversing from their abortive night march. The signal guns boomed in the thick, damp air of the early morning and the outposts were duly relieved. The raw wind stirred the silken folds of the colours as they were unfurled and the cold grey dawn, leaden with showers, suddenly enlivened by a great spilling of scarlet and yellow, blue and buff.

Though the Duke of Cumberland had paid for a generous measure of sprits so that each man might drink his health the evening before, and he would have drawn satisfaction from their cheers, he had been careful to remind them of their duty and the task that lay before them. It was time to make an end to the business of rebellion. Though something of a martinet, the Duke was not unpopular with his men; he took a feudal interest in their welfare and ensured that they had food in their bellies and shoes upon their feet. If he was not a great general, he had led them bravely if unsuccessfully over the bloody ground at Fontenoy, and if there had been no victory, nor was there shame. The army had fought long, well and hard, a high price had been paid and if the French marshal finally won the day then it was no fault of the British redcoat.

By four thirty the muster was taking shape, the cursing of sergeants affrighting the Calvinist air of Nairn. The skirl of the Campbells' pipes added to the steady tempo of the drums, a dozen miles of wet heath lay between the army and its next objective and the men were to have the spiritual sustenance of the chaplain's words before setting off. After the Word of God came Orders of the Day, more pragmatic but, for the assembled battalions, at least of equal weight. These were uncompromising. Anyone who shirked his duty faced the censure of a court martial and the likelihood of a hanging; clemency and compassion were not included in that day's strictures.

With the drums still beating out the steady roll of command and movement the army prepared to march, long lines of tramping redcoats, stamping in the cold air and deployed for the advance in three columns of foot, each of five battalions. The horse were concentrated in a fourth column which rode as a screen on the left; guns, baggage and sundries trundled less tidily behind the right-hand column.[17]

As they marched they faced toward Inverness and the great mass of the mountains that were crowding the western skyline. This was a hostile land, they a sea of scarlet and silk, yet lost in the immensity of the Highlands. It is not a difficult matter to trace the line of the army's advance today; what requires a greater shift of perspective is to imagine the landscape as it stood some 250 years ago.

This was still a largely untamed world, where the encroaching hand of man was yet to stamp its definitive grip. Snow-capped summits, dark glens, hidden valleys, tumbled slopes of scree and waste of peat and heather dominated, with only the huddled, grey and dirty towns, a scatter of farms and steadings, to proclaim man's presence. The balance of man and nature had not yet altered to its present, biased form and the wildness was a talisman of the enemy, the shrieking tartan horde who had so discomfited their regular opponents. This was their country and the presence of the Argyll militia scarcely afforded any comfort.

To the east the English warships bobbed in the Firth, to the west the wilderness of the central Highlands, somewhere before the Jacobite army. If

Johnstone is correct, Cumberland, whilst ready to fight, did not necessarily expect to do so, and if the Chevalier's observation was accurate the army was about to pitch tents when the presence of the rebel deployment was revealed.

Each marching column had its untidy trail of supply wagons, officers' horses, carriages and the regimental women, plodding in the muck unless they could hitch a ride on one of the carts. The more informal practice of allowing these ladies to keep pace with their men was forbidden on pain of the lash and the Duke was not a man who would flinch at a flogging or two. Regulations provided for the march to proceed at the rate of seventy-five paces a minute, thus the army would cover perhaps two and a half miles per hour. Given the poor conditions that obtained on the march, this might have been reduced to around two miles an hour. It would be late morning before the columns approached Culloden Moor where their exhausted and sodden enemies waited.

It was always a difficult and, in the face of the enemy, potentially hazardous move for the army to shift from column to line of battle, but this was one the government troops had practised extensively. When the order was given, the first, third and last battalion in each of the marching columns halted and stayed put whilst the second and fourth spread out onto the left flank of the first and third. By this means the entire army swiftly completed a deployment that created two lines each of six battalions, with a half-strength third or reserve line. This deployment was undertaken as soon as the rebel army was spotted, in the anticipation the Jacobites would advance further and attack. When it was obvious that no such threat existed the army re-formed and continued its own forward movement.

Unlike the sudden and furious onslaughts seen at Prestonpans and Falkirk, the fumbling at Clifton, the swiftness of the raids at Inverurie or in Atholl, this final battle proceeded with the formal elegance of a ball, the government army completing a textbook deployment before the rebels' inert ranks. Initially Cumberland deployed his six front-line battalions facing almost south-west. Barrell's on the extreme left with the flank anchored on the moor road. The second line behind at something of an angle to the left, with Wolfe's, on that flank, largely standing south of the highway and the reserve battalions in line to the rear. Hawley, commanding the cavalry, had the bulk of his squadrons, with the Campbells, massed to the south of Leanach, well down toward the Nairn and with the Culwhiniac enclosure before them. A single squadron from Cobham's was patrolling on the far right flank with Kingston's in two squadrons, one on either flank of the reserve line.

When Lord George Murray began his contentious manoeuvre on the Jacobite right, the Duke of Cumberland concluded, understandably, that this betokened a general shift of rebel forces to create a growing threat to his own right, whose flank was already rather 'in the air'. His response was to move forward two of the reserve battalions of foot, with Kingston's Horse, thus leaving only Blakeney's as a final reserve. As the moment drew inexorably closer when both sides would be irretrievably committed to fight, the government deployment was as follows.

In the first line, from the left: Barrell's, Monro's, Campbell's Royal North British Fusiliers, Price's, Cholmondeleys' and Pulteney's – a total force of 461 officers and NCOs with 2,623 other ranks,[18] stretched across a distance of nearly 1,000 yards. Brigadier Sempill held command, and he had detachments from both Kingston's and Cobham's guarding his exposed right flank.[19]

Huske was in charge of the second line, which comprised, again from the left: Wolfe's, Ligonier's, Sempill's, Bligh's, Fleming's and Battereau's. With a slightly shorter frontage the total manpower included some 707 officers and NCOs with 2,598 soldiers. Hawley and Bland, on the far left with the remaining mounted troops, led the rest of Cobham's and the whole of Kerr's, nearly 500 troopers.[20] Quite how many Highlanders were on this flank is not certain, perhaps a couple of hundred all told.

Lastly, the guns. The train included ten of the three-pounder battalion guns, posted a brace apiece between the original six battalions making up the initial front line – this was normal practice – and the half dozen Coehorns were sited in threes at either extremity of the second line. Lieutenant-Colonel Belford, dragged from the arms of his young wife, was in command; a highly competent officer, he was seconded by Captain-Lieutenant John Godwin with just over a hundred gunners, plus officers and detached volunteers.

Each battalion stood three ranks deep, divided into platoons. The men stood with their muskets held ready, eighteen inches of honed bayonet already fixed. Their gaiters and breeches were already caked with the muck of peat bogs, furze and last year's dead bracken, drenched and sodden from this and the corollary of freezing rain. The grenadier companies held the flanks of each of the battalions with the colours kept in the centre. Behind these the colonel took his stance, whilst the major stood on the flank, each company led by its captain also posted on the flank. Men would be busy

ensuring the barrels of their muskets and the locks stayed dry and that their
cartridges were not soaked, for on this day such details were the difference
between living and dying. Time, too, for a man to void bladder and bowels,
lest he be caught out when the firing began.

The royal army's deployment was carried out to the steady beat of drum
with the sergeants bellowing orders, the stately advance, then the rather
hurried reshuffle to conform with the perceived shift in the Jacobite axis of
attack. It was raining on the moor, a misery of squally showers, driven by the
bleak scurrying of the wind that whipped over the open expanse of moor,
driving the sleet into the faces of the rebels, drumming on the wool-coated
backs of the Hanoverians. From across the expanse of rain-slashed heather
and bog came the ranting wail of the pipes, the long lines of saffron and
plaid, muskets, Lochaber axes, the glint of uncertain light on drawn steel.

For both armies this was the time of waiting, of taut nerves and dry-
mouthed fears, before the wild exhilaration of battle takes over from rational
terror and red mist leads the way. Cumberland, mindful of this dangerous
emptiness, rode along the ranks of his arms, exhorting them to do their
duty. His speech was much elaborated by subsequent press reports, transformed into the wonderful, uplifting prose that those with greater ease and
less apprehension of immediate need might care to apply.

In reality few commanders soar to such Shakespearean heights, their
addresses short and pithy, couched in terms the soldiers, most of whom
would be unlettered, might readily understand. Essentially the message is
always the same: one, stand firm; two, kill the enemy. Whatever the content
of their general's exhortation, the men responded with a loud cheer and
the oft repeated refrain of 'Flanders, Flanders'. The men who had fought
with some costly resolution against the pride and potency of France's finest
would not now dissolve against a parcel of savages.

Having passed along the line the Duke and his staff took position
between the front and second lines, on the right just behind the Royals.
The Commander-in-Chief's aides made a glittering show, their uniforms
tailored and impeccable, the very image of the military artist's dramatic
vision. Invariably young men of rank and breeding; they included Joseph
Yorke, whose correspondence has been quoted from and whose father
was the Earl of Hardwicke, George Keppel, Lord Bury, Albemarle's son
and heir and Charles, Baron Cathcart. None of these was older than their
commander, several some years his junior, yet nearly all had seen action
at Dettingen or Fontenoy. Cathcart wore a suitably dramatic eye patch to

cover a facial injury which afforded him a buccaneering swagger. It is said, as John Prebble relates, that Lord Bury's accoutrement was splendid enough for a Prince, and a dissembling Highlander who had offered to surrender, thinking that this was the Duke of Cumberland, seized a musket and let fly. He missed and was instantly dispatched. Lord Bury, of course, did not permit so close a shave to disrupt his sang-froid.

The stage was now set. Across from the royal army the rebel lines were showing no sign of offensive movement. The skirl of the pipes did not falter, the men of the clan regiments standing or shuffling in knots and eddies, not a distinct line as such, a stark contrast to the well-dressed lines of scarlet opposite. Even to the most optimistic of the Jacobites, the ponderous and methodical advance of the Hanoverian army must have seemed heavy with intent.

This was not the untried, raw and unsupported army of Prestonpans, not the ill-deployed and unready force from Falkirk. This was a well-led, pro-fessional army of horse, foot and guns, against which the rebels, low on numbers, tired, hungry, ragged and soaking, ill-furnished with ordnance and cavalry, must now fight in open field. It is further said that Murray, whilst speaking to Lochiel and looking over at the strength of Cumberland's army, muttered: 'We are putting an end to a bad business.'

The Duke had little regard for Highlanders, a contempt he extended to those serving under him, whom he considered as fit for little more than guarding the baggage. These comprised three companies of the Argyll Militia[21] and a further company of Loudon's under Colin Campbell of Ballimore. The notion that they should be relegated to despised onlook-ers whilst there were scores to settle and glory to be won did not appeal. Ballimore, as a regular officer, took command and, as previously mentioned, his Highlanders had kept pace with the government cavalry on the left. Scouting the high wall of the Culwhiniac enclosure they were able to report that the obstacle was impassable to mounted troops.

Once the Campbells had advised General Bland of the nature of this man-made obstacle he simply ordered them to unmake it, to pull down a sufficient length to permit the cavalry to pass. The general was surprised to find the enclosure within apparently deserted, and immediately perceived that this created an opportunity to ride around the rebels' flank and fall upon them from the rear. The fact was that the horse had been posted on the left as there appeared to be no firm ground elsewhere, but here was an opportunity for a significant tactical gambit.

James Wolfe, no admirer of Hawley, was serving as the general's aide-de-camp and he and his commander were invited to survey the enclosure and consider the possibilities. The ageing martinet responded with firmness and decision, sending the swift-footed Highlanders across the open interior to create a similar breach in the far wall.[22] If the horse could successfully outflank the Jacobite right wing, not only would this assist mightily in procuring their defeat but it would ensure that the cavalry were best placed to exploit a rout and wreak havoc amongst the fugitives.

This activity did not, however, pass unnoticed. The possibility that the park walls might be successfully breached was one that had worried several Jacobite officers. As Murray was over on the left, discussing matters with Perth, Lochiel sent an urgent warning that the risk of the right being outflanked was imminent. According to an eyewitness, John Cameron, Lord George asked O'Sullivan, John Roy Stewart and Colonel Ker to investigate. The former apparently opined that few if any cavalry could get through and behind Murray's brigade by this means. Lord George remained unconvinced; clearly his views on the Irishman's capacities had not changed. O'Sullivan recounts that:

> The enemy appeared plainly in battle array, upon two lignes, and in very good order, as they were near the river side Ld George thought they were coming to take him in flank 'Never fear yt My Ld' says Sullivan 'They cant come between yu & the river, unless they break down the walls of those two parks yt are between yu & them, but yu can prevent them, but as I am sure they will not, & yt certainly their left will be against this park where yr right is. My advise wou'd be, as all their horse is on their left, yt, yt we shou'd make a breach in this wall, & set in this park Stonywood & the other Regimt yt is in Colloum behind yu, who will take their horse in flank, without fearing in the least yt they can come upon him. If the horse is taken in flanck, with such a wall as this between them, & those yt fires on 'em Il answer they'd break. If they are once broak, the foot will not stand, besides my Ld, if yu march to the enemy, as yu have no other party to take, for I suppose yu don't pretend to measure yr fire with English troops; in case yu are repulsed those same troops yt you'l set in the park will protect yr retrait.[23]

Sullivan was in fact correct in his analysis. Despite the fact that the government cavalry were able to pass through both sets of walls, their overall advantage was limited, hemmed in by the slope toward the river. The only available line of advance was following the line of the wall of the upper, or more northerly, of the two enclosures. The two weak battalions of Stonywood and Gordon of Avochie would, it seemed, be sufficient to counter the threat. No move was made to occupy the enclosure itself as O'Sullivan had earlier recommended; rather, the Stonywood and Gordon's foot were posted along a hollow way that followed the course of the stream running from south-west of Culchunaig, blocking an approach from that quarter.

It is possible that Lord George was reluctant to place men within the enclosure, as it would effectively remove them from what could well become a fast-changing tactical situation. Regardless of the reasoning, the government horse, their passage facilitated by the Campbells, were able to traverse the enclosure unmolested. The cavalry, however, now had to find a way to come upon their enemies if they were to be of service. The area of ground between the ditch that ran due southwards from Culchunaig toward the river was insufficient to allow the squadrons to deploy fully. This obliged Hawley to continue riding in a westerly direction to attempt a deployment along the line of the hollow which ran to the rear of the steading.[24]

This wide flanking movement from the cavalry considerably extended the potential threat to the Jacobite right: the deployment, once completed, would mean that Hawley's squadrons could simply roll up the line. Stonywood's and Avochie's battalions were ordered to conform and face toward the dragoons' line of advance. Murray also took the added precaution of ordering across Ogilvie's two additional battalions, to stiffen the ad hoc defensive line he was forming.

Hawley now made a cardinal error by leaving Ballimore's fleet Highlanders within the enclosure. Quite why is uncertain, whether he was so contemptuous he felt he had no further need or whether he felt the necessity of having his flank secured. Ballimore was, as he had demonstrated, both energetic and capable, and he was not simply content to assume a spectator role. It is again questionable if an offensive role was intended or whether he took it upon himself to engage. In recalling the situation, Duncan Campbell, commanding one of the militia companies, clearly states that the Campbells were ordered into the attack.

It seems likely that a brisk exchange of fire now occurred between the Campbells, using the remains of the park wall as cover, and the Jacobite right flank. Campbell of Airds states that the combat was between them and the men of the Royal Ecossois. Casualties in this encounter were light;

the Campbells lost barely half a dozen men, though Ballimore himself was amongst the slain. As the rattle of musketry flared on their right the dragoons were trotting northwards and deploying into two lines to face the Jacobite foot, lining the ground ahead. Murray had further reinforced his screen by sending up Elcho's Life Guards and Fitzjames's Horse. It would appear likely that the line comprised, from left to right, Stonywood's and Avochie's foot, the Jacobite horse and, on the right, Ogilvy's foot.

Without supporting infantry of their own it would be virtually impossible for Hawley and Bland to force a crossing. Although the shallow ravine was not a major obstacle, nor were the waters deep, the ascent was steep and uncertain, not to be attempted from a cold start under fire from infantry lining the opposing crest. The two generals must have made an odd pair – Hawley, the foul-mouthed old martinet, detested by friend and foe alike, and Bland, the leading military theorist in the army!

James Wolfe, who is likely to have been present, found little to admire in his superior's conduct that day. He had no time for Hawley at best, and writing next day to a friend, Major Henry Delabene, he observed that his commander made no effort to engage until the crescendo of firing, about to erupt over the rest of the field, had slackened and, presumably, the government victory assured. If nothing else, however, Hawley and Bland kept a fair proportion of the rebel forces tied down before them. Wolfe, with the priggishness of intellectual assurance, also wrote somewhat cynically to his father five years later:

> I have surveyed the field of Culloden with great exactness, and find room for a military criticism... The actors shine in the world too high and bright to be eclipsed; but it is plain they don't borrow much of their glory from their performance on that occasion... You would not have left those ruffians the only possible means of conquest, nor suffer multitudes to go off unhurt with the power to destroy.[25]

One of the anomalies of the battle, now about to erupt in earnest, is that there is some doubt as to exactly when it took place. Some who were present put it as early as noon, other half an hour later and yet others not until one. Wolfe, whom we may consider a very precise young man, felt it to have been around one o'clock. Across the moor, the Jacobite Sir Robert Strange felt that this was the time when the first shot was fired in earnest. It is generally agreed that the immediate target which inspired the rebel gunners to begin was the gorgeously attired Lord Bury, who had ridden forward to investigate what was taken to be additional Jacobite guns standing in the Leanach enclosure.

John Finlayson, an amateur artillerist and otherwise cartographer from Edinburgh, was in charge of the piece Lord Bury was intent on investigating and greeted the peer with its discharge. This initial crash produced a ragged cannonade from the generally ill-served Jacobite guns. These were not, however, entirely ineffective. The shot fell amongst the government foot and caused some casualties, a man killed here and there, others injured. Bligh's was badly hit – four men died and another sixteen were wounded, some of whom undoubtedly succumbed later to their injuries.

Belford's guns were not long in replying. Gunnery was not an art, very much a science, the gunner a man apart from his fellow officers. Artillery had yet to achieve dominance on the battlefield – that would be delayed until the advent of the quick-firer, prior to 1914. Frederick the Great had not yet instituted the overhaul of the artillery arm which would follow from his costly encounters with the Austrians, leading exponents of field artillery tactics. The three-pounder guns that Belford deployed were smaller pieces, but being less heavy they were easier to move over the hostile terrain. Moving the guns was a major feat of expertise, persistence and sweat and the batteries carried with them all the tools and impedimenta of their fearsome trade.

The matrosses would generally construct a basic emplacement from fascines they carried with them, to offer at least some protection from counter-battery fire and sharpshooters. The barrel of a three-pounder was around a metre or so in length, the mouth secured for transit by a wooden plug or tompion. Loading the piece required a pound and a half of black powder, which was fed into the barrel and rammed home. (The barrel would be sponged out between firings to eliminate any burning residue that could prematurely explode the new charge.) The ball was rolled down and wadded, a fine grade powder used to prime the touch hole, and the weapon, when discharged, would be touched off by the master gunner using a linstock.[26]

It was necessary to sight the gun after each round as the fixed wooden trails would kick back viciously on the report, the recoil worsening as the barrel grew progressively fouled. Guns were sighted using a carpenter's square inserted into the bore. The crack of detonation was ear-splitting, even from these smaller guns; gunners and matrosses would turn away, fingers in ears, mouths agape, to lessen the concussion which jolted the brain like a hammer blow. A man could easily be deafened by the hideous bark of these monsters, their roar accompanied by a pall of filthy, sulphurous smoke.

At Culloden the range was close enough to minimise the need for careful calculation, and the ten guns in the Hanoverian line spewed death with deadly proficiently. As previously noted, the gunner aims to cause his ball to bounce or 'graze' before striking the target to cause the most potent destruction. The shot will eviscerate, decapitate or otherwise mutilate not just the first man it strikes but several behind him. Even the steadiest of regular troops, standing helpless under such fire, will quail. Quoting from a later battle, the field of Waterloo, where Wellington's regulars had to endure the constant horror of bombardment, it is possible to appreciate just how horrible the experience must be:

> We had three companies almost shot to pieces, one shot killed and wounded twenty-five of the 4th Company, another of the same killed poor Fisher, my captain, and eighteen of our company… and another took the 8th and killed or wounded twenty-three… At the same time poor Fisher was hit, I was speaking to him, and I got all over his brains, his head was blown to atoms.[27]

For Highlanders, this was not war – their tactic was to charge, to close, to settle the business with hand strokes, not simply to stand and be shot at. Most of those who stood on the moor would have seen little real combat before the outbreak of the rebellion, and until now they had not faced cannon. Such a test would have been severe for seasoned regulars. Seeing a man cut down by the swing of a broadsword, his bright life's blood arcing over the heather was one thing, terrible in its way, but this impotent shrieking death was infinitely worse. If a man fell in the charge then his clansmen would bear his lifeless form back to the glens and the bards would weave his deeds that day into the stuff of legend.

But the guns killed from a distance, the shot bouncing on the springy turf and heather, smashing home into the ranks and files, scattering men like bloodied manikins. It was a ghastly death, men shredded, their entrails spilling, warm and stinking, blood and ordure mixing, the smell of horror to accompany the sights. No one in the Jacobite ranks had experienced this, had had to stand in the cold driving sleet and watch as the enemy gunners sponged and loaded, wadded and aimed. None had watched the great rippling sheets of flame as the guns bellowed, seen the balls come skipping over the heather, seeming almost innocuous as though a man might thrust out his foot and stop one like a cricket ball. This would have been very unwise indeed, to lose the foot.

Exactly for how long the clans were subjected to this regular, murderous fire is uncertain. Some reports suggested as long as half an hour, Wolfe thought perhaps fifteen minutes, though Campbell of Airds estimated no longer than nine and, in this, he is most probably correct. It would also be fair to assert that the real impact of the guns was more psychological than punitive. With the two sides separated on the government left by say 500 paces, and perhaps half as far again on the right, the guns were at maximum range. In the circumstance the rate of fire probably did not exceed one round per minute and the wet ground would soak up a number of these, while the uphill trajectory added to the gunners' burden and probably no more than half the shots struck home. Even if the fire continued for a full fifteen minutes, this leaves no more than between seventy and eighty balls finding their mark. Smoke also obscured the gunner's aim, with a tail wind blowing the residue across the field to spoil the aim.

There is evidence from the rebel side that many balls went overhead, and therefore we may speculate that the guns hit say two men with each of seventy or so rounds of whom perhaps a third were killed, a total of around 150 casualties. In tactical terms the number was not significant, but the overall effect upon the clansmen cannot be overestimated. For, when a man fell wounded and maimed, several of his comrades and kin would rush to his aid to try and stop the blood loss from a severed limb. Observers from the government side recalled how the whole mass of the clans seemed to be heaving, shifting under the weight of the bombardment, like a giant beast in torment, in a rage of frustration at their impotence.

After perhaps a couple of ragged volleys the rebel guns had fallen silent. Most of the amateur gunners, overawed by the weight of the government response, seem simply to have fled, abandoning their pieces which played no further part in the fight. At some point balls began to fall amongst the Prince and his staff. Sir Robert Strange noted the effect:

> One Austin, a very worthy, pleasant fellow, stood on my left; he rode a fine mare which he was accustomed to call his lady. He perceived her give a sudden shriek, and, on looking around him called out 'Alas, I have lost my lady!' One of her hind legs was shot and hanging by the skin. He had instantly dismounted and endeavouring to push her out of the ranks, she came to the

ground. He took his gun and pistols out of the holsters, stepped forward, joined the Foot but was never more heard of.[28]

One of the Prince's servants, Thomas Ca, was cut down by the flying round shot and Charles was exhorted to shift to the right with Fitzjames's Horse. As he turned a shot gouged the ground beside him, showering dirt. His Royal Highness was uninjured, though his own mount was less fortunate. 'I was riding to the right wing,' he later recalled,

> my horse began to kick, at which I was much surprised, being very quiet and peaceable formerly, and looking narrowly to him to see what was the matter with him I observed blood gushing out of his side. 'Oh, oh!' says I, speaking of the horse, 'if this is the story with you, you have no less reason to be uneasy.' Whereupon I was obliged to dismount and take another.[29]

Whatever the Prince was doing he did not appear to be exercising any direction over his army. The Hanoverian guns were playing upon his front line at will, and the only apparent course was for the Highlanders to charge as quickly as possible before their numbers were further reduced and their morale utterly destroyed. For the moment the Duke of Cumberland need do nothing; his gunners were performing admirably on his behalf, winnowing the enemy ranks at no cost to his army. Johnstone, standing with his friend Scothouse, was unimpressed.

> He [the Prince] saw that his orders [the movement of troops into the Culwhiniac enclosure] were carried out, but yet he never quitted his place on the eminence. This was a critical moment when he ought to have displayed the courage of a grenadier, by immediately advancing to put himself at the head of his army, and by commanding himself those manoeuvres which he wished to be executed. He would never have experienced disobedience on the part of his subjects who had exposed their lives and fortunes to establish him on the throne of his ancestors, and would have shed for him the last drop of their blood. There are occasions when a general ought to expose his person, and not remain beyond the reach of musketry, and surely there was never a more pressing occasion for disregarding a few shots than the one in question, as the gain or loss of the battle depended on it. In the desperate expedition on which he had entered, though it was proper that he should guard against danger, he ought to have done so in a manner which showed

that life or death was equally indifferent to him, conducting himself with valour and prudence, according to circumstances. But he was surrounded by Irish confidants, whose baseness of soul corresponded to the obscurity of their birth. The natives of Ireland are generally supposed, in England, to have a great confusion of ideas, and they are in general very bad counsellors. But the Prince blindly adopted their opinions.[30]

If the Jacobite army was to survive, the clans had to move forward to contact as soon as possible. It appears that Charles had already given the orders and on two occasions. In the first instance Murray refused to go forward, on the perfectly reasonable grounds that insufficient numbers of men had at that point mustered. Some time later, after the cannonade had begun, the Prince sent young Lachlan MacLachlan to convey the order but he was cut down, decapitated by round shot before accomplishing his mission. It was Colonel Ker who finally received confirmation of the order and duly rode along the line, starting on the left with Perth, then cantering along toward the left to give the order to Lord George.

With a great and sudden surge, the charge was underway, the clansmen leaping forward, an iridescent steel tipped avalanche – 'like hungry wolves'. The last charge of the Highland clans, the rain-lashed air rent with the rant of the pipes the howls of the Highlanders, the flash of steel. And it was with steel that they came; the horror of the cannonade had destroyed the more disciplined form of advance, and many just threw down their firearms and pelted toward the government lines. Joseph Yorke, he of the casual contempt for this savage foe, watched them come on:

> When our cannon had fired about two rounds, I could plainly perceive that the rebels fluctuated extremely, and could not remain long in the position they were then in without running away or coming down upon us; and according as I thought, in two or three minutes they broke from the centre in three large bodies, like wedges, and moved forward. At first they made a feint, as if they would come down upon our right, but seeing that wing so well covered, and imagining that they might surround the left because they saw no cavalry to cover it, two of those wedges bore down immediately upon Barrell's and Monroes regiments, which formed the left of the first line; and after firing very irregularly at a considerable distance, they rushed furiously in upon them, thinking to carry all before them, as they had done on former occasions.

Clearly some of the Highlanders did retain their firelocks and, certainly until they had let fly their single volley, they would likely have remained more or less in formation, but, thereafter they would begin to lose some cohesion, forming irregular blocks and wedges. These shifts were organic rather than in any sense tactical. Johnstone was one of those who closed in for the attack:

> As far as I could distinguish, at the distance of twenty paces, the English appeared to be drawn up in six ranks, the three first being on their knees, and keeping up a terrible running fire on us.[31]

As the swirling knots of clansmen closed to within 300 paces the gunners shifted from ball to canister. In the time it would take a fleet-footed Highlander to cover that distance – less than two minutes, even on such wet ground – a good artilleryman could fire off three or four rounds of shot. Canister, which operates like a giant shotgun cartridge, would deluge the leading ranks in a hail of lead, scything down any within its deadly arc. A single discharge could account for half a dozen to a dozen men. A Hanoverian volunteer with Bligh's recalled how, despite the press of attackers, the shot mowed a line clear through from front to rear, dropping men like skittles.

This was not tidy killing. The shot, being lead, would flatten in the air and strike bone and tissue with awful force, joints would be smashed and torn away, limbs half-severed, with gaping entry wounds in flesh and muscle. Charging men plucked at random into oblivion, their blood and tissue spurting liberally over the sodden ground. Most wounds to the head would be almost instantly fatal; sucking chest wounds and intestinal injuries mostly so, but far less quickly. A man might last for hours or even days with his entrails laid before him like a butcher's anatomy class. The wounded would writhe shrieking on the heather, clutching at spurting stumps, a thickening carpet of dead, maimed and dying.

When represented in a neat diagram, battles appear both relatively straightforward and orderly. The reality is completely different, an anarchy of movement, noise and utter confusion. Each man sees only that which immediately faces him, the red mist clouds his vision, the noise hammers at his senses. If the government artillery fired three rounds in the time it took the Highlanders to cover that dreadful gap, and if each round accounted for six men, then the clans would have lost at least 180 men, dead and wounded; in fact it was probably more, 200 at the very least. At this point the government had suffered no casualties, apart from those Campbells who had fallen in the exchange of fire on the rebel right.

At fifty paces the infantry would commence firing. The Long Land Pattern Brown Bess was a cumbersome beast, particularly so with the eighteen-inch fluted bayonet fixed. To prepare, the infantryman would, with wet, cold fingers, take out a paper cartridge and bite off the end, dribbling a thumbnail of powder into the pan of his weapon. The pan was covered by the hinged frizzen against which the flint, held in the jaws of the cock, would strike. He then poured the remaining powder down the barrel, wadded the paper and rammed the whole down with his wooden ramrod or scouring stick. The cock was pulled back to the halfway or safety position awaiting the order to fire. When he pulled the trigger the cock was released, the flint striking the frizzen, flinging it back, at once exposing the pan and showering the powder with sparks. These ignited and the flame leapt through the touch-hole to set off the main charge.

The report was loud, the recoil fierce. As with his illustrious comrades in the artillery the wind would whip the foul cloud toward the enemy, immediately obscuring his view. He might fire two rounds a minute, the kick worsening with every shot as residue fouled the heated barrel, his face blackened, mouth parched by the gritty black powder. The lead shot would have a similar effect to canister, flattening to create a gaping, funnel-shaped wound. If tissue damage and blood loss did not finish the job, the shock and later septicaemia could be expected to oblige. The prospects for a wounded man were poor indeed, especially if he was deemed a rebel and a traitor, undeserving of clemency.

It was not yet 1.30 p.m.

As the hail of grape flensed the Jacobite lines, the casualties were particularly high amongst officers, who in keeping with clan and regimental tradition led from the front. Clan Chattan appear to have charged first, with the Athollmen and Camerons pelting after. As the guns banged, each thunderclap a harbinger of death, the clansmen surged on, the swords raised high, targets held across the upper body to give some scant protection. They would at this point be able to see very little of their foes, the government lines obscured by the dense pall of smoke. John Prebble recounts how John Grant, who charged with Clan Chattan, would in later years recall how he went forward with Colonel Anne's Mackintoshes. His first glimpse was of a line of white gaiters on the claves of Cumberland's men with their neat rows of black buttons.

Topography now also came to the aid of Belford's gunners. Clan Chattan, almost at the point when the ordnance swapped to canister, became enmired, in a particularly wet stretch of moorland. This, coupled with the first murderous blast of grape, seems to have caused their axis of advance to shift markedly to the right, occurring just as they encountered the moor road. In so doing they literally collided with Murray's Athollmen, who were themselves echeloning to the left to avoid the obstacle posed by the Leanach enclosure. A gap thus opened between the Jacobite centre and left whilst the right was swift becoming a vast confusion.

Now presenting a dense, disorganised column, the centre/right presented the guns with an almost perfect target, enabling the sweating artillerymen to pour in several additional volleys, inflicting substantial casualties. Flayed by grape, the column was assailed from fifty paces by the musketry of Barrell's, Monro's and Campbell's Scots Fusiliers. A survivor from Monro's recalled the opening volleys of musketry:

> …they began to play their Cannon very briskly upon us; but as soon as we saw them pointed, we stoop'd down, and the Balls flew over our Heads. Two pieces of our Cannon play'd from our Left to their Right, which kill'd many of them and made their whole body determine to come down upon our Left, compos'd of Barrell's, Monro's and the Scots Fusiliers. When we saw them coming towards us in great Haste and Fury, we fired at about 50 Yards Distance, which made Hundreds Fall, notwithstanding which, they were so numerous, that they still advanced, and were almost upon us, before we had loaden again. We immediately gave them another full fire…[32]

Hawley was quite right when he described the swift onrush of the Highlanders confounding the regular, stately platoon volleys through sheer speed. The government left had discharged only two volleys, the second at point blank range. Both, given the mass of targets, will have taken effect, and the kill ratio may well have exceeded the period norm of one round in ten finding its mark. Clan Chattan were in fact pelting across the government front line, so that the weight of theirs and the Athollmen's charge fell upon Barrell's veterans on the extreme left.

Now it was time for the bayonet. Barrell's had stood firm at Falkirk and they did so again now:

There was scarce a soldier or officer of Barrel's and that part of Monroe's which engaged, who did not kill one or two men each with their bayonets and spontoons.[33]

A correspondent confirmed that:

...General Barrell's regiment gained the greatest reputation imaginable in the late engagement; the best of the clans having made their strongest efforts to break them, but without effect, for the old Tangerines bravely repulsed those boasters, with a dreadful slaughter, and convinced them that the broad sword and target is unequal to the musket and bayonet, when in the hands of veterans, who are determined to use them – After the battle there was not a bayonet in this regiment but was either bloody or bent.[34]

The new bayonet drill which Cumberland had adopted clearly proved its worth:

The alteration was mightily little, but of the last consequence. Before this, the bayonet man attacked the sword man right fronting him: now the left hand bayonet attacked the sword fronting his next right hand man. He was then covered by the enemy's shield where open on his left, and the enemy's right open to him. This manner made an essential difference, staggered the enemy, who were not prepared to alter their way of fighting, and destroyed them in a manner rather to be conceived than told. When the rebels made some impression on Barrel's regiment its giving ground proved fatal to Lord Robert Ker; who not observing his men's giving back, remained a few yards alone. He had struck his pike into the body of a Highland officer; but before he could disengage himself, was surrounded, and cut to pieces.[35]

Here, then was the crisis of the battle. If the massed confusion of Jacobites could rout Barrell's and destroy the government left as they had done before, then they might yet, despite the savage pounding they had taken, roll up the Duke's line and win a pyrrhic victory. This was warfare at its most basic, a Homeric contest of steel on steel, musket and bayonet against sword and target. A sweating, heaving, slashing, stabbing melee of primeval fury. No description or image, however vivid, can truly convey the horror and intensity of the contest. Highlanders slashed with broadswords aiming to inflict a killing cut to the neck, and some blows certainly struck home, inflicting a massive trauma, great geysers of bright arterial blood spurting. The redcoats lunged as they had been taught, the wicked sharp points driving into the exposed ribs or underarm of their opponents, a deep, potentially fatal stabbing.

A man wounded in this way would fall quite soon, shock, blood loss and tissue damage combining to bring him down. As he fell his opponent would likely strike down again either with the point or the butt of the clubbed musket, the brass plate smashing down like a heavy club. A wounded man at your feet is still dangerous, he must be rendered incapable as quickly as possible with a frenzied thrusting of the bayonet driving repeatedly into the torso, spraying blood, or clubbing the skull, spilling brain and shattered bone.

Joseph Yorke described the action:

> However, they [the clansmen] found themselves grossly mistaken; for though by the violence of the shock Barrell's regiment was alittle staggered, yet Major General Huske (who commanded the second line), perceiving where the weight was felt, rode up to the regiment, and bidding the men push home with their bayonets, was so weel obeyed by these brave fellows, that hundreds perished on their points. At the same instant the rebels who came around the left of Barrell's and in the pell-mell broke through the line, met their fate from the fire of Wolfe's and Ligonier's on the left of the second line. The broad-swords succeeding so ill, the rebels turned their backs, and in flying were so well received by the cavalry under Hawley and Bland, who had broke down two dry stone walls, and unperceived had gained their rear, that a general rout and slaughter ensured among them... in the meantime, that wedge which was designed to fall on our right, after making three feints, as if they were coming down upon us, in order to draw away our fire, seeing that the right kept shouldered with the greatest coolness, and the three squadrons were moving towards their flank, followed the example of their right wing and fled for it. Immediately the horse were in amongst 'em and the lines of foot advanced with shouts of victory and with the regularity of well disciplined troops.[36]

Clan Chattan began the battle with twenty-one officers in the first rank; only three returned from the charge. Some, like Gillies MacBean, hacked a bloody swathe through Barrell's and burst through to the second line where he was dispatched by the eager bayonets of the second line. Before falling he had already sustained several bayonet wounds, slashed across the forehead by an infantry hanger, and with his thigh already mangled by grape.

John MacGillivray is said to have hacked down a dozen redcoats before also falling against the second line. MacGillivray of Dunmaglass was another who slashed a frenzied path through the front line, sustaining multiple wounds; he finally crawled toward a spring in the rear where he finally succumbed. Fraser of Inverallochy was also killed. These and so many others died shrieking beneath the merciless bayonets, writhing on the bloodied heather, choking in their own blood.

Barrell's lost not only Lord Ker but suffered sixteen fatalities and over a hundred wounded; a number of these would inevitably die of their hurts. The broadswords would have lopped off limbs and inflicted dreadful slashing wounds, great arcing cuts to heads and upper torsos. Lieutenant-Colonel Robert Rich was amongst these, he lost a hand and suffered a number of cuts to the head as he bravely struggled to save the colours. We know that several of the wounded received pensions for disabling injuries sustained; thus Isaac Midgely, a native of Halifax, lost the use of his left hand and suffered an additional fourteen wounds in the fight.[37]

The great mass of clansmen seemed to engulf the struggling redcoats, swirling around the flanks of the regiment to hack down Sergeant Bristo's pair of guns, killing him and wounding several of his crew:

> Making a dreadful huzza, and even crying 'Run, ye dogs!', they broke in between the grenadiers of Barrel and Monro; but these had given their fire according to the general direction, and then parried them with their screwed bayonets. The two cannon on that division were so well served, that when within two yards of them they received a full discharge of cartridge shot, which made a dreadful havoc; and those who crowded into the opening received a full fire from the centre of Bligh's regiment, which still increased the number of the slain. However, such as survived possessed themselves of the cannon, and attacked the regiments sword in hand.[38]

As such eminent commentators as John Keegan have observed, most battles, from the eclipse of chivalry up to the era of industrialised warfare, were ultimately determined by infantry – by the taking and holding of ground. He who remains in possession of the field has won the day. Taking or holding the critical ground might involve both sides in fearful loss; in many of

Wellington's battles the losses of the victor were frequently almost as great as those of the loser.

Patterns of basic human behaviour are also relevant. Contact may occur at a distance, 'flight distance' or closer 'critical distance'. In the case of the former, a brave, aggressive show by the attacker might so disconcert the defenders that they break and flee. This reasoning might be applied to battles such as Prestonpans, where the savage rush of the Highlanders, coming on with the confidence and naked aggression of the victor, was sufficient to induce the enemy to run away. In short, the battle was won and lost before the first blow was struck.

At Culloden the matter came to strokes, within the 'critical' space, where the defender perceives he cannot flee and his resolution has surmounted the urge, if it arose as the foe approached. Barrell's men had withstood this critical test. Based on past performance the Highlanders may have believed it was only necessary for them to close to contact and the redcoats would rout. The whole ritual of clan warfare, the wild rant of the pipes, the hurling of insults, brandishing weapons, and the sheer confidence in the fury of the charge, was intended to move the enemy to flight before contact. In this instance the concept failed.

In the frightful melee of the contact there was simply no opportunity for flight on either side; it was an instinctive reaction that the only road to survival lay in killing your enemy before he killed you. Keegan describes the infantry clash as the 'Queen's Move' in black powder battles. At Culloden the Queen's Move was the Highland charge. Once committed the clans could not be recalled, nor was it likely, in the event of failure, that they could be reformed. The charge was essentially a 'one shot' weapon.

What we perhaps struggle to comprehend in the modern era is just how close and personal this type of warfare was. To kill a man with sword or bayonet you had practically to be touching him, to smell his sweat, see every strand of stubble, as close and intimate as a lover in the split second it took one of you to kill the other.[39]

Despite their spirited resistance, Barrell's seemed to have been pushed back, in good order, by the sheer weight of the attack, and effectively formed two wings with the Well of the Dead in between. It was now the turn of Monro's to feel the keen edge of the sword, though they, like Barrell's, stood their ground:

...the Front Rank charged their Bayonets Breast high, and the Center and Rear Ranks kept a continual Firing... the rebels designing to break or flank us; but our fire was so hot, most of us having discharged nine Shot each, that they were disappointed.[40]

It is from an officer in this regiment that we glean a vivid account of the fighting. The account was duly published in the *Newcastle Journal*:

The Hurry I am in going to collect the number of killed and wounded, scarce allows me time to tell you, that Yesterday we had the bloodiest Battle with the Rebels that ever was fought in the Memory of Man. The same morning we marched from Nairn, and met the Gentry about Noon near Culloden, the Lord President's House, three miles from hence, where we cannonaded each other for some Time; at last the Rebels advanc'd against the Left of our Line where was Barrel's Regiment, and the late Sir Robert Monro's, now Col. De Jean's. Barrel's behaved very well, but was obliged to give Way to their Torrent that bore down upon them; Their whole force then fell upon the Left of ours where I had the Honour to command the Grenadier platoon; our Lads fought more like Devils than Men. In short we laid (to the best of my Judgement) about 1600 dead on the Spot, and finished the Affair without the Help of any other Regiment. You may judge of the Work, for I had 18 men killed and wounded in my Platoon. I thank God I escaped free, but my Coat had six balls thro' it. I must now tell you, that in the midst of the Action, the Officer that led on the Camerons call'd to me to take Quarters, which I refus'd, and bid the rebel Scoundrel advance, he did and fir'd at me; but providentially miss'd his Mark; I then shot him dead, and took his Pistol and Dirk, which are extremely neat.

The French have all surrendered Prisoners of War: We have taken their Cannon and Baggage; Lords Kilmarnock and Cromarty are among the Prisoners of Distinction. Our Regiment had ample Revenge for the Loss of our late Colonel, Sir Robert, and the rest of our Officers, whom the Scoundrels murdered in cold blood, but (as I told Lord Kilmarnock) we had ample Revenge in hors. For I can with great Truth asure you, not one that attack'd us escaped alive, for we gave no Quarters nor would accept any. Our Regiment took three Stand of colours. Our wounded are Capt. Kinnier and Lieuts. Lord and King, and Ensign Dally kill'd. I now give you Joy of the Day; and be assur'd never was a more compleat Victory gained – Our Gaols are full of them and they are brought in by Hundreds.[41]

Contrary to certain accounts, Wolfe's regiment were not previously deployed en potence either within or in front of the Leanach enclosure, thus able to deliver a flanking fire on the attacking clansmen as they surged past. In fact Huske, from the second line, brought Wolfe's forward as a planned counterstroke on the left flank, swinging this and Ligonier's leftwards whilst also moving up Sempill's and Bligh's. James Wolfe, writing after the battle to his father, clearly refers to the regiment moving forward after the deluge struck Barrell's, and even though the young hero was posted elsewhere on the field he would take pains to ascertain his facts correctly. This general move served to consolidate the position. Even had the Jacobites completely overrun Barrell's and Monro's, this powerful deployment would have held the line; the attack simply had nowhere now to go.

Captain-Lieutenant Thomas Ashe Lee of Wolfe's confirms James Wolfe's understanding:

> Poor Barrell's regiment were sorely pressed by those desperadoes and outflanked. One stand of their coloours was taken; Collonel Riches hand cutt off in their defence… We marched up to the enemy, and our left, outflanking them, wheeled in upon them; the whole then gave them 5 or 6 fires with vast execution, while their front had nothing left to oppose us, but their pistols and broadswords; and fire from their center and rear, (as, by this time they were 20 or 30 deep,) was vastly more fatal to themselves, than us.[42]

These second-line regiments did sustain some casualties, never rising into double figures, but nothing compared to the crippling losses being sustained by the rebels. It may be that those who swept forward to swap strokes with Barrell's were the better armed; others of the commons may have hung back, not engaging, yet neither were they prepared to flee, rather they were simply shot down where they stood, their only reply to the redcoats' fire being to try and prise up stones and fling them at the line. Cumberland refers to this in his subsequent reportage as if no further proof of the rebels' base savagery need be observed.[43]

Lochiel was down, his ankles both smashed by canister. Lachlan MacLachlan, whose son, the Prince's aid, had already fallen, died in the charge long before he reached the government lines, and many of his name fell around him. MacLean of Drimmin, seeing Clan Chattan by now giving way, but hearing that at least one of his sons was already dead, resisted the exhortations of another to flee and ran on to his own certain death.[44] The Chisholms had already lost their colonel, Roderick Og, at first wounded, then finished off by round shot. What remained went forward to be winnowed by fire from, amongst others, the Royal Scots, where the two older sons stood under Hanoverian colours.

Lord George Murray was in the thick of the action, urging on his Athollmen, now hopelessly bunched with those who had drifted from the centre. His skittish horse bolted and carried its rider (now doubt cursing roundly) through the waiting bayonets and almost to the government rear. Amazingly, Murray, bereft of hat and wig, his sword broken and his coat slashed, passed through unscathed. Finally thrown by his panicked mount, he managed to regain the heaving mass of the Jacobite column. Help was obviously and urgently needed so he ran back toward the second line to bring forward such reinforcements as could be found. There would be only three units available, the Royal Ecossois, Kilmarnock's Footguards and the Irish Picquets. These did at least begin to advance and fire a volley but it was already, as Murray observed, too late – 'all was lost'.

Johnstone, standing with his friend Scothouse on the left, was a witness, albeit at a distance, to events on the Jacobite right:

> From the inequality of this marshy ground, our right and centre came first up with the enemy, our first line advancing a little obliquely; but, overpowered by a murderous fire in front and flank, our right could not maintain its ground and was obliged to give way, whilst our centre had already broken the enemy's first line and attacked the centre.[45]

Johnstone did not share the MacDonalds' concern that their flanks were insufficiently protected against cavalry, believing the morass achieved the purpose and besides O'Sullivan had brought up Perth's and Glenbucket's to shield the extreme left and repair the gaps left in the line by Lord George's 'changement'. Despite these reassuring factors the Jacobite left moved forward with far less panache than the centre and right and never came to contact. Johnstone states that the prime reason for this was the precipitate flight of the right, which developed before the MacDonalds could close with the government right:

> If our right could only have maintained its ground three minutes longer, the English army, which was very much shaken, would have been still more so by the shock of our left wing, which was yet at the distance of fifteen to twenty paces from the enemy, when the disorder began on the right…[46]

The left faltered and O'Sullivan, who places himself in the front line, recounts how Perth seized the colours of Clanranald and exhorted them by his brave example to fall on. He yelled that he would call himself a MacDonald thereafter, if they would but follow. The regiments moved forward but still refused to close. Cumberland himself later wrote that he had feared the greatest blow would fall upon his right, and he had taken station there accordingly:

> They began firing their cannon, which was extremely ill-served and ill-pointed. Ours immediately answered them which began their confusion. They then came running on in their wild manner & upon the right where I had placed Myself, imagining the greatest Push would be there, they came down three several Times within a Hundred Yards of our Men, firing their pistols and brandishing their Swords, but the Royals and Pulteneys hardly took their Firelocks from their shoulders, so that after those feint attempts they made off; and the little squadrons on our right were sent to pursue them. General Hawley had by the help of our Highlanders beat down two little stone walls, and came in upon the right flank of their second line.
>
> As their whole first line came down to attack at once, their right somewhat outflanked Barrel's regiment, which was our left, and the greatest part of the little loss we had was there, but Bligh's and Sempill's giving a fire upon those who had outflanked Barrell's soon repulsed them, and Barrel's regiment and the left of Monroe's fairly beat them with their bayonets; and I dare say there was neither soldiers nor officers of Barrell's and that part of Monroe's which engaged, who did not kill one or two men with their bayonets and spontoons, and they so fairly drove them back, that in their rage that they could not make any impression upon the battalions, they threw stones at them for at least a minute or two, before their total rout began.[47]

Many fell including Johnstone's friend Scothouse. Even had the Jacobite morale on the left been higher, the wet morass would have fatally hampered the advance. The MacDonalds were willing enough, but the deadly combination of ground and enemy fire was too much.

Keppoch was dead; he had been struck in the arm by a blast of canister that had scythed through the ranks of his regiment, killing his brother Donald, the same blast that also felled poor Scothouse. Despite his wound he made no attempt to quit the field. One of his clansmen, MacDonald of Kilchonat, tried to carry him to the rear but the old man was hit again, this time in the back, and left for dead. Despite his injuries the chief was still breathing and was eventually found by his son Angus Ban. He was carried to a bothy close by, though by now Keppoch was beyond help. The tiny space was crowded with badly wounded MacDonalds, a group of ragged scavengers lurking beside. It would soon be time for the crows to feed.

Clanranald was also wounded, the clan regiments decimated by the murderous fire. When it was seen that the right wing was disintegrating, the MacDonalds too began to run. 'What a spectacle of horror', wrote Johnstone:

> The same Highlanders, who had advanced to the charge like lions, with bold, determined countenances, were in an instant seen flying like trembling cowards in the greatest disorder. It may be said of the attack of the Highlanders, that it bears great resemblance to that of the French; that it is a flame, the violence of which is more to be dreaded than the duration.[48]

An NCO from Howard's was sufficiently impressed to write to his spouse: 'The Rebels, I must own, behaved with the greatest resolution.'[49] But for the army of the White Cockade, it was defeat.

13

DEFEAT – THE ROUT OF THE JACOBITE ARMY

EARLY TO MID-AFTERNOON, 16 APRIL, 2 P.M.–3 P.M.

They have not had such a thrashing since the days of Old Noll, and whatever the Jacobites may insinuate to lessen their losses; believe them not, for the country is covered with their dead bodies and arms and the gaols are full of their prisoners; what pity it is that so much resolution and bravery as our troops had that day, could not be united in the confederate arms and fall upon the grand enemy of the liberties of Europe bit I hope the time is coming when we shan't speak with him… I hope we shall soon finish this rebellion and bring their nobles in chains and their chiefs in fetters of iron.

Major Richard Webb[1]

Lord, what am I, that I should be spared when so many brave men lie dead upon this spot?

Attributed to the Duke of Cumberland

The rot usually starts from the rear. Those at the front are too hotly engaged and pushed on by the press behind. When the first trickle of fugitives begins is the time when true leaderships should come to the fore. At Culloden the Jacobite officers, Lord George Murray, Lochiel, Keppoch, had all behaved with the utmost gallantry, leading their men from the front and, with the cadre of junior officers below them, paying a fearful price. With many officers down, dead or wounded, the clansmen were deprived of leadership. The Prince and his entourage failed utterly to inspire the level of loyalty that might have facilitated a rally. As it was, the Highlanders just ran.

Men who had fought like Hectors dissolved in panicked rout. The surging tide of saffron and plaid flowed back over the moor, leaving the Hanoverian infantry with nothing to shoot at. The ground in front of the survivors of Barrell's and Munro's regiments was heaped with the bodies of the fallen, a broken, bloodied mass that writhed and shuddered in an ecstasy of pain.

There is a certain echo of the latter stages of the Battle of Flodden in the situation that had developed on the government left. The Highlanders had been pushed into a compressed single column, finally hemmed on three sides by the redcoats, firing now at point blank range. When they broke it was like the wave receding from the shore, the ebb and suck of the tide, as elemental as nature. The Jacobite position unravelled from right to left, the latter, as described, never having come fully to contact.

If he was never to be a great general, Cumberland at least recognised the moment when victory appeared in his palm. Nor did he waste that moment. Seeing that Cobham's dragoons on the extreme right of his line were already gearing up for an attack, he galloped over to add the necessary impetus of command: 'clapping some of them on the Shoulders, [he] call'd out, "One Brush my Lads, for the honour of Old Cobham"; upon which, rather like Devils than Men they broke through the Enemy's Flank, and a total Rout followed.'[2]

Neither Perth's nor Glenbucket's had shown any enthusiasm for advancing, leaving, as they had feared, the retreating MacDonalds' flank very much in the air. O'Sullivan, still on this wing, though without achieving anything, now thought only of securing the safety of the Prince, himself trying unsuccessfully to rally the fleeing clansmen in the centre. Charles Edward was already over-drawn on the goodwill and loyalty of his followers, his cause, in every sense, insolvent. O'Sullivan, as ever, gives a cool account of his actions, undoubtedly with a careful re-editing of history, implying some order into *sauve qui peut*:

About this time Lord George goes off with the most part of the right, Sullivan seeing this runs to Shea yt commanded fitz Jame's Squadron & tels him, 'yu see all is going to pot. Yu can be of no great succor, so before a general deroute wch will soon be, Seize upon the Prince & take him off.' The Prince was at this time rallying the right... the Prince wont retire notwithstanding all yt can be told him. Sullivan seeing a Regimt of horse yt was all the day upon a hight at a great distance but in a ligne with the right of the enemy, where it was thought Cumberland was, seeing this Regimt marching towards our left, as if they were to cut our retrait runs to the Prince, and tels him yt he has no time to lose, yt he'l be surrounded imediately if he does not retir 'Well,' says the Prince, 'they wont take me alive' Sullivan prays him to look behind him, & yt he'd see the whole moor cover'd with men yt were going off & yt half the Army was away. The Prince looks, sees it is true, everybody presses him, in short he retirs but does not go far, comes back again, sees this Regimt of horse very near on our left wch was the MccDonels, yt were quite uncovered, sees it is time & retirs.[3]

Thus Prince Charles Edward Stuart slipped away from the wrack of his cause and the final ruin of his dynasty. The death knell sounding in the hooves of Cobham's dragoons and the echo of the government guns, which were harassing the fleeing clans. It is said Lord Elcho, dismayed at the carnage and his Prince's flight, yelled after him: 'Run, you cowardly Italian!'[4]

The dragoons were having a field day, their backswords hacking down the broken remnants of the Jacobite left, the grey blades soon blooded. The wounded Lochiel, being loyally borne from the field by his clansmen, was for a moment surrounded by the horse in a bothy or barn. The Camerons made ready to sell their lives as dearly as possible but the expected attack never came, the moor was strewn with softer targets.

Lord Balmerino and the Earl of Kilmarnock were both taken, Lord Strathallan slain.[5] Cobham's however, did not have it all their own way. The Irish Picquets were withdrawing steadily and in good order, offering a measure of protection to the fleeing mass. Stapleton ordered his men to fire upon the advancing dragoons. Their regular volleys, augmented by shot from one of the previously abandoned guns,[6] was sufficient to see off the horse, at least for the moment, though Stapleton was mortally wounded either in the course of the encounter or the continued withdrawal.

After a sustained battering, which, as a survivor, Captain Hay of the Royal Ecossois estimated cost the Irish about half their number in dead and wounded, the rest surrendered their arms. As soldiers of France, in French uniform, they could expect the courtesies of war. The scale of their loss may be exaggerated as they most probably withdrew behind the walls of Culloden Park, and the pursuing dragoons certainly reported only trifling loss.[7]

On the Jacobite right the Royal Ecossois and the remains of Kilmarnock's Footguards were similarly harassed, both by musketry and round shot. The survivors fell back into the temporary shelter of the Leanach walls, where, in turn, they were exposed to sniping from Ballimore's men within the Culwhiniac enclosure. The Campbells, having fired on the Royal Ecossois, then charged — an ill advised move, the one which cost Ballimore and several others their lives, including Campbell of Achnaba, mortally wounded. The skirmish, though it resulted in few casualties, forced the French regulars back onto the expanse of the moor. Here they were assailed by the government horse, and after a further exchange of fire they laid down their arms. Lord Lewis Drummond was badly wounded, losing a leg, and, as Captain Hay estimates, the regiment suffered a total loss of perhaps half a hundred.

The situation on the far right of the rebel position had largely remained static throughout the main action. Hawley had shown no inclination to attack the Jacobite battalions drawn up opposite. With the great grinding roar of continuous fire now slackening, the General prepared for an immediate assault. He seems to have sent forward his six troops from Kerr's to form the front line, previously formed by the four troops of Cobham's. No charge as such took place – the nature of the small ravine confounded this; instead there was a brisk firefight, a popping or carbines and pistols, that left few men dead (though Kerr's reported the loss of nearly a score of horses).[8] Being less well armed, the rebel cavalry certainly appears to have sustained the greater loss.

Having gained fire superiority, the government dragoons crossed the stream and took possession of the higher ground beyond with the Jacobites falling doggedly back. Kerr's troopers kept up a steady pressure but the surviving rebel horse, with the remains of Gordon's and Ogilvy's, withdrew in good order and quit the field substantially unmolested. A part of the Royal Ecossois may also have escaped along with them. Johnstone was amongst those fleeing the stricken field:

We were on the left of our army and at the distance of about twenty paces from the enemy when the route began to become general. Almost at the same instant that I saw Scothouse fall – to add to the horror of the scene – I perceived all the Highlanders around me turning their back to fly, I remained for a time motionless, and lost in astonishment; then, in a rage, I discharged my blunderbuss and pistols at the enemy and immediately endeavoured to save myself like the rest. But having charged on foot and in boots I was so overcome by the marshy ground, the water on which reached to the middle of the leg, that instead of running I could scarcely walk. I had left my servant, Robertson, with my horses, on the eminence about six hundred yards behind us where the Prince remained during the battle, with orders to remain near the Prince's servants, that I might easily know where to find my horses in case of need. My first object on retreating was to turn my eyes toward the eminence to discover Robertson; but it was to no purpose. I neither saw the Prince, nor his servants, nor anyone on horseback. They had all gone off and were already out of sight. I saw nothing but the most horrible of all spectacles; the field of battle, from the right to the left of our army covered with Highlanders dispersed and flying as fast as they could to save themselves.[9]

Despite the horror of the rout, Johnstone records that the right wing of the defeated army did get off in reasonable order:

> The right wing of our army retreated towards the river Nairn and met in their way a body of English cavalry, which appeared as much embarrassed as the Highlanders; but the English commander very wisely opened a way for them in the centre and allowed them to pass at the distance of a pistol shot, without attempting to molest them or to take prisoners. One officer only of this body, wishing to take a Highlander prisoner, advanced a few paces to seize him, but the Highlander brought him down with his sword and killed him on the spot. Not satisfied with this, he stopped long enough to take possession of his watch, and then decamped with the booty... Our left, which fled towards Inverness, was less fortunate. Having been pursued by the English cavalry, the road from Culloden to that town was everywhere strewed with dead bodies. [10]

Johnstone also raises the spectre of atrocities committed by the government troops both on an off the field:

> The Duke of Cumberland had the cruelty to allow our wounded to remain amongst the dead on the field of battle, stripped of their clothes, from Wednesday, the day of our unfortunate engagement, till three o'clock in the afternoon of Friday, when he sent detachments to kill all those who were still in life. A great many, who had resisted the efforts of the continual rains which fell all that time, were then dispatched. He ordered a barn, which contained many of the wounded Highlanders, to be set on fire and the soldiers stationed round it drove back with fixed bayonets the unfortunate men who attempted to save themselves, into the flames, burning them alive in this horrible manner, as if they had not been fellow creatures. [11]

Evidence of the completeness of the Duke's victory is provided by the respective loss on both sides. The rebels suffered a very considerably, whilst casualties on the government side were substantially lighter. An early report, was given by Captain Thomas Davis, who wrote from Inverness, barely two days after the battle:

> ...of the complete and cheap victory his Royal Highness the Duke has gained over the rebels the 16th instant. Thank God the loss of our side was very

inconsiderable (viz.) Lt.-Col. Rich has lost a hand and received a wound in his head, poor Lord Robert Carr [Kerr] is killed and about ten officers more are killed and wounded with about 200 private men most of Barrell's and Monroe's regiment they being the two left battalions of the first line where the heat of the action was. His Royal Highness is extremely well pleased with the behaviour of his troops and returned the army thanks for their brave and gallant behaviour. There is not the least thing to be said against any one man that was in the action, which I hope will clear us from the scandal of Falkirk.

The action with cannonading and all did not last above half an hour in which about 1,500 of the rebels were killed and 700 taken prisoners... It is very certain that the proportion their officers killed is great. We likewise took ten pieces of their cannon which they had with them in the field beside eight more that were taken in town, and in the neighbourhood. Above 3,000 stand of arms with eleven stands of colours the Pretenders and all their baggage belonging to their army was likewise taken, al the French picquets with their ambassador surrendered themselves after the action. The Pretender is gone in the hills, with some of the rebels. This is very certain that of the 9,000 rebels there is not 1,000 of them left together, parties are out after him, and others, I pray God they may have success, in hopes of having revenge for the unnatural orders he gave out in the morning before the action not to give a man of us quarter, which *writen* orders have been found upon them [author's italics].[12]

This matter of the Jacobite orders of the day was highly contentious. Lord George Murray had indeed written out his orders and a copy had been found on the person of a captured Jacobite officer. The apparent reference to no quarter is regarded as a subsequent forged addition and that no such sentiment was officially expressed. This would certainly square with previous encounters, where the Jacobites had been generous and ready in accepting surrenders. Whilst there had certainly been instances, in the heat of the fight, where wounded Hanoverians had been killed, no deliberate policy of slaughter can be identified.

The actual wording of the suspect orders had stated that:

It is His Royal Highness positive Orders that every person attach themselves to some Corps of the Armie and to remain with that Corps night and day till the Battle and persute be finally over; and to give no quarters to the Elector's troops on any account whatsoever.

Forgery or not, this was enough to confirm government prejudice about the attitude of their vanquished foe. A subsequent order of Cumberland's issued in the wake of the battle has also been the subject of heated debate:

> A Captain and 50 foot to march directly and visit all the cottages in the neighbourhood of the field of battle, and to search for rebels. The officers and men will take notice that *the Public orders of the rebels yesterday was to give us no quarter* [author's italics]. [13]

It would certainly seem that such an order equates to an incitement to deal ruthlessly with any rebels found, be they under arms or lying helpless. It is difficult to view the Duke's order as anything more than a clear instruction to kill all they came across. The conduct of the army after the battle had left a bitter legacy in the minds of many Scots. In part this is part of the Romantic tradition (see Appendix 2), but the fury of the government response would tarnish the victor's laurels and earn him the unenviable epithet of 'Butcher' Cumberland.

Davis's estimate of losses seems to be fairly acceptable, though Joseph Yorke put the Jacobite casualties as nearer 2,000 with half as many captive, for the loss of only forty-four dead and 250 wounded on the government side. The Duke himself suggested 2,000 rebel dead and estimated that his dead and wounded, combined, barely exceeded 300. The exact figure for the clans cannot be accurately established; so many were missing, and many more would have escaped or been carried off the field but subsequently died of their wounds. In total though, the loss appears to approach almost half of those present on the field, a very grievous blow. [14] Johnstone, it has to be said, puts the overall toll on the field at no more than 1,200.

The nature and composition of the Highland army contributed to the death toll. It was an irregular army, untrained in the techniques of formal warfare. When it broke it did so completely, without a coherent reserve to cover the retreat. The French no doubt helped, but without covering detachments of horse to form a viable rearguard, the moor and the bloody road to Inverness were death traps. And Cobham's dragoons were the sharp-fanged jaws of the trap.

A body of fleeing Jacobite riders, including John Daniel and Lord John Drummond, were able to cut their way through to safety. Daniel had taken part in the desperate charge in which Lord Strathallan had fallen:

Coming to the place I was on before, and seeing it covered with the dead bodies of many of the Hussars who at the time of our leaving had occupied it, I pressed on, resolving to kill or be killed. Some few accompanied my standard, but soon left it.[15]

Despite sustaining a wound to the arm, Daniel survived.

Cobham's were already hallooing down the road to Inverness, their blades reaping a grim harvest amongst the rabble of fugitives, scarcely bothering to distinguish between Jacobite and bystander. Hawley, with victory of the left now also assured, ordered a more organised pursuit. The carnage was indeed terrific, 'a prodigious slaughter'.

Traditionally, it has always been the job of the victorious cavalry to pursue the beaten enemy and harry them without drawing rein or giving way to compassion. This is the moment when a tactical victory on the field becomes a strategic win – the defeated are driven like beasts to the butcher's block, given no chance to rally. It was a brutal and a bloody business but, by the rules which obtained, both necessary and justified.

Wolfe himself comments in his correspondence that the rebels had orders for no quarter. 'We had an opportunity for avenging ourselves for that and many other things, and indeed we did not neglect it, as few Highlanders were made prisoners as possible.'[16]

It is probably correct to assert that a number of civilians were caught up in the carnage. Obviously the clansmen and locals would resemble each other in dress; some of those who fell foul of the hacking sabres were undoubtedly the same spectators who had gathered to watch the armies fight. Soldiers habitually have little regard for these opportunistic voyeurs, who would descend like locusts to rob and silence the wounded. If the troopers were less than discriminating it is not altogether to be wondered at.

Prince Charles Edward had, ostensibly, detailed Captain O'Neill of Lally's to ride into Inverness and warn his supporters there that it was time now to be elsewhere. There was a fear amongst the government officers that Hanoverian prisoners, crammed into the Tolbooth and a nearby church, might become the objects of reprisal. In the event, however, all were released without injury.

The battle had probably lasted, from the first shot to the last, forty minutes at most.

On the government side of the field, the long lines of scarlet remained motionless. Those on the right had suffered no loss, the men leaning on their muskets, their faces, hands and uniforms caked in the filthy residue. Those on the left would be numbed, exhausted, their bayonets bent and bloodied, blood on their faces, their hands, over their coats, red on scarlet, over their breeches and gaiters, a lake of blood. The rebel dead, where they had clashed with Barrell's and Munro's, were stacked as many as four deep by the Well of the Dead where the slaughter had reached its zenith. The survivors, already beset with the particular listlessness that follows the red mist, the sheer, utter tiredness that great surges of adrenalin leave in their wake.

At last the great guns also fell silent, the mired, blackened, sweating gunners spent around their pieces, the barrels still hot, too hot to touch. As they stood their victorious commander rode along the line, saluting each of his regiments in turn, as well he might for all had done good service. He even found breath to praise his hitherto despised Highlanders, his 'brave Campbells'. The men, exhausted as they were, returned their general's blandishments with cheers, their black tricorne waved aloft on bayonets, cries of 'Billy' and 'Flanders' echoing over the stricken field.

Then the order to march was given, the men shouldered their muskets, the drums began their urgent summons and the army advanced to take possession of the field. They stamped over the deadly ground until they reached the line previously held by the rebels. Here the order to halt was given and the victory further cheered with several loud huzzas.

Meanwhile, James Ray, a volunteer with Kingston's Horse, was said to be the first man to ride, blooded and clattering, into the Highland capital, where according to a witness he dispatched a further pair of luckless fugitives sheltering in the well-house. The English had arrived.

Surgeon Grainger rode up behind the steady tramp of Pulteney's and, as he recorded in correspondence, took a most sanguine view of the field, expressing his joy at seeing so many rebels dead upon the ground: 'the whole field on their side was one continued scene of slaughter and dismay'.[17]

Another of his profession later made a meticulous tally, like a medieval herald, of the Jacobite dead and came to a figure of 750. This excluded those who died off the field and those hunted down in the immediate aftermath; the total is therefore probably about the figure Johnstone gives, perhaps 1,200.

For the medical services there would be much trade in the grim aftermath, the gory reckoning in the surgeons' lines which never features in anyone's victory parade. Comrades and the regimental women, who did invaluable service in getting wounded men off the field, would help the stream of casualties reach help. Many seriously wounded on the government side (there was no succour for rebels) would succumb to shock and blood loss. Battlefield trauma was not unknown, as men's senses failed to cope with the noise and horror. For these men there could be little treatment; some would recover, others would not.

Accounts from later battles speak of the effects of the various types of injury a casualty might sustain. An officer writing of Waterloo tells of a soldier struck on the knee by a round shot, how the whole leg above the joint immediately swelled 'till it became the size of the body'.[18] The same observer was injured when a chunk of another man's skull, splintered by a ball, struck his hand. He also witnessed the effect when two men were hit by a round shot passing between them:

> For they were both struck in exactly the same place, about four inches below the shoulder, the wounded arm being attached to the upper part by a small portion of skin and flesh, and being supported by the man taking hold of the hand of that arm by the other hand.[19]

The government army had only had to endure a few moments of largely ineffective cannonade from the rebels. Most injuries from flying round shot, other than those which merely sheared off limbs, were likely to be fatal. Musket balls also frequently caused fatalities. Many of the government wounded would have sustained their injuries from edged weapons, some, inevitably, being struck several more times after they were first felled. These slashing and piercing wounds, frightful enough, were apt to prove less fatal than wounds from missiles.

When a limb was mangled by round shot, grape or a soft lead musket ball, the surgeon generally had little option other than to amputate. These operations would be carried out under canvas, by lantern if the light failed and using instruments that were undisinfected. Anaesthetics were not available, the introduction of chloroform still some way off. Having decided upon amputation, the surgeon would make incisions both above and below the wound, taking care to leave a flap of skin on one side. Picking up his bonesaw, he would now saw through the bone until it was cut through. Using a sharp knife he would then make a further incision, cutting through the muscle and skin to the bone.

His assistant, having chucked aside the severed limb, would proceed to tie off the arteries using horsehair, silk or cotton thread, whilst the surgeon scraped back both the extremity and edges of the bone, so they could not cut through the skin and extrude. The flap of skin he had created before-hand would be pulled over and sewn up, leaving an aperture to permit the wound to drain, the stump would be bandaged and the patient put aside. The job might perhaps have taken ten minutes.

If the patient survived the operation there was always the strong pos-sibility of his being taken off by fever, pyaemia, a form of blood poisoning, tetanus, erysipelas or gangrene. Mortality rates from all of these were high.

Obviously the rebel wounded, moaning and writhing on the bloodied ground, were denied even this most basic care. Aside from those lying or piled on the moor, more would lie, horribly injured, along the corpse-strewn route to Inverness. Despite the enthusiasm with which the cavalry went about the bloodletting, some prisoners were taken. In his report Cumberland notes he held 326 assorted rebels and 222 serving under French colours (excluding officers).[20] This would confirm that the redcoats were certainly taking prisoners on the field, though undoubtedly some wounded men would have been dispatched; in the circumstances this was not neces-sarily done through cruelty.

The Duke's victorious soldiers were fed and refreshed upon the field, where a few sought diversion in shooting or bayoneting any of the scores of wounded who littered the ground. Their Commander-in-Chief rode into Inverness about four in the afternoon, where he gave orders for re-forming the regiments into column and marching the army into a new encampment.

That evening the bells of the city rang heartily to celebrate the royal victory, and men who had cheered the prince but a day before suddenly discovered new loyalties. Many had witnessed the slaughter on the road, had seen the bodies, some stripped and mutilated, of both sexes. If the citizens needed a reminder of the fate that awaited rebels, the stark and bloody corpses created a highly pertinent example.

If, on the evening of 16 April, the Duke of Cumberland was a contented young man, then he had cause. He had, that day, saved his father's kingdom and utterly destroyed the rebels in the field – a success that had eluded his predecessors in office. He had avenged the humiliations of Prestonpans and Falkirk, shattered the Pretender's army and ensured the Whig supremacy. The nation and particularly the administration had reason to be grateful.

His victory had been swift and decisive, the loss on the government side trifling. What remained of the campaign was likely to be purely punitive, the bulk of the army could be returned to the war in Flanders. The spectre of a long drawn out guerrilla-style insurgency was removed. If some innocent lives had been lost in the heat of the rout, what in the modern idiom would be termed 'collateral damage', then this was unavoidable, the victims persons of no account. The Duke was neither butcher nor fiend, but the 'police action' which followed on from this, his only triumph in the field, would damn his memory thereafter.

John Prebble, in his magnificent account of the battle, does not hesitate to accuse the Hanoverian army of widespread atrocities, mainly directed against the Jacobite wounded left on the field in the days following. Much of the evidence was gathered by the Reverend Robert Forbes, a known sympathiser. Recent historians, in seeking to exculpate the redcoats, have sought to cast doubts on his testimony. Whilst it may be the case that Forbes had a political axe to grind, there can be little real doubt that some savage and bloody retribution was meted out.

It has to be borne in mind that in a brutal age, the army contained hardened and violent men. The Jacobites were officially rebels and outlaws, clemency was not their entitlement. Moreover, the Duke's men were disposed to believe that the clansmen had murdered their fellows in the course of the rout at Prestonpans and that, according to the supposed Jacobite orders, they themselves could have expected little better had the rebels won the field. The soldiers, used to fighting regular opponents in Flanders, found these Highlanders outlandish, brute barbarians from a Celtic past. They had as little sympathy with them as their successors in the nineteenth century would find for Pathans, Zulus or Hottentots.

By their language, dress, faith, habitation and accoutrement, these clansmen were a race apart, *Untermenschen*. Their upland country was regarded as alien, harsh and barren; the Lowlander's admiration for the splendid vistas of the Highland landscape was a century away. Much show had been made of captured Jacobite arms, broadswords and Lochaber axes, to demonstrate what fiendish wounds these would make. As noted, however, there was no comparable demonstration of the effect of round shot or grape.

Forbes recounts that a number of wounded men were murdered at Culloden House by a unit of the Royals, and this seems to be supported by additional eyewitness testimony.[21] The injured rebels had, by Friday, lain for two bitterly cold nights upon the moor, with only the government sentries and their own agonies. Many would in that time have succumbed, stripped by the jackals prowling the field. Some of the Highland women, who had tried to gain access to the field and search for their loved ones, had been driven off by the guards. The government dead had been interred the day after the battle. A grim chore to bury the stiffening remains of comrades, slashed and dismembered, not an occupation that would be likely to inspire sympathy for the wounded rebels in the breast of the average redcoat.

Forbes reports that nearly a score of Jacobite wounded had been collected from the environs of the Lord President's house and Thomas Stewart, Forbes's secretary, had done what he could for them. On Friday all were taken by the Royals to a section of the park wall near Balloch. There they were lined up and shot at close quarters.[22] A further dozen injured men were lying in the house of William Rose, his lordship's grieve. On Friday they were removed, ostensibly to have their hurts attended to, 'upon which the poor men made a shift to get up and went along with the party with an air of cheerfulness and joy, being full of the thought that their wounds were to be dressed'.[23] Their optimism was misplaced, however, for all were shot.

Doubtless many other badly wounded men, lying naked and bloodied on that awful moor, suffered a similar fate, their skulls crushed by clubbed muskets, bone and brain tissue splattering with the puddled gore, or run through repeatedly with bayonets. It was a savage and horrible business which we would now unhesitatingly label as an atrocity, but at that time much harsher rules applied. Certain of these unsavoury tasks may well have been allotted to the despised 'Vestry' men, often those of the worst sort, unsuited to frontline duties but reliable enough to act as butchers.

There was also booty to be had. Dead men have no need of possessions and the homes of rebel sympathisers offered the lure of rich pickings. On the evening of the battle Colonel Cockayne, CO of Pulteney's, was instructed to march a detachment 200 strong to 'take up' Moy Hall, fifteen miles south of Inverness, and bring in 'Colonel Anne', Lady Mackintosh. Cockayne's volunteers determined to enjoy the spoils due to them as victors: the harsh upland through which they passed was stripped of livestock, and any locals discovered were abused, or worse, at will. Colonel Anne was at home, and resigned to captivity, her house was thoroughly pillaged and stripped as though by a plague of brigands.

One category of Jacobite prisoner which could have no expectation of clemency was those who had deserted the government forces. In the event, though nearly ninety of these unfortunates were identified, the majority serving under the French colours, only around a third of that number were actually hanged.[24]

The final flourish in the drama was not yet acted out. Those Jacobites who had successfully fled the carnage, in many instances, returned quietly to their homes. The surviving units from the Jacobite right wing, who had quit the field in good order, fell back on the night of the 16th to Corrybrough, south-east of Loch Moy, from where they marched to Ruthven Barracks. Most of those who mustered there comprised the survivors from the Lowland regiments, a few stragglers from the French, the remnant of Perth's regiment, a few of the cavalry and Cluny's MacPhersons, who had arrived too late for the fight. Johnstone was amongst these survivors:

> We were masters of the passes between Ruthven and Inverness, which gave us sufficient time to assemble our adherents. The clan of Macpherson of Clunie, consisting of five hundred very brave men, besides many other Highlanders, who had not been able to reach Inverness before the battle, joined us at Ruthven. Our numbers increased every moment, and I am thoroughly convinced that, in the course of eight days, we should have had a more powerful army than ever, capable of re-establishing without delay the state of our affairs and of avenging the barbarous cruelties of the Duke of Cumberland. But the Prince was inexorable and immoveable in his resolution of abandoning his enterprise, and terminating in this inglorious manner an expedition, the rapid progess of which had fixed the attention of all Europe.[25]

Lord Elcho had earlier found Charles Edward, disconsolate, in a bothy by the Nairn, surrounded only by his Irish cronies. The shock of the defeat had unmanned them all and the Prince now thought only of flight and a safe return to France. His brittle personality was incapable of seizing a fresh initiative. Elcho's entreaties accomplished nothing and the Pretender simply washed his hands of his army, which, if the Chevalier is to be believed, was still full of fight. He simply advised that the survivors should 'shift for themselves'. 'Our separation at Ruthven', wrote Johnstone,

> was truly affecting. We bade one another an eternal adieu. No one could tell whether the scaffold would not be his fate. The Highlanders gave vent to their grief in wild howlings and lamentations; the tears flowed down their cheeks when they thought that their country was now at the discretion of the Duke of Cumberland and on the point of being plundered, whilst they, and their children would be reduced to slavery and plunged, without resource, into a state of remediless distress.[26]

Notwithstanding some poetic licence from the author, the survivors, those who could neither take ship nor surrender, had every reason for anguish. Their Prince, in whose cause they had hazarded their lives and fortunes, was preparing simply to cut and run, to seek sanctuary in France. But for the rank and file there could be no refuge, they divined the quality of ruthless retribution to be unleashed upon them. Many must have roundly cursed the royal person of Prince Charles Edward Stuart.

John Daniel was another survivor from the field who appeared at Ruthven and corroborates Johnstone's assertions of brave talk. In reality there was no serious prospect of continuing the struggle. The rebels were bereft of cash, arms and ordnance, most of the Highland regiments were broken and scattered and they were to be deserted by their Prince. Most now simply dispersed at Ruthven, though Lord Ogilvy's regiment marched southward in a brave, final flourish, before disbanding.

From the stricken field with its dreadful human cargo of dead and dying, Joseph Yorke picked up a discarded rebel cockade, as a souvenir, which he sent home to his father. No doubt the ground was strewn with these mementoes, poignant proof that the cause they had blazoned was now dead, its badge now nothing more than a fit trinket for collectors. The '45 was done.

14
RETRIBUTION – THE DESTRUCTION OF THE CLANS

SPRING AND SUMMER, 1746

And it is further enacted. That from and after the 1st August 1747 no man or boy within Scotland, other than such as shall be employed as officers and soldiers in the King's forces, shall on any pretence whatsoever, wear or put on the cloaths commonly called Highland cloaths, that is to say, the plaid, philabeg or little kilt, trowse, shoulder-belts, or any part whatsoever of what peculiarly belongs to the Highland garb; and that no tartan or party-coloured plaids or stuff shall be used for great-coats, or for upper coats; and if any such persons shall, after said 1st August, wear or put on the aforesaid garments, or any part of them, every such person so offending, being convicted thereof by the mouth of one or more witnesses, before any court of judiciary, or any one or more Justices of the Peace for the shire or stewartry, or judge ordinary of the place where such offence shall be committed, shall suffer imprisonment, without bail, during six months and no longer; and being convicted of a second offence, before the court of judiciary or the circuits, shall be liable to be transported to any of his Majesty's plantations beyond the sea, for seven years.

Disarming Act 1746

They were kneeling in a small box-shaped pit sunk into the stone floor, huddled together in fear, their arms and hands entwined in support. Normally the hole would have been used to store grain and covered with the wooden trapdoor that now lay upright on its hinges behind their backs. It would have been the ideal place to hide. Close the lid and the pit would be nearly invisible. There would have been just enough room for three people to lie beneath it. What gave them away? I wondered. A cough? A sob?

Two of the women were in their twenties, the third was an old lady. Someone had shot her in the mouth and her shattered dentures cascaded with her own teeth down her front like mashed melon pips. One girl had been shot repeatedly in the chest. It was difficult to tell if the other had had her throat cut or been shot; a great gash of blood crescented her neck. The expression on their faces had survived the damage. It was so clear. A time valve that opened directly onto those last moments. So you saw what they saw. I hope beyond hope that I never see it again.[1]

That repugnant expression, 'ethnic cleansing', has become synonymous with modern atrocities, such as that described above, which occurred in the Balkans during the 1990s. Such dreadful scenes would have been all too familiar to the inhabitants of the western Highlands in the late spring and summer of 1746. Casual brutalities had, it is true, been a feature of inter-necine clan strife for centuries and the 'Age of Forays' had produced a fair crop of horrors.[2]

Stuart Reid, the most notable contemporary student of the battlefield, has argued that the continuing flame of resistance, orchestrated primarily by Lochiel, that kept the ghost of a cause spluttering on into the early summer, was the catalyst that caused the Duke of Cumberland to decide in favour of a policy of repression. It is argued that the Commander-in-Chief had issued what amounted to an amnesty for the commons and was contemplating extending this toward the officers. The edict actually stipulated that all those who had borne arms against the government should surrender their arms to the nearest magistrate and 'submit themselves to the King's Mercy'.

Neither the Duke's previous utterances, nor his subsequent conduct, would suggest that he was in any way inclined to reconciliation. The French had suggested that a general amnesty for the defeated Jacobites be included in the terms of a draft peace treaty proposed in May 1746. There was an urgent imper-ative to shift troops back to Flanders where Saxe was pressing Britain's Dutch allies hard. In the following year French arms would enjoy further successes, overrunning the Dutch part of Flanders. Bergen-op-Zoom was stormed and bloodily sacked, Cumberland again defeated by Saxe at Laffeldt.[3]

It is probably fair to say that the defeat of the last Jacobite rising strength-ened the overall position of the House of Hanover; the subsequent opprobrium incurred through public disquiet at the harsh treatment meted out in the glens fell mainly on Cumberland. When he addressed Parliament on 14 January 1746 the King had differentiated the position which obtained in his two kingdoms of Great Britain:

> The daring attempt, which the rebels have since made upon this part of my kingdom has been happily disappointed, and, as their precipitate flight, before a small number of my troops, must greatly dispirit their followers; so, that invi-olable duty, and loyalty, which have been so universally, and steadily shown by my faithful subjects, and shall never be forgotten by me, must convince them, how vain, and ill-grounded their hopes were of any addition of strength from such an enterprise.[4]

John Maule MP, writing from the capital on 4 March, over a month before the battle, was one of those who expressed disquiet over the redcoats' conduct toward the Highlanders:

> There are many here who much disapprove of the plundering that has been but too much practised by the Duke's army, no good can result from it, and the rebels will certainly make reprisals a hundred fold, so that the whole country will be a scene of blood and rapine and many a man that has merit with the government undone. In the meantime it is not lawful for any man to complain lest he be taxed with disaffection.[5]

Cumberland, needless to relate, would have no truck with those who thought in terms of moderation. On 4 April he wrote forcefully to Newcastle:

> The orders which were sent to the Governor and Commandant of Fort William, before it was threatened with a siege, to seize al the cattle and demolish the habitations of those in Lochaber, who were actually out in rebellion, has had a very good effect, as all the rebels of that country have deserted, to go home to their own habitations, it obliged them to undertake this siege, which will only discourage the men and add to their present distraction.[6]

Captain Caroline Scott of Guise's regiment, the defender of Fort William, would later that year earn a particular notoriety as a persecutor of rebels, or those suspected of such sympathies. That troops would behave badly toward a civilian population was a not uncommon phenomenon in the eighteenth century. The harsh realities of the Age of Reason were frequently experienced by hapless populations caught between warring armies – Saxe's capture of Bergen-op-Zoom was the scene of wholesale looting, slaughter and mass rape. Where the victims were distinguished in ethnic terms from the perpetrators, the scale of atrocity could be expected to escalate. It should be noted that several of the names which stand out as exemplars of barbarity in 1746, besides Captain Scott, were those of fellow countrymen: Captain Dunlop of Blakeney's, Major Lockhart of Cholmondeley's and Captain John Fergusson RN.

French support for the Stuart cause waned perceptibly after Culloden and never again reached the levels of 1744 and the winter of 1745–46. There were further alarums as long as the war in Europe continued to rage. In June 1746, an invasion of Ireland was feared. Early in 1747 the Prince, who had escaped from Scotland the previous September, was reported as having left Paris for Spain, there to beg for further aid and intervention. These fears resurfaced later that year, in October. The 1st Earl of Hardwicke summed up the prevailing view in correspondence penned in late summer:

> It surprises me that any of the sensible Jacobites, who know the world, can still, after all the experience they have had, really be persuaded that France means anything more than to make them the engines and dupes of her own politics, without being much in earnest to push the point they have in view. I don't believe that France has any immediate design of this nature; but I entirely concur in your lordship's doctrine, and have preached it all this year, that it is absolutely necessary to keep a sufficient body of troops in the northern parts to crush every tentative towards a rising.[7]

However, in that month Admiral Hawke roundly thrashed a French fleet in the second Battle of Cape Finisterre, to a degree offsetting Cumberland's failures on land. The inexorable growth in the power of the Royal Navy was a crucial factor in dissuading the French or Spanish from further intermeddling.

By the time 1748 came around, the major powers were growing weary and intimations of peace were in the air. The French might continue to use the Jacobites as pieces on the board, admittedly of minor importance, to be traded as expediency demanded, but the end of the war largely spelled the end of Stuart hopes. When hostilities broke out again, in the form of the Seven years War (1756–1763), the situation would be very different.

Cumberland's harsh regime might raise some disquiet in informed circles, but his fellow officers heartily agreed. Thomas Lee of Wolfe's wrote from Fort Augustus on 31 May, advising that his men were

> dispersed through the several parts of this heathenish country, converting them to Christianity, and propagating a new light among them. Some few of them bring in their arms, others skulk in the woods and mountains, but we take care to leave them no sustenance, unless they can browse like goats.[8]

This contempt for Highlanders in general was exacerbated by a general loathing for their country. Albemarle, who was to succeed Cumberland as Commander-in-Chief, wrote bitterly that 'to be ordered to remain in Scotland and to have no douceurs is intolerable and what no flesh and blood can bear. I have applied and shall again… to attend His Royal Highness abroad next spring.'[9]

When, as a result of the alarums of October 1747, it was proposed once again to shift British troops from Flanders, Cumberland protested to Newcastle that

> such alarums in England occasioned by the French troops sent to Calis and Dunkirk, as well as for the impertinencies and insolencies the Scotch Jacobites are every day committing… I always declared my opinion, that affairs in Scotland never would go right, in the manner they were then and are still administered. And though I think it of great importance to keep the Duke of Argyll and the Campbells in good humour and even so far as to put the Duke of Argyll at the head of His Majesty's Scotch affairs, yet I can never think it adviseable to have him sole and absolute disposer of all the King's favours in the kingdom. From what I am able to see at present I am not much alarmed for this winter in that part, as I know the number of Highlanders has been very much thinned, as well as by what they lost in the rebellion, as by the number of men drawn out of the country for the kings and the States General service and as I am of opinion they will not let themselves be deluded by French promises of assistance and little corps that France might contrive to send them, for which reasons I think our security in that country depends entirely upon the diligence of our fleet in preventing any considerable embarkation of troops from landing in a body in Scotland… The only real danger which I can forsee, which we might be liable to this winter, would be the French assembling a number of small vessels at Calais and Dunkirk and risking an embarkation which they might push over with a fair wind and land either in Kent, Sussex or Essex.[10]

Prince Charles Edward had, after a series of adventures, eluded capture and been taken off by boat on 20 September 1746. He had contributed nothing toward the succour of his supporters after the disaster at Culloden. Whilst the hunt for the fugitive Prince had been energetic, there was no clear view as to what fate should befall him if he were to be taken. Only the most extreme Whigs advocated the axe; more likely he would have been held as a pawn in the greater game being played out in Europe, his freedom bargained in return for diplomatic advantage.

The final cannonades and the death rattle of the execution squads were not the final echoes of the '45. On 30 April two French privateers, *Mars* and

Bellone, had anchored in Loch nan Uamh, where it had all begun the previous year. The Frenchmen were initially sniped by Jacobites on the shore who believed them to be Royal Navy. These Highlanders, including, Perth, Lord John Drummond and Lord Elcho, quickly acquainted their newly arrived allies with tidings of the disaster. The visitors were able to provide much needed supplies and took time to come ashore and marvel at the desperate poverty and general wretchedness of their hosts.

Lochiel, with Murray of Broughton and Sheridan, was in hiding by Loch Arkaig, still disabled from his wounds. The Cameron, to his credit, did not seek an early escape as he refused to abandon his people in the face of the storm that was bound to descend upon them. Captain Noel RN, on board the sloop *Greyhound*, was stationed barely thirty miles from Loch nan Uamh and was aware of the privateers' presence. The rest of the captain's small flotilla was widely dispersed, but by dawn on the 2 May, both *Greyhound* and another sloop, *Baltimore*, were under sail and later joined by a third, *Terror*. At first light the following morning, a little after 3 a.m., the three small British vessels crept into the loch.

John Daniel was that night sleeping amongst the other fugitives on the shore, and the sight of the British men o' war provided a most unwelcome jolt. The French, however, alerted by the sighting of an earlier patrol boat, were ready to fight. Captain Rouillée of *Mars* remained, unwisely, at anchor whilst Lory of *Bellone* got underway. To receive *Greyhound*'s broadsides whilst thus immured was very nearly fatal and *Mars* took a substantial pounding.

Nearly a score of the privateers were killed, the decks, according to an eyewitness, awash with blood. One of the Jacobite refuges, Major Hales, was amongst the dead: having been bidden to throw himself to the deck to avoid injury, he preferred the upright pose of quixotic contempt – in his case lethal.

Baltimore now bore down on *Mars* while *Greyhound* attacked *Bellone*. The two smaller British vessels were heavily outgunned and began, in turn, to take serious punishment. Both suffered damage to the rigging and Lory was manoeuvring to board. He failed, but the respite enabled Rouilée to cut his cables and get his battered ship underway. The tiny *Terror* weighed into the fray but was seen off by a broadside from *Bellone*. The two Frenchmen were now under sail, heading up the narrow confines of the loch with *Mars* taking shelter in a small bay, the three English ships snapping at *Bellone* like terriers.

For a good three hours the Jacobites on the shore were treated to the spectacle of a fierce little battle raging on the normally placid waters. It seemed as though *Mars* was crippled and could be picked off at leisure whilst the sloops directed their attention toward *Bellone*. Noel was not blind to the scurrying Highlanders on the shore, busily removing inland the ships' cargoes of arms and cash, the latter amounting to some £35,000 in bullion. Such a sum would have very possibly enabled the Prince to stave off the defeat at Culloden and guaranteed the continuance of the rebellion. Flying round shot from *Greyhound* added urgency to the work.

Having managed to jury-rig repairs to his damaged sails, Captain Howe of *Baltimore* once more brought his vessel to the attack. Both his sloop and the gallant little *Terror* suffered grievously, *Baltimore's* rigging and sails cut up, Howe himself among the wounded. After some six hours of battle the fight petered out. All of the English ships had suffered damage, if relatively few casualties.[11] *Bellone* unleashed a final broadside to speed the retreating ships on their way, though *Mars* was by now in a bad state, hit repeatedly below the water line and with twenty-nine dead and eighty-five wounded, littering the decks, slippery with their spilled blood.

The French, knowing that other British ships could soon be expected to enable Noel to renew the assault, worked feverishly to ensure the badly holed vessel was seaworthy. The Jacobites, onshore, enjoyed the plentiful liquor their guests had left them. MacDonald of Barisdale, whose regiment had missed the fight, had by now appeared and began by appropriating a portion of the cash before departing. The remaining Macleans also dispersed, whilst one of the inebriated rebels unwisely elected to smoke his pipe in close proximity to one of the barrels of powder and succeeded in blowing himself to bits, his befuddled comrades mistaking the noise for a fresh alarum!

As the privateers nursed the battered ships back toward their Breton lairs, they took off Perth, his brother and Lord Elcho. The Duke, his poor constitution already seriously undermined by the rigours of the campaign, was utterly exhausted and expired before reaching France. The gift of gold, as ever, proved a double-edged sword. Being in funds encouraged Lochiel and others, mainly from Clan Donald, that some manner of continued resistance was possible. This strategy was probably dictated solely by fear. None can now have believed that serious aid from France was forthcoming, and their erstwhile leader was a fugitive skulking in the Isles with only the brandy bottle for comfort. Not to resist, however, must surely mean that the full fury of the government would fall mainly on Camerons and MacDonalds, as the leading Tory clans.

Consequently, a further muster, a pale ghost of Glenfinnan, was held at Murlaggan by the head of Loch Arkaig. Here, Lochiel was joined by Lochgarry, Clanranald and the mercurial Barisdale. This sombre gathering must have been a pathetic shadow of the raising of the standard, a bitter token of defeat. Here the chiefs could ponder upon what prodigies of war they had accomplished in their advance to Derby and what a bitter harvest their efforts had sown.

A further muster was to be held at Invermallie in a week's time, where the remnant of Keppoch's with Cluny's MacPhersons were expected. The summons produced no more than a few hundred desperate men, those who could plainly see the ruin of their world staring them in the face. The wily Barisdale slipped off, ostensibly to raise fresh recruits, and melted into the hills. The White Cockade was a lost cause.

On 17 May, Howard's, Cholmondeley's and Price's regiments had marched from Inverness to occupy the shell of Fort Augustus and re-establish government control of the Great Glen. With these were eight companies of Highlanders, and the wounded Lochiel, at Achnacarry, mistook their plaids for those of friends. On the day after the final muster, the remaining Jacobites scattered and took to the heather.

It was from the bastion of Fort Augustus that a series of ruthless forays was launched during the summer months. Cumberland had brought up the rest of his regulars before handing over his baton to Albemarle in July. Most of the regiments were withdrawn from the immediate sphere of the Highlands, leaving Loudon's and seventeen independent Highland companies to carry on the good work of pacification. The Argyll Militia were disbanded whilst Fort William was garrisoned with Houghton's regiment, one that had previously been stationed in the south-west of England and had not seen prior service during the rebellion.

'Daddy' Huske had demonstrated an attitude toward the defeated rebels that was anything but paternal. At Fort Augustus he suggested a bounty of £5 be offered for the head of every disaffected clansmen brought in. This notion, apparently suggested by previous practice in Ireland,[12] was rejected on the basis that it was impossible to distinguish one severed head from another, but there were no objections on purely humanitarian grounds.

If these were the thoughts of one of the kinder spirits in the army, the general mood of the rest may well be guessed at. Correspondence from officers refers to much hanging, shooting and looting of livestock.[13] Throughout that long summer, whilst the fugitive prince carried a bounty of £30,000, patrols scoured the dark glens and barren hillsides. Many clansmen still waged a desperate, guerrilla-style form of resistance and the redcoats would never know when they could be ambushed or sniped at. The squalid settlements were torched with deadly monotony and the defenceless, the young, the old, the sick and lame, were driven onto the moors, where many simply perished of cold and hunger. Ministers of Highland parishes complained of the ruthless practices of the army but the patrols were acting without legal or moral restraint. This was the bitter reaping, the final sanction for a century of loyalty to the Stuarts.

By the Braes of Balquhidder the lands of Clan Gregor were despoiled. For the Macgregors this was nothing new and they riposted with a few forays of their own and a spree of traditional blackmailing. Glengarry's house and lands in Knoydart were wasted, Achnacarry, too, was razed, while Lochiel watched impotent from the heather as the final account of his Stuart adherence was rendered by the crown. Anyone unfortunate enough to cross the redcoats' path was lucky if they escaped with only a beating; shooting up 'vagrants' was a favoured distraction. Moidart, good MacDonald country, was singled out for special attention; any who resisted, or seemed likely to resist, were shot out of hand.

Major Lockhart took up Glenmoriston and then Strathglass with a singular, ruthless zeal that was to characterise his raids, notwithstanding the fact that the wretched people had already suffered extensively at the rapacious hands of the Macleods, the chief anxious to prove his Whig credentials. Captain Scott was active throughout Badenoch and Lochaber, his brutalities frequently too much even for the Campbells who had to serve under him. He had raided Glen Nevis immediately the siege of Fort William was lifted and, after Culloden, directed his attentions to the Appin country. Campbell of Mamore had already passed through the Stewart lands but, for a Campbell, had shown some mercy. Scott did not feel so constrained.

Ardshiel House was thoroughly slighted, even the roof slates were stripped, the door and window frames removed. For the armies of the period, plunder was not some occasional burst of excess but a carefully organised process —all of the looted materials were removed and sold on. In this climate of merciless rapine, life, particularly that of a clansman or his dependants, was very cheap indeed. Officers like Lockhart and Scott were frequently disposed simply to hang those who came in, foolishly relying on Cumberland's amnesty. The Isle of Raasay, lying between Skye and the mainland, had the dubious privilege of being visited by both Scott and Fergusson of the Royal Navy, and the inhabitants were given good cause to remember both. When the English were done the independent companies took their turn – the wretched victims were MacLeods, as were their most recent persecutors.

Fergusson was skipper of *Furnace* and, in April, before Culloden, his marines had engaged in a drink-fuelled foray against hapless MacDonald womenfolk on the island of Canna. Having finished with Canna, Fergusson moved his attentions to Eigg, where the business of rounding up rebels was leavened with additional pillage and rape. Captain Felix O'Neill of Lally's was one of his victims, captured and about to be tortured until an officer of the Royals intervened and faced the brutal captain down. In their hunt for the Prince the soldiers and sailors of the crown even descended in force upon St Kilda, the most remote and westerly of the Isles, whose terrified inhabitants must have seen these swarming redcoats as a vision of hell. Needless to say, the Prince was not to be found.

Such conduct did not escape censure; Cumberland's role would haunt him and his memory ever after. The admittedly pro-Jacobite *National Journal* featured a fictional letter from 'A True Modern Whig' in its edition of 12 June 1746. This reflected the savagery of the views undoubtedly held by many Whigs, and even advocated killing the rebel women to prevent the breeding of a future generation of rebels:

> Because there is no doubt that many of them will breed Jacobites and children generally suck in the principles of their mothers and nurses, which can never be eradicated but by great posts and pensions, and this, you know, is often a great disappointment as well as loss to us honest people. I am also of the opinion, that all the corn in Scotland, designed for seed, as well as all the cattle, ought to have been seized, and all implements of husbandry destroyed, except what belongs to the few that are known to be well affected, which would infallibly starve all those rebellious wretches in a year or two. This would effectually extirpate them, and save us the expense of transporting them to our colonies, where they may do great mischief by infecting the people with their principles.[14]

This may seem extreme, but Albemarle's correspondence to Newcastle, written three months later, indicates that satire, in this instance, was perilously close to the mark:

> I am one of those, that notwithstanding the hopes entertained by most that this kingdom was restored to peace and quiteness, always feared from the bad

inclination of the people in most of the northern counties and from their stubborn, inveterate disposition of mind, nothing could effect it but the laying of the whole country waste and in ashes, and removing all the inhabitants (excepting a few) out of the kingdom.[15]

The haul of prisoners, initially from the wrack of the army and latterly from the raids, had initially been dispersed around Inverness, in overcrowded, unsanitary conditions that had proved fatal to many of those already debilitated by wounds. These wretched sufferers were rowed out to the transports standing off the Moray Firth and incarcerated in the stinking holds before being shipped south to await His Majesty's pleasure. In total there may have been anywhere between three and four thousand; the 500 or so from the French service were eventually repatriated. A total of 120 finally faced the gallows, including the thirty deserters previously mentioned. A further 88 are known to have died in custody, 936 were transported, 58 escaped and the rest eventually released. More probably died in custody than the earlier figure suggests, but some found their way into the ranks of the British army![16]

Of the noble captives, both Kilmarnock and Balmerino were executed; they fell by the axe as their rank ensured and both met their fate with great gallantry. Kilmarnock, despite his earlier terrors, showed resolute courage on the scaffold, while Balmerino was almost sublime in his indifference. Cromarty, due to his wife's intervention, was first reprieved and then exonerated. The headsman was not yet done, however, for in April 1747 Simon Fraser, the aged fox, finally went to the block.

The last, and perhaps most quixotic, of the noble casualties was Charles Radcliffe, *de jure* 4th Earl of Derwentwater. He had been condemned thirty years before, in the wake of the '15 when his tragic elder brother lost his life and lands. Charles Radcliffe had lived quietly in exile in France, never abandoning his Jacobite adherence. He had served the Prince as secretary, took ship to join him in November 1745 and was captured at sea. The following December, the original sentence was carried out.

Lochiel eventually escaped into embittered exile as did Lord George Murray.[17] The Chevalier de Johnstone also made good his escape to France, via Holland. He joined the French service and served as aide-de-camp to the Marquis de Montcalm during the Seven Years War and at the battle on the Plains of Abraham. He thus had the unenviable distinction of being on the losing side twice. He returned to France, where his remaining years were spent in obscurity. John Daniel was another who survived and entered

French service as a captain in Ogilvy's, though he had been court-mar-tialled at Loch nam Uamh for allegedly filching some of the gold!

The Duke of Cumberland, though initially lionised, was dogged by the increasing revulsion over his treatment of the glens. His military career foundered. Firstly he was defeated by Saxe at Laffeldt; then, during the course of the Seven Years War, charged with defending Hanover with largely Germanic forces, he was beaten again at Hastenbeck and forced into a humiliating surrender. The terms so outraged both King and country that he was subsequently forced to resign from all of his appointments. His fail-ing political career never recovered and he died, forgotten and obese, in 1765.

It would have been far better for Prince Charles Edward Stuart had he died on the field at Culloden, so history might remember a handsome, if flawed, young man, whose army came within an ace of unseating the House of Hanover. Better by far than the long years of an embittered, wasted life, his cause in ruins, increasingly an unwelcome anachronism, whose only succour came from the bottle. He died, also forgotten, in Rome in 1788.

Not only were the rebel clans to be harried, slaughtered and despoiled, their habitations burnt, their beasts driven off and their dependants thrust out onto the hillsides, but their very way of life was to be erased. The Disarming Act of 1746 proscribed not only the possession of arms but the wearing of Highland dress. Catholic and nonjuring Episcopalian meeting-houses were also banned; arms, dress, religion, all were to be suppressed. Another legisla-tive casualty were the hereditable jurisdictions – legal powers were to be removed from the ancient grasp of local magnates and passed to the crown. Even the Campbells, perhaps the most over-mighty of Highland subjects, would not escape.

Culloden could be said to have ushered in a profound era of change in Scottish society; Brown Bess was not the only catalyst. The country, with Edinburgh as the hothouse, was poised to embark on an age of economic and intellectual growth unparalleled in its history. Scotland in the latter half of the eighteenth century would be the power house of the Enlightenment. The building of the New Town in Edinburgh would herald the arrival of the nation's capital as one of the great cities of Europe, a position that has never been relinquished.

The Union, so much despised, would generate unimagined opportuni-ties as Scots participated fully in the building of the great British Empire, as much a Scottish as an English phenomenon. The Seven Years War would witness Scottish soldiers fighting as redcoats around the globe, particularly in North America and Canada.

In the Highlands, the clan system died after Culloden, though it was undoubtedly moribund beforehand and the brutal transition ushered in by the failure of the '45 completed a process that would have occurred in time. In its way the savage repression was successful, for the old loyalties did die out − in the space of a generation the chiefs, no longer educated in Paris, became facsimiles of English gentlemen. Within a few decades the Highland Clearances would change the face of the landscape and add considerably to the diaspora begun by the events of 1746.

By the time of the Romantic revival in the 1820s, engineered by Sir Walter Scott, Jacobitism was a historical anomaly, an ancient grudge, as dead as the clansmen who had charged on the moor. Like all lost causes, it improved in the telling and acquired the romantic veneer which stills fuels a significant slice of the Scottish tourism industry.

Popular history and culture has, therefore, to a certain extent reversed the verdict on the day, and thrown a gloss of romanticism over the sheer grinding horror of it all. Perhaps then, those ragged, exhausted men who charged over the sodden ground, in the last bellow of defiance from the Highland clans, won some posthumous glory after all.

APPENDIX 1

ORDER OF BATTLE AT CULLODEN, 16 APRIL 1746

JACOBITE ARMY

Commander-in-Chief: Prince Charles Edward Stuart
Chief of Staff: Colonel John William Sullivan

Escort troop under Captain O'Shea, Life Guards and Fitzjames's Horse (32*)

FOOT

Front Line

Lord George Murray's Brigade – three battalions of Athollmen under Lord Nairn (500); Cameron of Lochiel's Regiment under Donald Cameron of Lochiel (650); the Appin Regiment under Charles Stewart of Ardshiel (150).
Lord John Drummond's Brigade – Lovat's Regiment under Charles Fraser of Inverallochie (500); Lady Mackintosh's Regiment under Alexander McGillivray of Dunmaglas (500); Monaltrie's Battalion under Francis Farquharson of Monaltrie (150); Battalion of Macleans and Maclachlans under Lachlan Maclachlan (182); Chisholm's Regiment under Roderick Og Chisholm (100).
Duke of Perth's Brigade – Keppoch's Regiment under MacDonald of Keppoch (200); Clanranald's Regiment under Ranald MacDonald of Clanranald (200); Glengarry's Regiment under Donald MacDonald of Glengarry (500).

Second Line

John Roy Stewart's Brigade – 1st Battalion Lord Lewis Gordon's Regiment under John Gordon of Avochie (300); 2nd Battalion under James Moir of Stoneywood (200); 1st Battalion Lord Ogilvy's Regiment under Thomas Blair of Glassclune (200); 2nd Battalion under Sir James Kinloch (300); John Roy Stuart's Regiment under Major Patrick Stuart (200); Footguards under Lord Kilmarnock (200); Glenbuchat's Regiment under John Gordon of Glenbuchat (200); Duke of Perth's Regiment under James Drummond, Master of Strathallan (300).
The Irish Brigade – 'Royal Ecossois' under Lieutenant Colonel Lord Lewis Drummond (350); Irish Picquets under Lieutenant Colonel Walter Stapleton (302).

HORSE

Commanded by Colonel Sir John MacDonald of Fitzjames's Horse. On the right, Fitzjames's Horse commanded on the field by Captain William Bagot (70); The Life Guards under Lord Elcho (30). On the left, Bagot's Hussars under Major John Bagot (36); Strathallan's Horse under Lord Strathallan (30).

GUNS

Eleven three-pounders under Captain John Finlayson and a single four-pounder under Captain du Saussay.

HANOVERIAN ARMY

Commander-in-Chief: William Augustus, Duke of Cumberland
Chief of Staff: Lieutenant General Henry Hawley

Escort Troop: Duke of Cumberland's Hussars (*c.* 20)

VANGUARD

Major General Humphrey Bland: 10th (Cobham's) Dragoons [*10th Hussars*] under Major Peter Chaban (276); 11th (Lord Mark Kerr's) Dragoons [*11th Hussars*] under Lieutenant Colonel William Lord Ancrum (267); Composite Highland Battalion under Lieutenant Colonel John Campbell of Mamore of 64th Highlanders (*c.* 300).

FRONT LINE

Major General William Anne, Earl of Albemarle: First Brigade –1st (Royal) Foot (St Clair's) [*Royal Scots*] under Lieutenant Colonel John Ramsay (401); 34th Foot (Cholmondley's) [*The Border Regiment*] under Lieutenant Colonel Charles Jeffreys (339); 14th Foot (Price's) [*The West Yorks Regiment*] under Lieutenant Colonel John Grey (304). Third Brigade – 21st Fusiliers (North British; Campbell's) under Major the Honourable Charles Colvill (358); 37th Foot (Munro's) [*The Hampshire Regiment*] under Colonel Louis Dejean (426); 4th Foot (Barrell's) [*The King's Own Royal Regiment*] under Lieutenant Colonel John Robert Rich (325).

SECOND LINE

Major General John Huske: Second Brigade – 3rd Foot (the Buffs) [*Royal East Kents*] under Lieutenant Colonel George Howard (413); 36th Foot (Fleming's) [*Worcesters*] under Lieutenant Colonel George Jackson (350); 20th Foot (Bligh's) [*Lancashire Fusiliers*] under Colonel Lord George Sackville (412). Fourth Brigade – 25th Foot (Sempill's) [*King's Own Scottish Borderers*] under Lieutenant Colonel David Cunynghame (429); 59th/48th Foot (Conway's) [*Northants Regiment*] under Colonel Henry Conway (325); 8th Foot (Wolfe's) [*King's Liverpool Regiment*] under Lieutenant Colonel Edward Martin (324).

RESERVE

Duke of Kingston's 10th Horse under Lieutenant Colonel John Mordaunt (211). Brigadier John Mordaunt: Fifth Brigade – 13th Foot (Pulteney's) [*Somerset Light Infantry*] under Lieutenant Colonel Thomas Cockmayne (410); 62nd Foot (Batereau's) under Colonel John Batereau (354); 27th Foot (Blakeney's) [*Royal Inniskilling Fusiliers*] under Lieutenant Colonel Francis Leighton (300).

GUNS

Major William Belford with Captain Lieutenant John Godwin – 10 three-pounders and 6 Coehorn Mortars (108**).

NOTES

*   Figures for both armies include officers and men.
** Includes NCOs and men.

Names in square brackets and italics are the later regimental names.

A degree of confusion ensued when a regiment had a new colonel appointed in mid-campaign as the unit was named after its commanding officer! Thus after Culloden Bligh's became Sackville's and Munro's Dejean's.

ROMANCE OF THE WHITE COCKADE

'Bonnie Prince Charlie' has become a tourist icon. His name has filled a thousand coaches from every corner of the globe, the annual flood of visitors who collectively add so much to the income of Scotland in general and the Highlands in particular. The tourists are, for the most part, lamentably deceived. The gimcrack souvenirs and Highland fripperies sold to them would be generally unrecognisable to any who followed the White Cockade. It probably doesn't matter, tourism is a major industry and needs its supports.

Besides, the process has a substantial pedigree. Martin Martin, who published his *Description of the Western Isles of Scotland* as early as 1703, was perhaps the first writer to breach the enigma of the Highlands. It was not until later in the century that the growth of the Romantic movement would glorify the rugged grandeur of the hills, and perhaps the most famous visitor to the dark glens, Dr Johnson, together with Boswell, pierced the veil.

It was, however, James MacPherson who created the influential Romantic cult of 'Ossian' – the alleged discovery and translation of a corpus of ancient Celtic verse that offered the clans their very own Homer:

> Now I beheld the chiefs in the pride of their former deeds. Their souls are kindled at the battles of old... Their eyes are flames of fire. They roll in search of the foes of the land. Their mighty hands are on their swords. Lightning pours from their sides of steel. They come like streams from the mountains; each rushes roaring from his hill. Bright are the chiefs of battle in the armour of their fathers, gloomy and dark their heroes follow, like the gathering of the rainy clouds behind the red meteors of heaven.[1]

This turgid melodrama chimes with the contemporary vision of the Noble Savage. The Highlander, follower of the White Cockade, his reality safely defeated and consigned to memory, was rehabilitated in fiction as the romantic hero. Even Napoleon Bonaparte, the arch-pragmatist, was said to be an admirer of Ossian. Dr Johnson, it has to be said, was not and it was his savage cynicism that largely brought about MacPherson's eclipse, that and the author's inability to validate any of his alleged texts!

By the third decade of the nineteenth century the Highlands had become an established tourist destination. Mendelssohn and Klingemann were just two more distinguished visitors. If a further boost was needed then Sir Walter Scott was the provider. With Sir Walter the Romantic Movement came of age; his poems such as *The Lord of the Isles* and novels such as *Rob Roy* inspired a generation of travellers. Even today his image of the swashbuckling Highlander, fierce but loyal and enduring, persists.

Johnson, initially discreetly, was the first to lay the foundations of the cult of Prince Charles Edward Stuart. The pair made their celebrated journey in 1773 when memories of the '45 were still fresh, too fresh for any overt admiration of the lost cause. Boswell did not write his own account until some ten years later and told of the meeting between Johnson and Flora MacDonald.

His working of the tale of the Pretender's escape sparked the genesis of the cult, this at a time when Charles Stuart, an embittered dipsomaniac, was still clinging to life in Rome. Once the aged relic was safely buried in 1788 his heroic status soared. Old Jacobite airs were revived, and any gaps were swiftly filled by a swelling chorus of nostalgic repertoire. From being a covert and dangerous expression of extremism the Jacobite movement re-emerged as a Romantic phenomenon, a relatively safe symbol of sentimental nationalism.

James Hogg, the 'Ettrick Shepherd' and Scott's collaborator was quick to leap on the fast moving bandwagon:

> Cam ye by Athol, lad wi' the philabeg
> Down by the Tummel, or banks o' the Garry;
> Saw ye our lads, wi' their bonnets and white cockades
> Leaving their mountains to follow Prince Charlie?
>
> Follow thee! Follow thee! Wha wadna follow thee?
> Lang hast thou loved and trusted us fairly:
> Charlie, Charlie, wha wadna follow thee,
> King o' the Highland hearts, bonnie Prince Charlie.[2]

It is doubtful that even Charles Stuart himself, in the wildest excess of alcohol-fuelled optimism, would have recognised himself in this turgid stream! Scott featured the '45 in *Waverley* (1814). Though he initially disdained fiction as inferior to verse, his iconic status meant that by the 1820s he was the recognised authority of all matters appertaining to Scottish history.

His great moment came in 1822 when he was appointed to organise the pomp and pageantry celebrating the state visit of George IV to Edinburgh. The King was to be treated to a spectacle of Jacobite fantasy, and kilted Highlanders would once again conquer the capital. This was a bold move – some lingering resentment of the Act of Union still festered, and Highland dress had remained proscribed until 1782. George IV, as easily in love with dressing up as Scott, entered fully into the spirit and donned a florid version of Highland kit for a reception at Holyrood on 17 April 1822.

Though some dissenters muttered, the Romantic Jacobite Revival had arrived. Scott was the hero of the hour, and the fact that the tartan had been repressed for so long merely fuelled the passion with which it was now embraced. By a supreme irony the revival was generally limited to the upper tiers of society and mainly concentrated in the Lowlands. The combination of Ossian, Bonnie Prince Charlie and Scott had otherwise proved unstoppable.

The fashion for Highland garb went on to spawn a whole industry devoted to the study and manufacture of tartan, an enduring fad that would totally have bemused any of those who stood on the field at Culloden. By the time Queen Victoria first toured the Highlands twenty years after George IV first dandified a plaid, the cult had become embedded and embellished with a historic pedigree of highly questionable provenance!

Together with her beloved consort the Queen fell for the Highland myth in its entirety. Their house at Balmoral created a whole style of 'Scottish Baronial' and inspired a rash of imitators from the wealthy strata of Victorian industrialists and tycoons seeking to invent pedigrees of their own.

Tartan abounded. The ageing Queen Empress, desolate at the loss of her beloved Albert, sought solace in her Stuart roots and the cult of Charles Edward, notwithstanding he was her family's foe and, had he succeeded, she would never have reached the throne. Her journal entry for 12 September 1873 records:

> I feel a sort of reverence in going over these scenes of [the Pretender's trekking across the western Highlands] in this most beautiful country, which I am proud to call my own, where there was such devoted loyalty to the family of my ancestors – for Stuart blood is in my veins, and I am now their representative.[3]

The Jacobite movement had thus succeeded in popular romance where it had so signally failed in historical reality. Whether any of those who shivered in the morning showers on the cold Culloden Moor, so many years before, would have appreciated the irony has to remain questionable.

THE BATTLEFIELD TRAIL

The Jacobites have no truly dedicated museum, if the visitor centres at Glenfinnan and Culloden are discounted. Scottish Highland edged weapons and firearms feature in a number of collections, particularly those of the Royal Armouries in Leeds, the National Museum of Scotland in Edinburgh and the Kelvingrove Museum in Glasgow. Armour Class, based in Glasgow, manufacture extremely good quality facsimiles to museum standard. The West Highland Museum situated at Fort William is also worth a visit.

In England, Carlisle Castle and the nearby Cathedral where some of the Jacobite prisoners were lodged both survive, and the events of the '45 are commemorated in the display housed in the great square Norman Keep. The name 'Military Road' is still used for the B6318, Wade's Highway running east to west from Tyne to Solway.

Berwick Barracks, built by the great Palladian architect Sir John Vanbrugh (1717–1721), still stand intact beside the Cow Port and inside the ring of the Elizabethan enceinte. The King's Own Scottish Borderers are based there with their regimental museum, and the permanent exhibition *By Beat of Drum* chronicles a soldier's life in the eighteenth and nineteenth century. Some traces of the garrison in the 1730s remain.

Any tour in Scotland should perhaps start at Glenfinnan. A suitably, almost impossibly romantic spot where the circular stone tower, erected by Alexander MacDonald of Glenaladale some seventy years after the raising of the standard there, provides magnificent views down the length of Loch Shiel, the narrow waters crowded by the blue hills around. The nearby visitor centre which, like the monument, is in the care of the National Trust for Scotland remains open from April to October.

Edinburgh Castle, the great fortress that dominates Scotland's flourishing capital, still looms over the city and affords some splendid vistas of both the Old and New Towns below. The Great Hall and the Imperial War Museum annexe both house some interesting exhibits, the latter having recently been extensively and attractively refurbished.

Stirling vies with Edinburgh for the greatest measure of visual impact. The great castle still lowers over the plain and town below and the walk up through the older portions is recommended. Like Edinburgh, Stirling has been a citadel for centuries; much of the present works date from the years 1708–1714, constructed by Captain Drury. The fortress also contains the regimental museum of the Argyll and Sutherland Highlanders.

The field of Prestonpans is identified by an earthen mound which stands just to the east of Preston, and Bankton House, Colonel Gardiner's former home, has been restored. It was in the garden of his property that the desperately wounded officer finally expired, bringing an end to an eventful military career.

Both Ruthven and Bernera barracks survive, ruined and roofless but still distinctive. Ruthven, stark and skeletal, planted on the old castle mound, seems a fitting location for almost the final act of in the rebellion of 1745. Bernera, close to the pleasant village of Glenelg, is altogether more cheerful in aspect. The road from Shiel Bridge maintains the line of the military road.

Predating both of these as a barracks is Kilchurn Castle, a superb medieval ruin which stands on the northern flank of Loch Awe. The seat of Campbell of Glenorchy, it was refurbished at the behest of Sir John Campbell, 1st Earl of Breadalbane. The barrack block, which dates from the 1690s, was a likely response to the perceived Jacobite menace, and was designed to contain a garrison able to maintain the Whig supremacy in the area.

Of the military roads built by Marshal Wade, numerous stretches can still be walked and, free from the encumbrances of traffic, road signs, power lines and the other plethora of modern manifestations, offer a unique insight into the eighteenth century. The battered but still walkable highways traverse the broad expanses of heather and gorse, with only the noise of your own footfalls and the mournful cry of the curlew to complement the perfect silence.

Fort William has little to show apart from the museum and the remains of the old Inverlochy castle which featured in the battle there in 1645, now isolated incongruously in the middle of a rather drab industrial estate, executed in a particularly appalling vernacular. Some traces of the fort begun in 1690, the sally port and a single demi-bastion survive north of the present railway station. The gateway of the Williamite fort was re-erected in the nineteenth century as the entrance to the cemetery, where it stands today, a somewhat incongruous reminder.

At Fort Augustus only a single bastion from the fort still stands, incorporated into the buildings forming the present Benedictine Abbey. At the time of writing this is shrouded in scaffolding as the place undergoes yet another transformation into a housing scheme. A visible trace of the earlier fort can be glimpsed (again behind the detritus of construction work) at the rear of the Lovat Arms Hotel.

Inverness, likewise, is devoid of remembrance, the present castle being a reconstruction dating from 1909. It still serves as a courthouse, however, and a trace of the original medieval wall survives. The Highland capital, pleasantly situated with the broad reaches of the river flowing through, does little to celebrate its Jacobite associations. The museum, housed in a ghastly 1960s building, is well worth a visit and the city is booming on the proceeds of North Sea industry and tourism.

From Inverness one would follow the B9006 for five miles to Culloden Moor. It has been suggested, quite properly, that the more energetic and determined visitor should walk the distance, following in the tracks of the Prince's army. By approaching on foot one obtains a completely different perspective, sharing the experience of the combatants (though hopefully better fed).

Culloden is perhaps one of the best preserved and most atmospheric battlefields in Britain. So many others are shamefully neglected – the very richness of our martial heritage seems to breed complacency and neglect!

I was first taken to the site as a small boy, having just seen the excellent TV dramatised documentary based on Prebble's book which was first shown late in 1964. The grainy black-and-white footage with a largely amateur cast does not detract from the effect.

The day was still, blanketed with mist and at that time the ground was hemmed in by intrusive forestry. The effect was electrifying, the slew of clan graves expressed the whole doleful eloquence of the place, a palpable sadness seemed to hang over the chill and quiet air. The impression has never vanished.

Contrary to some opinions, the land in the 1740s was not a wild expanse of blasted heath but rough grazing held in common by the tenants of the Culloden Estate; the subsequent forestation was, of course, a twentieth-century phenomenon. The National Trust for Scotland maintains the site and the visitor centre. At present an ambitious new exhibition facility is under construction, some 200 metres to the south of the existing building. At present some 200,000 visitors access the site annually.[1]

From 16 April–20 September 1996, in commemoration of the 250th anniversary of the battle, a very fine display of weapons and other artefacts, advertised as *The Swords and the Sorrows*, was mounted at the site. This was a dazzling area of fine arms – swords, dirks, Lochaber axes, firearms, powder horns, silverware and textiles. Perhaps the most complete tribute to the Jacobite movement yet created. A portion of that exhibition remains on permanent display.

Duncan Forbes, descendant and namesake of the Lord President, erected the present cairn in 1881, some 20 feet high and 18 feet in diameter, constructed in rubble and rather resembling a small-scale version of a Pictish broch. It was Forbes, the last resident owner of the Culloden estate, who planted the stone slabs over the various mass graves.

At present much work is being carried out on the site in addition to the construction of the new visitor centre. Battlefield archaeology has been employed to improve our understanding of the ground; however, the Trust still only owns about a third of the field and although the intrusive forestry has largely been cleared, resilient secondary growth is proving nearly as much of a hazard. This certainly obscures our understanding of the ground and provides a false feel for the conditions which obtained in 1746.

The tour begins at the visitor centre, and we proceed toward the left of the government line. To the left of Barrell's flank stands The English Stone, which is said to mark the pits wherein the Hanoverian dead were interred. Some yards further west lies the Well of the Dead, where the slain of Clan Chattan piled so thick.

As you continue to walk westwards you come to the slew of clan graves. In spite of the dubious provenance of Forbes's markers, these retain a strongly emotive aura. The memorial cairn, also from 1881, stands to your right. Its presence does nothing for the field, an overlay of Victorian romanticism, redolent with convenient myth. Forbes cannily avoided any reference to his distinguished ancestor, whose sympathies were staunchly Whiggish.

The path now proceeds toward the extreme right of the Jacobite line, and traces of the Leanach Enclosure may be viewed to your right. Reaching the position marked as that of the Atholl Brigade, the area to the south, that covered by the Culwhiniac Enclosure, lies outside the boundaries of the National Trust site. You now walk north-west along the Jacobite front line and note how the gap between the two armies funnels outwards.

At present, the current B9006 cuts off the extreme left where the line butted the now vanished walls of the Culloden Parks. In the midst of what would have been the second line stands the Strathallan stone, again a survivor from Forbes's day, together with two more recent additions, the French and Irish stones. The former is the most recent, erected by the White Cockade in 1994, whilst the latter was set up by the Military History Society of Ireland in 1963. The inscription reads: 'The breed of Kings, sons of Milheadh, Eager warriors and heroes'. One has to wonder if any of the Wild Geese, professional mercenaries, would have recognised themselves in this romanticised glow.

Retracing the ill-fated charge of Clan Donald from the rebel left, the width of the gap is obvious, and the notion that the clansmen should traverse such a distance under fire appears totally unsound. The ground is now generally dry, and roughly midway the Keppoch stone is said to mark the spot where the chief fell. Further east, closer to Cumberland's line, there is a marker indicating the grave pits into which so many of Clan Donald were tumbled.

A large stone boulder, a survivor from glacial deposit, lies to the east of the NT site, now largely obscured by trees. This is known as the Cumberland Stone, though whether the portly general dismounted to ascend for a better view of the field is conjectural. It must appear rather unlikely.

Old Leanach Cottage has been restored as an element of the permanent exhibition. Despite its appearance of great age it was probably built some twenty or so years after the battle when the estate was being improved.

A barn which may have once stood nearby is reputed to have been the setting for one of the atrocities committed by Hanoverian troops after the fight, when its complement of wounded Jacobites were burned to death as the place was torched. This may be apocryphal and it remains possible the building was used as a form of advanced dressing station by the government side.

The positions of forces from both sides are denoted by a helpful series of markers though their exact positioning may be open to some discussion. The walls of the Leannach and Culwhiniac enclosures are partly reconstructed and add greatly both to the visual impact and understanding the ground. The road in 1746 traversed the moor and has since been realigned, though tracing the line of the original is quite easy.

Culchunaig still stands but is beyond the Trust boundary. The track leading up to the abandoned steading follows what would have been the first Jacobite position on that flank prior to Lord George Murray's move. The buildings provide the anchor from which the Jacobite right flank began their doomed attack. Following the line of that fatal charge along the walls of the two enclosures brings you to the mass of the clan graves, the most telling evidence of the slaughter.

Beyond and north of Culchunaig it is possible to follow the course of the cavalry action as Hawley's squadrons first crossed the gully and then faced the Jacobites over the gap (note that this is now all private land). The ground is, if superficially changed, frequently still as wet underfoot and the visitor, suitably shod, can glean an understanding of how great an obstacle this sodden terrain creates.

Stand on the moor on a wet and windy day, when a keen-edged blast from the east sweeps unchecked over the plateau and the ground is heavy with surface water, and think, as you look from the government line, how that ragged army of desperate men surged across the gap into that storm of grape and musketry and how many of them now still lie here beneath the cold clay.

Lastly, Fort George at Ardersier, built to deter any future Jacobite pretenders in the following decade and completed in 1769. It remains a magnificent example of eighteenth-century defensive architecture, superbly located and preserved. Aside from the splendid defences and buildings within, the fort houses the Seafield collection of militaria and the regimental museum of the Queen's Own Highlanders.

RAISING THE GLENS –
THE HIGHLAND REGIMENTS

The trend was begun before the '45 with the raising of six Independent Companies of Highlanders, which were effectively recruited as a paramilitary police force. These were, in 1739, subsequently formed into the 43rd Regiment of Foot. Though they were provided with the ubiquitous red coat they retained their native plaid. The unit was subsequently renumbered as the 42nd – to be known as the Black Watch, one of the most distinguished in the British Army.

This rather ad hoc marriage of convenience between the uniform of the British regular and attire of the clansman created the mould for those Highland regiments raised subsequently. Their tartan, however, was an official or 'Government' pattern. Between the raising of the 43rd in 1739 and 1800, over a score of regular and no less than twenty-six fencible regiments were formed from the Highland region.[1] Only one of these, the 79th, wore a variant of the Government tartan.

Alan Cameron of Erracht, a cadet branch of the clan, was, despite the fact that he was not a great magnate or landowner, praised by Sir William Napier as one who 'brought to the ranks of the British Army more men than any other who, like himself, was commissioned to raise regiments'.[2] He had a colourful career in the American colonies and fought for the crown during the War of Independence, sustaining near crippling injuries when he shattered both ankles in a bungled bid to escape from Patriot captivity! He was able, however, on returning to London to cultivate important friends such as Pitt the Younger and Lord Melville. An advantageous marriage to a wealthy heiress significantly boosted his financial position and provided the funds for the raising of a regiment.

His early overtures were rejected, and it was not until war with revolutionary France broke out and his friend Melville was appointed as Secretary at War that the offer was finally taken up. In August 1793 Cameron was finally granted his Letter of Service which empowered him to raise a foot regiment for Crown service: 'By Beat of Drum or otherwise to raise so many men in any country or part of our Kingdom of Great Britain as shall be wanted to complete the said Regiment.'[3]

It was to prove an expensive business. Erracht's father-in-law (who had initially opposed his daughter's match) had already paid off his debts in the amount of £10,000, a very sizeable sum, and the cost of raising the new regiment was estimated to require a further investment of some £8,000. Though he already had an annual pension of £100 per annum awarded for his loyal service in the Americas, the crown was not a generous employer, his wife's health was uncertain and he had half a dozen offspring to support.

The purchase system meant that the regiment was run as a kind of joint stock company with the colonel, who often had little or nothing to do with the day-to-day business of seeking a return on his investment. Living like a gentleman was an expensive business, and a good match or a profitable campaign were both to be sought after!

Cameron's new Highland formation was to be known as the 79th Foot or Cameronian Volunteers. It was not until 1804 that the regiment was designated as the Cameron Highlanders, though in recruiting terms it was still styled the Cameron Volunteers or Reisimeid an Earrachd.[4]

Recruiting was directed from Stirling Castle and the volunteers were raised from the breadth of the country, from the dark glens to the sprawling new industrial slums of Glasgow. Erracht was partly hamstrung by the need to draw his cadre of officers from the Half Pay list, thus relieving the Crown of another fiscal burden, nor did he ever see any Bounty Money from the administration. Patriotism, it seems, was expected to be its own reward. This was a true example of privatisation – the officer in charge was effectively on his own.

If these difficulties were insufficient, he was obliged to contend with the enmity of a kinsman, Ewen Cameron of Fassfern, factor for the Clan Chief of Lochiel and related to Lord Adam Gordon, commander of land forces in Scotland.[5] Undeterred by this rival's influence at Fort William and in Lochaber, Erracht had moved there by November and his officers were soon actively recruiting. Resentment among the Fassfern faction ran deep and they were certainly not deterred from violence, though the recruits were likely to be safe enough within the walls of the fort!

As he had only three months from 17 August to bring his new regiment up to strength he could not afford to slacken in his efforts. By the latter part of October the recruits were ready to be marched south to Stirling. In order to make up the numbers he had been obliged to beg favours from his friends, including Lord Breadalbane, who had transferred some volunteers from his fencibles. However, this further enraged the Fassfern faction and Erracht found himself under fire due to Lord Gordon's partisan intermeddling.

Somehow the recruiting officers were able to make good the loss, but at a significant cost to their commander's already overstretched purse. Erracht was credited with raising some 800 men though the fiscal burden amounted to some £15,000, way above the original estimate. None of this pleased his enemies in Lochaber and the feud was still simmering the best part of a century later when the biographer of Ewen Fassfern's son, writing in 1877, remained dismissive:

> But to come to the 79th Highlanders & Sir Allan – it was late in the day when he entered the field, & being on the worst possible terms with Lochiel had not much chance of getting up men in Lochaber. But 1st he had plenty of money through a Miss Philip, a Welsh heiress of great property having fancied and married him. 2nd. He was a very cool clever fellow & knowing the value of a Highland regiment – he set up his Camp in Fort William on the Parade Ground between the fort and the village, had a couple of Pipers playing all day, & some soldiers in Cameron tartan swaggering about. Meantime he sent many agents to the towns in the south, Glasgow, Paisley etc. and some to the north of Ireland to get up recruits by every possible means, giving them a handsome bounty out of his wife's money...[6]

Despite Fassfern's active plotting, the regiment was mustered and passed its first inspection with only four men out of 654 being rejected.[7] Shipped to Ireland early in 1794, more recruits were sourced locally to make up the requisite numbers and Erracht's dream for the 79th Highlanders became a reality. He was a firm advocate of the kilt as a superlative form of battle dress and the regiment was soon tested when it took part in the expedition to Low Counties that August.

At some point an anomaly occurred in the weaving of the regimental tartan. This was no random error. Erracht did not care to adopt the Cameron sett as he felt the colours clashed with the scarlet coat — or, possibly, he was determined to take an additional swing at his enemies within the clan hierarchy. In any event the 'Cameron Erracht', said to have been woven to a pattern designed by his mother, became the standard issue for the 79th.

Despite all of his tribulations, threats to the regiment's very existence continued over the next few years and it was only their Colonel's resilient obduracy that prevented them being disbanded and the men drafted into other formations.

NOTES

1. THE MOOR

1 *Clan Donald's Greatest Defeat – The Battle of Harlaw 1411* (England 2005).
2 See A. Herman, *The Scottish Enlightenment* (London 2001), p. 117.
3 *Jacobite General* (London 1958).
4 See bibliography.
5 *Like Hungry Wolves: Culloden Moor 16 April 1746* (London 1994) and *1745: A Military History of the Last Jacobite Rising* (England 1996).

2. THE HOUSE OF STUART

1 J.D. Mackie, *A History of Scotland* (England 1964), p. 96.
2 Hector Boece in his *Historia* expounds the romantic view that the family were descended from Banquo and it is they, stretching in a long line from the murdered man's son Fleance, who haunts MacBeth.
3 See S. Boardman, *The Early Stewart Kings* (East Lothian 1996), p. xiii.
4 Robert III was disadvantaged by his given name of John; it was deemed unsuitable for a King of Scots due to the association with John Baliol, 'Toom Tabard', whose brief and inglorious tenure was clearly not likely to inspire! On a more practical note Robert also suffered from some form of impairment resulting from injuries sustained when he was kicked by a horse.
5 Patrick Dunbar, Earl of March, was one of the architects of the Scottish recovery under Robert II; his feud with Douglas prompted a shift of allegiance. Whilst he ably counselled the impetuous Hotspur and Homildon, he later acted as a military advisor to Henry IV in the campaign against the Percies which ended with Hotspur's defeat and death at Shrewsbury in 1403.
6 Rothesay died in rather suspicious circumstances whilst incarcerated under his uncle's control. Albany was cleared of any foul play, the Duke's death being ascribed to natural causes. Needless to say it was the Regent who also directed the investigation!
7 James I was murdered on the night of 20 February 1437 while he maintained his winter court in the Dominican Friary at Perth. The assassination was brutal and bloody. The King managed to lift the floorboards of his chamber and drop into the undercroft below but he was found and hacked to death; the Queen herself was wounded as she tried to assist.

8   So called because of a prominent birthmark which covered one side of his face.

9   This was in February 1452, after the King accused Douglas of his treachery in entering into a treasonable accord or 'band' with the Earls of Crawford and Ross. The 6th Earl of Douglas and his younger brother had also been summarily done to death at an earlier feast at Edinburgh castle in November 1440, the infamous 'Black Dinner'.

10 These killings occurred at Lauder, where the unfortunate courtiers were hanged from the parapet of the bridge!

11 Marie de Guise, who clearly did not lack a sense of humour, is said to have politely declined an offer of marriage from Henry VIII on the ground that 'her neck was too slender'.

12 'Montrose ranks by common consent with the greatest of his age, with Cromwell and Conde. The historian of the British Army has described him as "perhaps the most brilliant natural military genius disclosed by the Civil War."' Thus John Buchan extols the talent of his hero in *Montrose* (London 1928), p. 389. Modern writers tend to be somewhat more critical: see S. Reid, *The Campaigns of Montrose* (Edinburgh 1990).

13 The Battle of Marston Moor began in the early evening after the armies had confronted each other for the length of much of the afternoon. Cromwell commanded the Parliamentary Horse on the left, Fairfax those on the right. The future Lord Protector was wounded in the first clash and obliged to briefly withdraw for medical attention. Fairfax fared badly against Goring, and the Royalists came close to winning the infantry battle in the centre where several Scottish regiments gave way. Leven was preparing to quit the field, thinking the day lost. It was left to Cromwell to shore up the Parliamentary forces and tip the balance.

14 Or MacCholla; or even in the anglicised form Sir Alexander MacDonald (or MacDonnell). MacColla means 'son of Coll', his father being Alasdair MacColla Chiotaich. For a full discussion see D. Stevenson, *Highland Warrior: Alasdair MacColla and the Civil Wars* (Edinburgh 1980), pp. 1–5.

15 The principal fort was Mingary castle which still stands, dramatically perched on the coast of Ardnamurchan in Argyll, looking out toward Mull. It was here in 1495 that James IV accepted the submission of the Highland chiefs, and in 1644 MacColla, having overawed the Covenanting garrison which surrendered without a fight, used the place as a gaol.

16 'Great Chief' Argyll was on the one hand a leading magnate and politician on the national stage, whilst retaining his hereditary chieftainship of Clan Campbell. The rivalry between them and Clan Donald stretched back to the Lordship of the Isles. The Campbells has been steadily increasing their lands and powers before the abolition of the Lordship in 1493 and had subsequently risen to challenge Clan Donald's hegemony.

17 The courtyard wall or 'barnekin' still stands at Newark.

18 The remains of the castle at Ardvreck still occupy a spur of rock that juts out into Loch Assynt in Sutherland, the tall towers of the mountains crowding an almost impossibly romantic location, perhaps a fitting memorial to Montrose.

19 Tam Dalyell, an eccentric figure who, it is said, refused to cut his beard for the whole period between the execution of Charles I and the restoration of his son! Having quit the realm in disgust at the regicide, he served with some distinction in the armies of the Russian Tsar and returned with ample funds to construct his fine house of the Binns. The Covenanters believed he had sold his soul to the devil who, as part of the bargain, rendered him invulnerable to musketry 'shot proof'. They ascribed his (and later Claverhouse's) deliverance from their volleys to this infernal trade rather than their own limited marksmanship!

20 Quoted in M. Linklater and C. Hesketh, *For King and Conscience* (London 1989), p. 45.

21 Linklater and Hesketh op. cit., p. 55.

22 Sir George Mackenzie, the Lord Advocate.

3. THE WHITE COCKADE

1 The *Linn nan Creach*, usually considered to encompass the 150 years after the final demise of the Lordship in 1493. See C. Bingham, *Beyond the Highland Line* (London 1991), p. 97.

2 Stevenson op. cit., p. 267.

3 Ibid., pp. 270–271.

4 Sir Ewen Cameron of Lochiel, 13th Chief. He had a long and colourful career and is credited as being responsible for killing the last wolf in Scotland. He had previously been a ward of Argyll which had prevented him from being 'out' with Montrose, though, as a young man, he had ripped out the throat of a Cromwellian officer with his teeth in an encounter!

5 Stevenson op. cit., p. 272.

6 Effectively a bond for good behaviour.

7 Captain Edward Burt, who served with Marshal Wade, identified the chief's 'tail' or following as comprising: The Hanchman – a kind of secretary-cum-bodyguard, he would stand behind or at the 'haunch' of the chief whilst the latter was at table (hence our expression 'henchman'); Bard – the poet; Bladier – the spokesman or negotiator; Gilli-more – sword-bearer; Gilli-casflue – has the job of carting his chief over fords and mosses to save his dainty footwear; Gilly comstrainie – performs a like service, leading the chief's garron over difficult or wet ground; Gilly-trushanarnish – the baggage handler; Piper – a position of rank as the piper would himself be of gentlemanly stock, with his own gilly to cart the pipes themselves. For a good modern image of the chief with his tail on the move, see plate A from S. Reid, *Highland Clansman 1689–1746* (Osprey 'Military', 1997).

8 Stevenson op. cit., pp. 280–281.

9 Caterans appear in the fourteenth century and were a class of professional warriors attached to the household of a chief or magnate. They may be likened to the Irish 'kernes' who served the Anglo-Irish lords of Ireland at the same time. The broken men and outlaws who infested the Highlands during the restoration were possibly of a similar type or, often, otherwise ordinary tenants who had been made destitute by the troubles. The growth in the business of cattle droving, which was an important feature of the local economy, provided a form of camouflage as broken men could pass from one district to another in the guise of peaceable drovers. Cattle raiding and 'protection' offered sources of income. Chiefs might be willing to employ caterans as military muscle, thus offering them a cloak of respectability.

10 Stevenson op. cit., p. 283.

11 Ibid., p. 286.

12 Ibid., p. 288.

13 This was a finely balanced problem. Parliament could perhaps humble Argyll, yet, as a servant of the Crown, it would not do for his actions to be censured for fear this weakened the Royal Prerogative.

14 Stevenson op. cit., p. 290.

15 These companies were to be recruited from the ranks of the regulars and expected to live off the land; as such they were more likely to exacerbate than contain the problem of lawlessness.

16 Lochiel arranged a sham riot to pose a notional threat to the safety of the commissioners then appeared to intervene on their behalf, thus providing the pretext to 'escort' them from Lochaber. See Stevenson op. cit., p. 291.

17 Ibid., p. 294.

18 Ibid., p. 295.

19 Ibid., p. 293.

20 From the Latin 'Jacobus'.

21 The later barracks occupies the site of the medieval castle, still standing in 1689.

22 These were not uncommon during the period – the lined iron barrels were stiffened with alloy and splints, bound with iron wire and rope, coated with canvas wrapping, profiled in timber and then finally sheathed in leather. The idea was to provide a light weapon that could be easily transported and manhandled. See Col. H.C.B. Rogers, *Artillery Through the Ages* (London 1971), pp. 49–52.

23 The spot known as 'Soldier's Leap' is said to mark the spot where one of the redcoats made a spectacular jump over the Garry to avoid his pursuers. The feat certainly looks improbable, but on the other hand he had ample incentive!

24 One of the difficulties facing the Williamites was that the pike had, by now, been phased out and replaced by the bayonet. This was not the later socket type that fitted over the mouth of the barrel: the plug bayonet was effectively a long-bladed dagger that was pushed into the muzzle. It offered a very poor compromise and obviously prevented reloading whilst fixed in place. The flintlock muskets with their plug bayonets rammed in proved a very poor match for broadsword and target or Lochaber axe!

4. DEATH OF NATIONHOOD — THE ROAD TO UNION

1 A. Herman, *The Scottish Enlightenment* (London 2001), p. 116.

2 G.A. Hayes-McCoy, *Irish Battles* (Belfast 1969), p. 214.

3 Hayes-McCoy op. cit., p. 235.

4 As the eighteenth century progressed, the rise in English/British sea power was to become an important factor.

5 J. Black, *Culloden and the '45* (New York 1990), p. 15.

6 John Campbell of Glenorchy, 1st Earl of Breadalbane, was the chief of the main cadet branch of Clan Campbell and devoted his long career to establishing his personal position as the most influential Whig magnate in the Highlands. Kilchurn Castle on Loch Awe was a tower house which he had altered and extended in the 1680s to form a barracks for Highland companies – at once a practical move and a statement of power. See C. Tabraham and D. Grove, *Fortress Scotland and the Jacobites* (London 1995), pp. 42–45.

7 See J. Prebble, *Glencoe* (London 1966), pp. 136–141.

8 The epithet 'Glen o' Weeping' is a later romantic attachment created by Macaulay. It more likely means 'Glen of Dogs' after the legendary wolfhounds of Fionn MacCumhail whose warband, the Feinn, were said to have battled against Norse invaders pushing up Loch Leven. The Northmen arrived in forty galleys, but so fierce was the fight that only two were required to evacuate the survivors!

9 Glencoe still presents a wild and desolate appearance. The stone cairn which is allegedly the point at which the MacDonald chiefs were installed still stands towards the eastern end.

10 Hugh Mackay of Scourie had instigated the hurried reconstruction around the core of the earlier fort.

11 The Coire Gabhail and Devil's Staircase are still perfectly accessible though the climb in both cases is steep and difficult. Full protective clothing, stout boots and the relevant OS 1:25000 maps are essential.

12 The 'curse' of Glencoe is said to have haunted the Campbells of Glenlyon. One of the lairds, The Black Colonel, served as a redcoat for most of his career; dour and unmarried, he felt the cold hand of history ever on his shoulder. At the end of his service he was placed in command of a firing party tasked to execute deserters. In fact the wretched men were not to be killed but advised, at the last moment, of their reprieve. Unfortunately, as Campbell (who, as the officer in charge, was the only one aware of the changed orders) drew the reprieve from his pocket he let fall his handkerchief, the signal to fire, and the men died ignorant of their release! See Prebble op. cit., p. 259.

13 The 'Auld Alliance' had always been a marriage of expediency and the French would generally not hesitate to play their ally as a pawn on the larger board. The Scottish Reformation had finally alienated the relationship but the cultural ties still lingered.

14 Argyll's regiment and others fought hard for Dutch Billy and suffered great loss at Dottignies in July 1693. The Cameronians had been decimated a year earlier at Steenkirk. William's steadfast if uninspired generalship may have held the French at bay but it cost his armies dear. Duncanson went on to serve with some distinction, though his expenditure on his regiment placed him in debt. He was finally killed at the siege of Valencia de Alcantara.

15 Scottish merchants were trading with the English colonies in spite of such statutory restrictions as the Navigation Acts.

16 This colossal investment equated to something in the order of half the country's wealth. See Mackie op. cit., pp. 254–256.

17 Anne's tragedy was that she had in fact produced no fewer the eighteen children, none of which had survived infancy.

18 James, at his birth, had been labelled by Whig satirists as 'The Baby in the Bedpan' as it was suggested he was a substitute foundling!

19 The offending clauses were in fact struck out of the final draft of the Bill.

20 Mackie op. cit., p. 262.

21 Black op. cit., p. 18.

22 Ibid., p. 18.

23 The besiegers initially were Leven's Regiment, who fought at Killiecrankie, later the 25th Foot and now The King's Own Scottish Borderers.

24 Tabraham and Groves op. cit., p. 39.

25 The Scottish regiments continued to do good service and suffer grave losses at Blenheim and in the course of Marlborough's subsequent victories. The colonel of the Scots Fusiliers led the first rank of the assault on the fortified village of Blenheim, planting his swordpoint in the barricades before he fell.

26 Post Union, Dory's appointment was with the Board of Ordnance in London. This was a late medieval and Tudor institution which was charged with the supply of artillery, guns and munitions as well as being responsible for fortifications. See Tabraham and Stokes op. cit., pp. 48–49.

5. THE TIME OF 'BOBBING JOHN'

1 Traditional ballad, *The Battle of Sheriffmuir.*
2 From *The Flying Post*, 7 March 1723. Quoted in Black op. cit., p. 36.
3 'An Address to the Peers of England', ibid., p. 22.
4 This was despite his best attempts at sycophancy. Had Mar secured advancement under the Hanoverians, it seems highly unlikely he would have reverted to the House of Stuart.
5 Quoted in Black op. cit., p. 23.
6 When the Jacobites finally surrendered the total haul of prisoners was in the region of 1,600, including seventy-five Northumbrian gentry.
7 Forster subsequently managed to escape from Newgate Gaol and thus cheated the executioner. Derwentwater was less fortunate and went to the block on 24 February 1716; he became a symbol of a doomed, romantic attachment to the House of Stuart. His younger brother was taken at sea during the '45 and also executed. The Radcliffes' vast estates were attainted and most came into the care of Chelsea Hospital. Dilston Castle near Corbridge in Northumberland, the Earl's home, has been partly restored and is open to the public. Of his grand design, however, nothing remains except the block of the medieval hall tower and the delightful recusant chapel.
8 Wightman's battalions did succeed in firing several volleys, inflicting loss on Clan Donald, including the popular Captain of Clanranald. Glengarry rallied the waverers: 'Revenge, revenge. Today for revenge and tomorrow for mourning.' See D.J. Sadler, *Scottish Battles* (Edinburgh 1996), p. 189.
9 Jean de Robethon, quoted in Black op. cit., p. 25.
10 George Bubb, ibid., p. 25.
11 Ibid., p. 26.
12 1700–1721. Charles XII proved a most formidable military talent, defeating the Russians at Narva early in the war, though his army was finally and decisively beaten at Poltava.
13 Black op. cit., p. 28.
14 1663–1745.
15 Quoted in Black op. cit., p. 29.
16 Ibid., p. 30.
17 Eilean Donan Castle, traditionally a Mackenzie hold, was restored in 1912 and now remains one of the most photographed of all Scottish castles. It is said that the plan for the original layout was revealed to the architect in a dream.
18 The Coehorn Mortar is named after its creator, the 'Dutch Vauban' – Menno Van Coehorn (1641–1704).
19 Not all from the clan were Whigs; these were of Ormidale and Glendaruel.
20 Quoted in Black op. cit., pp. 31–32.
21 The tension which arose between Britain and Russia, ruled by Peter the Great, had led to a naval deployment in those waters, which obviously drained the Navy's available resources.
22 Quoted in Black op. cit., p. 33.
23 The War of Spanish Succession had left England with a crippling deficit of £10 million. A scheme was conceived whereby a private company limited by shares, the South Sea Company, would assume the entire risk at a rate of 6 per cent in return for monopolistic concessions over trade in the South Seas. The directors believed

the company could reap huge profits from slavery and other undertakings. Investors flocked to buy the first issue of shares, and then the next, and the share price soared. Even the outbreak of hostilities with Spain in 1718 did not calm the market, which continued to rise. By this time the directors had realised that the profits being generated could never provide adequate returns to investors and that the shares were hopelessly overvalued. They then began to try and offload their personal stock whilst the price was buoyant. This fuelled a crisis of confidence, the price plummeted as panic buying ensued and the debacle resulted in a stock market crash. Many investors lost heavily including Isaac Newton and Jonathan Swift.

24 The 'Wild Geese' were originally those 11,000 Irish troops who, under their commander Patrick Sarsfield, left their homeland after the ruin of Jacobite hopes and the siege of Limerick. They sailed from Cork to Brest, and in France James formed them into four regiments which entered the French Service – the Irish Brigade. Ireland had been exporting fighting men for centuries and an earlier mass defection had occurred when the rebel earls Hugh O'Neil and Rory O'Donnell fled in 1607 after the disastrous Battle of Kinsale.

25 The conspiracy is known as the Atterbury Plot after the Jacobite Bishop of Rochester.

26 George Tilson, quoted in Black op. cit., p. 34.

27 Ibid., p. 34.

28 Layer suffered the full ghastly horror of a traitor's death by hanging, drawing and quartering. It is possible he was also tortured beforehand.

6. ROADS, REDCOATS AND REBELS

1 Quoted in J. Prebble, *Culloden* (London 1961), p. 35.

2 As observed by a late seventeenth-century English traveller, William Sacheverell.

3 Long sections of Wade's roads can still be traversed on foot including the way over the Corrieyairack Pass – Ordnance Survey Landranger 1:50,000 series sheet 34.

4 Tabraham and Grove op. cit., p. 69.

5 A Disarming Act had been passed to deprive Highlanders of their arms; this measure was largely ineffective.

6 Quoted in Tabraham and Grove op. cit., p. 69.

7 Ibid., pp. 69–70.

8 Ibid., p. 70.

9 Ibid., p. 72.

10 Ironically, Wade's roads proved particularly useful to the Jacobites in 1745!

11 Tabraham and Grove op. cit., p. 73.

12 Ibid., p. 75.

13 William Augustus, born 1721, the future Duke of Cumberland.

14 All that now remains of the old fort is a single length of curtain wall loopholed for muskets, which survives to the rear of the Lovat Arms Hotel. Of Wade's fort, just a single well-preserved bastion stands within the complex of later, nineteenth-century religious buildings, currently being redeveloped for residential purposes.

15 Though now roofless, the layout of the barracks survives remarkably well and its commanding elevation atop the original motte is immediately apparent. The stable block was added in 1734. Though it initially resisted the first Jacobite attempt, the diminutive garrison surrendered in 1746.

16 Bernera Barracks were built between 1719–1723 and remain largely intact. The area
   is particularly lovely and contains the traces of earlier Pictish brochs, though it is of
   course uncertain as to whether these were intended as defensible.

17 Working with Romer, Robert Adam carried through a number of changes at
   Edinburgh. In 1737 the interior of the Great Hall was refurbished as additional
   accommodation, and the former Banqueting Hall was also converted into barracks.
   Similar upgrading took place at Dumbarton.

18 The substantive Georgian barrack piles at Berwick, which stand completely preserved
   within the Elizabethan Walls, were initially designed by Sir John Vanburgh. Presently in
   the care of English Heritage, they offer a number of museum displays and remain the
   home of the King's Own Scottish Borderers.

19 Burt's work, probably written in 1725–1726, was not published until 1754. Though he
   had little sympathy with his Highland hosts, Burt was fair-minded and meticulous in
   his observations. He found their sense of propriety at times alarming: 'I happened to
   be at the house of a certain chief, when the chieftain of another tribe came to make
   a visit. I told him I thought some of his people had not behaved toward me with that
   civility I expected of the clan. He started, clapped his hand to his broadsword and said,
   if I required it, he would send me two or three of their heads. I laughed thinking it a
   joke, but the chief insisted he was a man of his word.' We may fairly safely assume the
   Englishman did not take up the offer of decapitations! If not impressed by Highland
   notions of honour, considering them backward, he was mindful of their sincerity:
   '[This] oath they take upon a drawn dirk, which they kiss in a solemn manner,
   consenting if ever they prove perjured to be stabbed with the same weapon.' Whilst
   he deprecated their constant foraying over cattle he recorded that he had never been
   robbed by them, except for perhaps a missing pair of gloves. See Prebble op. cit., pp.
   42–43.

20 Quoted in M. Brander, *The Making of the Scottish Highlands* (London 1980), p. 101.

21 Brander op. cit., p. 101.

22 Ibid., p. 101.

23 Sage came to Lochcarron in 1726, immediately ran into local opposition and had to
   resort to bribing a single parishioner to attend! His persistence was rewarded and he
   remained as minister until his death nearly fifty years later. A man of great physical
   strength, Sage was happy to prove his point with fists if so challenged. See Brander
   op. cit., p. 102. The church of Rome was equally active, however, and in 1731 Hugh
   MacDonald of Morar had returned from Rome as Vicar-Apostolic to the glens. He
   recruited youngsters to the priesthood and held services in roofless chapels. Despite his
   personal charisma, and local tolerance of Popish presence, this was bound to spread
   alarm amongst the Whig clans. He was not alone: a number of distinguished Catholic
   clergy, including the Protestant Lochiel's brother Alexander Cameron, preached openly
   in the Highlands. See Prebble op. cit., p. 50.

24 Brander op. cit., p. 102.

25 During the sixteenth and seventeenth centuries the Highland pipes began to reach
   their full design and came to supplant the Highland harp (*clarsach*) as the preferred
   instrument. As early as 1500 the MacCrimmons had established a school for pipers on
   Skye. Burt and other commentators failed to comprehend that, in terms of martial
   music, the pipes were to the Highlands what the drums represented in English
   regiments. Major General David Stewart of Garth observed in 1822: 'Playing the
   bagpipes within doors is a Lowland or English custom. In the Highlands the piper

is always in the open air; and when people wish to dance to his music, it is on the green, if the weather permits; nothing but necessity makes them attempt a pipe dance in the house. The bagpipe was a field instrument intended to call the clans to arms and animate them in battle, and was no more intended for the house than a round of six-pounders.' From *Sketches of the Character, Manners and Present State of the Highlanders of Scotland with the details of the Military Service of the Highland Regiments.* Quoted in Brander op. cit., p. 103.

26 Stevenson op. cit., pp. 6–7.

27 Ibid., pp. 7–10.

28 These minority kingships were those of James II, James III, James IV, James V, Mary and James VI, all those who ruled following the assassination of James I.

29 Stevenson op. cit., p. 9.

30 Ibid., p. 10.

31 Ibid., p. 14.

32 'Blackmail' was the Highlander's custom of extorting money from his Lowland neighbours for 'protecting' his cattle from harm or theft, a handy adjunct to husbandry.

33 Quoted in Prebble op. cit., p. 47.

34 The blood feud or vendetta was endemic, not just in the Highlands but also, in the sixteenth century, amongst the Border 'Names'. A member of the clan accepted without question the quarrel of the chief or any of the name. This would be writ in blood and the antagonism could subsist for generations. Honour was all, and this tribalism was something that Lowland writers such as Burt could not truly fathom, so alien was the concept to the developing society south of the Highland line. In 1396 King Robert III and his court gathered to watch the bloody denouement of a feud between Clan Chattan (literally 'Clan of the Cats', an ancient confederation of minor clans) and Clan Kay. Thirty paladins from each fought literally to the death in a bespoke arena erected for the occasion on the North Inch of the Tay at Perth. Only a single survivor from Clan Kay's detachment survived by leaping into the river. From Clan Chattan eleven outlived the day. The Keiths and the Gunns, in 1464, arranged a similar bout with a dozen champions apiece but the feud was still going strong some three score years later!

35 Forbes's House at Culloden was to feature in the battle. The Lord President was a staunch Whig but received scant recognition from the government for his efforts. He was, in quieter times, well noted for his abundant hospitality.

36 Quoted in Prebble op. cit., p. 35.

37 Ibid., p. 36.

38 Ibid., p. 52.

39 Ibid., p. 53.

40 Dr Archibald Cameron, whose portrait (now in the Scottish National Portrait Gallery) shows him wearing Lowland rather than Highland attire, served as his brother's lieutenant colonel with the clan regiment during the '45. He escaped the immediate consequences by fleeing into exile but, on returning in 1753, was apprehended and subsequently executed.

41 Quoted in Prebble op. cit., p. 53.

42 Ibid., p. 45. Burt makes his point with an anecdote which tells of a Lowland lady's embarrassment when attempting to follow a Highland ghilly, clad in the plaid, uphill on a windy day!

43 Some late seventeenth-century and early eighteenth-century clothing has survived

from peat burials which suggest that breeches were commonly worn.

44 The early form of kilt was essentially a cut-down plaid with the tops of the pleats secured by stitching. It would appear a good deal more rough and ready than the present, sharply creased, pleated garment. Whether its invention was properly credited to Rawlinson, who was working in Lochaber during the 1720s, is not precisely clear. The mere fact that the credit attaches to an Englishman is likely to be a source of dispute.

45 The earliest reference comes from 1501 when James IV is recorded as having purchased an axe of the 'Lochaber fashion'. See D.H. Caldwell, *The Scottish Armoury* (Edinburgh 1979), pp. 19–20.

46 Caldwell op. cit., pp. 24–26.

47 Ibid., pp. 37–41. The backsword has only the leading edge sharpened, the rear edge is left blunted. Weapons of this type might be favoured by the mounted arm, ideal for the downward stroke.

48 These curved or Turkish (*Turcheach*) blades were by no means uncommon. The anonymous Penicuik artist who drew a series of vignettes of figures from the '45 shows several wielding blades of this type.

49 Caldwell op. cit., pp. 56–50.

50 This is an eyewitness account from an Edinburgh gentleman who witnessed the Highland army at close quarters. Its veracity might be open to question, but it does indicate that the Jacobite army, prior to Prestonpans, was very poorly equipped with muskets.

51 A Dutch design which spread to Britain, Scandinavia and as far afield as Africa. See H.L. Peterson, *The Book of the Gun* (London 1963), pp. 78–79.

52 Caldwell op. cit., pp. 64–70.

53 A *brosnachadh catha*, a Celtic 'incitement to battle'.

54 An eyewitness to the burying of the English dead after Falkirk noted that it was downward cuts to the head and neck that had caused death.

55 Quoted in S. Reid, *Highland Clansman* (England 1997), p. 16.

56 Sullivan's reputation has suffered, largely due to his differences with Lord George Murray whom certain writers identify as the most competent of the Prince's officers, this is particularly true of John Prebble who paints a very pejorative picture of the Irishman. Later authors, such as Stuart Reid, have attempted a more balanced view. See *Like Hungry Wolves* (London 1994), pp. 14–15.

57 A particular example from the '45 attaches to Campbell of Breadalbane, who sent the fiery cross around his tenantry by Loch Tay to raise troops for the government. The cross is said to have travelled 32 miles in three hours. See Prebble op. cit., p. 41.

58 The Highland charge would have been unlikely to develop prior to the seventeenth century, as the weapons which facilitated its adoption were not available. As Professor Stevenson points out, the double-handed sword tended to impede agility, and the fact the wearer, lacking a shield, had to resort to mail likewise added to his burden. The adoption of the single-handed, basket-hilted sword and the target dispensed with the need for body armour and increased the potential for greater mobility. It is also possible that the use of a rapid charge was influenced by Irish precedent and brought back to Scotland by 'redshanks' or mercenaries. The use of musketry, whilst not necessarily likely to cause widespread casualties amongst the lines to be assaulted, could be used both to target enemy officers and to provoke counter-fire at long range. The Highlanders could then close the gap by a rapid advance before their opponents had

time to reload. Actually abandoning their long guns, which seems completely contrary to any accepted tactical doctrine, was nonetheless a common-sense practice. The attack was delivered with edged weapons only, which, though technically outdated, were superior in the melee. In MacColla's time Lowland infantry had no bayonets whatsoever and were obliged to rely on clubbed muskets or munition-quality (i.e. mass-produced government issue) swords. The use of the plug bayonet was equally an abandonment of the firepower of the musket. Even Hawley, for all his contempt, appreciated that where regular troops had to rely on their bayonets they were disadvantaged. See Stevenson op. cit., pp. 82–84.

59 Quoted in Reid op. cit., p. 16.

7. WILDERNESS YEARS

1 Black op. cit., p. 52.

2 Ibid., p. 38.

3 Ibid., p. 38.

4 The diplomatic sphere was divided into two sections; the more distant Northern region embraced Russia, Turkey, Austria, Scandinavia, the German States and the Dutch.

5 Black op. cit., p. 39.

6 This was in 1727. Gibraltar had come into British possession earlier in the century.

7 These occurred in Glasgow. Black op. cit., p. 42.

8 Ibid., p. 42.

9 Ibid., p. 43.

10 Ibid., p. 43.

11 Ibid., pp. 44–46.

12 Ibid., p. 46.

13 The King had been born in 1683 and Walpole earlier in 1676.

14 Black op. cit., p. 47.

15 Gordon of Glenbucket, born around 1675, was an ardent Jacobite and one to whom George II is said to have had a particular aversion. He was 'out' with the '45 despite his years and was described by one eyewitness as being a crooked old man. He died in 1750.

16 Robert Jenkins preserved the ear lopped off by the Spanish and brought it home suitably pickled. The affair became something of a cause célèbre and he was able to produce the picked ear when questioned by the Commons. When asked of his reaction at the point of severance he exclaimed, 'I commended my soul to God and my cause to my country'.

17 The Spanish Queen is said to have muttered threats to the effect that Spain could stir up internal difficulties in England, presumably a reference to the exiled Stuarts. See Black op. cit., p. 47.

18 Ibid., p. 51.

19 Ibid., p. 51.

20 George II led a coalition army of British, Austrian and German contingents. This composite force pushed through western Germany with the strategic objective of driving a wedge between the French and the Bavarians. Marshal de Noailles marched across the Rhine and encircled the allies on the north bank of the Main. George

fell back toward Hanau. De Noailles detached de Grammont to block his retreat at Dettingen. On 27 June the battle opened with French artillery thundering over the Main. George swung his forces around to conform and de Grammont took the opportunity to attack. The King faced his line about and advanced to contact. The foot regiments making up the French right centre were seen off by sustained volley fire. A rather confused cavalry melee ensued with a series of charges and counter-charges. George proved an excellent battlefield commander in the thick of the fight. When the French horse finally retired the foot succumbed to panic and fled; many were drowned in the Main. Tactically it was a famous victory but the strategic consequences were limited.

21 A.J. Guy, 'The Army of the Georges' in D. Chandler (ed.), *Oxford History of the British Army*, p. 93.

22 *Oxford History* op. cit., p. 92.

23 Though duty against rioters and smugglers sounds unglamorous, the experience did provide officers and men with experience of what would now be described as 'low-intensity' warfare. Smuggling operations were organised on a grand scale and, in some cases, represented a form of guerrilla warfare.

24 S. Reid., *Like Hungry Wolves* (London 1994), pp. 29–30.

25 *Oxford History* op. cit., p. 99.

26 Ibid., p. 101.

27 Wolfe was by no means the only veteran of Culloden to serve in this campaign; the Chevalier Johnstone acted as his opponent the Marquis de Montcalm's aide de camp.

28 'Double shotted' i.e. with two balls in the load; the flintlock is remarkably robust, though the recoil is terrific.

29 Lt. Col. Russell was rather dismissive of the Royal Welch Fusiliers: 'a good sort of people, very well in their way, but low enough'. Oxford op. cit., p. 105.

30 P. Young, *The British Army 1642–1970* (London 1967), p. 62.

31 Now the Grenadier Guards.

32 Young op. cit., p. 63.

33 Ibid., p. 64.

34 Early military long guns tended to have wooden ramrods. These were obviously less strong than the later steel variety, but there were fears that steel could spark and thus ignite the charge prematurely.

35 *Oxford History* op. cit., p. 110.

36 The battalion comprised eight 'hatmen' and two flank or grenadier companies.

37 Colonel Lascelles still commanded his regiment in person at Prestonpans.

38 The colonel's company was led, in practice, by the senior regimental lieutenant.

39 Grenadiers were so named from the projectile weapons they carried, originally called grenadoes after the Spanish for pomegranates. These were essentially heavy infantry used for assaulting fortified positions, the steadiest and most experienced in the regiment.

40 The quality of the non-field officers varied. Many of the surgeons were highly competent professionals, though some of their clerical contemporaries were less highly regarded.

41 Kingston's Horse were a volunteer regiment raised during the '45.

42 When an officer who might have advanced through merit or sheer hard work came to retire, he did not own the commission he held. He could, however, go on the Half Pay list of a disbanded regiment, and the commission he had effectively vacated became available to another.

43 The dragoon owed his origins to Central Europe in the sixteenth and seventeenth centuries. Purely a mounted infantryman at the outset, he was named after the carbine or dragon he carried.

44 Col. H.C.B. Rogers, *Artillery through the Ages* (England 1971), p. 59.

45 Rogers op. cit., pp. 65–68.

8. RAISING THE STANDARD

1　Black op. cit., p. 59.

2　Henry Stuart, Cardinal Duke of York, on his brother's death the titular 'Henry IX'.

3　The Duke of Liria – Duke of Berwick on his father's death.

4　The agent in question was Ormonde's bastard, James Butler, who had reported in August 1743.

5　Black op. cit., p. 56.

6　Ibid., pp. 56–57.

7　Sir F. Maclean, *Bonnie Prince Charlie* (London 1998), p. 130.

8　Black op. cit., p. 59.

9　Spain was far more focused on likely gains in Italy and there was much campaigning down the length of the Peninsula. Franco-Spanish armies inflicted a severe reverse on Britain's ally Charles Emmanuel III of Sardinia at Bassignano on 27 September 1745. See Black op. cit., p. 60.

10 Ibid., p. 61.

11 Perhaps the most active of this rather shadowy clique was Antoine Walsh of Nantes. Formerly commissioned in the French service, the slave trade had made him enormously rich. Walsh had been introduced to the Prince by another of the Wild Geese, Lord Clare, who at that time commanded the Irish brigade. If the French Crown was keen to be seen to keep its distance, it would appear that, at various points down the line, the wheels were being greased. See J.S. Gibson, *Ships of the '45* (London 1967), p. 8.

12 Fontenoy is regarded as de Saxe's masterpiece, thought the day was hard fought and cost both sides around 7,000 casualties. De Saxe had formed a defensive line south-east of Tournai, deploying his men so as to form a salient with both flanks secured, his line strengthened by a series of emplacements. He reserved his strongest works for his left where, correctly, he believed Cumberland would attack with his British troops, entrusting the assault on the French right to his allies. Despite gallant and costly assaults the British were unable to force the position and Cumberland was obliged to withdraw. The victory cleared the way for significant French gains. For a good, concise account of the battle see D. Chandler, *A Guide to the Battlefields of Europe* (London 1989), p. 16.

13 Gibson op. cit., p. 9.

14 *L'Elisabeth* had formerly been a British ship, *Elizabeth*. A venerable vessel, she had been captured in the earlier wars of Queen Anne's reign and was therefore distinctly elderly.

15 Gibson op. cit., p. 11.

16 Maclean op. cit., pp. 33–34.

17 'Raking' occurred when one warship was able to cut across the bows or stern of her opponent and pour successive fire down the length of her gun decks, dismounting guns and producing fearful carnage.

18 *Lyon* lost 45 dead and 107 wounded in the action.

19 These ships were never properly identified, but were very possibly not men o' war at all; however, this was a risk Captain Durbe could scarcely afford to take.

20 Maclean op. cit., p. 41.

21 Arisaig is as beautiful today as it was in the eighteenth century, despite the construction of the modern road that skirts Loch nan Uamh. The author has fond memories of many childhood family holidays spent touring in a Austin A35, struggling to pull a Sprite 'Musketeer' caravan, in days when the road was considerably narrower and rather ill-provided with passing places.

22 MacLeod wasted no time in writing to Duncan Forbes, to ensure his options were kept fully open.

23 Lochiel, who was certainly no dreamer, attended the Prince with a view to persuading him to return to France and have no part in any putative rising. It is a tribute to Charles's eloquence that he was able to recruit the Cameron chief. Assurances that the French would lend support undoubtedly played a major part in Lochiel's conversion.

24 Maclean op. cit., p. 42.

25 Ibid., pp. 44–45.

26 19 August was the anniversary of the Battle of Otterburn in 1388, when the English had been worsted.

27 Charles might have been less welcoming if he had known that MacGregor was there in his capacity as a government agent, a tendency handed on from his father.

28 Maclean op. cit., p. 48.

9. ADVANCE — THE INVASION OF ENGLAND

1 This third verse was added to the National Anthem after Prestonpans.

2 Correspondence from diplomat Benjamin Keen, dated September 1745. Black op. cit., pp. 74–76.

3 The titular Duke of Perth. Diplomatic, popular and amiable, perhaps with more military skill than he is traditionally credited, he allowed Murray to assume the senior role. His health was always precarious and he died during his flight into exile.

4 Lord George Murray had forfeited a commission in the Royal Scots to join the '15 and was again active in the '19. He was pardoned in 1726, and from then until 1745 lived quietly on his estates. Initially he had sought to raise a volunteer regiment to join Cope, though how sincere an effort this represented may be judged. His conversion to the White Cockade was undoubtedly genuine, though he was regarded with some suspicion from the outset. Neither the Prince nor his Irish cronies would ever wholly trust Murray, particularly after the decision to retreat was taken at Derby.

5 Chevalier de Johnstone, *A Memoir of the '45*, ed. B. Rawson (1958 edn).

6 Gardiner had been famous as a trainer of horses and breaker of female hearts. He had fought courageously at Preston during the '15, where his colourful language was noted in an army scarcely renowned for moderate speech. His apparent religious conversion brought about a distinct personality shift. See K. Tomasson and F. Buist, *Battles of the '45* (London 1962), p. 31.

7 Tomasson and Buist op. cit., pp. 34–35.

8 Ibid., p. 38.

9 Black op. cit., p. 79.

10 Ibid., p. 82.

11 The Dutch were bound by a treaty of 1713; the forces available were the captured garrison of Tournai under General Schwartzenburg. The arrival of the French troops in December 1745 meant that they could not continue to serve, this now being contrary to the terms of their parole. Their complement was ten full battalions, one half battalion and a small detachment of gunners. See S. Reid, *Culloden Moor 1746* (England 2002), p. 33.

12 John Campbell, 4th Earl of Loudon. He cooperated with Duncan Forbes in raising loyalists around Inverness and reinforcing the Great Glen garrisons, including Fort Augustus. On 11 December 1745 Loudon laid hands on the troublesome Lord Lovat, though the Fraser soon gave him the slip. Lord Lewis Gordon's recruiting had been successful, and his forces confronted loyalists under Norman MacLeod and Grant of Grant in a raid on their position at Inverurie on 23 December in which the loyalists were routed.

13 This feature had figured in the earlier Battle of Pinkie in 1547 when an English army under the Duke of Somerset defeated a Scottish force under the Regent Arran.

14 The controversy as to which regiment was to have the honour of the right was to dog the Jacobite campaign until the bitter and bloody denouement. Traditionally this was a MacDonald privilege but a system had previously been put into effect whereby the matter was to be settled by drawing lots. The Prince had sought Murray's counsel – Lord George, as ever, was not at his best when diplomacy was needed, and snapped that none could truly claim the honour and that his own Athollmen had taken the right in Montrose's battles. See Tomasson and Buist op. cit., pp. 43–44.

15 Ibid., p. 63.

16 The stricken officer was conveyed to his nearby estate of Bankton where he expired. His premonition had been correct but his courage certainly had not, in the end, failed him.

17 Johnstone op. cit., p. 37.

18 Ibid., p. 37.

19 Ibid., p. 40.

20 Black op. cit., p. 82.

21 Johnstone op. cit., p. 42. The field now lies just north of the A1 and the A198; development of both Prestonpans and Port Seton has encroached to a not inconsiderable degree.

22 Black op. cit., p. 83.

23 Johnstone op. cit., pp. 44–45.

24 Tomasson and Buist op. cit., p. 74.

25 The red sandstone walls of the great border fortress still stand and the place is not that much changed. There is a small exhibition on the events of the '45 housed in the Keep. The magnificent cathedral is nearby – this is where the luckless Jacobite garrison were housed after their surrender.

26 Johnstone op. cit., pp. 55–56. By this time the Chevalier had quit his arduous post as an aide de camp and was commanding a company.

27 Tomasson and Buist op. cit., p. 79.

28 Johnstone op. cit., p. 62. The Bank proved equal to the crisis, resorting to a ruse of their own. Agents were posted in the queues of creditors all armed with notes, the placemen had priority and were paid in sixpences, the coin being doled out in a highly deliberate manner. On departing they promptly deposited the coin back with

the tellers and then came around again! Thus was the Bank's collapse averted.

29 Tomasson and Buist op. cit., p. 82.

30 Johnstone op. cit., p. 66.

31 Ibid., p. 67.

32 Major-General James Oglethorpe MP came from staunchly Jacobite stock and had flirted with the Stuart cause. He had resigned his commission in 1715 rather than bear arms against the Pretender; two year later he fought with the legendary Prince Eugene at Belgrade. Since then he had developed the British colony in Georgia and had all the outward show of a loyal Whig. His present commission had been granted in 1744. Despite his current, apparently impeccable Whig credentials, it is possible that Cumberland detected, or perceived that he detected, a lingering whiff of Jacobitism. Oglethorpe, despite credible protestations that delays had resulted from bad roads, bad weather and poor supply, was court-martialled. He was acquitted, but the experience led him once again to embrace Stuart sympathies. By then, of course, it was far too late.

33 Ibid., pp. 74–75.

34 Black op. cit., p. 131.

10. RETREAT — THE RETURN TO SCOTLAND AND THE BATTLE OF FALKIRK

1 Johnstone op. cit., p. 76.

2 *The Highland Medley or The Duke Triumphant.*

3 Henry Hawley, nicknamed 'Lord Chief Justice', was considered something of a martinet, dour and irascible, though perhaps possessed of a greater sense of humour than he is normally credited with. His commission dated from 1694; by 1746 he was in his late sixties. He had fought at Sheriffmuir, where he may have acquired the mistaken belief that Highlanders could not stand a cavalry charge. There was a story that he had denied surgeons the body of a deserter hanged before his window in Flanders as he enjoyed the spectacle, though, again, this may have been his macabre humour at work! His performance at both Falkirk and Culloden was sluggish. James Wolfe, who had served as his ADC, had nothing but contempt for his superior, portraying him as a brutal and rather stupid figure.

4 Lady Mackintosh, a most attractive young woman, may have been a genuine Jacobite, though as her husband held a commission in the Black Watch this may have been a case of the couple 'hedging their bets'.

5 Johnstone op. cit., pp. 76–77.

6 Ibid., pp. 77–78.

7 The rebel horse had entered the city a day earlier on Christmas Day 1745.

8 This ordnance comprised two 16-pounders, two 12-pounders and a further pair of 8-pounders.

9 Johnstone op. cit., p. 85.

10 The Third Foot (The Buffs).

11 The correspondent is Andrew Fletcher, Lord Milton. See Black op. cit., p. 137.

12 Tomasson and Buist op. cit., p. 91.

13 Ibid., p. 92.

14 Reid op. cit., p. 42.

15 Black op. cit., p. 137.

16 Colonel Bedford had pleaded illness after the capture of Carlisle, though Hawley cynically felt that he was more likely diverted by the charms of a young wife! His replacement, Captain Archibald Cuningham, was not to the General's liking. Cuningham had joined the Royal Regiment of Artillery seventeen years earlier and Hawley's prediction that they would soon fall out was uncannily accurate. See Tomasson and Buist op. cit., p. 93.

17 Major-General John Huske was a popular and highly competent officer whose care for the men earned him the sobriquet 'Daddy'. He had been with the colours for a considerable time, having been blooded under Marlborough, and had recently distinguished himself at Dettingen.

18 Tomasson and Buist op. cit., p. 94.

19 Johnstone op. cit., p. 83.

20 The Prince had found a diversion in the person of Miss Clementina Walkinshaw, niece to his host Sir Hugh Paterson. She was so devoted as to follow him into subsequent exile, where she bore him a daughter. See Tomasson and Buist op. cit., p. 94. The garrison left behind to mask the defenders of Stirling comprised a force of three battalions under Perth and Glenbucket.

21 Drummond's brigade comprised the horse with a grenadier company and picquet from his own Royal Ecossois with three of the Irish Picquets. The total numbers that Murray would be able to field amounted to 5,800 foot and 360 horse. See Reid op. cit., p. 44.

22 Johnstone op. cit., p. 87.

23 Formerly Gardiner's.

24 Johnstone op. cit., p. 88. He seems to overestimate both the number of horse on the field and, very probably, the effectiveness of the Jacobite volley.

25 Ibid., p. 88.

26 Reid op. cit., p. 45.

27 Johnstone op. cit., p. 89.

28 Tomasson and Buist op. cit., p. 111.

29 Johnstone op. cit., p. 92.

30 There is some discrepancy as to how Colonel Munro met his death. His son states that, fighting bravely, and having accounted for at least two assailants, he was brought down by a pistol shot to the groin and then hacked to death by cuts to the head and face. Killing a wounded foe in this way was not uncommon; indeed it was the norm in close quarter combat, where the prime objective was to ensure the fallen man was incapable of further harm. At least one other account claims the Colonel was done to death whilst being tended on the field by his brother, a surgeon, who was also cut down. Such stories served to feed the propagandist line that the clansmen gave no quarter.

31 Tomasson and Buist op. cit., pp. 111–112.

32 Black op. cit., p. 141. Cholmondeley does refer to Cobham's having broken a body of Jacobite foot, and it seems to have been the case that a body of the dragoons had passed around or through a battalion of MacDonalds and disordered Ogilvy's regiment in the second line.

33 Mackenzie was the second son of the Earl of Bute and Argyll was his uncle. The young man had formed a passionate if inappropriate liaison with a celebrated dancer and had sought to follow the ballerina to Venice. His uncle had acted speedily to remove the girl from the vicinity and to ensure his nephew was sent post-haste back to Britain.

See Black op. cit., p. 142.

34 Ibid., pp. 139–140.

35 The unfortunate Mirabel had become a butt for the Highlanders' humour, they having perceived that his purported knowledge was mere bluster.

36 The Hessian brigade was some 6,000 strong and was led by the future Frederick II of Hesse-Cassel, who was Cumberland's brother-in-law, having married the Princess Mary six years earlier.

37 S. Reid, *1745: A Military History of the Last Jacobite Rising* (England 1996), p. 105.

11. DECISION — THE WITHDRAWAL TO INVERNESS: CHOOSING GROUND

1 Black op. cit., p. 146.

2 Ibid., p. 146.

3 Ibid., p. 146.

4 The gallant Sgt. Molloy had been obliged to surrender his tiny garrison when Glenbuchat brought up guns on 11 February. His stout defence was rewarded with a well-earned commission.

5 Reid op. cit., p. 48.

6 Inverness was regarded by the majority of Lowland visitors as poor and squalid; even in an era when civic sanitation was largely unheard of its streets were considered particularly noisome. It had four streets, three of which met at the Cross. Burt and others found the dirt and filth of the place its most distinguishing feature. See Prebble op. cit., pp. 151–152.

7 Johnstone op. cit., p. 106.

8 Black op. cit., p. 149.

9 Ibid., p. 149.

10 Ibid., p 151, from correspondence of the Earl of Glenorchy.

11 Fort Augustus was besieged by Brigadier Stapleton and a lucky mortar round exploded in the powder magazine located in the north-west bastion. This disaster persuaded Major Wentworth to capitulate. See Tabraham and Grove op. cit., p. 90.

12 Johnstone op. cit., p. 109.

13 Scott's defence of Fort William was robust, and the Argyll militia were carrying out spoiling raids in Cameron country. The removal due to injury of Grant left the incompetent Mirabel in charge, which augured very badly for the continued conduct of the siege! See Tabraham and Grove op. cit., p. 91.

14 Johnstone op. cit., p. 115.

15 Ibid., p. 114.

16 Ibid., p. 109.

17 Frederick wished to negotiate an exchange of prisoner protocols, perfectly proper in formal warfare, but Cumberland would not brook such cordiality with rebels. See Black op. cit., p. 158.

18 Johnstone op. cit., p. 109.

19 Corgarff Castle was a sixteenth-century tower house used on numerous occasions by Jacobite armies. After 1746 it was strengthened into a government outpost. See Tabraham and Grove op. cit., p. 101.

20 Tomasson and Buist op. cit., p. 118.

21 Commissioned in 1704, Bland was one of the army's leading theoreticians. His work formed the guidance for the 1729 Regulations.

22 John Roy Stuart did possess some military experience and had commanded a grenadier company at Fontenoy whilst in the French service. Something of a swashbuckler and an inveterate conspirator, he was in his mid-forties, a fitting model for a fictional character from the pages of Dumas, Henty or Stevenson, whose Alan Breck Stuart could have been inspired by him!

23 Black op. cit., p. 159.

24 Reid op. cit., p. 52.

25 The crossing, in terms of lives lost, claimed a single dragoon and three female followers. These were all drownings, none was lost to enemy action. See Tomasson and Buist op. cit., p. 118.

26 Black op. cit., 153.

27 Ibid., p. 160.

28 Charles was noted as a serious imbiber even in a society that put little store on temperance. His drinking had not yet become a chronic addiction; the slide into dipsomania would attend the bitterness of defeat and the gnawing paranoia of betrayal.

29 Johnstone op. cit., p. 116.

30 *Hazard* had recently been sailing under British colours. An eighteen gun sloop, she had formed part of the blockading squadron and her gunfire had particularly annoyed the Jacobites at Montrose. Taking advantage of a thick mist, the Highlanders had set out in requisitioned small boats; whether or not a full cutting-out expedition was intended at the outset is uncertain, but the sight of their enemies emerging like vengeful wraiths from the fog unnerved the crew. They promptly surrendered and were made to sail the vessel into the port, where she was pressed into the French service. Returning under her new flag, she fell foul of HMS *Sheerness* on 24 March. Heavily outgunned, she dodged her pursuer all day before running aground. The action cost her some three dozen casualties. See Johnstone op. cit., p. 107.

31 Lochiel's uncle.

32 Reid op. cit., p. 55.

33 Tomasson and Buist op. cit., p. 119.

34 Ibid., p. 119.

35 Ibid., p. 120.

36 Ibid., p. 120.

37 Ibid., p. 121.

38 Johnstone op. cit., p. 121.

12. BATTLE — CULLODEN MOOR: 16 APRIL, MORNING AND EARLY AFTERNOON UNTIL 2 P.M.

1 Johnstone op. cit., pp. 121–122.

2 Ibid., p. 123.

3 A 'ferm-toun' was an agricultural holding in the ownership of a number of heritors, whose property rights passed by will or survivorship to their children.

4 Johnstone op. cit., pp. 122–123.

5 Reid op. cit., p. 81.

6 Some accounts have erroneously placed Lord George Murray's initial deployment as having its flank resting some halfway down the enclosure wall.

7 The Clan of the Cats was an ancient confederation, born out of Bruce's 'herschip' (harrying) of Buchan in the first decade of the fourteenth century. The feline connection is said to have been derived from Ciarbre, the cat-headed King of Ireland.

8 Angus Og. He had accidentally been shot by the careless discharge of a Clanranald firelock.

9 The total frontage occupied by the rebel army exceeded 1,100 yards, and the precise numbers on the moor at the outset are impossible to gauge accurately. Murray later opined that some 2,000 men were missing, though many of these would have straggled up in time for the action. See Reid op. cit., p. 82.

10 Ibid., p. 83.

11 Stapleton was dubious of the steadfastness of the clans: 'The Scots, are always good troops until things come to a crisis', he is reported to have commented. See Prebble op. cit., p. 77.

12 As well as his artist's impression, Sandby also produced a highly detailed map of the battle and he completed his survey in the immediate aftermath, on 23 April.

13 Reid op. cit., p. 84.

14 Prebble op. cit., p. 67.

15 There appears to have been a number of very young lads standing in the Jacobite regiments, most apparently unarmed. See Prebble op. cit., pp. 63–64.

16 Johnstone op. cit., p. 122.

17 The order of march was: 1st foot column: Monro, Barrell, Ligonier, Wolfe and Blakeney; 2nd foot column: Price, Campbell, Bligh, Sempill and Battereau; 3rd foot column: Royals, Cholmondely, Howard, Fleming and Pulteney. See Reid op. cit., p. 85.

18 Ibid., p. 86.

19 Ibid., p. 86.

20 Ibid., p. 86.

21 The three captains were (1) John Campbell of Achnaba, (2) Dugald Campbell of Achrossan, (3) Duncan Campbell. See Reid op. cit., p. 87.

22 It would seem that the breaches in the enclosure walls were effected some little distance south and downhill from Culchunaig. See Reid op. cit., p. 87.

23 Ibid., p. 87.

24 See Reid op. cit., pp. 88–89.

25 Ibid., p. 90.

26 The linstock was a timber device which was finished with a length of slow match, kept burning through the action.

27 Keegan op. cit., pp. 160–161.

28 Prebble op. cit., p. 86.

29 Ibid., p. 86.

30 Johnstone op. cit., p. 127. The Chevalier clearly allows a note of general prejudice to intrude but the Prince's coterie of Irish toadies had done little to advance his cause, and provided sycophancy rather than dispassionate advice.

31 Black op. cit., p. 170.

32 Reid op. cit., pp. 97–98.

33 Ibid., p. 99.

34 Ibid., p. 99.

35 Ibid., p. 99.

36 Black op. cit., p. 170.

37 Reid op. cit., p. 99.

38 Ibid., p. 100.

39 Keegan op. cit., pp. 161–175.

40 Reid op. cit., p. 100.

41 Ibid., p. 100.

42 Ibid., p. 100.

43 When the Mackintosh standard-bearer was shot down, a young clansman picked up the staff and then, when the rout ensued, tore off the colours and wrapped them around his torso. He and they returned home safely, and the lad was thereafter known as Donald 'of the Colours'. See Prebble op. cit., p. 98.

44 MacLean of Drimmin, undismayed by the retreat of Clan Chattan, tried to rally his own but found they would not proceed. Hearing from one son of the death of another, he charged on alone, eventually coming up against Cobham's troopers on the extreme right of the government line. Fighting bravely, he was finally ridden down by the dragoons. See Prebble op. cit., pp. 98–99.

45 Johnstone op. cit., p. 126.

46 Ibid., p. 128.

47 Black op. cit., p. 169.

48 Johnstone op. cit., p. p. 126–127.

49 Prebble op. cit., p. 110.

13. DEFEAT — THE ROUT OF THE JACOBITE ARMY: EARLY TO MID-AFTERNOON, 16 APRIL 2 P.M.— 3.P.M.

1   Writing on 21st April, 1746; 'Old Noll' = Oliver Cromwell. Black op cit. p. 165.

2   Reid op. cit., p. 107.

3   Ibid., p. 107.

4   Prebble op. cit., p. 112.

5   Kilmarnock had the misfortune to be taken when he mistook a knot of government troopers for his own. His son Lord Boyd was serving in the Royal Scots Fusiliers.

6   A French officer Du Saussay had rescued one of the four-pounders and managed to find a decently trained crew. See Reid op. cit., p. 108.

7   Kingston's Horse lost but one man wounded and three horses; Cobham's had a man killed, with nine horses lost or injured. Reid op. cit., p. 108.

8   Ibid., p. 110.

9   Johnstone op. cit., p. 138.

10 Ibid., p. 129.

11 Ibid., pp. 129–130.

12 Black op. cit., p. 174.

13 Prebble op. cit., p. 132.

14 Black op. cit., p. 174.

15 Prebble op. cit., p. 114.

16 Reid op. cit., p. 113.

17 Prebble op. cit., p. 117.

18 Keegan op. cit., p. 198.

19 Ibid., pp. 198–199.

20 Reid op. cit., p. 115.

21 Ibid., p. 117.
22 One of these was a John Fraser, called MacIver, who, having been felled by a ball in his knee, had crawled toward Culloden House. When, on Friday, the Royal Scots called on their mission of frightfulness, Maciver was shot but again not killed. Desperately wounded, he crawled away until he was discovered by Kilmarnock's son Lord Boyd. He begged the young officer to put him from his misery but Boyd, who had seen enough of killing that day, helped the wounded man, who survived, though he was crippled for life. See Prebble op. cit., pp. 134–135.
23 Prebble op. cit., pp. 135–136.
24 Reid op. cit., p. 119.
25 Johnstone op. cit., pp. 130 –131.
26 Ibid., p. 131.

14. RETRIBUTION — THE DESTRUCTION OF THE CLANS: SPRING AND SUMMER, 1746

1 A. Loyd, *My War Gone By, I Miss It So* (London 1999), pp. 152–153.
2 A good example was the Battle of the Spoiling of the Dyke in 1578. Here a party of warring MacDonalds from Uist herded the MacLeod congregation at Trumpan on Skye into their church. They then set fire to the structure, incinerating all within, save for one burnt and dying girl who lived long enough to flee and raise the alarm. The MacLeod, big with vengeance, sallied from Dunvegan and fell upon the raiders in Ardmore Bay. None survived and the corpses were interred by the simple expedient of tipping the turves from a wall over the bodies, thus 'spoiling' the dyke. See Bingham op. cit., p. 107.
3 One of Saxe's aides at Laffeldt was none other than Colonel O'Sullivan. The Irishman and the Prince had been somewhat estranged when Charles discovered he was sharing Clementina Walkinshaw's favours with O'Sullivan!
4 Black op. cit., p. 177.
5 Ibid., p. 177.
6 Ibid., p. 178.
7 Ibid., p. 180.
8 Ibid., p. 178.
9 Ibid., p. 178.
10 Ibid., p. 182.
11 It was customary for French naval gunnery to concentrate upon an enemy's rigging and steering, to disable her prior to boarding. See Gibson op. cit., pp. 36–41.
12 Prebble op. cit., p. 203.
13 Ibid., p. 204.
14 Black op. cit., p. 186.
15 Ibid., p. 186.
16 Reid op. cit., pp. 122–123.
17 Lord George Murray escaped to Holland where he remained for the rest of his life, dying in Medemblick. He and the Prince were never reconciled, indeed the passing years saw only a widening of the gulf, to the sorrow of James 'III' who had a high regard for Murray and was probably aware of his son's deficiencies of character. The Prince increasingly shifted the burden of failure onto Murray, a ridiculous notion

that failed to endear the increasingly embittered Pretender to his shrinking band of
adherents.

APPENDIX 2: ROMANCE OF THE WHITE COCKADE

1　*The Poems of Ossian etc., Containing the poetical works of James MacPherson with notes and
illustrations by Malcolm Laing*, 2 vols (Edinburgh 1805); 'Fingal', book 1 vol. I, pp. 13–14.
2　Quoted in C. Bingham, *Beyond the Highland Line: Highland History and Culture*
(London 1991), p. 179.
3　J. MacInnes, D. Thompson (ed.), *Companion to Gaelic Scotland*, p. 58; quoted in Bingham
op. cit., p. 183

APPENDIX 3: THE BATTLEFIELD TRAIL

1　Figure supplied by National Trust for Scotland.

APPENDIX 4: RAISING THE GLENS — THE HIGHLAND REGIMENTS

1　The term 'fencible' is an ancient Scots expression for someone able to serve in the
militia – 'defensible'. On the outbreak of the Seven Years War the administration,
realising the Scottish militia system was archaic, decided to raise two battalions of
'Fencibles' in proven loyalist regions. See S. Reid, *King George's Army 1740–1793 (2)*,
'Men at Arms' series no. 289 (Osprey), pp. 41–42. The six Highland regiments that
survived into the post-Second World War era were: The Black Watch or Royal
Highland Regiment (42nd & 73rd); The Highland Light Infantry (71st & 74th);
The Seaforth Highlanders (72nd & 78th); The Gordon Highlanders (75th & 92nd);
The Queen's Own Cameron Highlanders (79th); and the Argyll and Sutherland
Highlanders (91st & 93rd).
2　Sir William Napier, 'Obituary of Sir Alan Cameron of Erracht' in *The Gentleman's
Magazine*, April 1828.
3　Quoted in L. Maclean of Dochgarroch, *The Raising of the 79th Highlanders* (Scotland
1980), p. 6.
4　Maclean of Dochgarroch op. cit., p. 9.
5　His estranged Duchess, the famous or perhaps infamous Jane, had boosted her son the
Marquis of Huntly's recruiting for the 92nd Gordon Highlanders by her legendary
offer of a kiss to all new recruits!
6　Maclean of Dochgarroch op. cit., pp. 15–16.
7　Ibid., p. 16.

BIBLIOGRAPHY

Anderson, M.S., *War and Society in Europe of the Old Regime 1618–1789* (London 1988).
Anderson, P., *Culloden Moor and the Story of the Battle* (Scotland 1920).
Bailey, D.W., *British Military Longarms 1715–1865* (London 1986).
Baynes, J., *The Jacobite Rising of 1715* (London 1970).
Bingham, C., *Beyond the Highland Line* (London 1991).
Black, J., *Culloden and the 45* (New York 1990).
Black, J. (ed.), *Britain in the Age of Walpole* (London 1984).
Blaikie, W.B., *The Itinerary of Prince Charles Edward Stuart* (Edinburgh 1897).
Blaikie, W.B. (ed.), *Origins of the '45* (Scottish History Society 1916).
Blackmore, H.L., *British Military Firearms 1650–1850* (London 1961).
Bland, H., *Treatise on Military Discipline* (London 1727).
Brander, M., *The Making of the Scottish Highlands* (London 1980).
Bruce, A., *The Purchase System in the British Army* (Royal Historical Society 1980).
Buchan, J., *Montrose* (London 1928).
Caldwell, D.H., *The Scottish Armoury* (Edinburgh 1979).
Chambers, R., *History of the Rebellion in Scotland 1745* (1869).
Chandler, D.A. (ed.), *Oxford History of the British Army*
Chandler, D.A., *Guide to the Battlefields of Europe* (London 1989).
Chandler, D.A., *The Art of Warfare in the Age of Marlborough* (London 1976).
Cruickshanks, E. (ed.), *By Force or Default? The Revolution of 1688–1689* (Edinburgh 1989).
Cruickshanks, E. (ed.), *Ideology and Conspiracy: Aspects of Jacobitism 1689–1759* (Edinburgh 1982).
Cruicksanks, E., and J. Black (eds), *The Jacobite Challenge* (Edinburgh 1988).
Cruickshanks, E., *Political Untouchables. The Tories and the '45* (London 1979).
Forbes, D., *Culloden Papers* (1815).
Gibson, J., *Playing the Scottish Card. The Franco-Jacobite Invasion of 1708* (Edinburgh 1988).
Gibson, J.S., *Ships of the '45* (London 1967).
Gibson, J.S., *Lochiel of the '45* (Edinburgh 1994).
Hayes-McCoy, G.A., *Irish Battles* (Belfast 1969).
Henderson, A., *The History of the rebellion, 1745 & 1746* (1748), 2nd edn.
Herman, A., *The Scottish Enlightenment* (London 2001).
Hill, J.M., *Celtic Warfare* (Edinburgh 1986).
Home, J., *The History of the Rebellion in the Year 1745* (1802).
Hopkins, P., *Glencoe and the End of the Highland War* (Edinburgh 1986).
Houlding, J.A., *Fit for Service: The Training of the British Army 1715–1795* (Oxford 1981).
Hughes, B.P., *Firepower: Weapons Effectiveness on the Battlefield, 1630–1850* (London 1974).

Jarvis, R.C., *Collected Papers on the Jacobite Risings* (England 1972).

Johnstone, Chevalier de, *Memoirs of the Rebellion in Scotland*, ed. B. Rawson (1958 edn).

Jones, G.H., *The Main Stream of Jacobitism* (Cambridge, Mass. 1954).

Keegan, J., *The Face of Battle* (London 1976).

Lenman, B., *The Jacobite Risings in Britain 1689–1746* (London 1980).

Lenman, B., *The Jacobite Clans of the Great Glen 1650–1784* (London 1984).

Linklater, M., and C. Hesketh, *For King and Conscience* (London 1989).

Lodge, R., *Studies in Eighteenth Century Diplomacy 1740–1748* (London 1930).

Loyd, A., *My War Gone by I Miss It So* (London 1999).

McLynn, F., *France and the Jacobite Rising of 1745* (Edinburgh 1981).

McLynn, F., *Charles Edward Stuart* (London 1988).

McLynn, F., *The Jacobite Army in England* (Edinburgh 1983).

Mackie, J.D., *A History of Scotland* (England 1964).

Maclean, Sir F., *Bonnie Prince Charlie* (London 1998).

Maclean of Docharroch, L., *The Raising of the 79th Highlanders* (Scotland 1980).

MacPherson, J. and M. Laing, *The Poems of Ossian etc.*, 2 vols. (Edinburgh 1805).

Napier, Sir. W., 'Obituary of Sir Alan Cameron of Erracht' in *The Gentleman's Magazine*, April 1828.

Newcastle Gazette, 1745–1746.

Newcastle Journal, 1745–1746.

Parker, G., *The Military Revolution* (Cambridge 1988).

Peterson, H.L., *The Book of the Gun* (London 1963).

Prebble, J., *Culloden* (London 1961).

Prebble, J., *Glencoe* (London 1966).

Reid, S., *The Campaigns of Montrose* (Edinburgh 1990).

Reid, S., *Eighteenth Century Highlanders* (London 1993).

Reid, S., *Like Hungry Wolves: Culloden Moor 16 April 1746* (London 1994).

Reid, S., *1745: A Military History of the Last Jacobite Rising* (England 1996).

Reid, S., *Culloden Moor 1746* (England 2002).

Reid, S., *Highland Clansman 1689–1746* (England 1997).

Richmond, H.W., *The Navy in the War of 1739–1748* (London 1920).

Roberts, M., *The Military Revolution 1560–1660* (Belfast 1956).

Rogers, Col. H.C.B., *Artillery Through The Ages* (London 1971).

Sadler, D.J., *Scottish Battles* (Edinburgh 1996).

Sadler, D.J., *Clan Donald's Greatest Defeat: The Battle of Harlaw 1411* (England 2005).

Scott, A.M., *Bonnie Dundee, John Graham of Claverhouse* (Edinburgh 1989).

Seymour, W., *Battles in Britain*, vol. 2 (London 1989).

Smith, A.M., *Jacobite Estates of the '45* (Edinburgh 1982).

Speck, W.A., *The Butcher, the Duke of Cumberland and the Suppression of the '45* (Oxford 1981).

Speck, W.A., *Reluctant Revolutionaries, Englishmen and the Revolution of 1688* (Oxford 1988).

Stevenson, D., *Highland warrior: Alasdair MacColla and the Civil Wars* (Edinburgh 1980).

Tabraham, C., and D. Grove, *Fortress Scotland and the Jacobites* (London 1995).

Taylor, A. & H., *1745 and After* (London 1938) (narratives of Colonel O'Sullivan and Sir John McDonnell).

Tomasson, K, and F. Buist, *Battles of the '45* (London 1962).

Tomasson, K., *The Jacobite General* (London 1958).

Young, Brig. P., *The British Army 1642–1970* (London 1967).

LIST OF MAPS AND ILLUSTRATIONS

All illustrations are from the author's collection, unless otherwise stated.

INDEX

TEMPUS REVEALING HISTORY

 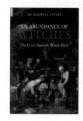  

William Wallace
The True Story of Braveheart
CHRIS BROWN
'The truth about Braveheart' *The Scottish Daily Mail*
£17.99
0 7524 3432 2

An Abundance of Witches
The Great Scottish Witch-Hunt
P.G. MAXWELL-STUART
'An amazing account of Scots women in league with the Devil' *The Sunday Post*
£17.99
0 7524 3329 6

The Roman Conquest of Scotland
The Battle of Mons Graupius AD 84
JAMES E. FRASER
'Challenges a long held view' *The Scottish Sunday Express*
£17.99
0 7524 3325 3

Scottish Voices from the Great War
DEREK YOUNG
'A treasure trove of personal letters and diaries from the archives'
Trevor Royle
£17.99
0 7524 3326 1

Culloden
The Last Charge of the Highland Clans
JOHN SADLER
£25
0 7524 3955 3

The Scottish Civil War
The Bruces & the Balliols & the War for the Control of Scotland
MICHAEL PENMAN
'A highly informative and engaging account' *Historic Scotland*
£16.99
0 7524 2319 3

The Pictish Conquest
The Battle of Dunnichen 685 & the Birth of Scotland
JAMES E. FRASER
£12.99

Scottish Voices from the Second World War
DEREK YOUNG
'Poignant memories of a lost generation… heart-rending' *The Sunday Post*
£17.99
0 7524 3710 0

If you are interested in purchasing other books published by Tempus, or in case you have difficulty finding any Tempus books in your local bookshop, you can also place orders directly through our website

www.tempus-publishing.com

TEMPUS REVEALING HISTORY

Scotland
From Prehistory to the Present
FIONA WATSON
The Scotsman **Bestseller**
£9.99
0 7524 2591 9

Flodden
NIALL BARR
'Tells the story brilliantly'
The Sunday Post
£9.99
0 7524 2593 5

1314 Bannockburn
ARYEH NUSBACHER
'Written with good-humoured verve as befits a rattling "yarn of sex, violence and terror"'
History Scotland
£9.99
0 7524 2982 5

Scotland's Black Death
The Foul Death of the English
KAREN JILLINGS
'So incongruously enjoyable a read, and so attractively presented by the publishers'
The Scotsman
£14.99
0 7524 2314 2

David I The King Who Made Scotland
RICHARD ORAM
'Enthralling... sets just the right tone as the launch-volume of an important new series of royal biographies' *Magnus Magnusson*
£17.99
0 7524 2825 X

The Second Scottish Wars of Independence 1332–1363
CHRIS BROWN
'Explodes the myth of the invincible Bruces... lucid and highly readable' *History Scotland*
£12.99
0 7524 3812 3

The Kings & Queens of Scotland
RICHARD ORAM
'A serious, readable work that sweeps across a vast historical landscape' *The Daily Mail*
£12.99
0 7524 3814 X

Robert the Bruce: A Life Chronicled
CHRIS BROWN
'A masterpiece of research'
The Scots Magazine
£30
0 7524 2575 7

If you are interested in purchasing other books published by Tempus, or in case you have difficulty finding any Tempus books in your local bookshop, you can also place orders directly through our website

www.tempus-publishing.com